BORDER CROSSINGS

CULTURAL WORKERS AND THE POLITICS OF EDUCATION

HENRY A. GIROUX

ROUTLEDGE NEW YORK AND LONDON

First published in 1992 by Routledge, Chapman and Hall

Reprinted in 1993 by

Routledge
An imprint of Routledge, Chapman and Hall, Inc.
29 West 35 Street
New York, NY 10001

Published in Great Britain by

Routledge
11 New Fetter Lane
London EC4P 4EE

Library of Congress Cataloging in Publication Data

Giroux, Henry A.
      Border crossings : cultural workers and the politics of education /
by Henry A. Giroux.
        p.   cm.
Includes bibliographical references.
ISBN 0-415-90466-8   ISBN 0-415-90467-6 (pbk.)
      1. Education—United States—Philosophy.   2. Educational an-
thropology—United States. 3. Politics and education—United States.
I. Title.
LB885.G47B67   1991
370.19—dc20   91-754
                                                    CIP

British Library cataloguing in publication data also available.

*This book is dedicated
to the memory of my mother and father
and to James Baldwin,
who was my first teacher.*

Contents

WITHDRAWN

Acknowledgments

In developing this book, I received a great deal of support, intellectual and otherwise, from a number of people too numerous to mention. But I do want to thank my wife and friend, Jeanne Brady, for her intellectual advice, patience, and moral support. My colleagues Peter McLaren, Roger I. Simon, Richard Quantz, Dennis Carlson, Larry Grossberg, Donaldo Macedo, Candy Mitchell, Harvey Kaye, Stanley Aronowitz, Ralph Page, David Trend, and bell hooks have been enormously helpful in getting me to think through the implications of various aspects of the work in this book. Graduate students at the Center for Education and Cultural Studies: Martin O'Neill, Jeanne Brady, Honor Fagan, Adriana Hernandez, and Steven Haymes were a constant source insight about many of the problems I take up in this book. I am also indebted to the graduate students I taught at The Ontario Institute for Studies in Education in the Fall of 1990. Their insights on the politics and pedagogical implications of post-colonial theory and the identity politics were very much appreciated. I most grateful to Martin O'Neill who consistently provided me with new research, texts, and readings of my work. I could not have finished this manuscript without his help, intelligence, and support. I also want to thank my editor at Routledge, Jayne M. Fargnoli, who encouraged me to write this manuscript and whose vision and generosity were a constant source of support.

Portions of this book have appeared elsewhere in different form. I extend my gratitude to the publishers for permission to make use of the folling materials: the current version of Chapter 1 was first published in *The Journal of Education* 170 (1989). This is a slightly edited version of an interview that appeared in the *Civic Arts Review*, Volume 1, Number 1 (Summer 1988) and is reprinted by permission. Versions of Chapter 3 first appeared in *College Literature* 17 (199), © West Chester University, and in *Postmodernism, Feminism, and Cultural Politics* (1990), © State University of New York Press; a much different version Chapter 4 appeared originally in *South Atlantic Quarterly* 89 (1990), © Duke University Press; Chapter 5 was published in a shorter version in *Postmodernism, Feminism, and Cultural Politics* (1990), © State University of New York Press; Chapter 9 was first published in *Exposure*. The interview in Chapter 5 was published in *Afterimage* 18 (1990). Different versions of Chapters 8 and 10 were published in *Cultural Studies*.

Introduction

The various essays that appear in this book represent a shift in both my politics and my theoretical work. Over the past decade, most of my writing has been concerned specifically with schooling. Within this context, I worked within a political project aimed primarily at reforming the sites of teacher education, public schools, higher education, and certain aspects of community education. While I still believe that these sites are crucial for encouraging students to be educated for critical citizenship, that is, as political subjects capable of exercising leadership in a democracy, I no longer believe that the struggle over education can be reduced to these sites, nor do I believe that pedagogy as a form of political, moral, and social production can be addressed primarily as a matter of schooling. This is not to suggest that I ever believed that schools alone could change society. I have never believed or supported such a view. Yet I chose to focus my political and theoretical energies on these sites because I believed they deserved such a focus.

These concerns were not misplaced, but in arguing that schools of education and public schooling were capable of becoming agencies of larger social reform, I vastly underestimated both the structural and ideological constraints under which teachers labor as well as the hold that the prevailing conservatism has in shaping the curriculum and vision of most schools of education in the United States. However, these are not the only circumstances that have altered my theoretical analyses regarding schooling and education.

Demoralized by the ravages inflicted by federal and state policies on education during the Reagan/Bush Era, many progressive and critical educators in the last decade became their own worst enemies. The inability to form constructive alliances both within and outside of the educational field, the reductionistic refusal to treat the complexity of social theory and educational practice as a promising possibility for opening new pedagogical spaces, and the emergence of new forms of ideological and political separatism had the effect of greatly reducing the influence that critical educators might play as public intellectuals.

With notable exceptions, radical and critical educators have generally ignored the sea changes in social theory that have been taking place in other fields. Locked within traditional disciplinary boundaries and recycling old orthodoxies, many critical educators risk becoming like shadows dancing on the wall of an obscure academic conference, oblivious to an outside world that is filled with real threats to democracy, society, and the schools. I have also witnessed among a sizeable number of educators in the United States a rising anti-intellectualism that is thinly coded under calls for "real" practice, accessible language, and grassroot-level politics. While none of these issues in themselves are unimportant, given the contexts in which they appear they often translate either into a self-congratulatory call for practical solutions or an unwillingness to engage the serious social and political problems facing public and higher education. In some cases, educational criticism itself has been transformed into a reductionistic celebration of experience that resurrects the binary opposition between theory and practice, with the latter becoming an unproblematic category for invoking the voice of pedagogical authority. In this instance, theory is dismissed as either incidental to educational reform or simply as the discourse of bookish academics who have little to say to those working in the field.

The decade has also witnessed the rise of forms of educational criticism that can be construed as nothing less than mean-spirited attacks on colleagues, attacks that are closer to the spirit of the McCarthy Era than the politics of conscientious and concerned criticism, dialogue, and collective struggle that the field of education so desperately needs.

Contemporary forms of critical educational theory with their narrowed vision and truncated view of the possibilities opened by new theoretical perspectives have kept the field too insular. It needs to make new connections, take up new paradigms, and open up different spaces with new allies in order to work simultaneously on changing the schools and the wider social order. Most of the leading journals in education have ignored the theoretical ruptures and new discourses that have emerged in a number of other academic fields and as a result have become increasingly irrelevant in addressing the key problems facing public schools, higher education, and the larger society. The real action theoretically is elsewhere. The wider movements in feminist theory, poststructuralism, postmodernism, cultural studies, literary theory, and in the arts are now addressing the issue of pedagogy within a politics of cultural difference that offers new hope for a deteriorating field. Theorists such as bell hooks, Cornel West, Stuart Hall, Edward Said, Chandra Mohanty, Larry Grossberg, Gayatri C. Spivak, and others are redefining both the meaning of critical pedagogy and the notion of cultural politics. Refusing to reduce the concept to the practice of knowledge and skills transmission, the new work on pedagogy has been taken up as a form of political and cultural production deeply implicated in the construction of knowledge, subjectivities, and social relations. In the shift away from pedagogy as dehistoricized, atheoretical practice, there is an increasing attempt by various cultural workers to engage pedagogical practice as a form of cultural politics. Both in and outside the academy this has meant a concern with analyses of the production and representation of meaning and how these practices and their effects are implicated in the dynamics of social power.

This book is an attempt to broaden the parameters of how we think about schooling, education, pedagogy, and cultural politics. As such, in both form and content, it intends to rupture the conventional codes of how to both read and construct such a book. For instance, each of the chapters has its own perspective and can be read independently of the others, though Chapter 2 provides a theoretical framework for engaging critically with other chapters in the book. Moreover, this book attempts to develop a new discourse that proposes radically new questions, analyses, and forms of ethical address. I make no apology for the language used. I believe that creating a new language is both an urgent and central task today in order to reconstitute the grounds on which cultural and educational debates are to be waged. In effect, I agree with Ernesto Laclau, who is quite insightful regarding the use of new discourses. He writes:

> "the important epistemological breaks have not occurred when new solutions have been given to old problems, but when a radical change in the ground of the debate strips the old problems of their sense. This is what seems central to me today if one wishes to push forward the political debate. . . . it is necessary to construct a new language—and a new language means . . . new objects, new problems, new values, and the possibility of discursively constructing new antagonisms and forms of struggle"[1].

Moreover, the production and accessibility of language cannot be divorced from its readership; there are many reading publics, and I hope it can be understood that books are read differently by diverse audiences. My one caveat is that I don't believe that teachers are "too dumb" to read theoretical books. I suggest that those critics who claim they can read theoretical literature but that public school teachers are either too busy or incapable of engaging a critical discourse may be suffering from an overdose of the kind of vanguardism that underestimates and undermines the basic intelligence of most teachers.

I also think that the generally unexamined complaint that a theoretical text should be linked directly to providing specific forms of classroom practice is one that needs to be refuted through a broader sense of what pedagogy actually is and does. This is a central concern of this book. Indeed, such a task demands a rewriting of the meaning of pedagogy itself. It means comprehending pedagogy as a configuration of textual, verbal, and visual practices that seek to engage the processes through which people understand themselves and the ways in which they engage others and their environment. It recognizes that the symbolic presentations that take place in various spheres of cultural production in society manifest contested and unequal power relations. As a form of cultural production, pedagogy is implicated in the construction and organization of knowledge, desires, values, and social practices. At stake here is developing a notion of pedagogy capable of contesting dominant forms of symbolic production. As a cultural practice, pedagogy in Roger Simon's terms, both contests and refigures the construction, presentation, and engagement of various forms of images, text, talk, and action.[2] This results in the production of meaning, which informs cultural workers, teachers, and students in regard to their individual and collective futures.

As described here, pedagogy is less about providing a universalized set of prescriptions than it is about rewriting the relationship between theory and practice as a form of cultural politics. This means respecting the complexity of the relationship between pedagogical theories and the specificity of the sites in which they might be developed. Pedagogical theory is not a substitute for the particular practices taken up by historically specific subjects who work in concrete social, political, and cultural contexts. On the contrary it is a discursive practice, an unfinished language, replete with possibilities, that grows out of particular engagements and dialogues. It offers up new categories, examples, and insights for teachers and others to engage and rethink everything from the purpose and meaning of schooling to the role that educators might play as cultural workers. Its specificity and value lie in its success in providing a language that ruptures the business-as-usual relationship between theory and practice, pedagogy and teaching, and schools and critical public cultures.

I also argue that pedagogy is a discourse that should extend the principles and practices of human dignity, liberty, and social justice by engaging in social criticism that acknowledges the serious threats faced by schools, critical cultural spheres, and the state of democracy itself. For example, it has become fashionable in the Bush Era to construct "domestic enemies" (such as the American Civil Liberties Union, affirmative action advocates, gay activists, and leftist academics) and then wage a war against them in the name of an "unproblematic" principle such as the public's right to free speech. Beneath the surface of this rhetoric is a politics of erasure. Racism, poverty, sexism, ecological ruin, and a host of other problems are no longer addressed in serious terms; instead, it has become commonplace to deflect or mask one's complicity with these practices by labeling those who argue against them ideological tyrants who are attempting to impose a form of "political correctness." To complicate matters, a new form of McCarthyism threatens the university, but it is not a McCarthyism of the Left; it is the intolerance being mustered by those who in the centers of power can no longer legitimate their ideologies and practices so easily. For instance, within the academy attempts to challenge the debilitating effects of Eurocentric perspectives on identity and difference are being seized upon by neoconservatives as an excuse to label such challenges as a violation of academic freedom. The same tactic is used to denounce anyone who dares utter the slightest protest against social practices that subjugate, violate, and oppress. The oppressors are now the victims. In being asked to become responsible for their actions, neoconservatives have responded with a vengeance by claiming that the universities and schools are filled with radicals (surely one of the great overstatements of the century, especially in the United States) and diverse cultural others who represent a threat to what they call "a common culture."

This book makes no claim for political correctness, but it does make a claim for taking a political position and addressing various injustices while attempting to avoid duplicating the means that create such injustices in the first place. These are bad times; greed is everywhere; commodification and mediocrity dominate the mass culture; a whole generation of poor, young people of color is being lost to the excruciating devastation of bad schooling, poverty, hopelessness, and joblessness. The 1990s has made visible the colonialism at work in both cities in the United States and in other advanced industrial countries.

This book attempts to address many of these issues by drawing upon new paradigms in order to rewrite the meaning of pedagogy, education, and their implications for a new politics of cultural difference, radical democracy, and a new generation of cultural workers. The concept of "cultural worker" has traditionally been understood to refer to artists, writers, and media producers. In this book, I extend the range of cultural work to people working in professions such as law, social work, architecture, medicine, theology, education, and literature. In doing so, my intention is to rewrite the concept and practice of cultural work by inserting the primacy of the political and the pedagogical. The pedagogical dimension of cultural work refers to the process of creating symbolic representations and the practices within which they are engaged. This includes a particular concern with the analysis of textual, aural, and visual representations and how such representations are organized and regulated within particular institutional arrangements. It also addresses how various people engage such representations in the practice of analysis and comprehension. The political dimension of cultural work informs this process through a project whose intent is to mobilize knowledge and desires that may lead to minimizing the degree of oppression in people's lives. What is at stake is a political imaginary that extends the possibilities for creating new public spheres in which the principles of equality, liberty, and justice become the primary organizing principles for structuring relationships between the self and others.

At the current time, a new generation of cultural workers is beginning to emerge in both the United States and other countries. A growing number of social movements and theorists starting to fight back after the abysmal decade of the 1980s. This book is written with the desire that such groups can see the relevancies in each others' work so that they can talk, work together, organize, and struggle against real problems.

REFERENCES

[1] Ernesto Laclau, *New Reflections on the Revolution of Our Time* (London: Verso Press, 1990), p. 162.

[2] Roger I. Simon, *Teaching Against the Grain* (New York: Bergin and Garvey Press, 1992).

I

SCHOOLING AND CULTURAL POLITICS

I

The Hope of Radical Education:
A Conversation with Henry Giroux

The School of Education at Miami University in Oxford, Ohio, is housed in McGuffey Hall, named after the author of the famous nineteenth century readers and a long-time professor at Miami University. As one approaches the building from the west, a large statue of McGuffey rears from the shrubbery. The inscription reads:

Wm. Holmes McGuffey
1800–1878

Who while professor in Miami University
compiled the famous McGuffey readers
Which established the social standards
of the great Middle West of the United States.

Eminent Divine and Philosopher
Peer of College Teachers
Inspirer of young men.

On another panel are chiseled the first words from the first lesson of the first McGuffey reader:

Here is John
And there are Ann and John.
Ann has got a new Book.
Ann must keep it nice and clean.
John must not tear the book.
But he may see how fast he can learn.

It was both appropriate and ironic that Henry Giroux, a leading spokesperson for radical education in America today, should have his offices in a building named after McGuffey—appropriate because both attained a measure of recognition in the educational world and ironic because one could scarcely imagine two more dissimilar philosophies. When we met Giroux in his third floor offices he commented on the irony. "McGuffey was pretty conservative in his thinking but he was a committed educator. We share that in common." We had not come to talk about McGuffey but to get some perspective on a movement in education that is gaining considerable prominence. So we began our business with a leading question.

Q—What is a radical education?

Giroux—Radical education doesn't refer to a discipline or a body of knowledge. It suggests a particular kind of practice and a particular posture of questioning received institutions and received assumptions. I would say in a general way that the basic premises of radical education grew out of the crisis in social theory. More specifically, we can distinguish three traits: radical education is interdisciplinary in nature, it questions the fundamental categories of all disciplines, and it has a public mission of making society more democratic. This last point is perhaps the principal reason why radical education as a field is so exciting. We can take ideas and apply them.

Q—Almost like having your own laboratory?

Giroux—Something like that. I prefer to think of it as a public sphere. Most disciplines don't have that. As a result their attempts to construct a public discourse become terribly academized and limited. That is why I find radical education so exciting both theoretically and politically.

Q—How close is the tie between the two?

Giroux—Very close. We can add that as another distinguishing trait. Radical education joins theory and praxis.

Q—Is radical synonymous with critical?

Giroux—Yes, I think they have to be. I can't conceive of a radical position that is not at the same time, and even in the first instance, critical both in historical terms about the ways schools have evolved in this country and ideologically in terms of the particular kinds of values that operate in our schools and in our practices of education. Critical education operates on two basic assumptions. One, there is a need for a language of critique, a questioning of presuppositions. Radical educators, for example, criticize and indeed reject the notion that the primary purpose of public education is economic efficiency. Schools are more than company stores. They have the much more radical purpose of educating citizens. Which is why the second base assumption of radical education is a language of possibility. It goes beyond critique to elaborate a positive language of human empowerment.

Q—*We hear a lot about empowerment these days. How do you understand that term?*

Giroux—It is the ability to think and act critically. This notion has a double reference: to the individual and to society. The freedom and human capacities of individuals must be developed to their maximum but individual powers must be linked to democracy in the sense that social betterment must be the necessary consequence of individual flourishing. Radical educators look upon schools as social forms. Those forms should educate the capacities people have to think, to act, to be subjects, and to be able to understand the limits of their ideological commitments. That's a radical paradigm. Radical educators believe that the relationship between social forms and social capacities is such that human capacities get educated to the point of calling into question the forms themselves. What the dominant educational philosophies want is to educate people to adapt to those social forms rather than critically interrogate them. Democracy is a celebration of difference, the politics of difference, I call it, and the dominant philosophies fear this.

Q—*Is your position that our assumptions were at one time sound and became outmoded or were they faulty to begin with?*

Giroux—If we are talking about traditional perspectives, I think the traditionalists have always been wrong about the nature of education.

Q—*How can you say such a thing?*

Giroux—Let me put it differently and say that within the field of education the languages that have dominated have generally been languages that have highly instrumentalized the purposes of schooling by either privileging certain groups of elites who become the managers of society or narrowing the scope of education so severely that schools become mere factories to train the work force. The traditionalists lack a language of possibility about how schools can play a major role in shaping public life.

Q—*But surely the liberal arts tradition has not been instrumentalist in that way?*

Giroux—I say that liberal education in any ideal sense of that term has always occupied a subordinate position vis-à-vis the dominant languages. And that is unquestionably true in this country since the 1950s. If we are talking about the public schools then the instrumentalist argument is very, very powerful. And this has been true from the beginning. If we are talking about higher education then it depends on what kinds of schools we have in mind. We all know our educational system is tiered. Some institutions are vocational. Others are places of real learning, although primarily for the elite. Harvard will never define itself as an institution whose primary mission is the promotion of industrial growth! It appeals to the life of the mind, the good life, and so forth. The higher rhetoric! We can distinguish different missions. But if we look at higher education in general I argue that the instrumentalist ideology prevails.

Q—*Hasn't the wave of reforms we have had lessened the dominance of that ideology?*

Giroux—I don't think so. Most of them have to my way of thinking been misguided. What has been the thrust of these reforms? Back to basics, merit pay, a standardized curriculum, raising test scores, evaluation criteria, and the like. This is just another version of the technological fix that ignores the philosophical questions. It is quantifying the educational process in a belief that the outcome will be some kind of excellence or economic competence. All of this suggests to me that those who are pushing these reforms have no educational philosophy at all. We have to ask what the purposes of education are, what kind of citizens we hope to produce. To say that test scores are the answer is to beg the question of "What do test scores measure anyway?"

Here is a story that perfectly illustrates the point. Joe Clark, a school principal in Newark, has been touted by many reformers as the paragon of what an inner school educator should be. How does Clark operate? He marches through the halls of his school with a bullhorn and a baseball bat, publicly berating anybody who flouts his authority. When students misbehave they must learn the school anthem and sing it over the P.A. system. Clark is given credit for restoring authority to the school and for raising the test scores of his students. What that report omits is that some nine hundred students, most of them minorities, have been expelled to roam the streets with bleak prospects. One has to ask: What educational philosophy motivates this kind of action? What sense of learning do students get? How do teachers teach in such a context?

Q—*Has there ever been a time when schools met your criteria?*

Giroux—No, although there is a discernible tradition of dissent and vision that argues for a connection and the imperatives of a critical democracy. It is an important and powerful tradition, particularly during the 1920s and 1930s in this country. But we are not talking about much history here. Prior to the twentieth century there wasn't much education of the sort we think appropriate for a democracy for the simple reason there wasn't much democracy.

Q—*Does democracy have to be critical democracy to be genuine?*

Giroux—That's what I mean. Dewey talked about democracy as a way of life that has to be made and remade by each generation.

Q—*The existentialists use the word appropriation to cover all questions of making our ideals meaningful in a lived context.*

Giroux—I like that word. It brings to the fore for me the crucial role of pedagogy and the question of how we learn to become subjects who engage not only our own self formation but the possibilities for society at any given time. How does one come to self-understanding? How does one situate oneself in history? How do we relate questions of knowledge to power? How do we understand the limitations of our institutions, or even of our age? Those are pedagogical questions. Radical educators understand them to be political questions as well. But let's face it, this is a lost discourse. None of the many recent reports about educational reform even scratches the surface of this problem.

Q—*What problem is that again?*

Giroux—The relationship between pedagogy and power.

Q—*Are radical educators a heard voice in the land?*

Giroux—They are an argument on the block, especially since 1976 when Samuel Bowles and Herbert Gintis published their path-breaking *Schooling in Capitalist Society*. I would argue that that book, along with some seminal works in the sociology of education, provided the foundation for a new language that went beyond the earlier critical tradition of Dewey and his colleagues. In the last ten years this influence has become quite evident in what is published, what is taught, and what is talked about at professional meetings.

Q—*Does radical education draw its inspiration primarily from Marxism?*

Giroux—It did. Bowles and Gintis did. But as I look at the work of radical educators today I would find it difficult to say that Marxism is the primary influence on it. And where the Marxist influence exists in education it can sometimes be overly reductionistic and one-dimensional.

Q—*You mean not good Marxism?*

Giroux—It is more a question of how good Marxism is to begin with. We can appropriate a number of good things from Marxism but do we want to appropriate the paradigm itself?

Q—*It seems the radical educator has to do just that in some sense because Marxism has supplied the principal language of critique in the 20th century. Where else would you look?*

Giroux—I would say that to be a radical educator today you have to engage the Marxist tradition. And there is no question that Marxist discourse dominated in the beginning because in the beginning most work in radical education was about reproduction theory.

Q—*What is that?*

Giroux—It is a Marxist category which says that the basic function of the schools is to reproduce the dictates of the state in the economic order. It was a rather simple and mechanistic view but not entirely false and it had important consequences for politicizing the debate about the purpose of schools, which is something that the paradigm itself completely ignored.

Q—*But are there other traditions?*

Giroux—I myself draw from a number of positions. There are critical traditions in feminist literature, in literary theory, and in liberation theology that I find useful. But it is hard to put a label on all of this. I would like to call myself a good working-class, radical American.

Q—*As in populist?*

Giroux—Sure. A critical populist who includes some elements of the IWW, Bill Haywood, C. Wright Mills, Martin Luther King, and Michael Harrington. In other words, people who speak to people in a language that dignifies their history and their experience. I don't understand how you can speak to people if you don't celebrate their voices.

Q—How did you become interested in this field?

Giroux—I went to college on a basketball scholarship. I started off in the sciences but then the Vietnam War came along and all of a sudden social theory became very important. The more I read the more I became interested in teaching. Not only did I see that as a way to make an impact but I saw teaching as a wonderfully noble profession. And I still feel that way. One of the things I try to impress upon my students is how important this field is.

Q—What did you do your PhD dissertation on?

Giroux—It was a study of curriculums. I was interested in the different ways kids learn in schools and the ways in which subject matters get selected for the curriculum. Where I grew up learning was a collective activity. But when I got to school and tried to share learning with other students that was called cheating. The curriculum sent the clear message to me that learning was a highly individualistic, almost secretive, endeavor. My working-class experience didn't count. Not only did it not count, it was disparaged. I was being reproduced according to a different logic. I think schools should be about ways of life. They are not simply instruction sites. They are cultures which legitimize certain forms of knowledge and disclaim others. The language for understanding this phenomenon in some pretty sophisticated ways is now starting to emerge.

Q—For example?

Giroux—Take the work being done on ideology and language in schools. It's very rich. If you believe that language actively constructs as well as reflects social reality, that language always develops out of a sense of difference—if something is this it is not that—and that language always embodies particular kinds of values then you can raise questions. You can ask: What is the relationship between what is learned and the pedagogies in place? Where does the language they use come from? Whose interests does it promote? What are its value assumptions? And the like.

Q—One thinks of inner city schools. It seems to be the case there that the kind of education offered mismatches the experience of those to whom it is offered.

Giroux—In my mind we have instrumentalized the process of education so much that we have forgotten that the referent out of which we operate is a white, upper-middle-class logic that not only modulizes but actually silences subordinate voices. If you believe that schooling is about somebody's story, somebody's history, somebody's set of memories, a particular set of experiences, then it is clear that just one logic will not suffice.

Q—Not many people believe that.

Giroux—Well, I'm surprised how many do. Even people of a very conservative cast are much more open to the kind of argument I am making. They, too, see schools as cultural institutions, as cultural frontiers if you will, and not merely boot camps for the economy. They see the value dimension. Unfortunately, their understanding is not very democratic. My point is that learning has to be meaningful to students before it can become critical. Our problem is that we have a theory of knowledge but no theory of pedagogy.

Q—Isn't this all pretty abstract? After all, schools are run bureaucratically on the principles of delegated responsibility and dictated policies. And that seems clearly what the majority of Americans want.

Giroux—But that's another question altogether, although related to the first question. The first question is: Can learning take place if in fact it silences the voices of the people it is supposed to teach? And the answer is: Yes. People learn that they don't count. The second question is: What are the necessary conditions to educate teachers to be intellectuals so they can engage critically the relationship between culture and learning and change the conditions under which they work? As I put it in some of my writings, we need to redefine the role of teachers as transformative intellectuals.

Q—Would you elaborate on that intriguing idea?

Giroux—Michael Waltzer speaks of intellectuals as engaged critics. They do not operate from an aloof perspective that legitimizes the separation of facts from values. They understand the nature of their own self-formation, have some vision of the future, see the importance of education as a public discourse, and have a sense of mission in providing students what they need to become critical citizens. So to give you a somewhat schematic sense of what I mean by teachers as transformative intellectuals, I would say, first, that teachers are engaged. They are partisans, not doctrinaire. They believe something, say what they believe, and offer their belief to others in a framework that always makes it debatable and open to critical inquiry. Second, to talk about teachers as intellectuals is to say they should have an active role in shaping the curriculum. Think of intelligence as a form of currency that enables teachers to have a role in shaping school policy, defining educational philosophies, and working with their communities in a variety of capacities. Transformative intellectuals are aware of their own theoretical convictions and are skilled in strategies for translating them into practice. Above all, finally, it means being able to exercise power. Pedagogy is always related to power. In fact educational theories, like any philosophy, are ideologies that have an intimate relation to questions of power. So learning must be linked not just to learning in the schools but extended to shaping public life and social relationships. The proletarianization of the teaching profession has made educators too dependent and powerless. Does that give you some idea?

Q—That's fine. Wouldn't you want, for much the same reasons, all professionals to be transformative intellectuals?

Giroux—To be sure. But bear in mind that the teaching profession alone has the primary responsibility to educate critical citizens whereas we might argue that the first responsibility of, say the medical profession, is healing. Educators have a public responsibility that by its very nature involves them in the struggle for democracy. This makes the teaching profession a unique and powerful public resource.

Q—Are schools of education moving toward this thinking?

Giroux—The short answer is that they are starting to move but very slowly. And I have to say, without naming names, that some of our most progressive schools of education have become disappointingly reactionary. They tend more and more to hire people in the business manager mode and there are few, very few, critical voices to be heard.

Q—*Talk a little about your teaching experience.*

Giroux—It's both very gratifying and very challenging.

Q—*Tell us about the challenging part.*

Giroux—Most of our students are very comfortable with defining themselves as technicians and clerks. For them to be all of a sudden exposed to a line of critical thinking that both calls their own experience into question and at the same time raises fundamental questions about what teaching should be and what social purposes it might serve is very hard for them. They don't have a frame of reference or a vocabulary with which to articulate the centrality of what they do. They are caught up in market logic and bureaucratic jargon. We can't defend what we do that way. We can't make our best case. We always wind up on the defensive and appear to others as second rate and marginal. If, on the other hand, we make the case for critical democracy we can at the same time make the case for the centrality of the teaching profession. Of one thing I am sure, the older paradigm is dying not only in terms of its effectiveness but in terms of its legitimacy as well.

Q—*That's usually referred to as positivism and it has been stated more than once that positivism is dead. Yet it seems to be a very lively corpse.*

Giroux—Oh, it's not dead. I am not saying that at all. What you call positivism I would want to call technocratic rationality or scientism which identifies the idea of progress with an idea of efficiency, which in turn defines itself by abstracting its discourse from questions of power and politics and values. What I am saying is: that paradigm is breaking down, not dead. Look at the urban school systems. They are falling apart all over the country.

Q—*Do you find some teaching techniques more effective than others?*

Giroux—My courses are all seminars. I prescribe the materials I think are important but the students have to write papers and defend their positions. This is the basis of a 15-week working-through process. I don't care what positions the students take. I want them to be able to justify whatever position they do take so they come out with a clearer sense of what they believe in and what effects that might have. I think what I really do is politicize the process of education in the minds of the students. As soon as you say people can be agents in the act of learning you politicize the issue of schooling. It becomes political in the best sense of the word, which is to say that students have to become self-conscious about the kinds of social relationships that undergird the learning process. That's a political issue. Another thing I take very seriously in my teaching is illustrating principles with a sense of voice, with somebody's story. There are experiences out there that illuminate larger questions of educational philosophy. We can, for example, talk about the hidden curriculum of racism, about what black kids have to give up to become academically successful and we can do this through their own voices. Or we can talk about people who have no community of memories. We can talk about people who are defined by such a nonbelief in the common good that they can't even imagine an alternative vision according to anything other than highly individualistic and egotistical norms. Those stories are important. That is one of the reasons I have a lot of trouble with liberal and procedural morality. It eliminates the stories in favor of abstract rules. Of course, we need to understand that these stories by themselves do not always speak for themselves. But they can become the basis for analyzing a whole range of considerations that are often hidden in the stories. Experience never simply speaks for itself. The language that we bring to it determines its meaning.

Q—*Speak further to the point about student voices. How do you deal with the objection that students are virtual* tabula rasas *who don't have much to bring to the table?*

Giroux—Let me say what student experience is not. It is not a romantic celebration of adolescence as it sometimes was in the '60s. It is something very different. I am arguing that the notion of experience has to be situated within a theory of learning, within a pedagogy. You can't deny that students have experiences and you can't deny that these experiences are relevant to the learning process even though you might say that these experiences are limited, raw, unfruitful, or whatever. Students have memories, families, religions, feelings, languages, and cultures that give them a distinctive voice. We can critically engage that experience and we can move beyond it. But we can't deny it.

Q—*What about the white, middle-class voice?*

Giroux—That's a voice too.

Q—*But isn't it more than a voice? Isn't it the model we set? Doesn't it encapsulate the best experiences we want to emulate? To be blunt, isn't the best voice an urban minority student can adopt that of the white middle class?*

Giroux—In an instrumental sense that is true. But it is a truth that conceals dangers. The problem with that position is that it makes it hard for people to realize how important the question of voice is. We become unquestioning and fail to realize the symbolic violence the dominant voice can exercise. And I will say this: even for the white middle-class majority education often, most often, functions to silence rather than empower them.

Q—*A telling point. You make teaching sound like very hard work.*

Giroux—It is very hard work. That is why teachers need to be intellectuals, to realize that teaching is a form of mediation between different persons and different groups of persons and we can't be good mediators unless we are aware of what the referents of the mediation we engage in are. Teaching is complex, much more complex than mastering a body of knowledge and implementing curriculums. The thing about teaching is that the specificity of the context is always central. We can't get away with invoking rules and procedures that cut across contexts.

Q—*Your view of education seems to make tradition irrelevant.*

Giroux—As I mentioned before, the nature of our educational problems is new and unprecedented. In that sense there is no tradition to appeal to. But there are elements of a critical pedagogy in all traditions. The radical educator deals with tradition like anything else. It must be engaged and not simply received. Traditions are important. They contain great insights, both for undestanding what we want to be and what we don't want to be. The question is: In what context do we want to judge tradition? Around what sense of purpose? We need a referent to do that. If we don't have a referent then we have no context to make sense of tradition. It doesn't supply its own referent.

Q—Your referent is probably clear by now but could you state it briefly again?

Giroux—My referent is how do we make this country a real critical democracy.

Q—Where do you stand on liberal arts education?

Giroux—A lot of people think everyone should have a liberal arts education. I disagree with that vehemently. Schooling has its own context. Often that context generates methods of inquiry that aren't likely to surface in the liberal arts disciplines.

Q—Can you, as the clock winds down, summarize your educational philosophy?

Giroux—Probably not, but I'll try. I find myself frequently falling back on a distinction John Dewey made over forty years ago between "education as a function of society" and "society as a function of education." In other words, are schools to uncritically serve and reproduce the existing society or challenge the social order to develop and advance its democratic imperatives? Obviously, I opt for the latter. I believe schools are the major institutions for educating students for public life. More specifically, I believe that schools should function to provide students with the knowledge, character, and moral vision that build civic courage.

Q—The expression "civic courage" has a nice ring to it.

Giroux—We are going to need a lot of it.

Q—We'll talk again sometime.

Giroux—I hope we do.

2

Postcolonial Ruptures/Democratic Possibilities

> The choice of language and the use to which it is put is central to a people's definition of themselves in relation to their natural and social environment, indeed in relation to the entire universe.[1]

I begin this chapter with a quote from Ngugi Wa Thiong'O, an African writer who is in the forefront of postcolonial struggles to redefine meaning as a historical and social construction. At stake here is not merely the refusal to take language for granted but to understand how it is produced and rewritten within the ideological and material legacies of imperialism and colonialism. Hence, it is in the domain of language that the traces of a theoretical and political journey begin to emerge as part of a broader attempt to engage meaning as a form of social memory, social institutions as powerful carriers and legitimators of meaning, and social practices as sites in which meaning is re-invented in the body, desire, and in the relations between the self and others.

Language in all of its complexity becomes central not only in the production of meaning and social identities but also as a constitutive condition for human agency. For it is in language that human beings are inscribed and give form to those modes of address that constitute their sense of the political, ethical, economic, and social.

This book is about what is often called the crises in meaning and authority that have beset many of the Western democracies in the 1990s. Of course, any one crisis can be refigured to secure the authority of a specific ideological position. My interest is not to secure the authority of a totalizing narrative that enshrines truth as a science and agency as a universalizing category. Rather I attempt to challenge the authority and discourses of those practices wedded to the legacy of a colonialism that either directly constructs or is implicated in social relations that keep privilege and oppression alive as active constituting forces of daily life within the centers and margins of power. Within the currency of the language of cultural crisis and authority, postcolonial discourses have pushed against the politics of such crises by inserting the primacy of a politics of difference and struggle. They scan the surface language that constructs such crises and ask: which crisis, for whom is there a crisis, and Who speaks in the name of such a crisis? "How do we construct a discourse, which displaces the effects of the colonizing gaze while we are still under its influence."[2] Postcolonialism challenges how imperial centers of power construct themselves through the discourse of master narratives and totalizing systems; they contest monolithic authority wielded through representations of "brute institutional relations" and the claims of universality. Postcolonial theorists offer resistance to social practices that relegate Otherness to the margins of power; they interrogate how centers of power and privilege are implicated in their own politics of location as forms of imperializing appropriation; and, of crucial importance, postcolonialism contests the dominant Eurocentric writing of politics, theory, and history. In effect, postcolonial discourses have not only redefined a new cultural politics of difference, they have also helped to create a new amalgam of cultural workers whose distinctive features are, according to Cornel West:

> to trash the monolithic and homogeneous in the name of diversity, multiplicity, and heterogeneity; to reject the abstract, general, and universal in light of the concrete, specific, and particular; and to historicize, contextualize and pluralize by highlighting the contingent, provisional, variable, tentative, shifting, and changing ... what makes these [gestures] novel—along with the cultural politics they produce—is how and what constitutes difference, the weight and gravity it is given in representation, and the way in which highlighting issues like exterminism, empire, class, race, gender, sexual orientation, age, nation, nature, and region at this historical moment acknowledges some of the discontinuity and disruption from previous forms of cultural critique.[3]

Postcolonial discourses have also made clear that the old legacies of the political left, center, and right can no longer be so easily defined. Indeed, postcolonial theorists have gone further and provided important insights into how such discourses either actively construct colonial relations or are implicated in their construction. From this perspective, Robert Young argues that postcolonialism is a dislocating discourse that raises theoretical questions regarding how dominant and radical theories "have themselves been implicated in the long history of European colonialism—and, above all, the extent to which [they] continue to determine both the institutional conditions of knowledge as well as the terms of contemporary institutional practices—practices which extend beyond the limits of the academic institution."[4] This is especially true for many of the new social movements that have taken up the language of difference and a concern with the politics of the other. Many theorists within these movements have addressed a number of pressing political and pedagogical issues through the construction of binary oppositions that represent both a new vanguardism while simultaneously falling into the trap of simply reversing the old colonial legacy and problematic of oppressed vs. oppressor. In doing so, they have often unwittingly imitated the colonial model of erasing the complexity, complicity, diverse agents, and multiple situations that constitute the enclaves of colonial/hegemonic discourse and practice.[5]

In this chapter, and throughout this book, I will argue that postcolonial theory, in its many varieties, provides the possibility of both challenging and transforming a cultural politics formed in binary oppositions that both silence and invite people to deskill themselves as educators and cultural workers. The challenge that postcolonialism presents to educators and cultural workers calls for new ideas, pedagogical strategies, and social movements capable of constructing a politics of difference within critical public cultures forged in the struggle to deepen and extend the promise of radical and cultural democracy. This suggests a politics and pedagogy developed around new languages capable of acknowledging the multiple, contradictory, and complex subject positions people occupy within different social, cultural, and economic locations. At issue here is a challenge to the growing anti-intellectualism and theoretical reductionism that have become characteristic of so much critical educational theory within the last decade.

Central to this book is the need to take up the relationship between language and the issues of knowledge and power on the one hand, and to retheorize language within a broader politics of democracy, culture, and pedagogy on the other. This suggests creating a new language that extends the meaning of pedagogy as a form of cultural production that takes place in a variety of sites and is produced by a diverse number of cultural workers. It also proposes appropriating some of the most insightful aspects of postcolonial discourse to further our understanding of the limits and possibilities of what it means to recognize that every new paradigm has to create its own language because the old paradigms, through their use of particular language forms, produce knowledge and social relations that often serve to legitimate specific relations of power. Oppositional paradigms provide new languages through which it becomes possible to deconstruct and challenge dominant relations of power and knowledge legitimated in traditional forms of discourse. These oppositional paradigms offer the possibility for producing constructive languages that provide the opportunity for educators to understand and engage the experiences of both the classroom and other cultural sites. This opposition often reflects major changes in thinking that are mediated and produced through related shifts in new ways of speaking and writing. Oppositional languages are generally unfamiliar, provoking questions and pointing to social relations that will often appear alien and strange to many educators (what Roger Simon calls the fear of theory). What is at stake here is whether such languages offer a vision and practice for new forms of understanding, social practice, and collective struggle.

In this book, I argue that the varied discourses of postmodernism, feminism, modernism and postcolonialism provide diverse but theoretically provocative and valuable insights for educators and cultural workers to construct an oppositional and transformative politics. A dialogical encounter between these discourses offers cultural workers the opportunity to reexamine the partiality of their respective views. Similarly, such an encounter points to new possibilities for sharing and integrating the best insights of these varied discourses as part of a broader radical democratic project. In effect, this is a call for educators and cultural workers to become border crossers engaged in an effort for create alternative public spheres. In my mind, alternative public spheres are central not only for creating the conditions for "the formation and enactment of social identities," but also for enabling the conditions "in which social equality and cultural diversity coexist with participatory democracy."[6] It is through the development of such public spheres that the discourses of democracy and freedom can address what it means to educate students for forms of citizenship forged in a politics of difference that educate people in the Gramscian sense of governing as agents who can locate themselves in history, while simultaneously shaping the present as part of a discourse and practice that allows people to imagine and desire beyond society's existing limitations and practices.

A caveat must be noted here. To appropriate the discourses of postcolonialism, modernism, postmodernism, and feminism is not another academic attempt to construct new topologies, nor is it meant to suggest a textual encounter based on a refusal of politics. On the contrary, I am taking a subject position, a point of view that argues that without a political project, there can be no ground on which to engage questions of power, domination, human suffering, and the possibilities of human struggle. In this case, I embrace a point of view rooted in a discourse of emancipation that recognizes that subjective and objective forms of domination need to be addressed as part of an educational project that is the starting point for political engagement. Hence, the varied theoretical positions critically appropriated in this book become important to the degree that they provide the categories and theoretical practice by which to engage in forms of transgression that challenge knowledge and social relations structured in dominance. This suggests a political project that goes beyond merely discursive struggles, one that also attempts to transform nondiscursive and institutional relations of power by connecting educational struggles with broader struggles for the democratization, pluralization, and reconstruction of public life.

In what follows, I want to briefly analyze some of the central theoretical assumptions that characterize the diverse work of a number of postcolonial theorists.[7] In doing so, I want to critically appropriate these assumptions as part of an effort to both enter into dialogue with this body of work and also engage its criticisms as part of an attempt to challenge some of the primary categories that construct current forms of radical educational theory and practice (including my own work). At the same time, I want to use some of the central insights of postcolonial theories to problematize and extend the possibilities that have emerged within the complex and sometime contradictory discourses of modernism, feminism, and postmodernism. Finally, I want to define the central theoretical categories around which I develop the notions of border crossing and border pedagogy as forms of cultural politics.

Colonizing Language and the Politics of Reversals

> Must we always polarize in order to polemicize? Are we trapped in a politics of struggle where the representation of social antagonisms and historical contradictions can take no other form than a binarism of theory vs. politics? Can the aim of freedom or knowledge be the simple inversion of the relation of oppressor and oppressed, margin and periphery, negative image and positive image? Is our only way out of such dualism the espousal of an implacable oppositionality or the invention of an originary counter-myth of radical purity? Must the project of our liberationist aesthetics be forever part of a totalizing, Utopian vision of Being and History that seeks to transcend the contradictions and ambivalences that constitute the very structure of human subjectivity and its systems of cultural representations.[8]

The logic of binary oppositions appears to have become an obsessive fatal attraction. More obviously, this is true for neoconservatives who consistently attempt to maintain imperial control over the Other through categories of discourse developed in repressive totalities and exclusions. For many neoconservatives, the issues of complexity, absence, difference, and specificity constitute a threat to monumentalism, cultural homogeneity, and master narratives that maintain the varied dimensions of Eurocentrism. This is evident in the current debates within the United States regarding the politics, content, and use of the academic canon. Neoconservatives such as members of the National Association of Scholars see these debates as less of an expression of academic freedom than as a threat to the very nature of Western civilization. The attack on a politics of cultural difference is also evident in the struggles being waged by the English First movement, which is indicative of the emerging new nativism that has gained credibility in the Reagan–Bush Era. The opposition to cultural democracy is further evident in the numerous attacks on radical approaches to multiculturalism that display a renewed interest in forms of democracy that challenge the violence of racism, bigotry, and cultural chauvinism.[9]

But the violence of master narratives formed in the language of binary oppositions is not simply characteristic of neoconservative discourse; it is also a major problem in the work of many critical cultural workers and educators. Women of color have made this quite clear in their criticism of those largely middle class, white feminist theorists who have developed theories of patriarchy and feminism that either excluded class and racial differences or simply reduced patriarchy to a struggle between men and women.[10]

More recently, some radical educational feminists have employed the language of binary oppositions to develop positions that may actually reproduce rather than challenge the assumptions and practices of Eurocentrism. For example, a case has been made for feminist pedagogy by defining it against what is alleged to be the unified discourse of critical pedagogy. Beyond the theoretical and political problem of refusing to deal with the differences, heterogeneity, and complexity of the varied discourses that constitute critical pedagogy, this view of feminist pedagogy is often constructed in terms of a violent opposition that reproduces the very problematic of center and margin that characterizes colonial discourses. Unfortunately, within such polarities there is little room for understanding the points of resistance, multiplicities, complicities, oppressions, and liberating elements that undermine all binary oppositions. Within this discourse, "heterogeneity is repressed in the monolithic figures and stereotypes of colonialist representation."[11]

What is at issue here is not simply the specifics of the arguments made by such theorists but the debilitating effects of a problematic encoded in the simple reversal of colonial binarisms that reproduce a reductionistic "us" against "them" discourse. Implicit in these oppositions is the assumption that feminist pedagogues have become the central bearers of knowledge and social practice while those educators who define themselves within the discourses of critical pedagogy have nothing to say or contribute. Such oppositions make it extremely difficult for critical educators to interrogate their own complicity with forms of domination that connect and refigure the centers and peripheries of power. Within this discourse of dualisms, there is little understanding of the Other as multiple complex subjects who both reproduce and refuse systems of domination. Similarly, there is a refusal to acknowledge the multiple rather than monolithic forms of power exercised through various institutions and diverse forms of representation. Finally, there are, as Gayatri Spivak has noted, few attempts to call into question the binary opposition of colonizer/colonized (in its many expressions) in order to "examine the heterogeneity of 'colonized power' and to disclose the complicity of the two poles of that opposition as it constitutes the disciplinary enclave of the critique of imperialism."[12]

Another example of how binary oppositions have undermined critical educational theory can be seen in the debate over language that has been enjoined by a growing number of educational writers.[13] These authors have constructed a defense and critique of radical discourse through the binary opposition of clarity vs. complexity. The theoretically flawed nature of such an argument is quite extensive and includes a number of the following considerations: it often subscribes to a universal referent for clarity and linguistic unity that is elitist as well as antiintellectual; it tends to simplify the politics of representation, reducing it to an unproblematic issue of clarity that is never deconstructed as perhaps complicitous with the construction of domination; and it reproduces a troublesome politics of erasure by claiming to represent a universal standard of literacy while failing to consider a plurality of audiences and constituencies. Hence, it eliminates the complexity and specificity of a readership that occupies multiple, diverse public cultures.

The clarity vs. complexity binarism is based on the presupposition that a simple invocation to clear language can by itself confer sense. This position ignores what Homi Bhabha calls a central feature of political maturity: "that there are many forms of political writing whose different effects are obscured when they are divided between the 'theoretical' and the 'activist' [whose corresponding correlates are complexity and clarity].[14] Similarly, the clarity vs. complexity argument also disregards how language and power come together in complex ways to exclude diverse narratives that rupture dominant codes and open up new spaces and possibilities for reading, writing, and acting within rather than outside of a democratic politics of difference. Inherent in this call to clarity is an assumed rather than demonstrated consensus about what clarity actually is and why it can only be taken up in progressive terms. Implicitly, this position represents a politics of containment, one that is silent about its own role in legitimating universalizing referents that marginalize and exclude multiple narratives expressed through a variety of complex discursive forms.

By ignoring these concerns, many critical educators appeal to a universal standard of literacy and clarity that is never examined. Such an appeal suppresses questions of context such as who reads what, and under what conditions. It also strongly suggests that the power of language is defined through a stylized aesthetic of clarity, one that presupposes the commonsense assumption that language is a transparent medium merely expressing existing facts that need only be laid out in an agreed-upon fashion. As previously suggested, this position does more than deny the politics of representation by situating language outside of theory, politics, and struggle. It also refuses to explore the complex issue of how language that challenges traditional educational paradigms is obligated to create new categories in order to reclaim new spaces for resistance, to establish new identities, or to construct new knowledge/power relations. Most importantly, the binary opposition that constructs this view of language appears to reproduce a central criticism posed by postcolonial critics regarding how the legacy of colonialism continually reasserts itself in a Eurocentric discourse and practice forged in relations in which the Other is subsumed or erased in the violence of binary oppositions. At work here is a form of Eurocentricism that refuses to interrogate the grounds of its own narration, its own sense of location, and how it is inscribed in a politics of difference. By refusing to interrogate how Eurocentricism may be complicit with the formation of their own identity as it is constructed in the interplay of language and difference, critical educational theorists find it difficult to understand how language itself can be used to shut down partiality, possibilities, and a politics of representation that is central to the construction of multiple social identities, public cultures, and forms of political practice.[15]

The Politics of Location, Agency, and Struggle in Postcolonial Discourse

The first set of problems is concerned with . . . issues like who writes or studies [the Other], in what institutional or discursive setting, for what audience, and with what ends in mind, the second set of problems [focuses on] . . . how the production of knowledge best serves communal, as opposed to factional, ends, how knowledge that is nondominative and noncoercive can be produced in a setting that is deeply inscribed with the politics, the considerations, the positions, and the strategies of power.[16]

As a radical standpoint, perspective, position, 'the politics of location' necessarily calls those of us who would participate in the formation of counter-hegemonic cultural practice to identify the spaces where we begin the process of revision. . . . [It] is that place which enables and promotes varied and everchanging perspectives, a place where one discovers new ways of seeing reality, frontiers of difference.[17]

Edward Said and bell hooks illuminate different aspects of the debate on the politics of location that have become fundamental to a number of theoretical paradigms, including various versions of feminism and postmodernism. Central to all of these positions is the importance of challenging, remapping, and renegotiating those boundaries of knowledge that claim the status of master narratives, fixed identities, and an objective representation of reality. Within feminist and postmodern discourses, this has expressed itself in recognizing the situated nature of knowledge, the partiality of all knowledge claims, the indeterminacy of history, and the shifting, multiple and often contradictory nature of identity.[18] At question here is the issue of who speaks, under what conditions, for whom, and how knowledge is constructed and translated within and between different communities located within asymmetrical relations of power. In addition, there is the important issue of how identity itself is constituted and what the enabling conditions might be for human agency. What the various discourses on the politics of location have made clear is that the relationship between knowledge and power on the one hand and the self and others on the other is as much an issue of ethics and politics as it is one of epistemology.[19] The legacy of a politics of location has provided a new vocabulary for analyzing how we are situated differently in the interplay of power, history, and culture. It also engages issues about how our psyches, desires, and bodies provide a reference point "to be able to name our location, to politicize our space and to question where our particular experiences and practice fit within the articulations and representations that surround us."[20] In various feminist and postmodern discourses, the politics of location has fruitfully pointed to how social identities occupy contradictory and shifting locations in which it becomes possible to open up new spaces for conversations and forms of solidarity. Rejecting the discourse of universality and essentialism, feminist theorists in particular have argued that politics and epistemology must be connected, not in an empty relativism, but in forms of discourse that are always "interpretive, critical, and partial. . . . [Where there] is a ground for conversation, rationality, and objectivity, which is power-sensitive, not 'pluralist' conversation."[21] In this context, a politics of location provides both a form of address as well as a historically constituted site from which expression and action proceed.

Postcolonial discourse has extended the parameters of this debate in a number of ways. First, it has made it clear that the relationship of history and the politics of difference is often informed by a legacy of colonialism that must be called into question so as to make visible the exclusions and repressions that allow specific forms of privilege to remain unacknowledged in the language of Western educators and cultural workers. At stake here is deconstructing not only those forms of privilege that benefit males, whiteness, heterosexuality, and property holders, but also those conditions that have disabled others to speak in places where those who are privileged by virtue of the legacy of colonial power assume authority and the conditions for human agency. This suggests, as Spivak has pointed out, that more is at stake than problematizing discourse; more importantly, educators and cultural workers must be engaged in "the unlearning of one's own privilege. So that, not only does one become able to listen to that other constituency, but one learns to speak in such a way that one will be taken seriously by that other constituency."[22] In this instance, postcolonial discourse extends the radical implications of difference and location by making such concepts attentive to providing the grounds for forms of self-representation and collective knowledges in which the subject *and* object of European culture are problematized, though in ways radically different from those taken up by Western radicals and conservatives.

Second, postcolonial discourse rewrites the relationship between the margin and the center by deconstructing the colonialist and imperialist ideologies that structure Western knowledge, texts, and social practices. Here, there are attempts to demonstrate how European culture and colonialism "are deeply implicated in each other."[23] This suggests more than rewriting or recovering the repressed stories and social memories of the Other; it means understanding and rendering visible how Western knowledge is encased in historical and institutional structures that both privilege and exclude particular readings, voices, aesthetics, authority, representations, and forms of sociality. The West and Otherness relate not as polarities or binarisms in postcolonial discourse but in ways in which both are complicitous and resistant, victim and accomplice. While it cannot be forgotten that the legacy of colonialism has meant large-scale death and destruction as well as cultural imperialism for the Other, the Other is not merely the opposite of Western colonialism, nor is the West a homogeneous trope of imperialism.

This suggests a third insight provided by postcolonial discourses. The current concern with the "death of the subject" cannot be confused with the necessity of affirming the complex and contradictory character of human agency. Postcolonial discourse reminds us that it is ideologically convenient and politically suspect for Western intellectuals to talk about the disappearance of the speaking subject from within institutions of privilege and power. This is not to suggest that postcolonial theorists accept the humanist notion of the subject as a unified and fixed identity. On the contrary, postcolonial discourse agrees that the speaking subject must be decentered but does not mean that all notions of human agency and social change must be dismissed. Understood in these terms, the postmodernist notion of the subject must be accepted and modified in order to extend rather than erase the possibility for enabling human agency. At the very least, this would mean coming to understand the strengths and limits of practical reason, the importance of affective investments, the discourse of ethics as a resource for social vision, and the availability of multiple discourses and cultural resources that provide the very grounds and necessity for agency.

Postcolonial discourses represent a space in which to retheorize, locate, and address the possibilities for a new politics based on the construction of new identities, zones of cultural difference, and forms of ethical address that allow cultural workers and educators alike to transform the languages, social practices, and histories that are part of the colonial inheritance. This position offer new hope for expanding both the practice of cultural work and the liberatory possibilities of crossing borders that open up new political and pedagogical possibilities. It is to these issues that I will now turn.

Border Pedagogy: An Introduction

In what follows, I want to delineate what might be some useful and transformative aspects of border pedagogy by situating it within those broader cultural and political considerations that are beginning to redefine our traditional view of community, language, space, and possibility. Border pedagogy is attentive to developing a democratic public philosophy that respects the notion of difference as part of a common struggle to extend the quality of public life. It presupposes not merely an acknowledgment of the shifting borders that both undermine and reterritorialize different configurations of culture, power, and knowledge. It also links the notions of schooling and the broader category of education to a more substantive struggle for a radical democratic society.

What does this suggest for redefining radical educational theory and practice as a form of border pedagogy? There are a number of theoretical considerations that need to be unpacked in reference to this question. First, the category of border signals a recognition of those epistemological, political, cultural, and social margins that structure the language of history, power, and difference. The category of border also prefigures cultural criticism and pedagogical processes as a form of border crossing. That is, it signals forms of transgression in which existing borders forged in domination can be challenged and redefined. Second, it also speaks to the need to create pedagogical conditions in which students become border crossers in order to understand otherness in its own terms, and to further create borderlands in which diverse cultural resources allow for the fashioning of new identities within existing configurations of power.

Third, border pedagogy makes visible the historically and socially constructed strengths and limitations of those places and borders we inherit and that frame our discourses and social relations. Moreover, as part of a broader politics of difference, border pedagogy makes primary the language of the political and ethical. It stresses the political by examining how institutions, knowledge, and social relations are inscribed in power differently; it highlights the ethical by examining how the shifting relations of knowing, acting, and subjectivity are constructed in spaces and social relationships based on judgments that demand and frame "different modes of response to the other; that is, between those that transfigure and those that disfigure, those that care for the other in his/her otherness and those that do not."[24] As part of a radical pedagogical practice, border pedagogy points to the need for conditions that allow students to write, speak, and listen in a language in which meaning becomes multiaccentual and dispersed and resists permanent closure. This is a language in which one speaks *with* rather than exclusively *for* others. Border pedagogy necessitates combining the modernist emphasis on the capacity of individuals to use critical reason to address the issue of public life with a postmodernist concern with how we might experience agency in a world constituted in differences unsupported by transcendent phenomena or metaphysical guarantees. In that way, border pedagogy can reconstitute itself in terms that are both transformative and emancipatory.

Border Pedagogy and the Representation of Practice

Central to the notion of border pedagogy is an understanding of how the relationship between power and knowledge works as both the practice of representation and the representation of practice to secure particular forms of authority.[25] But challenging such representations and practices entails more than revealing the Eurocentric, patriarchal, racist, and class-specific interests that are both produced and legitimated by the canon at various levels of schooling. Although the borders of existing disciplinary knowledge do need to be challenged and refigured, it is also crucial to recognize that knowledge formation is, as Spivak has also pointed out, both "the conditions of institutions and the effects of institutions."[26] In this case, border pedagogy must take up the dual task of not only creating new objects of knowledge but also addressing how inequalities, power, and human suffering are rooted in basic institutional structures. I want to develop certain aspects of border pedagogy as they relate specifically to schooling, but at the same time I want to maintain that many of the practices at work here apply to other cultural sites as well (this is demonstrated in other chapters in this book).

As a pedagogical process intent on challenging existing boundaries of knowledge and creating new ones, border pedagogy offers the opportunity for students to engage the multiple references that constitute different cultural codes, experiences, and languages. This means educating students to both read these codes historically and critically while simultaneously learning the limits of such codes, including the ones they use to construct their own narratives and histories. In this case, partiality becomes the basis for recognizing the limits built into all discourses and necessitates taking a critical view of authority as it is used to secure all regimes of truth that deny gaps, limits, specificity, and counter-narratives. Within this discourse, students should engage knowledge as border-crossers, as people moving in and out of borders constructed around coordinates of difference and power.[27]

These are not only physical borders, they are cultural borders historically constructed and socially organized within rules and regulations that limit and enable particular identities, individual capacities, and social forms. In this case, students cross over into realms of meaning, maps of knowledge, social relations, and values that are increasingly being negotiated and rewritten as the codes and regulations that organize them become destabilized and reshaped. Border pedagogy decenters as it remaps. The terrain of learning becomes inextricably linked to the shifting parameters of place, identity, history, and power. Border pedagogy shifts the emphasis of the knowledge/power relationship away from the limited emphasis on the mapping of domination toward the politically strategic issue of engaging the ways in which knowledge can be remapped, reterritorialized, and decentered in the wider interests of rewriting the borders and coordinates of an oppositional cultural politics. This is not an abandonment of critique as much as it is an extension of its possibilities.

In this sense, border pedagogy extends the meaning and importance of demystification as a central pedagogical task. Depending upon the level of schooling, students must be offered opportunities to read texts that both affirm and interrogate the complexity of their own histories. They must also be given the opportunity to engage and develop a counter discourse to the established boundaries of knowledge. For example, educators such as William Bigelow and Norman Diamond have created alternative curriculum materials dealing with the history of work and workers in the United States.[28] Simon and his cohorts at The Ontario Institute for Studies in Education have produced curriculum materials as a student-based approach to work education.[29] Equally important is the need for students to be able to create their own texts. In this regard, Katie Singer has worked with students at South Boston High School in Massachusetts to conduct oral histories of their communities, family life, neighborhood, and other issues as part of a broader project to produce anthologies to be used in the writing and bilingual programs.[30] In these examples, not only are borders being challenged, crossed, and refigured, but borderlands are being created in which the very production and acquisition of knowledge is being used by students to rewrite their own histories, identities, and learning possibilities.

In addition to reading different texts and refiguring the grounds on which knowledge is produced, border pedagogy takes up the important tasks of establishing conditions for dominant and subordinate texts to be read differently. Texts must be decentered and understood as historical and social constructions marked by the weight of a range of inherited and specified readings. Hence, texts can be read by focusing on how different audiences might respond to them, thus highlighting the possibilities of reading against, within, and outside their established boundaries.[31] Texts must also be understood in terms of the principles that structure them. This suggests not only identifying precise ideological interests, whether they be racist, sexist, or class specific, but also understanding how distinctive practices actually frame such texts by looking at the elements that produce them within established circuits of power.[32] This implies analyzing the political economy of publishing companies, the forces outside of the schools that render certain texts legitimate objects of knowledge, particular forms of state legislation and assessment that privilege certain readings of texts, and how students from different social formations and locations might read texts differently and why. As such, border pedagogy reads against totalizing curriculum and pedagogical practices that marginalize diverse student cultures and histories by taking up issues of production, audience, address, and reception. Similarly, border pedagogy reads against the grain of transmission teaching or what Paulo Freire has called "banking education" by opposing learning premised on the voyeuristic consumption of texts.[33] By "interrupting" representational practices that make a claim to objectivity, universality, and consensus, critical educators can develop pedagogical conditions in which students can read and write within and against existing cultural codes while simultaneously having the opportunity to create new spaces for producing new forms of knowledge, subjectivity, and identity. Within such a discourse, important social and political realities would be engaged rather than excluded from the school curriculum and the process of reading differently and critically would be aimed not only at dominant texts but also inwardly upon itself.

More specific examples of border pedagogy can be found in some of the recent work being done on educational theory and popular culture.[34] Three important issues are being worked out within the parameters of this work. First, there is a central concern for understanding how the production of meaning is related to affective investments and the production of pleasure.[35] In this view, it is necessary for teachers to incorporate into their pedagogies a theoretical understanding of how the production of meaning and economies of pleasure become mutually constitutive of students' identities, how students view themselves, and how students construct a particular vision of their future. Second, the nature of how students are inscribed in and take up different affective economies needs to be rethought in light of a number of important pedagogical considerations. One such consideration is that the production and regulation of desire must be seen as a crucial aspect of how students mediate, relate, resist, and create particular cultural forms and forms of knowing. Another concern is that popular culture be seen as a legitimate aspect of the everyday lives of students and be analyzed as a primary force in shaping the various and often contradictory subject positions that students take up. Third, popular culture needs to become a serious object of study in the official curriculum. This can be done by treating popular culture either as a distinct object of study within particular academic disciplines such as media studies or by drawing upon the resources it produces for engaging various aspects of the official curriculum. I take up this issue in more detail in another section of this book.

In all of these examples, important elements of a border pedagogy point to ways in which those master narratives based on white, patriarchal, and class-specific versions of the world can be challenged critically and effectively deterritorialized. That is, by offering a theoretical language for establishing new boundaries with respect to knowledge most often associated with the margins and the periphery of the cultural dominant, border pedagogy opens up the possibility for incorporating into the curriculum cultural and social practices that no longer need be mapped or referenced solely on the basis of the dominant models of Western culture. In this case, knowledge forms emanating from the margins can be used to redefine the complex, multiple, heterogeneous realities that constitute those relations of difference that make up the experiences of students who often find it impossible to define their identities through the cultural and political codes that characterize the dominant culture.

Border Pedagogy and the Politics of Identity and Community

If the concept of border pedagogy is to be linked to the imperatives of a critical democracy, as it must be, educators must possess a theoretical grasp of the ways in which difference is constructed through various representations and practices that name, legitimate, marginalize, and exclude the voices of subordinate groups in American society. Two considerations need to frame this project. First, the liberal notion of multiculturalism that links difference within the horizon of a false equality and a depoliticized notion of consensus must be replaced by a radical notion of cultural difference and citizenship that recognizes the "essentially contested character of the signs and signifying material we use in the construction of our social identities."[36] Second, the central values of a democratic revolution— freedom, equality, liberty, and justice—must provide the principles by which differences are affirmed within rather than outside of a politics of solidarity forged through diverse public spheres.

Central to this task is the need for critical educators to take up culture as a vital source for developing a politics of identity, community, and pedagogy. In this perspective, culture is not viewed as monolithic or unchanging, but as a shifting sphere of multiple and heterogeneous borders where different histories, languages, experiences, and voices intermingle amid diverse relations of power and privilege. For example, within the pedagogical cultural borderland known as school, subordinate cultures push against and permeate the alleged unproblematic and homogeneous borders of dominant cultural forms and practices. Critical educators cannot be content to merely map how ideologies are inscribed in the various relations of schooling, whether they be the curriculum, forms of school organization, or in teacher-student relations. A more viable critical pedagogy needs to go beyond these concerns by analyzing how ideologies are actually taken up in the contradictory voices and lived experiences of students as they give meaning to the dreams, desires, and subject positions that they inhabit. Critical educators need to provide the conditions for students to speak differently so that their narratives can be affirmed and engaged critically along with the consistencies and contradictions that characterize such experiences. They must not only hear the voices of those students who have been traditionally silenced, they must take seriously what all students say by engaging the implications of their discourse in broader historical and relational terms. Equally important is the need to provide safe spaces for students to critically engage teachers, other students, as well as the limits of their own positions as border-crossers who do not have to put their identities on trial each time they address social and political issues that they do not experience directly. Put simply, students must be encouraged to cross ideological and political borders as a way of furthering the limits of their own understanding in a setting that is pedagogically safe and socially nurturing rather than authoritarian and infused with the suffocating smugness of a certain political correctness. More specifically, student experience has to be analyzed as part of a broader democratic politics of voice and difference.

As part of a project of voice and difference, a theory of border pedagogy needs to address the question of how representations and practices that name, marginalize, and define difference as the devalued Other are actively learned, internalized, challenged, or transformed. That is, it is imperative that such a pedagogy acknowledge and critically interrogate how the colonizing of differences by dominant groups is expressed and sustained through representations in which the humanity of the Other is either ideologically disparaged or ruthlessly denied. In addition, such a pedagogy needs to address how an understanding of these differences can be taken up in order to challenge the prevailing relations of power that sustain them. Border pedagogy must provide the conditions for students to engage in cultural remapping as a form of resistance. Students should be given the opportunity to engage in systematic analyses of the ways in which the dominant culture creates borders saturated in terror, inequality, and forced exclusions. Students need to analyze the conditions that have disabled others to speak in the places where those who have power exercise authority. Thus, critical educators must give more thought to how the experience of marginality at the level of everyday life lends itself productively to forms of oppositional and transformative consciousness. Similarly, those designated as Other must both reclaim and remake their histories, voices, and visions as part of a wider struggle to change those material and social relations that deny radical pluralism as the basis of democratic political community. This suggests a pedagogy in which occurs a critical questioning of the omissions and tensions that exist between the master narratives and hegemonic discourses that make up the official curriculum and the self-representations of subordinated groups as they might appear in "forgotten" or erased histories, texts, memories, experiences, and community narratives.

At issue here is a pedagogical practice that is not concerned with simply marking difference as a historical construct; rather, it is also attentive to inserting difference within a cultural politics that attempts to create within schools, universities, and other educational sites what Chandra Mohanty calls "public cultures of dissent." By this she means:

creating spaces for epistemological standpoints that are grounded in the interests of people and which recognize the materiality of conflict, of privilege, and of domination. Thus, creating such cultures is fundamentally about making the axes of power transparent in the context of academic, disciplinary, and institutional structures as well as in interpersonal relationships (rather than individual relations in the academy).[37]

Furthermore, students must appropriate in a similarly critical fashion, when necessary, the codes and knowledges that constitute broader and less familiar historical and cultural traditions. Underlying this pedagogical practice is the importance of understanding how subjectivities are produced within those configurations of knowledge and power that exist outside of the immediacy of one's experience but are central to forms of self and social determination, the obligations of critical citizenship, and the construction of critical public cultures. Border pedagogy also points to the need to raise fundamental questions regarding how students make particular investments of meaning and affect, how they are inscribed within triad relations of knowledge, power, and pleasure, and why students might be indifferent to the forms of authority, knowledge, and values that are produced and legitimated within our classrooms and universities.

In addition, the concept of border pedagogy suggests more than simply opening diverse cultural histories and spaces to students. It also means understanding how fragile identity is as it moves into borderlands crisscrossed within a variety of languages, experiences, and voices. There are no unified subjects here, only students whose multilayered and often contradictory voices and experiences intermingle with the weight of particular histories that will not fit easily into the master narrative of a monolithic culture. Such borderlands should be seen as sites for both critical analysis and as a potential source of experimentation, creativity, and possibility. Moreover, these pedagogical borderlands where blacks, whites, latinos, and others meet demonstrate the importance of a multicentric perspective that allows students to recognize and analyze how the differences within and between various groups can expand the potential of human life and democratic possibilities.

Border Pedagogy and the Discourse of Teacher Location

Central to the notion of border pedagogy are a number of important pedagogical issues regarding the role that teachers might play at the interface of a number of concerns taken up in the discourses of postcolonialism introduced in the first part of this chapter.

Border pedagogy provides opportunities for teachers to deepen their own understanding of the discourse of various others in order to effect a more dialectical self-critical understanding of the limits, partiality, and particularity of their own politics, values, and pedagogy. By being able to listen critically to the voices of their students, teachers also become border-crossers through their ability both to make different narratives available to themselves and to legitimate difference as a basic condition for understanding the limits of one's own knowledge. What border pedagogy makes undeniable is the relational, constructed, and situated nature of one's own politics and personal investments. But at the same time, border pedagogy emphasizes the primacy of a politics in which teachers assert rather than retreat from the pedagogies they utilize in dealing with the various differences represented by the students who come into their classes.

At stake here is an important theoretical issue that is worth repeating. Knowledge and power come together not to merely reaffirm difference but to also interrogate it, to open up broader theoretical considerations, to tease out its limitations, and to engage a vision of community in which student voices define themselves in terms of their distinct social formations and their broader collective hopes. For critical educators, this entails speaking *to* important social, political, and cultural issues from a deep sense of the politics of their own location and the necessity to engage and often unlearn the habits of institutional (as well as forms of racial, gender, and class-specific) privilege that buttress their own power while sometimes preventing others from becoming questioning subjects. This does not suggest that as educators we should abandon our authority as much as we should transform it into an emancipatory practice that provides the conditions for us to speak and be taken seriously. Of course, as teachers we can never speak inclusively *as* the Other, though we may be the Other with respect to issues of race, class, or gender; but we can certainly work *with* diverse Others to deepen both our own and their understanding of the complexity of the traditions, histories, knowledges, and politics that they bring to the schools. More specifically, while teachers may not speak as others whose experiences they do not share, they certainly can speak about and to the experiences of racism, sexism, class discrimination, and other concerns as historical and contingent issues that affect public life. In other words, as a heterosexual, white, middle/working class educator, I cannot, for example, speak as or for Afro-Americans or women, but I can speak self-reflectively from the politics of my own location about the issues of racism and sexism as ethical, political, and public issues, which implicate in their web of social relations all those who inhabit public life, though from different spheres of privilege and subordination. Extending the logic of such a position is to create conditions within particular institutions that allow both teachers and students to locate themselves and others in histories that mobilize rather than destroy their hopes for the future. Such a position reconstructs teachers as intellectuals whose own narratives must be situated and examined as discourses that are open, partial and subject to ongoing debate and revision.

In conclusion, I think it is essential that educators and other cultural workers address the issues at stake in the new cultural politics of difference as pedagogical and political concerns. These concerns need to be taken up within broader mobilizing articulations such as public life, nationalism, and citizenship. The pedagogical issue at work here is to articulate difference as part of the construction of a new type of politics, language, and subject, which would be both multiple and democratic.

REFERENCES

[1] Ngugi Wa Thiong'O, *Decolonizing the Mind: The Politics of Language in African Literature* (London and Nairobi: Heinemann, 1986), 4.

[2] Linda Hutcheon, "Circling the Downspout of Empire," in Ian Adam and Helen Tiffin, eds. *Past the Last Post* (Calgary: University of Calgary Press, 1990), 176.

[3] Cornel West, "The New Cultural Politics of Difference," *October* 53 (Summer 1990), 93.

[4] Robert Young, *White Mythologies: Writing History and the West* (London: Routledge, 1990), viii.

[5] For an excellent discussion of these issues as they specifically relate to postcolonial theory, see Benita Parry, "Problems in Current Theories of Colonial Discourse," *The Oxford Literary Review* Vol. 9 (1987), 27–58; Abdul JanMohamed, *Manichean Aesthetics: The Politics of Literature in Colonial Africa* (Amherst: University of Massachusetts Press, 1983); Gayatri C. Spivak, *The Post-Colonial Critic: Interviews, Strategies, Dialogues*, Sarah Harasym, ed. (New York: Routledge, 1990).

[6] Both quotes are taken from: Nancy Fraser, "Rethinking the Public Sphere: A Contribution to the Critique of Actually Existing Democracy," *Social Text* Nos. 25/26 (1990), 68, 69.

[7] The literature on anticolonialism and postcolonialism is far too vast to cite here, but would include some of the following: Frantz Fanon, *The Wretched of the Earth* (New York: Grove Press, 1963); *Black Skin, White Masks* (New York: Grove Press, 1967); Kwame Nkrumah, *Consciencism* (New York: Monthly Review Press, 1964); Albert Memmi, *The Colonizer and the Colonized* (Boston: Beacon Press, 1965); Paulo Freire, *Pedagogy in Process: The Letters to Guinea-Bissau* (New York: Seabury Press, 1978); Ngugi Wa Thiong'O, *Decolonizing the Mind*; Jan Carew, *Fulcrums of Change* (Trenton, N.J.: Africa World Press, 1988); Edward W. Said, *Orientalism* (New York: Vintage Books, 1979); Rinajit Guha and Gayatri C. Spivak, eds., *Selected Subaltern Studies* (New York: Oxford University Press, 1988); Special Issue of *Inscriptions* on "Feminism and the Critique of Colonial Discourse," Nos. 3/4 (1988); James Clifford, *The Predicament of Culture* (Cambridge: Harvard University Press, 1988); Bill Ashcroft, Gareth Griffiths, and Helen Tiffin, eds., *The Empire Writes Back: Theory and Practice in PostColonial Literatures* (London: Routledge, 1989); Howard Adams, *Prison of Grass: Canada From a Native Point of View* (Saskatoon: Fifth House Publishers, 1989); Homi K. Bhabha, ed., *Nation and Narration* (London: Routledge, 1990); Gayatri C. Spivak, *The Post-Colonial Critic*; Ian Adam and Helen Tiffin, eds., *Past the Last Post: Theorizing Post-Colonialism and Post-Modernism* (Calgary, Canada: University of Calgary Press, 1990); Marianna Torgovnick, *Gone Primitive: Savage Intellects, Modern Lives* (Chicago: University of Chicago Press, 1990); Robert Young, *White Mythologies*.

[8] Homi Bhabha, "The Commitment to Theory," *New Formations* 5 (Summer 1988), 5. See also Tony Crowley, *Standard English and the Politics of Language* (Urbana: University of Illinois Press, 1989).

[9] For an example of how these issues are taken up around the struggle over multiculturalism in the academy, see Gregory S. Jay, "The End of 'American' Literature: Toward a Multicultural Practice," *College English* 53:3 (March 1991), 264–281.

[10] I take up this issue extensively in this book, see especially Chapters 3 and 5.

[11] The most influential example of this position can be found in Elizabeth Ellsworth, "Why Doesn't This Feel Empowering? Working Through the Repressive Myths of Critical Pedagogy," *Harvard Educational Review* 59:3 (1989), 297–324. Ellsworth isn't alone in constructing com-

fortable binary oppositions that simply reverse the violence of one hierarchical opposition for another. See Patti Lather, *Getting Smart: Feminist Research and Pedagogy with/in the Postmodern* (New York: Routledge, 1991); Jennifer M. Gore, "What Can We Do for You! What *Can* "We" Do for "You"?" *Educational Foundations* 4:2 (Summer 1990), 5–26. For a brilliant deconstruction of the debilitating effects of the binarisms inherent in Lather's position, see Peter McLaren, "Introduction: Postmodernism, Post-colonialism, and Pedagogy," in Peter McLaren, ed., *Post-modernism, Post-colonialism, and Pedagogy* (Albert Park, Australia: James Nicholas Publishers, in press). Of course, women of color have consistently refused to construct binary oppositions between varied critical pedagogies and the discourses of race and feminism. See, for example Chandra T. Mohanty, "On Race and Voice: Challenges for Liberal Education in the 1990s," *Cultural Critique* No. 14 (Winter 1990), 179–208. See also bell hooks, *Talking Back* (Boston: South End Press, 1989); *Yearnings* (Boston: South End Press, 1990); Michele Wallace, *Invisibility Blues* (London: Verso Press, 1991). What is interesting in these works is how they both critically engage and selectively appropriate the various positions taken up in critical pedagogy. hooks, in particular, is deeply influenced by the work of Paulo Freire, but does not suggest that because he does not make race and gender central to his work that it should simply be dismissed.

[12] Gayatri C. Spivak, quoted in Angela McRobbie, "Strategies of Vigilance: An Interview with Gayatri Chakravorty Spivak," *Block* 10 (1985), 9.

[13] See, for example Michael Apple, "Introduction" in Daniel P. Liston, *Capitalist Schools* (New York: Routledge, 1989); William Profriedt, "Review of *Capitalist Schools* and *Schooling and the Struggle for Public Life*" in *Socialism and Democracy* No. 9 (Fall/Winter 1989), 173–78; Jennifer M. Gore, "What Can We Do for You! What *Can* "We" Do for "You"? *Educational Foundations* 4:3 (Summer 1990), 5–26; Stan Karp, "A Review of Peter McLaren's *Life in Schools*," *Radical Teacher* No. 39 (Winter 1991), 32–34. See my extended response to the issue of clarity and language in Henry A. Giroux, "Writing for the Masses and Other Liberal Simplicities," *Socialism and Democracy* No. 11 (September 1990), 163–71; Henry A. Giroux and Peter McLaren, "Language, Schooling, and Subjectivity: Beyond a Pedagogy of Reproduction and Resistance," in Kathryn Borman, Piyush Swami, and Lonnie Wagstaff, eds., *Contemporary Issues in U.S. Education* (Norwood, N.J.: Ablex Publishing, 1991), 1–59.

[14] Bhabha, "The Commitment to Theory," 7.

[15] Related to this argument around clarity is a broader issue. The political and strategic inadequacy of much of what constitutes critical and radical versions of educational theory is largely evident in its overall refusal to engage the theoretical gains that have come to characterize the fields of literary studies, Marxist studies, feminist theory, poststructuralism, postmodernism, and democratic theory. Theoretically isolated from the many innovations taking place in the larger world of social theory, many educational theorists have removed themselves from critically engaging the limitations of the political projects implicit in their own work and have resorted instead to preaching the importance of the accessibility of theoretical language and the privileging of practice over theory. The call to writing in an educational language that is touted as clear and familiar appears to have become the political and ideological equivalent of a moral and political vision that increasingly collapses under the weight of its own anti-intellectualism and self-referential elitism. Similarly, educational theory is increasingly dissolved into practice under the vote-catching call for the importance of focusing on the concrete as the all-embracing sphere of educational strategy and relevance. To argue against these concerns is not meant as a clever exercise intent on merely reversing the relevance of the categories so that theory is prioritized over practice, or abstract language over the language of popcorn imagery. Nor am I merely suggesting that critical educators mount an equally reductionist argument against the use of clear language or the importance of practice. At issue here is the need to both question and reject the reductionism and exclusions that characterize the binary oppositions that inform these overly pragmatic tendencies.

[16] Edward W. Said, "Orientalism Reconsidered," *Cultural Critique* No. 1 (Fall 1985), 91.

[17] hooks, Chapter 15 *Yearning*, 145, 149.

[18] One important reference for this position is Donna Haraway, "Situated Knowledges: The Science Question in Feminism and the Privilege of Partial Perspective," *Feminist Studies* 14:3 (Fall 1989), 575–599.

[19] Ibid.

[20] Joan Borsa, "Towards a Politics of Location," *Canadian Woman Studies* (Spring 1990), 36.

[21] Donna Haraway, "Situated Knowledges," 589.

[22] Gayatri C. Spivak, *The Post-Colonial Critic*, 42.

[23] Robert Young, *White Mythologies*, 119.

[24] Richard Kearney, *The Wake of Imagination* (Minneapolis: University of Minnesota Press, 1988), 369.

[25] Gayatri C. Spivak, "The Making of Americans, the Teaching of English, and the Future of Cultural Studies," *New Literary History*, 21:4 (1990), 781–798.

[26] Ibid., 785.

[27] For example, see Guillermo Gomez-Peña, "The Other Vanguard," in Ivan Kapp, Christine Kreamer, and Steven Lavine, eds., *Museums and Communists: The Politics of Public Culture* (Washington, DC: Smithsonian Institution Press, 1992) pp. 65–75.

[28] William Bigelow and Norman Diamond, *The Power in Our Hands* (New York: Monthly Review Press, 1988).

[29] Roger I. Simon, Don Dippo, and Arleen Schenke, *Learning Work* (New York: Bergin and Garvey Press, 1991).

[30] Katie Singer, *Mosaic: Coming of Age in Boston—Across the Generations* (South Boston: Mosaic, 1984).

[31] Tony Bennett, *Outside Literature* (London: Routledge, 1990).

[32] Richard Johnson, "What is Cultural Studies Anyway?" *Social Text* No. 16 (Winter 1986/87), 38–80.

[33] Paulo Freire, *Pedagogy of the Oppressed* (New York: Seabury Press, 1973).

[34] Henry A. Giroux and Roger I. Simon, eds., *Popular Culture, Schooling, and Everyday Life* (New York: Bergin and Garvey Press, 1988).

[35] Lawrence Grossberg, "The Context of Audiences and the Politics of Difference," *Australian Journal of Communication*, No. 16 (1989), 13–35.

[36] Kobena Mercer, quoted in Lorraine Kenny, "Traveling Theory: The Cultural Politics of Race and Representation: An Interview with Kobena Mercer," *Afterimage* (September 1990), 8.

[37] Chandra T. Mohanty, "On Race and Voice," *Cultural Critique* No. 14 (Winter 1989/90), 207.

3

Crossing the Boundaries of Educational Discourse: Modernism, Postmodernism, and Feminism

We have entered an age that is marked by a crisis of power, patriarchy, authority, identity, and ethics. This new age has been described, for better or worse, by many theorists in a variety of disciplines as the age of postmodernism.[1] It is a period torn between the ravages and benefits of modernism; it is an age in which the notions of science, technology, and reason are associated not only with social progress but also with the organization of Auschwitz and the scientific creativity that made Hiroshima possible.[2] It is a time in which the humanist subject seems to no longer be in control of his or her fate. It is an age in which the grand narratives of emancipation, whether from the political right or left, appear to share an affinity for terror and oppression. It is also a historical moment in which culture is no longer seen as a reserve of white men whose contributions to the arts, literature, and science constitute the domain of high culture. We live at a time in which a strong challenge is being waged against a modernist discourse in which knowledge is legitimized almost exclusively from a European model of culture and civilization. In part, the struggle for democracy can be seen in the context of a broader struggle against certain features of modernism that represent the worst legacies of the Enlightenment tradition. And it is against these features that a variety of oppositional movements have emerged in an attempt to rewrite the relationship between modernism and democracy. Two of the most important challenges to modernism have come from divergent theoretical discourses associated with postmodernism and feminism.

Postmodernism and feminism have challenged modernism on a variety of theoretical and political fronts, and I will take these up shortly, but there is another side to modernism that has expressed itself more recently in the ongoing struggles in Eastern Europe. Modernism is not merely about patriarchy parading as universal reason, the increasing intensification of human domination over nature in the name of historical development, or the imperiousness of grand narratives that stress control and mastery.[3] Nor is modernism simply synonymous with forms of modernization characterized by the ideologies and practices of the dominating relations of capitalist production. It exceeds this fundamental but limiting rationality by offering the ideological excesses of democratic possibility. By this I mean that, as Ernesto Laclau and Chantal Mouffe have pointed out, modernism becomes a decisive point of reference for advancing certain and crucial elements of the democratic revolution.[4]

Beyond its claims to certainty, foundationalism, and epistemological essentialism, modernism provides theoretical elements for analyzing both the limits of its own historical tradition and for developing a political standpoint in which the breadth and specificity of democratic struggles can be expanded through the modernist ideals of freedom, justice, and equality. As Mark Hannam points out, modernism does have a legacy of progressive ambitions, that have contributed to substantive social change, and these ambitions need to be remembered in order to be reinserted into any developing discourses on democracy. For Hannam, these include: "economic redistribution towards equality, the emancipation of women, the eradication of superstition and despotism, wider educational opportunities, the improvement of the sciences and the arts, and so forth. Democratization was one of these ambitions and frequently was perceived to be a suitable means towards the realization of other, distinct ambitions."[5] What is important to note is that the more progressive legacies of modernism have been unleashed not in the West, where they have been undermined by modernism's undemocratic tendencies, but in Eastern Europe where the full force of political modernism has erupted to redraw the political and cultural map of the region. What this suggests is neither the death of modernism nor the facile dismissal of the new oppositional discourses that have arisen within postmodernism and feminism, but a rethinking of how the most critical aspects of these discourses can be brought to bear to deepen the democratic possibilities within the modernist project itself. For what is at stake here is not simply the emergence of a new language in order to rethink the modernist tradition, but also the reconstruction of the political, cultural, and social preconditions for developing a radical conception of citizenship and pedagogy.

That we live in an age in which a new political subject is being constructed can be seen most vividly in the events that have recently taken place in Eastern Europe within the last few years: the Berlin Wall has fallen; the Stalinist communist parties of the Eastern bloc are, for all intents and purposes, in disarray; the Soviet Union is radically modifying an identity forged in the legacy of Leninism and Bolshevism; and the master narratives of Marxism are being refigured within the shifting identities, cultural practices, and imaginary possibilities unleashed in the nascent discourse of a radical democracy. In Eastern Europe, the theoretical and political preconditions for a postmodern citizen are being constructed, even if only at the present they exist as a faint glimmer. This is a political subject that rejects the authoritarianism of master narratives, that refuses traditions that allow only for a reverence of what already is, that denies those instrumental and universalized forms of rationality that eliminate the historical and the contingent, that opposes science as a universal foundation for truth and knowledge, and that discredits the Western notion of subjectivity as a stable, coherent self. What these shifting perspectives and emergent social relations have done is to radicalize the possibilities of freedom and affirm the capacity of human beings to shape their own destinies as part of a larger struggle for democracy.

In the Western industrial countries, the revolutions in Eastern Europe for freedom, equality, and justice appear in the dominant media as the valiant struggle of the Other against enslavement through communism. But in the United States these are events that take place on the margins of civilization, related but not central to the political and cultural identity of the West except as mimesis. In the mass media, the struggles for equality and freedom in Eastern Europe have been analyzed through the lens of a modernist discourse that reproduces highly problematic notions of the Enlightenment tradition. For example, many Western theorists view the redrawing of the political and social borders of Eastern Europe in reductionist modernist terms as the "end of history," a metaphor for the already unquestionable triumph of capitalist liberal democracy. In this scenario, the ideological characteristics that define the center of civilization through the discourse of the Western democracies has now been extended to the culturally and politically "deprived" margins of civilization.

This is a curious position, because it fails to recognize that what the revolutions in Eastern Europe may be pointing to is not the "end of history" but to the exhaustion of those hierarchical and undemocratic features of modernism that produce state oppression, managerial domination, and social alienation in various countries in both the East and the West. It is curious because the "end of history" ideology, when applied to the Western democracies, is quite revealing; that is, it points to a political smugness, that presupposes that democracy in the West has reached its culmination. Of course, beneath this smugness lies the indifference of Western-style democracy toward substantive political life; in effect, what has become increasingly visible in this argument is the failure of democracy itself. Hannam captures this point. "Formal democracy has failed because it has generated indifference towards many of the substantive goals of political activity. Western democracy believes itself to be at its own endpoint; it has given up the ambition of social change, of which it was once a central, but never an exclusive part."[6]

While Western ruling groups and their apologists may choose to see only the triumph of liberal ideology beneath the changes in Eastern Europe, there is more being called into question than they suspect. In fact, the revolutions in Eastern Europe call into question not only the master narrative of Marxism, but all master narratives that make a totalizing claim to emancipation and freedom. In this case, the events taking place in Eastern Europe and in other places like South Africa represent part of a broader struggle of oppressed peoples against all totalizing forms of legitimation and cultural practice that deny human freedom and collective justice. What the West may be witnessing in Eastern Europe is the emergence of a new discourse, one that does not pit socialism against capitalism, but democracy against all forms of totalitarianism. In opposition to a limited modernist version of democracy, the struggles in Eastern Europe implicitly suggest the conditions for creating a radical democracy, one in which people control the social and economic forces that determine their existence. In this case, the struggle for democracy exceeds its modernist framework by extending the benefits of freedom and justice beyond the strictly formal mechanisms of democracy. What appears at work in these revolutions is a discourse that has the potential to deepen the radical implications of modernism through considerations of a rather profound set of questions: What set of conditions is necessary to create social relations for human liberation within historically specific formations? How might individual and social identities be reconstructed in the service of human imagination and democratic citizenship? How can the assertion of history and politics serve to deconstruct all essentialisms and totalizing rationalities? How can political and social identities be constructed within a politics of difference that is capable of struggling over and deepening the project of radical democracy while constantly asserting its historical and contingent character? Put another way, what can be done to strengthen and extend the oppositional tendencies of modernism?

I want to argue that modernism, postmodernism, and feminism represent three of the most important discourses for developing a cultural politics and pedagogical practice capable of extending and theoretically advancing a radical politics of democracy. While acknowledging that all three of these discourses are internally contradictory, ideologically diverse, and theoretically inadequate, I believe that when posited in terms of the interconnections between *both* their differences and the common ground they share for being mutually correcting, they offer critical educators a rich theoretical and political opportunity for rethinking the relationship between schooling and democracy. Each of these positions has much to learn from the theoretical strengths and weaknesses of the other two discourses. Not only does a dialogical encounter among these discourses offer them the opportunity to re-examine the partiality of their respective views. Such an encounter also points to new possibilities for sharing and integrating their best insights as part of broader radical democratic project. Together these diverse discourses offer the possibility for illuminating how critical educators might work with other cultural workers in various movements to develop and advance a broader discourse of political and collective struggle. At stake here is an attempt to provide a political and theoretical discourse, that can move beyond a postmodern aesthetic and a feminist separatism in order to develop a project in which a politics of difference can emerge within a shared discourse of democratic public life. Similarly, at issue is also the important question of how the discourses of modernism, postmodernism, and feminism might be pursued as part of a broader political effort to rethink the boundaries and most basic assumptions of a critical pedagogy consistent with a radical cultural politics.

I want to develop these issues through the following approach. First, I will analyze in schematic terms some of the central assumptions that characterize various modernist traditions, including Jürgen Habermas's spirited defense of social and political modernism. Second, I will analyze some of the central issues that postmodernism has made problematic in its encounter with modernism. Third, I will highlight the most progressive aspects of what can be loosely labeled post-modern feminist theory to be used in the service of advancing both its own critical tendencies and the most radical aspects of modernism and postmodernism. Finally, I will indicate how these three discourses might contribute to developing some important principles in the construction of a critical pedagogy for democratic struggle. It is to these issues that I will now turn.

Mapping the Politics of Modernism

To invoke the term "modernism" is to immediately place oneself in the precarious position of suggesting a definition that is itself open to enormous debate and little agreement.[7] Not only is there a disagreement regarding the periodisation of the term, there is enormous controversy regarding to what it actually refers. To some it has become synonymous with terroristic claims of reason, science, and totality.[8] To others it embodies, for better or worse, various movements in the arts.[9] And to some of its more ardent defenders, it represents the progressive rationality of communicative competence and support for the autonomous individual subject.[10] It is not possible within the context of this essay to provide a detailed history of the various historical and ideological discourses of modernism even though such an analysis is essential to provide a sense of the complexity of both the category and the debates that have emerged around modernism.[11] Instead, I want to focus on some of the central assumptions of modernism. The value of this approach is that it serves not only to highlight some of the more important arguments that have been made in the defense of modernism, but also to provide a theoretical and political backdrop for understanding some of the central features of various postmodernist and feminist discourses. This is particularly important with respect to postmodernism, which presupposes some idea of the modern and also various elements of feminist discourse, which have increasingly been forged largely in opposition to some of the major assumptions of modernism, particularly as these relate to notions such as rationality, truth, subjectivity, and progress.

The theoretical, ideological, and political complexity of modernism can be grasped by analyzing its diverse vocabularies with respect to three traditions: the social, the aesthetic, and the political. The notion of social modernity corresponds with the tradition of the new, the process of economic and social organization carried out under the growing relations of capitalist production. Social modernity approximates what Matei Calinescu calls the bourgeois idea of modernity, which is characterized by:

The doctrine of progress, the confidence in the beneficial possibilities of science and technology, the concern with time (a measurable time, a time that can be bought and sold and therefore has, like any other commodity, a calculable equivalent in money), the cult of reason, and the ideal of freedom defined within the framework of an abstract humanism, but also the orientation toward pragmatism and the cult of action and success.[12]

Within this notion of modernism, the unfolding of history is linked to the "continual progress of the sciences and of techniques, the rational division of industrial work, which introduces into social life a dimension of permanent change, of destruction of customs and traditional culture."[13] At issue here is a definition of modernity, that points to the progressive differentiation and rationalization of the social world through the process of economic growth and administrative rationalization. Another characteristic of social modernism is the epistemological project of elevating reason to an ontological status. Modernism in this view becomes synonymous with civilization itself, and reason is universalized in cognitive and instrumental terms as the basis for a model of industrial, cultural, and social progress. At stake in this notion of modernity is a view of individual and collective identity in which historical memory is devised as a linear process, the human subject becomes the ultimate source of meaning and action, and a notion of geographical and cultural territorality is constructed in a hierarchy of domination and subordination marked by a center and margin legitimated through the civilizing knowledge/power of a privileged Eurocentric culture.[14]

The category of aesthetic modernity has a dual characterization that is best exemplified in its traditions of resistance and formal aestheticism. But it is in the tradition of opposition, with its all consuming disgust with bourgeois values and its attempt through various literary and avant-garde movements to define art as a representation of criticism, rebellion, and resistance that aesthetic modernism first gained a sense of notoriety. Fueling this aesthetic modernism of the nineteenth and early twentieth centuries was an alienation and negative passion whose novelty was perhaps best captured in Bakunin's anarchist maxim, "To destroy is to create."[15] The cultural and political lineaments of this branch of aesthetic modernism are best expressed in those avant-garde movements that ranged from the surrealism and futurism to the conceptualism of the 1970s. Within this movement, with its diverse politics and expressions, there is an underlying commonality and attempt to collapse the distinction between art and politics and to blur the boundaries between life and aesthetics. But in spite of its oppositional tendencies, aesthetic modernism has not fared well in the latter part of the twentieth century. Its critical stance, its aesthetic dependency on the presence of bourgeois norms, and its apocalyptic tone became increasingly recognized as artistically fashionable by the very class it attacked.[16]

The central elements that bring these two traditions of modernism together constitute a powerful force not only for shaping the academic disciplines and the discourse of educational theory and practice, but also for providing a number of points where various ideological positions share a common ground. These elements can be recognized in modernism's claim for the superiority of high culture over and against popular culture, its affirmation of a centered if not unified subject, its faith in the power of the highly rational, conscious mind and its belief in the unequivocal ability of human beings to shape the future in the interest of a better world. There is a long tradition of support for modernism and some of its best representatives are as diverse as Marx, Baudelaire, and Dostoevsky. This notion of the unified self based on the universalization of reason and the totalizing discourses of emancipation have provided a cultural and political script for celebrating Western culture as synonymous with civilization itself and progress as a terrain that only needed to be mastered as part of the inexorable march of science and history. Marshall Berman exemplifies the dizzying heights of ecstasy made possible by the script of modernism in his own rendition of the modernist sensibility;[17]

> Modernists, as I portray them, are simultaneously at home in this world and at odds with it. They celebrate and identify with the triumphs of modern science, art, technology, communications, economics, politics—in short, with all the activities, techniques, and sensibilities that enable mankind to do what the Bible said God could do to "make all things new." At the same time, however, they oppose modernizations's betrayal of its own human promise and potential. Modernists demand more profound and radical renewals: modern men and women must become the subjects as well as the objects of modernization; they must learn to change the world that is changing them and to make it their own. The modernist knows this is possible: the fact that the world has changed so much is proof that it can change still more. The modernist can, in Hegel's phrase, "look at the negative in the face and live with it." The fact that "all that is solid melts into air" is a source not of despair, but of strength and affirmation. If everything must go, then let it go: modern people have the power to create a better world than the world they have lost.[18]

Of course, for many critics, the coupling of social and aesthetic modernism reveals itself quite differently. Modernist art is criticized for becoming nothing more than a commercial market for the museums and the corporate boardrooms and a depoliticized discourse institutionalized within the universities. In addition, many critics have argued that under the banner of modernism, reason and aesthetics often come together in a technology of self and culture that combines a notion of beauty, that is white, male, and European with a notion of mastery that legitimates modern industrial technologies and the exploitation of vast pools of labor from the "margins" of Second and Third World economies. Robert Merrill gives this argument a special twist in claiming that the modernist ego with its pretensions to infallibility and unending progress has actually come to doubt its own promises. For example, he argues that many proponents of modernism increasingly recognize that what has been developed by the West in the name of mastery actually indicates the failure of modernism to produce a technology of self and power that can deliver on the promises of providing freedom through science, technology, and control. He writes:

[A loss of faith in the promises of modernism] . . . is no less true for corporate and governmental culture in the United States which displays a . . . desperate quest for aestheticization of the self as modernist construct—white, male, Christian, industrialist—through monumentally styled office buildings, the Brooks Brothers suit (for male and female), designer food, business practices which amount only to the exercise of symbolic power, and most of all, the Mercedes Benz which as the unification in design of the good (here functional) and the beautiful and in production of industrial coordination and exploitation of human labor is pre-eminently the sign that one has finally achieved liberation and master, 'made it to the top' (even if its stylistic lines thematize what can only be called a fascist aesthetics).[19]

It is against the claims of social and aesthetic modernism that the diverse discourses of postmodernism and feminism have delivered some of their strongest theoretical and political criticism, and these will be taken up shortly. But there is a third tradition of modernism that has been engaged by feminism but generally ignored by postmodernism. This is the tradition of political modernism, which, unlike its related aesthetic and social traditions, does not focus on epistemological and cultural issues as much as it develops a project of possibility out of a number of Enlightenment ideals.[20] It should be noted that political modernism constructs a project that rests on a distinction between political liberalism and economic liberalism. With the latter, freedom is conflated with the dynamics of the capitalist market place, whereas with the former, freedom is associated with the principles and rights embodied in the democratic revolution that has progressed in the West over the last three centuries. The ideals that have emerged out of this revolution include "the notion that human beings ought to use their reason to decide on courses of action, control their futures, enter into reciprocal agreements, and be responsible for what they do and who they are."[21] In general terms, the political project of modernism is rooted in the capacity of individuals to be moved by human suffering so as to remove its causes, to give meaning to the principles of equality, liberty, and justice; and to increase those social forms that enable human beings to develop those capacities needed to overcome ideologies and material forms that legitimate and are embedded in relations of domination.

The tradition of political modernism has largely been taken up and defended in opposition to and against the discourse of postmodernism. Consequently, when postmodernism is defined in relation to the discourse of democracy it is pitted against the Enlightenment project and seen as reactionary in its political tend-encies,[22] grafted onto a notion of economic liberalism that converts it into an apology for rich Western democracies,[23] or portrayed in opposition to the eman-cipatory project of Marxism[24] and feminism.[25] I want to examine next some of the challenges that Jürgen Habermas presents to various versions of postmodernism and feminism through his defense of modernity as an unfinished emancipatory project.

Habermas and the Challenge of Modernism

Habermas has been one of the most vigorous defenders of the legacy of modernism. Habermas's work is important because in forging his defense of modernism as part of a critique of the postmodernist and poststructuralist discourses that have emerged in France since 1968, he has opened up a debate between these seemingly opposing positions. Moreover, Habermas has attempted to revise and reconstruct the earlier work of his Frankfurt School colleagues, Theodor Adorno and Max Horkheimer, by revising their pessimistic view of rationality and democratic struggle.

Habermas identifies postmodernity less as a question of style and culture than as one of politics. Postmodernism's rejection of grand narratives, its denial of epistemological foundations, and its charge that reason and truth are always implicated in relations of power are viewed by Habermas as both a retreat and a threat to modernity. For him, postmodernism has a paradoxical relation with modernism. On the one hand, it embodies the worst dimensions of an aesthetic modernism. That is, it extends those aspects of the avant-garde that "live in the experience of rebelling against all that is normative."[26] In this sense, postmodernism echoes surrealism's attempt to undermine the cultural autonomy of art by removing the boundaries that separate it from everyday life. On the other hand, postmodernism represents a negation of the project of social modernity by rejecting its language of universal reason, rights, and autonomy as a foundation for modern social life. According to Habermas, postmodernism's argument that realism, consensus, and totality are synonymous with terror represents a form of political and ethical exhaustion that unjustifiably renounces the unfinished task of the rule of reason.[27]

In Habermas's terms, the postmodernist thinkers are conservatives whose philosophical roots are to be found in various irrationalist and counter-Enlightenment theories that resemble a peculiar political kinship with fascism. Hence, postmodernism undermines the still unfolding project of modernity, with its promise of democracy through the rule of reason, communicative competence, and cultural differentiation. Postmodernism is guilty of the dual crime, in this case, of both rejecting the most basic tenets of the modernist ethos and failing to recognize its most emancipatory contributions to contemporary life. In the first instance, postmodernism recklessly overemphasizes the play of difference, contingency, and language against all appeals to universalized and transcendental claims. For the postmodernist, theory without the guarantee of truth redefines the relationship between discourse and power and in doing so destabilizes the modernist faith in consensus and reason. For Habermas, postmodernism represents a revolt against a substantive view of reason and subjectivity and negates the productive features of modernism.

Modernity offers Habermas the promise of integrating the differentiating spheres of science, morality, and art back into society not through an appeal to power, but through the rule of reason, the application of a universal pragmatics of language, and the development of forms of learning based on the dictates of communicative competence. While Habermas accepts the excesses of technological rationality and substantive reason, he believes that it is only through reason that the logic of scientific–technological rationality and domination can be subordinated to the imperatives of modernist justice and morality.[28] Habermas admires Western culture and argues that "bourgeois ideals" contain elements of reason that should be at the center of a democratic society. He writes:

> I mean the internal theoretical dynamic which constantly propels the sciences-and the self-reflection of the sciences as well-beyond the creation of merely technologically exploitable knowledge; furthermore, I mean the universalist foundations of law and morality which have also been embodied (in no matter how distorted and imperfect a form) in the institutions of constitutional states, in the forms of democratic decision-making, and in individualistic patterns of identity formation; finally, I mean the productivity and the liberating force of an aesthetic experience with a subjectivity set free from the imperatives of purposive activity and from the conventions of everyday perception.[29]

Central to Habermas's defense of modernity is his important distinction between instrumental rationality and communicative rationality. Instrumental rationality represents those systems or practices embodied in the state, money, and various forms of power that work through "steering mechanisms" to stabilize society. Communicative rationality refers to the world of common experience and discursive intersubjective interaction, a world characterized by various forms of socialization mediated through language and oriented toward social integration and consensus. Habermas accepts various criticisms of instrumental rationality, but he largely agrees that capitalism, in spite of its problems, represents more acceptable forms of social differentiation, rationalization, and modernization than have characterized past stages of social and instrumental development. On the other hand, he is adamant about the virtues of communicative rationality, with its emphasis on the rules of mutual understanding, clarity, consensus, and the force of argument. Habermas views any serious attack on this form of rationality as irrational itself. In effect, his notion of communicative rationality provides the basis not only for his ideal speech situation but also for his broader view of social reconstruction. With its distinctions between an outer world of systemic steering practices and a privileged inner world of communicative process, rationality in this case represents in part a division between a world saturated with material power expressed in the evolution of ever-growing and complex subsystems of rational modernization and one shaped by universal reason and communicative action. At the core of this distinction is a notion of democracy in which struggle and conflict are not based on a politics of difference and power, but on conceptual and linguistic search for defining the content of what is rational.[30]

Habermas's defense of modernity is not rooted in a rigorous questioning of the relationship between discourses, institutional structures, and the interests they produce and legitimate within specific social conditions. Instead, he focuses on linguistic competence and the principle of consensus with its guiding problematic defined by the need to uproot the obstacles to "distorted communication." Not only does this point to a particular view of power, politics, and modernity, it also legitimates, as Stanley Aronowitz points out, a specific notion of reason and learning:

> [Habermas] admonishes us to recognize modernity's unfinished tasks: the rule of reason. Rather than rules of governance based on power or discursive hegemonies, we are exhorted to create a new imaginary, one that would recognize societies able to resolve social conflicts, at least provisionally, so as to permit a kind of collective reflexivity. Characteristically, Habermas finds that the barriers to learning are not found in the exigencies of class interest, but in distorted communication. The mediation of communication by interest constitutes here an obstacle to reflexive knowledge. "Progressive" societies are those capable of learning—that is, acquiring knowledge that overcomes the limits of strategic or instrumental action.[31]

Habermas's work has been both opposed and taken up by a number of critical and radical groups. He has been highly criticized by feminists such as Nancy Fraser[32] and also embraced by radicals who believe that his search for universal values represents a necessary ingredient in the struggle for human emancipation.[33] In many respects, his writing provides a theoretical marker for examining how the debate over foundationalism and democracy, on the one hand, and a politics of difference and contingency, on the other, has manifested itself as a debate on the left between those who line up for or against different versions of modernism or postmodernism.

A more constructive approach to both the specifics of Habermas's work as well as to the larger issue of modernism is that neither should be accepted or rejected as if the only choice was one of complete denial or conversion. Habermas, for example, is both right and wrong in his analyses of modernism and postmodernism. He is right in attempting to salvage the productive and emancipatory aspects of modernism and for attempting to develop a unifying principle, that provides a referent for engaging and advancing a democratic society. He is also right in claiming that postmodernism is as much about the issue of politics and culture as it is about aesthetics and style. In this sense, Habermas provides a theoretical service by trying to keep alive as part of a modernist discourse the categories of critique, agency, and democracy. For better or worse, Habermas injects into the modernist versus postmodernist debate the primacy of politics and the role that rationality might play in the service of human freedom and the imperatives of democratic ideology and struggle. As Thomas McCarthy points out, Habermas:

> believes that the defects of the Enlightenment can only be made good by further enlightenment. The totalized critique of reason undercuts the capacity of reason to be critical. It refuses to acknowledge that modernization bears developments as well as distortions of reason. Among the former, he mentions the "unthawing"

and "reflective refraction" of cultural traditions, the universalization of norms and generalization of values, and the growing individuation of personal identities—all prerequisites for that effectively democratic organization of society through which alone reason can, in the end, become practical.[34]

It is around these concerns that postmodern theorists have challenged some of the basic assumptions of modernism. For Habermas, these challenges weaken rather than mobilize the democratic tendencies of modernism. But as I hope to demonstrate in the remainder of this chapter, Habermas is wrong in simply dismissing all forms of postmodernism as antimodernist and neoconservative. Moreover, given his own notion of consensus and social action, coupled with his defense of Western tradition, his view of modernity is too complicitous with a notion of reason that is used to legitimate the superiority of a culture that is primarily white, male, and Eurocentric. Habermas speaks from a position that is not only susceptible to the charge of being patriarchal but is also open to the charge that his work does not adequately engage the relationship between discourse and power and the messy material relations of class, race, and gender. Postmodern and feminist critiques of his work cannot be dismissed simply because they might be labeled as antimodern or antirationalist. In what follows, I want to take up some of the challenges that postmodernism has developed in opposition to some of the central assumptions of modernism.

Postmodern Negations

If postmodernism means putting the Word in its place . . . if it means the opening up to critical discourse the line of enquiry which were formerly prohibited, of evidence which was previously inadmissible so that new and different questions can be asked and new and other voices can begin asking them; if it means the opening up of institutional and discursive spaces within which more fluid and plural social and sexual identities may develop; if it means the erosion of triangular formations of power and knowledge with the expert at the apex and the "masses" at the base, if, in a word, it enhances our collective (and democratic) sense of possibility, then I for one am a postmodernist.[35]

Dick Hebdige's guarded comments regarding his own relationship to postmodernism are suggestive of some of the problems that have to be faced in using the term. As the term is increasingly employed both in and out of the academy to designate a variety of discourses, its political and semantic currency repeatedly becomes an object of conflicting forces and divergent tendencies. Postmodernism has not only become a site for conflicting ideological struggles—denounced by different factions on both the left and the right, supported by an equal number of diverse progressive groups, and appropriated by interests that would renounce any claim to politics—its varied forms have also produced both radical and reactionary elements. Postmodernism's diffuse influence and contradictory character is evident within many cultural fields—painting, architecture, photography, video, dance, literature, education, music, mass communications—and in the varied contexts of its production and exhibition. Such a term does not lend itself to the usual topology of categories that serve to inscribe it ideologically and politically within traditional binary oppositions. In this case, the politics of postmodernism cannot be neatly labeled under the traditional categories of left and right.

That many groups are making a claim for its use should not suggest that the term has no value except as a buzzword for the latest intellectual fashions. On the contrary, its widespread appeal and conflict-ridden terrain indicate that something important is being fought over, that new forms of social discourse are being constructed at a time when the intellectual, political, and cultural boundaries of the age are being refigured amidst significant historical shifts, changing power structures, and emergent alternative forms of political struggle. Of course, whether these new postmodernist discourses adequately articulate rather than reflect these changes is the important question.

I believe that the discourse of postmodernism is worth struggling over, and not merely as a semantic category that needs to be subjected to ever more precise definitional rigor. As a discourse of plurality, difference, and multinarratives, postmodernism resists being inscribed in any single articulating principle in order to explain either the mechanics of domination or the dynamic of emancipation. At issue here is the need to mine its contradictory and oppositional insights so that they might be appropriated in the service of a radical project of democratic struggle. The value of postmodernism lies in its role as a shifting signifier that both reflects and contributes to the unstable cultural and structural relationships that increasingly characterize the advanced industrial countries of the West. The important point here is not whether postmodernism can be defined within the parameters of particular politics, but how its best insights might be appropriated within a progressive and emancipatory democratic politics.

I want to argue that while postmodernism does not suggest a particular ordering principle for defining a particular political project, it does have a rudimentary coherence with respect to the set of "problems and basic issues that have been created by the various discourses of postmodernism, issues that were not particularly problematic before but certainly are now."[36] Postmodernism raises questions and problems so as to redraw and re-present the boundaries of discourse and cultural criticism. The issues that postmodernism has brought into view can be seen, in part, through its various refusals of all "natural laws" and transcendental claims that by definition attempt to "escape" from any type of historical and normative grounding. In fact, if there is any underlying harmony to various discourses of postmodernism it is in their rejection of absolute essences. Arguing along similar lines, Laclau claims that postmodernity as a discourse of social and cultural criticism begins with a form of epistemological, ethical, and political awareness based on three fundamental negations.

> The beginning of postmodernity can ... be conceived as the achievement of multiple awareness: epistemological awareness, insofar as scientific progress ap-

pears as a succession of paradigms whose transformation and replacement is not grounded in any algorithmic certainty; ethical awareness, insofar as the defense and assertion of values is grounded on argumentative movements (conservational movements, according to Rorty), which do not lead back to any absolute foundation; political awareness, insofar as historical achievements appear as the product of hegemonic and contingent—and as such, always reversible—articulations and not as the result of immanent laws of history.[37]

Laclau's list does not exhaust the range of negations that postmodernism has taken up as part of the increasing resistance to all totalizing explanatory systems and the growing call for a language that offers the possibility to address the changing ideological and structural conditions of our time. In what follows, I shall address some of the important thematic considerations that cut across what I define as a series of postmodern negations. I shall address these negations in terms of the challenge they present to what can be problematized as either oppressive or productive features of modernism.

Postmodernism and the Negation of Totality, Reason, and Foundationalism

A central feature of postmodernism has been its critique of totality, reason, and universality. This critique has been most powerfully developed in the work of Jean-Francois Lyotard. In developing his attack on Enlightenment notions of totality, Lyotard argues that the very notion of the postmodern is inseparable from an incredulity toward metanarratives. In Lyotard's view, "The narrative view is losing its functors, its great hero, its great dangers, its great voyages, it great goal. It is being dispersed in clouds of narrative language elements—narrative, but also denotative, prescriptive, descriptive, and so on.[38] For Lyotard, grand narratives do not problematize their own legitimacy; rather, they deny the historical and social construction of their own first principles and in doing so wage war on difference, contingency, and particularity. Against Habermas and others, Lyotard argues that appeals to reason and consensus, when inserted within grand narratives that unify history, emancipation and knowledge, deny their own implications in the production of knowledge and power. More emphatically, Lyotard claims that within such narratives are elements of mastery and control in which "we can hear the mutterings of the desire for a return of terror, for the realization of the fantasy to seize reality."[39] Against metanarratives, which totalize historical experience by reducing its diversity to a one-dimensional, all-encompassing logic, Lyotard posits a discourse of multiple horizons, the play of language games, and the terrain of micropolitics. Against the formal logic of identity and the transhistorical subject, he invokes a dialectics of indeterminacy, varied discourses of legitimation, and a politics based on the "permanence of difference." Lyotard's attack on metanarratives represents both a trenchant form of social criticism and a philosophical challenge to all forms of foundationalism that deny the historical, normative, and the contingent. Nancy Fraser and Linda Nicholson articulate this connection well:

For Lyotard, postmodernism designates a general condition of contemporary Western civilization. The postmodern condition is one in which "grand narratives of legitimation" are no longer credible. By "grand narratives" he means, in the first instance, overarching philosophies of history like the Enlightenment story of the gradual but steady progress of reason and freedom, Hegel's dialectic of Spirit coming to know itself,and, most important, Marx's drama of the forward march of human productive capacities via class conflict culminating in proletarian revolution. . . . For what most interests [Lyotard] about the Enlightenment, Hegelian, and Marxist stories is what they share with other nonnarrative forms of philosophy. Like ahistorical epistemologies and moral theories, they aim to show that specific first-order discursive practices are well formed and capable of yielding true and just results. True and just here mean something more than results reached by adhering scrupulously to the constitutive rules of some given scientific and political games. They mean, rather, results that correspond to Truth and Justice as they really are in themselves independent of contingent, historical social practices. Thus, in Lyotard's view, a metanarrative . . . purports to be a privileged discourse capable of situating, characterizing, and evaluating all other discourses, but not itself infected by the historicity and contingency that render first-order discourses potentially distorted and in need of legitimation.[40]

What Fraser and Nicholson imply is that postmodernism does more than wage war on totality, it also calls into question the use of reason in the service of power, the role of intellectuals who speak through authority invested in a science of truth and history, and forms of leadership that demand unification and consensus within centrally administered chains of command. Postmodernism rejects a notion of reason that is disinterested, transcendent, and universal. Rather than separating reason from the terrain of history, place, and desire, postmodernism argues that reason and science can only be understood as part of a broader historical, political, and social struggle over the relationship between language and power. Within this context, the distinction between passion and reason, objectivity and interpretation no longer exist as separate entities but represent, instead, the effects of particular discourses and forms of social power. This is not merely an epistemological issue, but one that is deeply political and normative. Gary Peller makes this clear by arguing that what is at stake in this form of criticism is nothing less than the dominant and liberal commitment to Enlightenment culture. He writes:

Indeed the whole way that we conceive of liberal progress (overcoming prejudice in the name of truth, seeing through the distortions of ideology to get at reality, surmounting ignorance and superstition with the acquisition of knowledge) is called into question. Postmodernism suggests that what has been presented in our social-political and our intellectual traditions as knowledge, truth, objectivity, and reason are actually merely the effects of a particular form of social power, the victory of a particular way of representing the world that then presents itself as beyond mere interpretation, as truth itself.[41]

By asserting the primacy of the historical and contingent in the construction of reason, authority, truth, ethics, and identity, postmodernism provides a politics of representation and a basis for social struggle. Laclau argues that the postmodern attack on foundationalism is an eminently political act because it expands the possibility for argumentation and dialogue. Moreover, by acknowledging questions of power and value in the construction of knowledge and subjectivities, postmodernism helps to make visible important ideological and structural forces, such as race, gender, and class. For theorists such as Laclau, the collapse of foundationalism does not suggest a banal relativism or the onset of a dangerous nihilism. On the contrary, Laclau argues that the lack of ultimate meaning radicalizes the possibilities for human agency and a democratic politics. He writes:

> Abandoning the myth of foundations does not lead to nihilism, just as uncertainty as to how an enemy will attack doe not lead to passivity. It leads, rather, to a proliferation of discursive interventions and arguments that are necessary, because there is no extradiscursive reality that discourse might simply reflect. Inasmuch as argument and discourse constitute the social, their open-ended character becomes the source of a greater activism and a more radical libertarianism. Humankind, having always bowed to external forces—God, Nature, the necessary laws of History—can now, at the threshold of postmodernity, consider itself for the first time the creator and constructor of its own history.[42]

The postmodern attack on totality and foundationalism is not without its drawbacks. While it rightly focuses on the importance of local narratives and rejects the notion that truth precedes the notion of representation, it also runs the risk of blurring the distinction between master narratives that are monocausal and formative narratives, that provide the basis for historically and relationally placing different groups or local narratives within some common project. To draw out this point further, it is difficult to imagine any politics of difference as a form of radical social theory if it doesn't offer a formative narrative capable of analyzing difference within rather than against unity. I will develop these criticisms in more detail in another section.

Postmodernism as the Negation of Border Cultures

Postmodernism offers a challenge to the cultural politics of modernism at a number of different levels. That is, it not only provides a discourse for retheorizing culture as fundamental to the construction of political subjects and collective struggle, it also theorizes culture as a politics of representation and power. Emily Hicks has presented the postmodern challenge to modernist culture as one framed within the contexts of shifting identities, the remapping of borders, and nonsynchronous memory.[43] In her terms, modernist culture negates the possibility of identities created within the experience of multiple narratives and "border" crossings; instead, modernism frames culture within rigid boundaries that both privilege and exclude around the categories of race, class, gender, and ethnicity. Within the discourse of modernism, culture, in large part, becomes an organizing principle for constructing borders that reproduce relations of domination, subordination, and inequality. In this case, borders do not offer the possibility to experience and position ourselves within a productive exchange of narratives. Instead, modernism constructs borders framed in the language of universals and oppositions. Within the cultural politics of modernism, European culture becomes identified with the center of civilization, high culture is defined in essentialist terms against the popular culture of the everyday, and history as the reclaiming of critical memory is displaced by the proliferation of images. In effect, postmodernism constitutes a general attempt to transgress the borders sealed by modernism, to proclaim the arbitrariness of all boundaries, and to call attention to the sphere of culture as a shifting social and historical construction.

I want to approach the postmodern challenge to a modernist cultural politics by focusing briefly on a number of issues. First, postmodernism has broadened the discussion regarding the relationship between culture and power by illuminating the changing conditions of knowledge embedded in the age of electronically mediated information systems, cybernetic technologies, and computer engineering. In doing so, it has pointed to the development of new forms of knowledge that significantly shape traditional analyses relevant to the intersection of culture, power, and politics. Second, postmodernism raises a new set of questions regarding how culture is inscribed in the production of center/margin hierarchies and the reproduction of postcolonial forms of subjugation. At issue here is not only a reconsideration of the intersection of race, gender, and class, but also a new way of reading history; that is, postmodernism provides forms of historical knowledge as a way of reclaiming power and identity for subordinate groups.[44] Third, postmodernism breaks down the distinction between high and low culture and makes the everyday an object of serious study.[45]

In the first instance, postmodernism points to the increasingly powerful and complex role of the new electronic medium in constituting individual identities, cultural languages, and new social formations. Postmodernism has thus provided a new discourse that enables us to understand the changing nature of domination and resistance in late capitalist societies.[46] This is particularly true in its analyses of how the conditions for the production of knowledge have changed within the last two decades with respect to the electronic information technologies of production, the types of knowledge produced, and the impact they have had at both the level of everyday life and in larger global terms.[47] Postmodern discourses highlight radical changes in the ways in which culture is produced, circulated, read, and consumed; moreover, they seriously challenge those theoretical models that have inadequately analyzed culture as a productive and constituting force within an increasingly global network of scientific, technological, and information-producing apparatuses.

In the second instance, postmodernism has provided an important theoretical service in mapping the relations of the center and periphery with respect to three related interventions into cultural politics. First, it has offered a powerful challenge to the hegemonic notion that Eurocentric culture is superior to other cultures and traditions by virtue of its canonical status as a universal measure of Western civilization. In exposing the particularity of the alleged universals that constitute Eurocentric culture, postmodernism has revealed that the "truth" of Western culture is by design a metanarrative that ruthlessly expunges the stories, traditions, and voices of those who by virtue of race, class, and gender constitute the Other. Postmodernism's war on totality is defined, in this case, as a campaign against Western patriarchal culture and ethnocentricity. To the extent that postmodernism has rejected the ethnocentricism of Western culture, it has also waged a battle against those forms of academic knowledge that serve to reproduce the dominant Western culture as a privileged canon and tradition immune from history, ideology, and social criticism.[48]

Central to such a challenge is a second aspect of postmodernism's refiguring of the politics of the center and the margins. That is, postmodernism not only challenges the form and content of dominant models of knowledge, but it also produces new forms of knowledge through its emphasis on breaking down disciplines and taking up objects of study that were unrepresentable in the dominant discourses of the Western canon.

Postmodern criticism provides an important theoretical and political service in assisting those deemed "Other" to reclaim their own histories and voices. By problematizing the dominant notion of tradition, postmodernism has developed a power-sensitive discourse that helps subordinated and excluded groups to make sense out of their own social worlds and histories, while simultaneously offering new opportunities to produce political and cultural vocabularies by which to define and shape their individual and collective identities. At stake here is both the rewriting of history within a politics of difference that substitutes totalizing narratives of oppression with local and multiple narratives, that assert their identities and interests as part of a broader reconstruction of democratic public life. Craig Owens captures the project of possibility that is part of reclaiming voices that have been relegated to the marginal and, therefore, seem to be unrepresentable. While women emerge as the privileged force of the marginal in this account, his analysis is equally true for a number of subordinated groups.

> It is precisely at the legislative frontier between what can be represented and what cannot that the postmodernist operation is being staged—not in order to transcend representation, but in order to expose that system of power that authorizes certain representations while blocking, prohibiting, or invalidating others. Among those prohibited from Western representation, whose representations are denied all legitimacy, are women. Excluded from representation by its very structure, they return within it as a figure for—a presentation of—the unrepresentable.[49]

Postmodernism's attempt to explore and articulate new spaces is not without its problems. Marginality as difference is not an unproblematic issue, and differences have to be weighted against the implications they have for constructing multiple relations between the self and the other. Moreover, resistance takes place not only on the margins but also at various points of entry within dominant institutions.

Needless to say, any notion of difference and marginality runs the risk of mystifying as well as enabling a radical cultural politics. But what is crucial is that postmodernism does offer the possibility for developing a cultural politics that focuses on the margins, for reclaiming, as Edward Said points out, "the right of formerly un- or misrepresented human groups to speak for and represent themselves in domains defined, political and intellectually, as normally excluding them, usurping their signifying and representing functions, over-riding their historical reality."[50]

This leads to a third dimension of a postmodern cultural politics. As part of a broader politics of difference, postmodernism has also focused on the ways in which modernity functions as an imperialist masternarrative that links Western models of industrial progress with hegemonic forms of culture, identity, and consumption. Within this context, the project of modernity relegates all non-Western cultures to the periphery of civilization, outposts of insignificant histories, cultures, and narratives.

In the discourse of neocolonial modernism, the culture of the Other is no longer inscribed in imperialist relations of domination and subordination through the raw exercise of military or bureaucratic power. Power now inscribes itself in apparatuses of cultural production that easily transgress national and cultural borders. Data banks, radio transmissions, and international communications systems become part of the vanguard of a new global network of cultural and economic imperialism. Modernity now parades its universal message of progress through the experts and intellectuals it sends to Third World universities, through the systems of representations that it produces to saturate billboards all over Latin America, and/or and through advertising images it sends out from satellites to the television sets of inhabitants in Africa, India, and Asia.

Postmodernism makes visible both the changing technological nature of postcolonial imperialism and the new forms of emerging resistance that it encounters. On the one hand, it rejects the notion that the colonial relationship is an "uninterrupted psychodrama of repression and subjugation."[51] There is an attempt to understand how power is not only administered, but also taken up, resisted, and struggled over. The Other in this scenario does not suffer the fate of being generalized out of existence, but bears the weight of historical and cultural specificity. In part, this has resulted in a radical attempt to read the culture of the Other as a construction rather than a description, as a form of text that evokes rather than merely represents.[52] Within this scenario, the relationship between the subject and the object, invention and construction is never innocent and is always implicated in theorizing about the margins and the center. At issue here is an attempt to make problematic the voices of those who try to describe the margins, even when they do so in the interest of emancipation and social justice.[53] This suggests yet another aspect of postcolonial discourse that postmodernism has begun to analyze as part of its own cultural politics.

In the postmodern age, the boundaries that once held back diversity, otherness, and difference, whether in domestic ghettoes or through national borders policed by custom officials, have begun to break down. The Eurocentric center can no longer absorb or contain the culture of the Other as something that is threatening and dangerous. As Renato Rosaldo points out, "the Third World has imploded into the metropolis. Even the conservative national politics of containment, designed to shield 'us' from 'them,' betray the impossibility of maintaining hermetically sealed cultures."[54] Culture in neocolonial discourse becomes something that Others have; it is the mark of ethnicity and difference. What has changed in this hegemonic formulation/strategy is that diversity is not ignored in the dominant cultural apparatus, but promoted in order to be narrowly and reductively defined through dominant stereotypes. Representation does not merely exclude, it also defines cultural difference by *actively* constructing the identity of the Other for dominant and subordinate groups. Postmodernism challenges postcolonial discourse by bringing the margins to the center in terms of their own voices and histories. Representation, gives way to opposition and the struggle over questions of identity, place, and values.[55] Difference holds out the possibility of not only bringing the voices and politics of the Other to the centers of power, but also understanding how the center is implicated in the margins. It is an attempt to understand how the radicalizing of difference can produce new forms of displacement and more refined forms of racism and sexism. Understandably, the best work in this field is being done by writers from the "margins."

Finally, it is well known that postmodernism breaks with dominant forms of representation by rejecting the distinction between elite and popular culture and by arguing for alternative sites of artistic engagement and forms of experimentation.[56] As an antiaesthetic, postmodernism rejects the modernist notion of privileged culture or art; it renounces "official" centers for "housing" and displaying art and culture along with their interests in origins, periodization, and authenticity. Moreover, postmodernism's challenge to the boundaries of modernist art and culture has, in part, resulted in new forms of art, writing, film-making, and various types of aesthetic and social criticism. For example, films like *Whetherby* and television movies like *Twin Peaks* deny the structure of plot and seem to have no recognizable beginning or end, photographer Sherrie Levine uses a "discourse of copy" in her work in order to transgress the notions of origin and originality, and Connie Hatch focuses on the act of looking itself.[57] Writer James Sculley blurs the lines between writing poetry and producing it within a variety of representational forms.[58] The Talking Heads, an American band, adopt an eclectic range of aural and visual signifiers to produce a pastiche of styles in which genres are mixed, identities shift, and the lines between reality and image are purposely blurred.[59]

Most importantly, postmodernism conceives of the everyday and the popular as worthy of serious *and* playful consideration. In the first instance, popular culture is analyzed as an important sphere of contestation, struggle, and resistance. In doing so, postmodernism does not abandon the distinctions that structure varied cultural forms within and between different levels of social practice. Instead, it deepens the possibility for understanding the social, historical, and political foundation for such distinctions as they are played out within the intersection of power, culture, and politics. In the second instance, postmodernism cultivates a tone of irony, parody, and playfulness as part of an aesthetic, that desacralizes cultural aura and "greatness" while simultaneously demonstrating that "contingency penetrates all identity" and that "the primary and constitutive character of the discursive is . . . the condition of any practice."[60] Richard Kearney has noted that the postmodern notion of play, with its elements of undecidability and poetical imagining, challenges constricted and egocentric levels of selfhood and allows us to move toward a greater understanding of the Other.

> The ex-centric characteristics of the play paradigm may be construed as tokens of the poetical power of imagination to transcend the limits of egocentric, and indeed anthropocentric, consciousness—thereby exploring different possibilities of existence. Such "possibilities" may well be deemed impossible at the level of the established reality.[61]

Central to the postmodern rejection of elite culture as a privileged domain of cultural production and repository of "truth" and civilization is an attempt to understand modernist cultural practices in their hegemonic and contradictory manifestations. Postmodernism also rejects the notion of popular culture as structured exclusively through a combination of commodity production and audience passivity, a site for both dumping commercial junk and the creation of consumer robots. Instead, postmodernism views popular culture as a terrain of accommodation and struggle, a terrain whose structuring principles should be analyzed not in the reductionistic language of aesthetic standards, but rather through the discourse of power and politics. Of course, it must be stated that the postmodern elements of a cultural politics that I have provided need to be interrogated more closely for their excesses and absences. I will take up this issue in another section, but in what follows I will analyze the third postmodern negation regarding language and subjectivity.

Postmodernism, Language, and the Negation of the Humanist Subject

Within the discourse of postmodernism, the new social agents become plural; that is, the discourse of the universal agent, such as the working class, is replaced by multiple agents forged in a variety of struggles and social movements. Here we have a politics that stresses differences between groups. But it is worth noting that subjectivities are also constituted within difference. This is an important distinction and offers an important challenge to the humanist notion of the subject as a free, unified, stable, and coherent self. In fact, one of the most important theoretical and political advances of postmodernism is its stress on the centrality of language and subjectivity as new fronts from which to rethink the issues of meaning, identity, and politics. This issue can best be approached by first analyzing the ways in which postmodernism has challenged the conventional view of language.

Postmodern discourse has retheorized the nature of language as a system of signs structured in the infinite play of difference, and in doing so has undermined the dominant, positivist notion of language as either a genetic code structured in permanence or simply a linguistic, transparent medium for transmitting ideas and meaning. Theorists such as Jacques Derrida, Michel Foucault, Jacques Lacan, and Laclau and Mouffe, in particular, have played a major role in retheorizing the relationship among discourse, power, and difference.[62] For example, Derrida has brilliantly analyzed the issue of language through the principle of what he calls "differance." This view suggests that meaning is the product of a language constructed out of and subject to the endless play of differences between signifiers. What constitutes the meaning of a signifier is defined by the shifting, changing relations of difference that characterize the referential play of language. What Derrida, Laclau and Mouffe, and a host of other critics have demonstrated is "the increasing difficulty of defining the limits of language, or, more accurately, of defining the specific identity of the linguistic object."[63] But more is at stake here than theoretically demonstrating that meaning can never be fixed once and for all.

The postmodern emphasis on the importance of discourse has also resulted in a major rethinking of the notion of subjectivity. In particular, various postmodern discourses have offered a major critique of the liberal humanist notion of subjectivity, which is predicated on the notion of a unified, rational, self-determining consciousness. In this view, the individual subject is the source of self-knowledge, and his or her view of the world is constituted through the exercise of a rational and autonomous mode of understanding and knowing. What postmodern discourse challenges is liberal humanism's notion of the subject "as a kind of free, autonomous, universal sensibility, indifferent to any particular or moral contents."[64] Teresa Ebert in her discussion of the construction of gender differences offers a succinct commentary on the humanist notion of identity:

> Postmodern feminist cultural theory breaks with the dominant humanist view . . . in which the subject is still considered to be an autonomous individual with a coherent, stable self constituted by a set of natural and pre-given elements such as biological sex. It theorizes the subject as produced through signifying practices which precede her and not as the originator of meaning. One acquires specific subject positions—that is, existence in meaning, in social relations—being constituted in ideologically structured discursive acts. Subjectivity is thus the effect of a set of ideologically organized signifying practices through which the individual is situated in the world and in terms of which the world and one's self are made intelligible.[65]

The importance of postmodernism's retheorizing of subjectivity cannot be overemphasized. In this view, subjectivity is no longer assigned to the apolitical wasteland of essences and essentialism. Subjectivity is now read as multiple, layered, and nonunitary; rather than being constituted in a unified and integrated ego, the self is seen as being "constituted out of and by difference and remains contradictory."[66] No longer viewed as merely the repository of consciousness and creativity, the self is constructed as a terrain of conflict and struggle, and subjectivity is seen as a site of both liberation and subjugation. How subjectivity relates to issues of identity, intentionality, and desire is a deeply political issue that is inextricably related to social and cultural forces that extend far beyond the self-consciousness of the so-called humanist subject. Both the very nature of subjectivity and its capacities for self- and social determination can no longer be situated within the guarantees of transcendent phenomena or metaphysical essences. Within this postmodern perspective, the basis for a cultural politics and the struggle for power has been opened up to include the issues of language and identity. I now want to take up how various feminist discourses reinscribe some of the central assumptions of modernism and postmodernism as part of a broader cultural practice and political project.

Postmodern Feminism as Political and Ethical Practice

Feminist theory has always engaged in a dialectical relationship with modernism. On the one hand, it has stressed modernist concerns with equality, social justice, and freedom through an ongoing engagement with substantive political issues, specifically the rewriting of the historical and social construction of gender in the interest of an emancipatory cultural politics. In other words, feminism has been quite discriminating in its ability to sift through the wreckage of modernism in order to liberate its victories, particularly the unrealized potentialities that reside in its categories of agency, justice, and politics. On the other hand, postmodern feminism has rejected those aspects of modernism in which universal laws are exalted at the expense of specificity and contingency. More specifically, postmodern feminism opposes a linear view of history, that legitimates patriarchal notions of subjectivity and society; moreover, it rejects the notion that science and reason have a direct correspondence with objectivity and truth. In effect, postmodern feminism rejects the binary opposition between modernism and postmodernism in favor of a broader theoretical attempt to situate both discourses critically within a feminist political project.

Feminist theory has both produced and profited from a critical appropriation of a number of assumptions central to both modernism and postmodernism. The feminist engagement with modernism has been taken up primarily as a discourse of self-criticism and has served to radically expand a plurality of positions within feminism itself. Women of color, lesbians, and poor and working-class women have challenged the essentialism, separatism, and ethnocentrism that have been expressed in feminist theorizing and in doing so have seriously undermined the the Eurocentricism and totalizing discourse that has become a political straitjacket within the movement. Fraser and Nicholson offer a succinct analysis of some of the issues involved in this debate, particularly in relation to the appropriation by some feminists of "quasi-metanarratives."

> They tacitly presuppose some commonly held but unwarranted and essentialist assumptions about the nature of human beings and the conditions for social life. In addition, they assume methods and/or concepts that are uninflected by temporality or historicity and that therefore function *de facto* as permanent, neutral matrices for inquiry. Such theories, then, share some of the essentialist and ahistorical features of metanarratives: they are insufficiently attentive to historical and cultural diversity; and they falsely universalize features of the theorist's own era, society, culture, class, sexual orientation, and/or ethnic or racial group. . . . It has become clear that quasi-metanarratives hamper, rather than promote, sisterhood, since they elide differences among women and among the forms of sexism to which different women are differentially subject. Likewise, it is increasingly apparent that such theories hinder alliances with other progressive movements, since they tend to occlude axes of domination other than gender. In sum, there is a growing interest among feminists in modes of theorizing that are attentive to differences and to cultural and historical specificity.[67]

Fashioning a language that has been highly critical of modernism has not only served to make problematic what can be called totalizing feminisms, but has also called into question the notion that sexist oppression is at the root of all forms of domination.[68] Implicit in this position are two assumptions that have significantly shaped the arguments of mostly Western white women. The first argument simply inverts the orthodox Marxist position regarding class as the primary category of domination with all other modes of oppression being relegated to a second rate consideration. Here, patriarchy becomes the primary form of domination, while race and class are reduced to its distorted reflection. The second assumption recycles another aspect of orthodox Marxism that assumes that the struggle over power is exclusively waged between opposing social classes. The feminist version of this argument simply substitutes gender for class and in doing so reproduces a form of "us" against "them" politics that is antithetical to developing community building within a broad and diversified public culture.

Both of these arguments represent the ideological baggage of modernism. In both cases, domination is framed in binary oppositions, which suggests that workers or women cannot be complicit in their own oppression and that domination assumes a form that is singular and uncomplicated. The feminist challenge to this ideological straitjacket of modernism is well expressed by bell hooks, who avoids the politics of separatism by invoking an important distinction between the role that feminists might play in asserting their own particular struggle against patriarchy as well as the role they can play as part of a broader struggle for liberation.

> Feminist effort to end patriarchal domination should be of primary concern precisely because it insists on the eradication of exploitation and oppression in the family context and in all other intimate relationships. . . . Feminism, as liberation

struggle, must exist apart from and as a part of the larger struggle to eradicate domination in all of its forms. We must understand that patriarchal domination shares an ideological foundation with racism and other forms of group oppression, that there is no hope that it can be eradicated while these systems remain intact. This knowledge should consistently inform the direction of feminist theory and practice. Unfortunately, racism and class elitism among women has frequently led to the suppression and distortion of this connection so that it is now necessary for feminist thinkers to critique and revise much feminist theory and the direction of the feminist movement. This effort at revision is perhaps most evident in the current widespread acknowledgement that sexism, racism, and class exploitation constitute interlocking systems of domination—that sex, race, and class, and not sex alone, determine the nature of any female's identity, status, and circumstance, the degree to which she will or will not be dominated, the extent to which she will have the power to dominate.[69]

I invoke the feminist critique of modernism to make visible some of the ideological territory it shares with certain versions of postmodernism and to suggest the wider implications that a postmodern feminism has for developing and broadening the terrain of political struggle and transformation. It is important to note that this encounter between feminism and postmodernism should not be seen as a gesture to displace a feminist politics with a politics and pedagogy of postmodernism. On the contrary, I think feminism provides postmodernism with a politics, and a great deal more. What is at stake here is using feminism, in the words of Meaghan Morris, as "a context in which debates about postmodernism might further be considered, developed, transformed (or abandoned)."[70] Critical to such a project is the need to analyze the ways in which feminist theorists have used postmodernism to fashion a form of social criticism whose value lies in its critical approach to gender issues and in the theoretical insights it provides for developing broader democratic and pedagogical struggles.

The theoretical status and political viability of various postmodern discourses regarding the issues of totality, foundationalism, culture, subjectivity and language are a matter of intense debate among diverse feminist groups.[71] I am less concerned with charting this debate or focusing on those positions that dismiss postmodernism as antithetical to feminism. Instead, I want to focus primarily on those feminist discourses that acknowledge being influenced by postmodernism but at the same time deepen and radicalize the assumptions most important in the interest of a theory and practice of transformative feminist democratic struggles.[72]

Feminism's relationship with postmodernism has been both fruitful but problematic.[73] Postmodernism shares a number of assumptions with various feminist theories and practices. For example, both discourses view reason as plural and partial, define subjectivity as multilayered and contradictory, and posit contingency and difference against various forms of essentialism.

At the same time, postmodern feminism has criticized and extended a number of assumptions central to postmodernism. First, it has asserted the primacy of social criticism and in doing so has redefined the significance of the postmodern challenge to founding discourses and universal principles in terms that prioritize political struggles over epistemological engagements. Donna Haraway puts it well in her comment that "the issue is ethics and politics perhaps more than epistemology."[74] Second, postmodern feminism has refused to accept the postmodern view of totality as a wholesale rejection of all forms of totality or metanarratives. Third, it has rejected the postmodern emphasis on erasing human agency by decentering the subject; it has also resisted defining language as the only source of meaning and has therefore linked power not merely to discourse but also to material practices and struggles. Fourth, it has asserted the importance of difference as part of a broader struggle for ideological and institutional change rather than emphasizing the postmodern approach to difference as either an aesthetic (pastiche) or as a expression of liberal pluralism (the proliferation of difference without recourse to the language of power). Since it is impossible within this chapter to analyze all of these issues in great detail, I will take up some of the more important tendencies implied in these positions.

Postmodern Feminism and the Primacy of the Political

> Working collectively to confront difference, to expand our awareness of sex, race, and class as interlocking systems of domination, of the ways we reinforce and perpetuate these structures, is the context in which we learn the true meaning of solidarity. It is this work that must be the foundation of feminist movement. Without it, we cannot effectively resist patriarchal domination; without it, we remain estranged and alienated from one another. Fear of painful confrontation often leads women and men active in feminist movement to avoid rigorous critical encounter, yet if we cannot engage dialectically in a committed, rigorous, humanizing manner, we cannot hope to change the world. . . . While the struggle to eradicate sexism and sexist oppression is and should be the primary thrust of feminist movement, to prepare ourselves politically for this effort we must first learn how to be in solidarity, how to struggle with one another.[75]

bell hooks speaks eloquently to the issue of constructing a feminism that is self-consciously political. In solidarity with a number of feminists, she provides a much-needed corrective to the postmodern tendency to eclipse the political and ethical in favor of issues that center on epistemological and aesthetic concerns. Not only does hooks assert that intellectual and cultural work must be driven by political questions and issues, she also performs the theoretically important task of affirming a feminist politics, which attempts to understand and contest the various ways in which patriarchy is inscribed at every level of daily life. But what is different and postmodern about hooks's commentary is that argues for a postmodern feminist practice that is oppositional in its appeal "to end sexism and sexist oppression,"[76] and she also calls into question those feminisms that reduce domination to a single cause, focus exclusively on sexual difference, and ignore women's differences as they intersect across other vectors of power, particularly with regards to race and class. In this version of postmodern feminist politics there is an attempt to reaffirm

the centrality of gender struggles while simultaneously broadening the issues associated with such struggles. Similarly, there is an attempt to connect gender politics
to a broader politics of solidarity. Let me be more specific about some of these
issues.

Central to the feminist movement in the United States since the 1970s has
been the argument that the personal is political. This argument suggests a complex
relationship between material social practices and the construction of subjectivity
through the use of language. Within this context, subjectivity was analyzed as a
historical and social construction, en-gendered through the historically weighted
configurations of power, language, and social formations. The problematization of
gender relations in this case has been often described as the most important
theoretical advance made by feminists.[77] Postmodern feminism has extended the
political significance of this issue in important ways.

First, it has strongly argued that feminist analyses cannot downplay the dialectical significance of gender relations. That is, such relations have to focus not
only on the various ways in which women are inscribed in patriarchal representations and relations of power, but also on how gender relations can be used to
problematize the sexual identities, differences, and commonalities of both men and
women. To suggest that masculinity is an unproblematic category is to adopt an
essentialist position, that ultimately reinforces the power of patriarchal discourse.[78]

Second, feminist theorists have redefined the relationship between the personal
and political in ways that advance some important postmodern assumptions. In
part, this redefinition of the relationship has emerged out of an increasing feminist
criticism that rejects the notions that sexuality is the only axis of domination and
that the study of sexuality should be limited theoretically to an exclusive focus on
how women's subjectivities are constructed. For example, theorists such as Teresa
de Lauretis have argued that central to feminist social criticism is the need for
feminists to maintain a "tension between (the personal and the political) precisely
through the understanding of identity as multiple and even-self contradictory."[79]
To ignore such a tension often leads to the trap of collapsing the political into the
personal and limiting the sphere of politics to the language of pain, anger, and
separatism. bell hooks elaborates on this point by arguing that when feminists
reduce the relationship between the personal and the political merely to the naming
of one's pain in relation to structures of domination they often undercut the
possibilities for understanding the multifaceted nature of domination and for creating a politics of possibility. She writes:

> That powerful slogan, "the personal is political," addresses the connection between
> the self and political reality. Yet it was often interpreted as meaning that to name
> one's personal pain in relation to structures of domination was not just a beginning
> stage in the process of coming to political consciousness, to awareness, but all
> that was necessary. In most cases, naming one's personal pain was not sufficiently
> linked to overall education for critical consciousness of collective political resist-
> ance. Focusing on the personal in a framework that did not compel acknowl-

edgement of the complexity of structures of domination could easily lead to misnaming, to the creation of yet another sophisticated level of non- or distorted awareness. This often happens in a feminist context when race and/or class are not seen as factors determining the social construction of one's gendered reality and most importantly, the extent to which one will suffer exploitation and domination.[80]

The construction of gender must, therefore, be seen in the context of the wider relations in which it is structured. At issue here is the need to deepen the postmodern notion of difference by radicalizing the notion of gender through a refusal to isolate it as a social category while simultaneously engaging in a politics, that aims at transforming the self, community, and society. Within this context, postmodern feminism offers the possibility of going beyond the language of domination, anger, and critique.

Third, postmodern feminism attempts to understand the broader workings of power by examining how it functions other than through specific technologies of control and mastery. At issue here is understanding how power is constituted productively. Teresa de Lauretis develops this insight by arguing that while postmodernism provides a theoretical service in recognizing that power is "productive of knowledges, meanings, and values, it seems obvious enough that we have to make distinctions between the positive effects and the oppressive effects of such production."[81] Her point is important because it suggests that power can work in the interests of a politics of possibility, that it can be used to rewrite the narratives of subordinate groups not merely in reaction to the forces of domination but in response to the construction of alternative visions and futures. The exclusive emphasis on power as oppressive always runs the risk of developing as its political equivalent a version of radical cynicism and antiutopianism. Postmodern feminism offers the possibility for redefining both a negative feminist politics[82] and a more general postmodern inclination towards a despair that dresses itself up in irony, parody, and pastiche. Linda Alcoff put it well in arguing that "As the Left should by now have learned, you cannot mobilize a movement that is only and always against: you must have a positive alternative, a vision of a better future that can motivate people to sacrifice their time and energy toward its realization."[83] Central to this call for a language of possibility are the ways in which a postmodern feminism has taken up the issue of power in more expansive and productive terms, one that is attentive to the ways in which power inscribes itself through the force of reason, and constructs itself at the levels of intimate and local associations.

Postmodern Feminism and the Politics of Reason and Totality

Various feminist discourses have provided a theoretical context and politics for enriching postmodernism's analyses of reason and totality. Whereas postmodern theorists have stressed the historical, contingent, and cultural construction of reason, they have failed to show how reason has been constructed as part of a masculine discourse.[84] Postmodern feminists have provided a powerful challenge to this position, particularly in their analyses of the ways in which reason, language, and representation have produced knowledge/power relations, legitimated in the discourse of science and objectivity, to silence, marginalize, and misrepresent women.[85] Feminist theorists have also modified the postmodern discussion of reason in two other important ways. First, while recognizing that all claims to reason are partial, they have argued for the emancipatory possibilities that exist in reflective consciousness and critical reason as a basis for social criticism.[86] In these terms, reason is not merely about a politics of representation structured in domination or a relativist discourse that abstracts itself from the dynamics of power and struggle, it also offers the possibility for self-representation and social reconstruction. For example, Haraway has qualified the postmodern turn towards relativism by theorizing reason within a discourse of partiality that "privileges contestation, deconstruction, passionate construction, webbed connections, and hope for transformation of systems of knowledge and ways of seeing."[87] Similarly, hooks and others have argued that feminists who deny the power of critical reason and abstract discourse often reproduce a cultural practice that operates in the interest of patriarchy.[88] That is, it serves to silence women and others by positioning them in ways that cultivate a fear of theory, which in turn often produce a form of powerlessness buttressed by a powerful antiintellectualism. Second, feminists such as Jane Flax have modified postmodernism's approach to reason by arguing that reason is not the only locus of meaning:

> I cannot agree . . . that liberation, stable meaning, insight, self-understanding and justice depend above all on the "primacy of reason and intelligence." There are many ways in which such qualities may be attained—for example, political practices, economic, racial and gender equality; good childrearing; empathy; fantasy; feelings; imagination; and embodiment. On what grounds can we claim reason is privileged or primary for the self or justice?[89]

At issue here is not the rejection of reason but a modernist version of reason that is totalizing, essentialist, and politically repressive. Postmodern feminism has also challenged and modified the postmodern approach to totality or master narratives on similar terms. While accepting the postmodern critique of master narratives that employ a single standard and make a claim to embody a universal experience, postmodern feminism does not define all large or formative narratives as oppressive. At the same time, postmodern feminism recognizes the importance of grounding narratives in the contexts and specificities of peoples' lives, communities, and cultures, but supplements this distinctly postmodern emphasis on the contextual with an argument for metanarratives that employ forms of social criticism that are dialectical, relational, and holistic. Metanarratives play an important theoretical role in placing the particular and the specific in broader historical and relational contexts. To reject all notions of totality is to run the risk of being trapped in particularistic theories that cannot explain how the various diverse relations that constitute larger social, political, and global systems interrelate or mutually determine and constrain one another. Postmodern feminism recognizes that we need a notion of large narratives that privileges forms of analyses in which it is possible to make visible those mediations, interrelations, and interdependencies that give shape and power to larger political and social systems. Fraser and Nicholson make very clear the importance of such narratives to social criticism.

> Effective criticism . . . requires an array of different methods and genres. It requires, at minimum, large narratives about changes in social organization and ideology, empirical and social-theoretical analyses of macrostructures and institutions, interactionist analyses of the micropolitics of everyday life, critical-hermeneutical and institutional analyses of cultural production, historically and culturally specific sociologies of gender. . . . The list could go on.[90]

Postmodern Feminism and the Politics of Difference and Agency

Many feminists exhibit a healthy skepticism toward the postmodern celebration of difference. Many feminist theorists welcome the postmodern emphasis on the proliferation of local narratives, the opening up of the world to cultural and ethnic differences, and the positing of difference as a challenge to hegemonic power relations parading as universals.[91] But at the same time, postmodern feminists have raised serious questions about how differences are to be understood so as to change rather than reproduce prevailing power relations.[92] This is particularly important since difference in the postmodern sense often slips into a theoretically harmless and politically deracinated notion of pastiche. For many postmodern feminists, the issue of difference has to be interrogated around a number of concerns. These include questions regarding how a politics of difference can be constructed that will not simply reproduce forms of liberal individualism, or how a politics of difference can be "rewritten as a refusal of the terms of radical separation?"[93] Also at issue is the question regarding how a theory of difference can be developed that is not at odds with a politics of solidarity. Equally important is the issue of how a theory of the subject constructed in difference might sustain or negate a politics of human agency. And there is the question of how a postmodern feminism can redefine the knowledge/power relationship in order to develop a theory of difference that is not static, one that is able to make distinctions between differences that matter and those that do not. All of these questions have been addressed in a variety of feminist discourses, not all of which support postmodernism. What has increasingly emerged from this engagement is a discourse that radically complicates and amplifies the possibilities for reconstructing difference within a radical political project and set of transformative practices.

In the most general sense, the postmodern emphasis on difference serves to dissolve all pretensions to an undifferentiated concept of truth, man, woman, and subjectivity, while at the same time refusing to reduce difference to "opposition, exclusion, and hierarchic arrangement."[94] Postmodern feminism has gone a long way in framing the issue of difference in terms that give it an emancipatory grounding, that identify the "differences that make a difference" as an important political act. Below, I want to briefly take up the issue of difference and agency that has been developed within a postmodern feminist discourse.

Joan Wallach Scott has provided a major theoretical service by dismantling one of the crippling dichotomies in which the issue of difference has been situated. Rejecting the idea that difference and equality constitutes an opposition, Scott argues that the opposite of equality is not difference but inequality. In this sense, the issue of equality is not at odds with the notion of difference, but depends on an acknowledgment of those differences that promote inequality and those that do not. For Scott, the category of difference is central as a political construct to the notion of equality itself. The implication this has for a feminist politics of difference involves two important theoretical moves:

> In histories of feminism and in feminist political strategies there needs to be at once attention to the operations of difference and an insistence on differences, but not a simple substitution of multiple for binary difference, for it is not a happy pluralism we ought to invoke. The resolution of the "difference dilemma" comes neither from ignoring nor embracing difference as it is normatively constituted. Instead it seems to me that the critical feminist position must always involve two moves: the first, systematic criticism of the operations of categorical difference, exposure of the kinds of exclusions and inclusions—the hierarchies—it constructs, and a refusal of their ultimate "truth." A refusal, however, not in the name of an equality that implies sameness or identity but rather (and this is the second move) of an equality that rests on differences—differences that confound, disrupt, and render ambiguous the meaning of any fixed binary opposition. To do anything else is to buy into the political argument that sameness is a requirement for equality, an untenable position for feminists (and historians) who know that power is constructed on, and so must be challenged from, the ground of difference.[95]

According to Scott, challenging power from the ground of difference by focusing on both exclusions and inclusions allows one to avoid slipping into a facile and simple elaboration or romanticization of difference. In more concrete terms, E. Ann Kaplan takes up this issue in arguing that the postmodern elimination of all distinctions between high and low culture is important, but postmodernism goes too far in overlooking the important differences at work in the production and exhibition of specific cultural works.[96] By not discriminating among differences of context, production, and consumption, postmodern discourses run the risk of suppressing the differences at work in the power relations that characterize these different spheres of cultural production. For example, to treat all cultural products as texts may situate them as historical and social constructions, but it is imperative that the institutional mechanisms and power relations in which different texts are produced be distinguished so that it becomes possible to understand how such texts, in part, make a difference in terms of reproducing particular meanings, social relations, and values.

A similar issue is at work regarding the postmodern notion of subjectivity. The postmodern notion that human subjectivities and bodies are constructed in the endless play of difference threatens to erase not only any possibility for human agency or choice, but also the theoretical means for understanding how the body becomes a site of power and struggle around specific differences that do matter with respect to the issues of race, class, and gender. There is little sensibility in many postmodern accounts toward the ways in which different historical, social, and gendered representations of meaning and desire are actually mediated and taken up subjectively by real, concrete individuals. Individuals are positioned within a variety of "subject positions," but there is no sense of how they actually make choices, promote effective resistance, or mediate between themselves and others. Feminist theorists have extended the most radical principles of modernism in modifying the postmodern view of the subject. Theorists such as de Lauretis, Rita Felski, and others insist that the construction of female experience is not constructed outside of human intentions and choices, however limited. They argue that the agency of subjects is made possible through shifting and multiple forms of consciousness constructed through available discourses and practices, but always open to interrogation through the process of a self-analyzing practice. For de Lauretis and others like Alcoff, such a practice is theoretical and political. Alcoff's own attempt to construct a feminist identity–politics draws on de Lauretis' work and is insightful in its attempt to develop a theory of positionality.

> . . . the identity of a woman is the product of her own interpretation and reconstruction of her history, as mediated through a cultural discursive context to which she has access. Therefore, the concept of positionality includes two points: First . . . the concept of woman is a relational term identifiable only with a (constantly moving) context; but second, that the position that women find themselves in can be actively utilized (rather than transcended) as a location for the construction of meaning, a place where a meaning can be discovered (the meaning of femaleness). The concept . . . of positionality shows how women use their positional perspective as a place from which values are interpreted and constructed rather than as a locus of an already determined set of values.[97]

Feminists have also raised a concern with the postmodern tendency to portray the body as so fragmented, mobile, and boundary-less that it invites a confusion over how the body is actually engendered and positioned within concrete configurations of power and forms of material oppression. The postmodern emphasis on the proliferation of ideas, discourses, and representations underplays both the different ways in which bodies are oppressed and how bodies are constructed differently through specific material relations. Feminists such as Sandra Lee Bartky have provided a postmodern reading of the politics of the body by extending Foucault's notion of how the growth of the modern state has been accompanied by an unprecedented attempt at disciplining the body.[98] Where Bartky differs from Foucault is that she employs a discriminating notion of difference by showing how gender is implicated in the production of the body as a site of domination, struggle, and resistance. For example, Bartky points to the disciplinary measures of dieting, the tyranny of slenderness and fashion, the discourse of exercise, and other technologies of control. She also goes beyond Foucault in arguing that the body must be seen as a site of resistance and linked to a broader theory of agency.

Postmodern feminism provides a grounded politics that employs the most progressive aspects of modernism and postmodernism. In the most general sense, it reaffirms the importance of difference as part of a broader political struggle for the reconstruction of public life. It rejects all forms of essentialism but recognizes the importance of certain formative narratives. Similarly, it provides a language of power that engages the issue of inequality and struggle. In recognizing the importance of institutional structures and language in the construction of subjectivities and political life, it promotes social criticism that acknowledges the interrelationship between human agents and social structures, rather than succumbing to a social theory without agents or one in which agents are simply the product of broad structural and ideological forces. Finally, postmodern feminism provides a radical social theory imbued with a language of critique and possibility. Implicit in its various discourses are new relations of parenting, work, schooling, play, citizenship, and joy. These are relations that link a politics of intimacy and solidarity, the concrete and the general; they provide a politics, that in its various forms needs to be taken up as central to the development of a critical pedagogy. That is, critical educators need to provide a sense of how the most critical elements of modernism, postmodernism, and postmodern feminism might be taken up by teachers, educators, and cultural workers so as to create a postmodern pedagogical practice. Finally, I want to briefly outline what some of the principles are that inform such a practice.

Towards a Postmodern Pedagogy

As long as people are people, democracy in the full sense of the word will always be no more than an ideal. One may approach it as one would a horizon, in ways that may be better or worse, but it can never be fully attained. In this sense, you too, are merely approaching democracy. You have thousands of problems of all kinds, as other countries do. But you have one great advantage: You have been approaching democracy uninterrupted for more than 200 years.[99]

How on earth can these prestigious persons in Washington ramble on in their subintellectual way about the "end of history?" As I look forward into the twenty-first century I sometimes agonize about the times in which my grandchildren and their children will live. It is not so much the rise in population as the rise in universal material expectations of the globe's huge population that will be straining its resources to the very limits. North–South antagonisms will certainly sharpen, and religious and national fundamentalisms will become more intransigent. The struggle to bring consumer greed within moderate control, to find a level of low growth and satisfaction that is not at the expense of the disadvantaged and poor, to defend the environment and to prevent ecological disasters, to share more equitably the world's resources and to insure their renewal—all this is agenda enough for the continuation of "history."[100]

> A striking character of the totalitarian system is its peculiar coupling of human demoralization and mass depoliticizing. Consequently, battling this system requires a conscious appeal to morality and an inevitable involvement in politics.[101]

All these quotations stress, implicitly or explicitly, the importance of politics and ethics to democracy. In the first, the newly elected president of Czechoslovakia, Vaclav Havel, addressing a joint session of Congress reminds the American people that democracy is an ideal that is filled with possibilities but one that always has to be seen as part of an ongoing struggle for freedom and human dignity. As a playwright and former political prisoner, Havel is the embodiment of such a struggle. In the second, E. P. Thompson, the English peace activist and historian, reminds the American public that history has not ended but needs to be opened up in order to engage the many problems and possibilities that human beings will have to face in the twenty-first century. In the third, Adam Michnik, a founder of Poland's Workers' Defense Committee and an elected member of the Polish parliament, provides an ominous insight into one of the central features of totalitarianism, whether on the Right or the Left. He points to a society that fears democratic politics while simultaneously reproducing a sense of massive collective despair. All of these writers are caught up in the struggle to recapture the Enlightenment model of freedom, agency, and democracy while simultaneously attempting to deal with the conditions of a postmodern world.

These statements serve to highlight the inability of the American public to grasp the full significance of the democraticization of Eastern Europe in terms of what it reveals about the nature of our own democracy. In Eastern Europe and elsewhere there is a strong call for the primacy of the political and the ethical as a foundation for democratic public life, whereas in the United States there is an ongoing refusal of the discourse of politics and ethics. Elected politicians from both sides of the established parties complain that American politics is about "trivialization, atomization, and paralysis." Politicians as different as the late Lee Atwater, the former Republican Party chairman, and Walter Mondale, former vice president, agree that we have entered into a time in which much of the American public believes that "Bull permeates everything . . . (and that) we've got a kind of politics of irrelevance."[102] At the same time, a number of polls indicate that while the youth of Poland, Czechoslovakia, and Germany are extending the frontiers of democracy, American youth are both unconcerned and largely ill-prepared to struggle for and keep democracy alive in the twenty-first century.

Rather than being a model of democracy, the United States has become indifferent to the need to struggle for the conditions that make democracy a substantive rather than lifeless activity. At all levels of national and daily life, the breadth and depth of democratic relations are being rolled back. We have become a society that appears to demand less rather than more of democracy. In some quarters, democracy has actually become subversive. What does this suggest for developing some guiding principles in order to rethink the purpose and meaning of education and critical pedagogy within the present crises? In what follows, I want to situate some of the work I have been developing on critical pedagogy over the last decade by placing it within a broader political context. That is, the principles that I develop below represent educational issues that must be located in a larger framework of politics. Moreover, these principles emerge out of a convergence of various tendencies within modernism, postmodernism, and postmodern feminism. What is important to note here is the refusal to simply play off these various theoretical tendencies against each other. Instead, I try to critically appropriate the most important aspects of these theoretical movements by raising the question of how they contribute to creating the conditions for deepening the possibilities for a radical pedagogy and political project that aims at reconstructing democratic public life so as to extend the principles of freedom, justice, and equality to all spheres of society.

At stake here is the issue of retaining modernism's commitment to critical reason, agency, and the power of human beings to overcome human suffering. Modernism reminds us of the importance of constructing a discourse that is ethical, historical, and political. At the same time, postmodernism provides a powerful challenge to all totalizing discourses, places an important emphasis on the contingent and the specific, and provides a new theoretical language for developing a politics of difference. Finally, postmodern feminism makes visible the importance of grounding our visions in a political project, redefines the relationship between the margins and the center around concrete political struggles, and offers the opportunity for a politics of voice that links rather than severs the relationship between the personal and the political as part of a broader struggle for justice and social transformation. All the principles developed below touch on these issues and recast the relationship between the pedagogical and the political as central to any social movement that attempts to effect emancipatory struggles and social transformations. All of these issues are dealt with in more detail throughout this book.[103]

1. Education needs to be reformulated so as to give as much attention to pedagogy as it does to traditional and alternative notions of scholarship. This is not a question of giving pedagogy equal weight to scholarship as much as it is of assessing the important relationship between them. Education must be understood as the production of identities in relation to the ordering, representation, and legitimation of specific forms of knowledge and power. As Chandra Mohanty reminds us, questions about education cannot be reduced to disciplinary parameters, but must include issues of power, history, self-identity, and the possibility of collective agency and struggle.[104] Rather than rejecting the language of politics, critical pedagogy must link public education to the imperatives of a critical democracy. Critical pedagogy needs to be informed by a public philosophy defined, in part, by the attempt to create the lived experience of empowerment for the vast majority. In other words, the language of critical pedagogy needs to construct schools as democratic public spheres.

In part, this means that educators need to develop a critical pedagogy in which the knowledge, habits, and skills of critical citizenship, not simply good citizenship, are taught and practiced. This means providing students with the opportunity to develop the critical capacity to challenge and transform existing social and political forms, rather than simply adapt to them. It also means providing students with the skills they will need to locate themselves in history, find their own voices, and provide the convictions and compassion necessary for exercising civic courage, taking risks, and furthering the habits, customs, and social relations that are essential to democratic public forms.

In effect, critical pedagogy needs to be grounded in a keen sense of the importance of constructing a political vision from which to develop an educational project as part of a wider discourse for revitalizing democratic public life. A critical pedagogy for democracy cannot be reduced, as some educators, politicians, and groups have argued, to forcing students to either say the pledge of allegiance at the beginning of every school day or to speak and think only in the language of dominant English. A critical pedagogy for democracy does not begin with test scores but with questions. What kinds of citizens do we hope to produce through public education in a postmodern culture? What kind of society do we want to create in the context of the present shifting cultural and ethnic borders? How can we reconcile the notions of difference and equality with the imperatives of freedom and justice?

2. Ethics must be seen as a central concern of critical pedagogy. This suggests that educators attempt to understand more fully how different discourses offer students diverse ethical referents for structuring their relationship to the wider society. But it also suggests that educators go beyond the postmodern notion of understanding how student experiences are shaped within different ethical discourses. Educators must come to view ethics and politics as a relationship between the self and the other. Ethics, in this case, is not a matter of individual choice or relativism but a social discourse that refuses to accept needless human suffering and exploitation. Ethics becomes a practice that broadly connotes one's personal and social sense of responsibility to the Other. Thus, ethics is taken up as a struggle against inequality and as a discourse for expanding basic human rights. This points to a notion of ethics attentive to both the issue of abstract rights and those contexts that produce particular stories, struggles, and histories. In pedagogical terms, an ethical discourse needs to be taken up with regard to the relations of power, subject positions, and social practices it activates. This is an ethics of neither essentialism nor relativism. It is an ethical discourse grounded in historical struggles and attentive to the construction of social relations free of injustice. The quality of ethical discourse is not simply grounded in difference but in the issue of how justice arises out of concrete historical circumstances and public struggles.

3. Critical pedagogy needs to focus on the issue of difference in an ethically challenging and politically transformative way. There are at least two notions of

difference at work here. One, difference can be incorporated into a critical pedagogy as part of an attempt to understand how student identities and subjectivities
are constructed in multiple and contradictory ways. In this case, identity is explored
through its own historicity and complex subject positions. The category of student
experience should not be limited pedagogically to students exercising self-reflection
but opened up as a race, gender, and class specific construct to include the diverse
ways in which students' experiences and identities have been constituted in different
historical and social formations. Two, critical pedagogy can focus on how differences between groups develop and are sustained around both enabling and disabling
sets of relations. In this instance, difference becomes a marker for understanding
how social groups are constituted in ways that are integral to the functioning of
any democratic society. Examining difference in this context does not only focus
on charting spatial, racial, ethnic, or cultural differences structured in dominance,
but also analyzes historical differences that manifest themselves in public struggles.

As part of a language of critique, teachers can make problematic how different
subjectivities are positioned within a historically specific range of ideologies and
social practices that inscribe students in various subject positions. Similarly, such
a language can analyze how differences within and between social groups are
constructed and sustained within and outside of the schools in webs of domination,
subordination, hierarchy, and exploitation. As part of their use of a language of
possibility, teachers can explore the opportunity to develop knowledge/power relations in which multiple narratives and social practices are constructed around a
politics and pedagogy of difference that offers students the opportunity to read
the world differently, resist the abuse of power and privilege, and construct alternative democratic communities. Difference in this case cannot be seen as simply
either as a register of plurality or as a politics of assertion. Instead, it must be
developed within practices in which differences can be affirmed *and* transformed
in their articulation with historical and relational categories central to emancipatory
forms of public life: democracy, citizenship, and public spheres. In both political
and pedagogical terms, the category of difference must not be simply acknowledged
but defined relationally in terms of antiracist, antipatriarchal, multicentric, and
ecological practices central to the notion of democratic community.

4. Critical pedagogy needs a language that allows for competing solidarities and
political vocabularies that do not reduce the issues of power, justice, struggle, and
inequality to a single script, a master narrative that suppresses the contingent, the
historical, and the everyday as serious objects of study. This suggests that curriculum knowledge should not be treated as a sacred text but developed as part of
an ongoing engagement with a variety of narratives and traditions that can be
reread and reformulated in politically different terms. At issue here is how to
construct a discourse of textual authority that is power-sensitive and developed as
part of a wider analysis of the struggle over culture fought out at the levels of
curricula knowledge, pedagogy, and the exercise of institutional power. This is not

merely an argument against a canon, but one that refigures the meaning and use of canon. Knowledge has to be constantly re-examined in terms of its limits and rejected as a body of information that only has to be passed down to students. As Laclau has pointed out, setting limits to the answers given by what can be judged as a valued tradition (a matter of argument also) is an important political act.[105] What Laclau is suggesting is the possibility for students to creatively appropriate the past as part of a living dialogue, an affirmation of the multiplicity of narratives, and the need to judge those narratives not as timeless or as monolithic discourses, but as social and historical inventions that can be refigured in the interests of creating more democratic forms of public life. Here is opened the possibility for creating pedagogical practices characterized by the open exchange of ideas, the proliferation of dialogue, and the material conditions for the expression of individual and social freedom.

5. Critical pedagogy needs to create new forms of knowledge through its emphasis on breaking down disciplinary boundaries and creating new spheres in which knowledge can be produced. In this sense, critical pedagogy must be reclaimed as a cultural politics and a form of social-memory. This is not merely an epistemological issue, but one of power, ethics, and politics. Critical pedagogy as a cultural politics points to the necessity of inserting the struggle over the production and creation of knowledge as part of a broader attempt to create a number of diverse critical public cultures. As a form of social-memory, critical pedagogy starts with the everyday and the particular as a basis for learning. It reclaims the historical and the popular as part of an ongoing effort to critically appropriate the voices of those who have been silenced and to help move the voices of those who have been located within narratives that are monolithic and totalizing beyond indifference or guilt to emancipatory practice. At stake here is a pedagogy that provides the knowledge, skills, and habits for students and others to read history in ways that enable them to reclaim their identities in the interests of constructing more democratic and just forms of life.

This struggle deepens the pedagogical meaning of the political and the political meaning of the pedagogical. In the first instance, it raises important questions about how students and others are constructed as agents within particular histories, cultures, and social relations. Against the monolith of culture, it posits the conflicting terrain of cultures shaped within asymmetrical relations of power, grounded in diverse historical struggles. Similarly, culture has to be understood as part of the discourse of power and inequality. As a pedagogical issue, the relationship between culture and power is evident in questions such as "Whose cultures are appropriated as our own? How is marginality normalized?"[106] To insert the primacy of culture as a pedagogical and political issue is to make central how schools function in the shaping of particular identities, values, and histories by producing and legitimating specific cultural narratives and resources. In the second instance, asserting the pedagogical aspects of the political raises the issue of how difference and culture can be taken up as pedagogical practices and not merely as political categories. For example, how does difference matter as a pedagogical category if educators and cultural workers have to make knowledge meaningful before it can become critical and transformative? Or what does it mean to engage the tension between being theoretically correct and pedagogically wrong? These concerns and tensions offer the possibility for making the relationship between the political and the pedagogical mutually informing and problematic.

6. The Enlightenment notion of reason needs to be reformulated within a critical pedagogy. First, educators need to be skeptical regarding any notion of reason that purports to reveal the truth by denying its own historical construction and ideological principles. Reason is not innocent, and any viable notion of critical pedagogy cannot exercise forms of authority that emulate totalizing forms of reason that appear to be beyond criticism and dialogue. This suggests that we reject claims to objectivity in favor of partial epistemologies that recognize the historical and socially constructed nature of their own knowledge claims and methodologies. In this way, curriculum can be viewed as a cultural script that introduces students to particular forms of reason, that structure specific stories and ways of life. Reason in this sense implicates and is implicated in the intersection of power, knowledge, and politics. Second, it is not enough to reject an essentialist or universalist defense of reason. Instead, the limits of reason must be extended to recognizing other ways in which people learn or take up particular subject positions. In this case, educators need to understand more fully how people learn through concrete social relations, through the ways in which the body is positioned through the construction of habit and intuition, and through the production and investment of desire and affect.

7. Critical pedagogy needs to regain a sense of alternatives by combining a language of critique and possibility. Postmodern feminism exemplifies this in both its critique of patriarchy and its search to construct new forms of identity and social relations. It is worth noting that teachers can take up this issue around a number of considerations. First, educators need to construct a language of critique that combines the issue of limits with the discourse of freedom and social responsibility. In other words, the question of freedom needs to be engaged dialectically not only as one of individual rights but also as part of the discourse of social responsibility. That is, whereas freedom remains an essential category in establishing the conditions for ethical and political rights, it must also be seen as a force to be checked if it is expressed in modes of individual and collective behavior that threaten the ecosystem or produce forms of violence and oppression against individuals and social groups. Second, critical pedagogy needs to explore in programmatic terms a language of possibility that is capable of thinking risky thoughts, that engages a project of hope, and points to the horizon of the "not yet". A language of possibility does not have to dissolve into a reified form of utopianism; instead, it can be

developed as a precondition for nourishing convictions that summon up the courage to imagine a different and more just world and to struggle for it. A language of moral and political possibility is more than an outmoded vestige of humanist discourse. It is central to responding not only with compassion to human beings who suffer and agonize but also with a politics and a set of pedagogical practices that can refigure and change existing narratives of domination into images and concrete instances of a future that is worth fighting for.

There is a certain cynicism that characterizes the language of the Left. Central to this position is the refusal of all utopian images, all appeals to "a language of possibility." Such refusals are often made on the grounds that "utopian discourse" is a strategy employed by the Right and is therefore ideologically tainted. Or the very notion of possibility is dismissed as an impractical and therefore useless category. In my mind, this represents less a serious critique than a refusal to move beyond the language of exhaustion and despair. What is central to develop in response to this position is a discriminating notion of possibility, one that makes a distinction between a language that is "dystopian" and one that is utopian. In the former, the appeal to the future is grounded in a form of nostalgic romanticism that calls for a return to a past, which more often than not serves to legitimate relations of domination and oppression. Similarly, in Constance Penley's terms, a "dystopian" discourse often "limits itself to solutions that are either individualist or bound to a romanticized notion of guerrilla-like small-group resistance. The true atrophy of the utopian imagination is this: we can imagine the future but we *cannot* conceive the kind of collective political strategies necessary to change or ensure that future."[107] In contrast to the language of dystopia, a discourse of possibility rejects apocalyptic emptiness and nostalgic imperialism and sees history as open and society worth struggling for in the image of an alternative future. This is the language of the "not yet," one in which the imagination is redeemed and nourished in the effort to construct new relationships fashioned out of strategies of collective resistance based on a critical recognition of both what society is and what it might become. Paraphrasing Walter Benjamin, this is a discourse of imagination and hope that pushes history against the grain. Nancy Fraser illuminates this sentiment by emphasizing the importance of a language of possibility for the project of social change: "It allows for the possibility of a radical democratic politics in which immanent critique and transfigurative desire mingle with one another."[108]

8. Critical pedagogy needs to develop a theory of educators and cultural workers as transformative intellectuals who occupy specific political and social locations. Rather than defining teacher work through the narrow language of professionalism, a critical pedagogy needs to ascertain more carefully what the role of teachers might be as cultural workers engaged in the production of ideologies and social practices. At one level this suggests that cultural workers first renounce the discourse of objectivity and decenteredness and then embrace a practice that is capable of revealing the historical, ideological, and ethical parameters that frame its discourse

and implications for the self, society, culture, and the other. Cultural workers need to unravel not only the ideological codes, representations, and practices that structure the dominant order, they also need to acknowledge "those places and spaces we inherit and occupy, which frame our lives in very specific and concrete ways, which are as much a part of our psyches as they are a physical or geographical placement."[109] The practice of social criticism becomes inseparable from the act of self-criticism; one cannot take place without the other; nor does one have priority over they other, instead they must be seen as both relational and mutually constitutive.

At another level, cultural workers need to develop a nontotalizing politics that makes them attentive to the partial, specific, contexts of differentiated communities and forms of power. This is not a call to ignore larger theoretical and relational narratives, but to deepen power of analyses by making clear the specificity of contexts in which power is operationalized, domination expresses itself, and resistance works in multiple and productive ways. In this case, teachers and cultural workers can undertake social criticism within and not outside of ethical and political discourses; they can address issues that give meaning to the contexts in which they work, but at the same time relate them to broader articulations that recognize the importance of larger formative narratives. Critique, resistance, and transformation in these terms is organized through systems of knowledge and webs of solidarity that embrace the local and the global. Cultural workers need to take seriously Foucault's model of the specific intellectual who acknowledges the politics of personal location. This is important, but not enough; cultural workers must also actively struggle as public intellectuals who can relate to and address wider issues that affect both the immediacy of their location and the wider global context. Transformative intellectuals must create webs of solidarity with those that share localized experiences and identities but must also develop a politics of solidarity that reaches out to those others who live in a global world whose problems cannot be dismissed because they do not occupy a local and immediate space. The issues of human rights, ecology, apartheid, militarism, and other forms of domination against both humans and the planet affect all of us directly and indirectly. This is not merely a political issue; it is also a deeply ethical issue that situates the meaning of the relationship between the self and the other, the margins and the center, and the colonizer and colonized in broader contexts of solidarity and struggle. Educators need to develop pedagogical practices that not only heighten the possibilities for critical consciousness but also for transformative action. In this perspective, teachers and other cultural workers would be involved in the invention of critical discourses, practices, and democratic social relations. Critical pedagogy would represent itself as the active construction rather than transmission of particular ways of life. More specifically, as transformative intellectuals, cultural workers and teachers can engage in the invention of languages so as to provide spaces for themselves, their students, and audiences to rethink their experiences in terms that both name relations of oppression and also offer ways in which to overcome them.

9. Central to the notion of critical pedagogy is a politics of voice that combines a postmodern notion of difference with a feminist emphasis on the primacy of the political. This engagement suggests taking up the relationship between the personal and the political in a way that does not collapse the political into the personal but strengthens the relationship between the two so as to engage rather than withdraw from addressing those institutional forms and structures that contribute to forms of racism, sexism, and class exploitation. This suggests some important pedagogical interventions. First, the self must be seen as a primary site of politicization. That is, the issue of how the self is constructed in multiple and complex ways must be analyzed both as part of a language of affirmation and a broader understanding of how identities are inscribed in and between various social, cultural, and historical formations. To engage issues regarding the construction of the self is to address questions of history, culture, community, language, gender, race, and class. It is to raise questions regarding what pedagogical practices need to be employed that allow students to speak in dialogical contexts that affirm, interrogate, and extend their understandings of themselves and the global contexts in which they live. Such a position recognizes that students have several or multiple identities, but also affirms the importance of offering students a language that allows them to reconstruct their moral and political energies in the service of creating a more just and equitable social order, one that undermines relations of hierarchy and domination.

Second, a politics of voice must offer pedagogical and political strategies that affirm the primacy of the social, intersubjective, and collective. To focus on voice is not meant to simply affirm the stories that students tell, nor to simply glorify the possibility for narration. Such a position often degenerates into a form of narcissism, a cathartic experience that is reduced to naming anger without the benefit of theorizing in order to both understand its underlying causes and what it means to work collectively to transform the structures of domination responsible for oppressive social relations. Raising one's consciousness has increasingly become a pretext for legitimating hegemonic forms of separatism buttressed by self-serving appeals to the primacy of individual experience. What is often expressed in such appeals is an antiintellectualism that retreats from any viable form of political engagement, especially one willing to address and transform diverse forms of oppression. The call to simply affirm one's voice has increasingly been reduced to a pedagogical process that is as reactionary as it is inward looking. A more radical notion of voice should begin with what bell hooks calls a critical attention to theorizing experience as part of a broader politics of engagement. In referring specifically to feminist pedagogy, she argues that the discourse of confession and memory can be used to "shift the focus away from mere naming of one's experience . . . to talk about identity in relation to culture, history, and politics."[110] For hooks, the telling of tales of victimization, or the expression of one's voice is not enough; it is equally imperative that such experiences be the object of theoretical and critical analyses so that they can be connected rather than severed from a broader notions of solidarity, struggle, and politics.

Conclusion

This chapter attempts to analyze some of the central assumptions that govern the discourses of modernism, postmodernism, and postmodern feminism. But in doing so, it rejects pitting these movements against each other and tries instead to see how they converge as part of a broader political project linked to the reconstruction of democratic public life. Similarly, I have attempted here to situate the issue of pedagogical practice within a wider discourse of political engagement. Pedagogy is not defined as simply something that goes on in schools. On the contrary, it is posited as central to any political practice that takes up questions of how individuals learn, how knowledge is produced, and how subject positions are constructed. In this context, pedagogical practice refers to forms of cultural production that are inextricably historical and political.

Pedagogy is, in part, a technology of power, language, and practice that produces and legitimates forms of moral and political regulation, that construct and offer human beings particular views of themselves and the world. Such views are never innocent and are always implicated in the discourse and relations of ethics and power. To invoke the importance of pedagogy is to raise questions not simply about how students learn but also how educators (in the broad sense of the term) construct the ideological and political positions from which they speak. At issue here is a discourse that both situates human beings within history and makes visible the limits of their ideologies and values. Such a position acknowledges the partiality of all discourses so that the relationship between knowledge and power will always be open to dialogue and critical self-engagement. Pedagogy is about the intellectual, emotional, and ethical investments we make as part of our attempt to negotiate, accommodate, and transform the world in which we find ourselves. The purpose and vision that drives such a pedagogy must be based on a politics and view of authority, that links teaching and learning to forms of self- and social empowerment that argue for forms of community life that extend the principles of liberty, equality, justice, and freedom to the widest possible set of institutional and lived relations.

As defined within the traditions of modernism, postmodernism, and post-modern feminism, pedagogy offers educators an opportunity to develop a political project that embraces human interests that move beyond the particularistic politics of class, ethnicity, race, and gender. This is not a call to dismiss the postmodern emphasis on difference as much as it is an attempt to develop a radical democratic politics that stresses difference within unity. This effort means developing a public language that can transform a politics of assertion into one of democratic struggle. Central to such a politics and pedagogy is a notion of community developed around a shared conception of social justice, rights, and entitlement. Such a notion is especially necessary at a time in our history in which the value of such concerns have been subordinated to the priorities of the market and used to legitimate the interests of the rich at the expense of the poor, the unemployed, and the homeless.

A radical pedagogy and transformative democratic politics must go hand in hand in constructing a vision in which liberalism's emphasis on individual freedom, postmodernism's concern with the particularistic, and feminism's concern with the politics of the everyday are coupled with democratic socialism's historic concern with solidarity and public life.

As I mentioned in Chapter 2, we live at a time in which the responsibilities of citizens extend beyond national borders. The old modernist notions of center and margin, home and exile, and familiar and strange are breaking apart. Geographic, cultural, and ethnic borders are giving way to shifting configurations of power, community, space, and time. Citizenship can no longer ground itself in forms of Eurocentrism and the language of colonialism. New spaces, relationships, and identities have to be created that allow us to move across borders, to engage difference and otherness as part of a discourse of justice, social engagement, and democratic struggle. Academics can no longer retreat into their classrooms or symposiums as if they were the only public spheres available for engaging the power of ideas and the relations of power. Foucault's notion of the specific intellectual taking up struggles connected to particular issues and contexts must be combined with Gramsci's notion of the engaged intellectual who connects his or her work to broader social concerns that deeply affect how people live, work, and survive.

But there is more at stake here than defining the role of the intellectual or the relationship of teaching to democratic struggle. The struggle against racism, class structures, sexism, and other forms of oppression needs to move away from simply a language of critique, and redefine itself as part of a language of transformation and hope. This shift suggests that educators combine with other cultural workers engaged in public struggles in order to invent languages and provide critical and transformative spaces both in and out of schools that offer new opportunities for social movements to come together. By doing this, we can rethink and re-experience democracy as a struggle over values, practices, social relations, and subject positions that enlarge the terrain of human capacities and possibilities as a basis for a compassionate social order. At issue here is the need for cultural workers to create a politics that contributes to the multiplication of sites of democratic struggles. Within such sites cultural workers can engage in specific struggles while also recognizing the necessity to embrace broader issues that enhance the life of the planet while extending the spirit of democracy to all societies.

In rejecting certain conservative features of modernism, the apoliticism of some postmodern discourses, and separatist versions of feminism, I attempt to critically appropriate the most emancipatory features of these discourses in the interest of developing a postmodern feminist pedagogy. Of course, the list of principles I provide is far from complete; I develop them in greater depth theoretically throughout this book. But the critical appropriation of emancipatory features does offer the opportunity for educators to analyze how it might be possible to reconceive as pedagogical practice some of the insights that have emerged from the discourses I analyze in this chapter. Far from being exhaustive, the principles offered are only meant to provide some fleeting images of a pedagogy that can address the importance of democracy as an ongoing struggle, the meaning of educating students to govern, and the imperative of creating pedagogical conditions in which political citizens can be educated within a politics of difference that supports rather than opposes the reconstruction of a radical democracy.

REFERENCES

[1] Representative analyses of the range of disciplines, genres, and writers who inhabit the slippery landscape known as postmodernism can be found in H. Foster, ed., *The Anti-Aesthetic: Essays on Postmodern Culture* (Port Townsend, Wash.: Bay Press, 1983); Ihab Hassan, *The Postmodern Turn: Essays in Postmodern Theory and Culture* (Columbus: Ohio State University Press, 1987), Dick Hebdige, "Postmodernism and the Other Side," *Journal of Communication Inquiry* 10:2, (1986), 78–99; Andreas Huyssen, *After the Great Divide* (Bloomington: Indiana University Press, 1986); Dick Hebdige, *Hiding in the Light* (New York: Routledge, 1989), Linda Hutcheon (1988), "Postmodern Problematics," in R. Merrill, (ed.), *Ethics/Aesthetics: Post-Modern Positions* (Washington, D.C.: Maisonneuve Press, 1988), 1–10; Linda Hutcheon, *The Politics of Postmodernism* (London: Routledge, 1989); Linda Hutcheon, *The Poetics of Postmodernism* (London: Routledge, 1988); L. Appignanensi and Bennington, G., eds., *Postmodernism: ICA Documents 4* (London: Institute of Contemporary Arts, 1986); Stanley Aronowitz, "Postmodernism and Politics," *Social Text* No. 18, (1987/1988) 94–114; Steven Connor, *Postmodernist Culture: In Introduction to Theories of the Contemporary* (New York: Basil Blackwell, 1989); Fredric Jameson, *Postmodernism or, the Cultural Logic of Late Capitalism* (Durham: Duke University, 1990); Scott Lash, *Sociology of Postmodernism* (New York: Routledge, 1990); Jane Flax, *Thinking Fragments: Psychoanlysis, Feminism, and Postmodernism in the Contemporary West* (Berkeley: University of California Press, 1990).

[2] Mark Poster, *Critical Theory and Poststructuralism* (Ithaca: Cornell University Press, 1989).

[3] Jean-Francois Lyotard, *The Postmodern Condition* (Minneapolis: University of Minnesota Press, 1984).

[4] Ernesto Laclau and Chantal Mouffe, *Hegemony and Socialist Strategy* (London: Verso Press, 1985).

[5] Mark Hannam, "The Dream of Democracy," *Arena* No. 90 (1990), 113.

[6] Ibid.

[7] Eugene Lunn, *Marxism and Modernism* (Berkeley: University of California Press, 1982); David Kolb, *The Critique of Pure Modernity* (Chicago: University of Chicago Press, 1986); Neil Larsen, *Modernism and Hegemony* (Minneapolis: University of Minnesota Press, 1990); Anthony Giddens, *The Consequences of Modernity* (Stanford: Stanford University Press, 1990).

[8] Lyotard, *The Postmodern Condition.*

[9] Charles Newman, *The Post-Modern Aura* (Evanston: Northwestern University Press, 1985); Charles Newman, "Revising Modernism, Representing Postmodernism," in L. Appignanensi and G. Bennington, eds., *Postmodernism: ICA Documents 4* (London: Institute of Contemporary Arts, 1986), 32–51.

[10] Jürgen Habermas, "Modernity Versus Postmodernity," *New German Critique* 8:1 (1981), 3–18; Jürgen Habermas, "The Entwinement of Myth and Enlightenment," *New German Critique* 9:3 (1982), 13–30; Jürgen Habermas, "Modernity—An Incomplete Project," in H. Foster, ed., *The Anti-Aesthetic: Essays on Postmodern Culture* (Port Townsend, Wash.: Bay Press, 1983),

3–16; Jürgen Habermas, *The Philosophical Discourse of Modernity*, trans by F. Lawrence (Cambridge: MIT Press, 1987).

[11] The now-classic defense of modernity in the postmodern debate can be found in Habermas, "An Incomplete Project" and *Philosophical Discourse*. An interesting comparison of two different views on modernity can be found in Marshall Berman, "Why Modernism Still Matters," *Tikkun* 4:11 (1988), 81–86, and Nelly Richard, "Postmodernism and Periphery," *Third Text*, No. 2 (1987/88), 5–12.

[12] Matei Calinescu, *Five Faces of Modernity: Modernism, Avant-Garde, Decadence, Kitsch, Postmodernism* (Durham: Duke University Press, 1987), 41.

[13] Jean Baudrillard, "Modernity," *Canadian Journal of Political and Social Theory*, 11:3 (1987), 65.

[14] Aronowitz, "Postmodernism and Politics," No. 18 (1987/1988), 94–114.

[15] Cited in Calinescu, *Five Faces of Modernity*, 117.

[16] Roland Barthes, *Critical Essays* (New York: Hill and Wang, 1972).

[17] Marshall Berman, *All That is Solid Melts into Air: The Experience of Modernity* (New York: Simon & Schuster, 1982); Marshall Berman, "Why Modernism Still Matters," *Tikkun* 4:1, (1988), 81–86.

[18] Berman, *All That is Solid*, 11.

[19] Robert Merrill, "Forward-Ethics/Aesthetics: A Post-Modern Position," in R. Merrill, ed., *Ethics/Aesthetics: Post-Modern Positions*, 9.

[20] See, for example, Chantal Mouffe, "Radical Democracy: Modern or Postmodern?" in A. Ross, ed., *Universal Abandon? The Politics of Postmodernism* (Minneapolis: University of Minnesota Press, 1988), 31–45.

[21] Mark Warren, *Nietzsche and Political Thought* (Cambridge: MIT Press, 1988), 9–10.

[22] Habermas, "Modernity versus Postmodernity," "An Incomplete Project," *Philosophical Discourse*.

[23] Richard Rorty, "Habermas and Lyotard on Postmodernity," in Richard Bernstein, ed., *Habermas and Modernity* (Cambridge: MIT Press, 1985), 161–76.

[24] Perry Anderson, "Modernity and Revolution," *New Left Review* No. 144 (1984), 96–113.

[25] Nancy Hartsock, "Rethinking Modernism: Minority vs. Majority Theories," *Cultural Critique*, No. 7 (1987), 187–206.

[26] Habermas, "An Incomplete Project," 5.

[27] Jürgen Habermas, *Communication and the Evolution of Society* (Boston: Beacon Press, 1979).

[28] Douglas Kellner, "Postmodernism as Social Theory: Some Challenges and Problems," *Theory, Culture, and Society* 5:2 & 3 (1988), 239–69.

[29] Habermas, "Myth and Enlightenment," 18.

[30] Michael Ryan, *Politics and Culture: Working Hypotheses for a Post-Revolutionary Society* (Baltimore: The Johns Hopkins University Press, 1989).

[31] Aronowitz, "Postmodernism and Politics," 103.

[32] Nancy Fraser, "What is Critical about Critical Theory? The Case of Habermas and Gender," *New German Critique* 12:2 (1985), 97–131.

[33] Barbara Epstein, "Rethinking Social Movement Theory," *Socialist Review* 20:1 (1990) 35–65.

[34] Thomas McCarthy, "Introduction," in Habermas, *Philosophical Discourse*, xvii.

[35] Hebdige, *Hiding in the Light* (1989) 226.

[36] Hutcheon, "Postmodern Problematics," in R. Merrill, ed., *Ethics/Aesthetics: Post-Modern Positions*, 5. For a more extensive treatment of Hutcheon's work on postmodernism, see *The Politics of Postmodernism*, and *The Poetics of Postmodernism*.

[37] "Building a New Left: An Interview with Ernesto Laclau," *Strategies* 1:1 (1988), 10–28.

[38] Lyotard, *The Postmodern Condition*, 24.

[39] Ibid., 82.

[40] Nancy Fraser and Linda Nicholson, "Social Criticism Without Philosophy: An Encounter Between Feminism and Postmodernism," in A. Ross, ed., *Universal Abandon? The Politics of Postmodernism*, 86–87.

[41] Gary Peller, "Reason and the Mob: the Politics of Representation," *Tikkun* 2:3 (1987), 30.

[42] Ernesto Laclau, (1988a), "Politics and the Limits of Modernity," in A. Ross, ed., *Universal Abandon? The Politics of Postmodernism*, 79–80.

[43] Emily Hicks, "Deterritorialization and Border Writing," in R. Merrill, ed., *Ethics/Aesthetics: Post-Modern Positions*, 47–58.

[44] This issue is taken up in a number of brilliant essays in Russell Ferguson, Martha Gever, Trinh T. Minh-ha, and Cornel West, eds., *Out There: Marginalization and Contemporary Cultures* (Cambridge: MIT Press, 1990. See also bell hooks, *Yearning: Race, Gender, and Cultural Politics* (Boston: South End Press, 1990); Stanley Aronowitz and Henry A. Giroux, *Postmodern Education: Politics, Culture, and Social Criticism* (Minneapolis: University of Minnesota Press, 1991).

[45] Jim Collins, *Uncommon Cultures: Popular Culture and Post-Modernism*, (New York: Routledge, 1989).

[46] Scott Lash and John Urry, *The End of Organized Capitalism* (Madison: University of Wisconsin Press, 1987).

[47] Poster, *Critical Theory and Poststructuralism*.

[48] Aronowitz and Giroux, *Postmodern Education*.

[49] Craig Owens, "The Discourse of Others: Feminists and Postmodernism," in Foster, H., ed., *The Anti-Aesthetic: Essays on Postmodern Culture*, 59.

[50] Edward W. Said, quoted in Connor, *Postmodernist Culture*, 233.

[51] Richard Roth, "The Colonial Experience and its Postmodern Fate," *Salmagundi* 84 (Fall 1989), 250.

[52] James Clifford and George Marcus, eds., *Writing Culture: The Poetics and Politics of Ethnography* (Berkeley: University of California Press, 1986); James Clifford, *The Predicament of Culture: Twentieth Century Ethnography, Literature, and Art* (Cambridge: Harvard University Press, 1988).

[53] Trinh Minh-ha, *Women, Native, Other: Writing Postcoloniality and Feminism.* (Bloomington: Indiana University Press, 1989).

[54] Renato Rosaldo, *Culture and Truth: The Remaking of Social Analysis* (Boston: Beacon Press, 1989) 44.

[55] Gayatri Spivak, *In Other Worlds: Essays in Cultural Politics* (New York: Methuen, 1987); Gayatri Spivak, *The Post-Colonial Critic*, edited by Minh-ha, *Women, Native, Other.*

[56] Hal Foster, *Recordings, Art, Spectacle, Cultural Politics* (Seattle: Bay Press, 1985); Brian Wallis, ed., *Art After Modernism: Rethinking Representation* (New York: Godine, 1989).

[57] See the discussion of various postmodern photographers in Abigail Solomon-Godeau, *Photography at the Dock* (Minneapolis: University of Minnesota Press, 1990).

[58] James Sculley, *Line Break: Poetry as Social Practice* (Seattle: Bay Press, 1988).

[59] Hebdige, *Hiding in the Light*, 1988.

[60] Laclau, "Building a New Left, 17.

[61] Kearney, *The Wake of Imagination*, 366–367.

[62] Jacques Derrida, *Of Grammatology*. G. Spivak, trans. (Baltimore: Johns Hopkins University Press, 1976); Michel Foucault, Foucault, M. (1977a). *Language, Counter-Memory, Practice: Selected Essays and Interviews*. D. Bouchard, ed., (Ithaca: Cornell University Press, 1977a); *Power and Knowledge: Selected Interviews and Other Writings*. G. Gordon, ed., (New York: Pantheon, 1977b). *Discipline and Punish: The Birth of the Prison.* (New York: Vintage Books, 1979); *The History of Sexuality, Volume 1: An Introduction.* (New York: Vintage Books, 1980); Jacques Lacan, *Speech and Language in Psychoanalysis*, trans. by A. Wilden (Baltimore: The Johns Hopkins University Press, 1988); Laclau & Mouffe, *Hegemony and Socialist Strategy.*

[63] Laclau, "Politics and the Limits of Modernity," p. 67.

[64] Terry Eagleton, "The Subject of Literature," *Cultural Critique* No. 2 (1985/86), 101.

[65] Teresa Ebert, "The Romance of Patriarchy: Ideology, Subjectivity, and Postmodern Feminist Cultural Theory," *Cultural Critique* 10 (Fall 1988), 22–23.

[66] Lawrence Grossberg, "On Postmodernism and Articulation: An interview with Stuart Hall," *Journal of Communication* 10:2 (1986), 56.

[67] Fraser and Nicholson, "Social Criticism Without Philosophy," in A. Ross, ed., *Universal Abandon? The Politics of Postmodernism*, 92, 99.

[68] M. Malson, J. O'Barr, S. Westphal-Wihl, and M. Wyer, "Introduction." In M. Malson, J. O'Barr, S. Westphal-Wihl,and M. Wyer, eds., *Feminist Theory in Practice and Process*. (Chicago: University of Chicago Press, 1989a), 1–13.

[69] hooks, *Talking Back*, 22.

[70] Meaghan Morris, *The Pirate's Fiancee: Feminism, reading, postmodernism* (London: Verso Press, 1988), 16.

[71] A number of feminist theorists take up these issues while either rejecting or problematizing any relationship with postmodernism. For instance, see Nancy Hartsock, "Postmodernism and Political Change: Issues for Feminist Theory," *Cultural Critique* No. 14 (Winter 1989–1990), 15–33; Rita Felski, "Feminism, Postmodernism, and the Critique of Modernity," *Cultural Critique*, No. 13 (Fall 1989), 33–56; For a range of feminist theoretical analyses concerning the construction of gender and modes of social division, see the two special issues of *Cultural Critique*, Nos. 13 and 14 (1989, 1989–90).

[72] Of course, as a number of feminists have pointed out, many of the issues taken up in postmodernist discourses have also been analyzed, albeit in different ways, in much of the literature written by feminists since the 1970s. See Morris, *The Pirate's Fiancee*, and hooks, *Yearnings*, for comments and references on this issue.

[73] E. Ann Kaplan, "Introduction," in E. Ann Kaplan, ed., *Postmodernism and Its Discontents* (London: Verso Press, 1988), 1–6.

[74] Donna Haraway, "Situated Knowledges: The Science Question in Feminism and the Privilege of Partial Perspective," *Feminist Studies* 14:3, (1989), 579.

[75] hooks, *Talking Back*, 25.

[76] Ibid., 23.

[77] Elaine Showalter, "Introduction: The Rise of Gender," in E. Showalter, ed., *Speaking of Gender* (New York: Routledge, 1989), 1–13.

[78] This issue is taken up in a number of feminist works. Some important and varied analyses include: hooks, *Yearnings*; Rita Felski, *Beyond Feminist Aesthetics* (Cambridge: Harvard University Press, 1989); Judith Butler, *Gender Trouble* (New York: Routledge, 1990); Carol Pateman, *The Sexual Contract* (Stanford: Stanford University Press, 1988); and Michele Wallace, *Invisibility Blues* (London: Verso Press, 1990).

[79] Teresa de Lauretis, ed., "Feminist Studies/Critical Studies: Issues, Terms, Contexts," in T. de Lauretis, *Feminist Studies/Critical Studies* (Bloomington: Indiana University Press, 1986), 9.

[80] hooks, *Talking Back*, 32. See also Felski, *Beyond Feminist Aesthetics*.

[81] de Lauretis, *Feminist Studies/Critical Studies*, 18.

[82] Julia Kristeva, "Oscillation between Power and Denial," in E. Marks and I. de Courtivron eds., *New French Feminisms*, (New York: Schocken Books, 1988), 165–67.

[83] Linda Alcoff, "Cultural Feminism vs. Poststructuralism: The Identity Crisis in Feminist Theory," *Signs*, 13:3 (1988), 418–19.

[84] Irene Diamond and Lee Quinby, "American Feminism and the Language of Control," in I. Diamond and L. Quinby, eds., *Feminism & Foucault: Reflections on Resistance*, (Boston: Northeastern University Press, 1988), 193–206.

[85] For example, see the work of Allison Jagger, *Feminist Politics and Human Nature* (Totawa, N.J.: Rowman & Allanheld, 1983) Sandra Harding, *The Science Question in Feminism* (Ithaca: Cornell University Press, 1986); Patricia Jagentowicz Mills, *Women, Nature, and Psyche*

(New Haven: Yale University Press, 1987); Donna Haraway, *Primate Visions: Gender, Race, and Nature in the world of Modern Science* (New York: Routledge, 1989); Sandra Harding, *Whose Science? Whose Knowledge? Thinking from Women's Lives* (Ithaca, N.Y.: Cornell University Press, 1991).

[86] For example, see Sharon Welch, *Communities of Resistance and Solidarity: a Feminist Theology of Liberation* (Maryknoll: Orbis Books, 1985); Sharon Welch, A *Feminist Ethic of Risk* (Minneapolis: Fortress Press, 1990); de Lauretis, "Studies/Critical Studies."

[87] Haraway, "Situated Knowledges," 585.

[88] For example, see hooks, *Talking Back; Yearnings*, 1990; Felski, *Beyond Feminist Aesthetics*; Nancy Fraser, *Unruly Practices: Power, Discourse and Gender in Contemporary Social Theory* (Minneapolis: University of Minnesota Press, 1989).

[89] Jane Flax, "Reply to Tress," *Signs* 14:1 (1988), 202.

[90] Fraser and Nicholson, "Social Criticism Without Philosophy," p. 91.

[91] See, for example, Jane Flax, "Postmodernism and Gender Relations in Feminist Theory," in M. Malson et al., eds., *Feminist Theory in Practice and Process*, 51–73; hooks, *Yearnings*; Harding, *The Science Question.*

[92] For example, see Audre Lorde, *Sister Outsider* (Freedom, CA: The Crossing Press, 1984); hooks, *Talking Back*; Trinh T. Minh-ha, *Woman, Native, Other* (Bloomington: Indiana University Press, 1989).

[93] Caren Kaplan, "Deterritorializations: The Rewriting of Home and Exile in Western Feminist Discourse," *Cultural Critique*, No. 6 (1987), 194.

[94] Malson, et al., "Introduction," in M. Malson, et al., eds., *Feminist Theory in Practice and Process*, 4.

[95] Joan Scott, *Gender and the Politics of History* (New York: Columbia University Press, 1988), 176–77.

[96] Kaplan, "Introduction," in E. Ann Kaplan, ed., *Postmodernism and Its Discontents.*

[97] Alcoff, "Cultural Feminism vs. Poststructuralism," 434.

[98] Sandra Lee Bartky, "Foucault, Femininity, and the Modernization of Patriarchal Power," in Diamond and Quinby, eds., *Feminism and Foucault*, 61–86.

[99] Vaclav Havel quoted in M. Oreskes, "America's Politics Loses Way as Its Vision Changes World," *New York Times*, (1990), 16.

[100] E. P. Thompson, "History Turns on a New Hinge," *The Nation* (January 29, 1990), 120.

[101] Adam Michnik, "Notes on the Revolution," *New York Times Magazine*, March 11, 1990, 44.

[102] Oreskes, "America's Politics Loses Way," 16.

[103] Some representative collections of current literature on diverse discourses in critical pedagogy can be found in: Cary Nelson, ed., *Theory in the Classroom* (Urbana: University of Illinois Press, 1986); David Livingstone, ed., *Critical Pedagogy and Cultural Power* (New York: Bergin and Garvey Press, 1986); Henry A. Giroux and Roger Simon, eds., *Popular Culture, Schooling and Everyday Life* (New York: Bergin and Garvey, 1988); Henry A. Giroux and Peter McLaren, eds., *Critical Pedagogy, the State, and Cultural Struggle* (Albany: Suny Press, 1989); Patricia Donahue and Ellen Quandahl, eds., *Reclaiming Pedagogy: The Rhetoric of the Classroom* (Carbondale: Southern Illinois University Press, 1989); Susan L. Gabriel and Isaiah Smithson, eds., *Gender in the Classroom* (Urbana: University of Illinois Press, 1990); Donald Morton and Mas'ud Zavarzadeh, eds., *Theory/Pedagogy/Politics: Texts for Change* (Urbana: University of Illinois Press, 1991); See also Roger I. Simon, *Teaching Against the Grain* (New York: Bergin and Garvey, 1992).

[104] Chandra T. Mohanty, "On Race and Voice: Challenges for Liberal Education in the 1990s," *Cultural Critique* (Winter 1989–1990), 179–208.

[105] Laclau, "Politics and the Limits of Modernity," in A. Ross, ed., *Universal Abandon? The Politics of Postmodernism*, 63–82.

[106] Thomas Popkewitz, "Culture, Pedagogy, and Power: Issues in the Production of Values and Colonialization," *Journal of Education* 170:2 (1988), 77.

[107] Constance Penley, *The Future of an Illusion: Film, Feminism, and Psychoanalysis* (Minneapolis: University of Minnesota, 1989), 122.

[108] Fraser, *Unruly Practices*, 107.

[109] Joan Borsa, "Towards a Politics of Location," *Canadian Women Studies* (Spring 1990), 36.

[110] hooks, *Talking Back*, 110.

4

Decentering the Canon: Refiguring Disciplinary and Pedagogical Boundaries

I will begin with what has become a controversial but not insignificant assertion: that the most important questions facing both the liberal arts and higher education in general are moral and political.[1] By invoking the category of the political, I wish to separate myself from a species of neoconservativism that claims that the relationship between the liberal arts and politics is one that taints the scholarship and teaching of those who dare even suggest that such a relationship exists. Nor do I believe that the fashionable but derogatory label of "politically correct" used by liberals and neo-conservatives adequately captures the complex set of motives, ideologies, and pedagogies of diverse progressive and radical scholars trying to engage the relationship between knowledge and power as it is expressed through the history and process of disciplinary canon formation. In fact, the charge that radical scholars are to be condemned for exercising a form of theoretical terrorism appears to be nothing more than a rhetorical ploy that barely conceals the highly charged ideological agenda of neoconservative scholars who refuse to address in any substantive way the political and theoretical considerations currently being raised within the academy by feminists, people of color, and other minority groups.[2]

What is being protested as the intrusion of politics into academic life is nothing less than a refusal to recognize that the canon and the struggle over the purpose and meaning of the liberal arts has displayed a political struggle from its inception. There are no disciplines, pedagogies, institutional structures, or forms of scholarship that are untainted by the messy relations of worldly values and interests.[3] For example, the history, configuration, and legitimation of the canon in the liberal arts cannot be removed from the issue of securing authority. As Gayatri Spivak points out, "canons are the condition and function of institutions, which presuppose particular ways of life and are inescapably political."[4]

More specifically, the various questions that have been raised recently about either defending, reconstructing, or eliminating a particular canon in higher education can only be understood within a broader range of political and theoretical considerations that bear directly on the issue of whether a liberal arts education should be considered a privilege for the few or a right for the vast majority of citizens. This is not merely a matter of deciding who is eligible or can financially afford a liberal arts education; it is fundamentally part of a wider discourse that has increasingly challenged the American public in the last decade to rethink the role of higher education and its relationship to democratic public life.

This debate raises new and important questions regarding the social and political implications of viewing curriculum as a historically specific narrative and pedagogy as a form of cultural politics. What must be asked about these specific narratives is whether they enable or silence the differentiated human capacities that allow students to speak from their own experiences, locate themselves in history, and act so as to create liberatory social forms that expand the possibility of democratic public life.[5] I believe that the current debate on higher education opens up new possibilities for rethinking the role that university educators might play as critically engaged public intellectuals. While neoconservatives generally view the extensive debate about the fundamental place of literature, culture, ethics, and politics in the academy and the wider society as symptomatic of a crisis of authority and an unmitigated assault on Western civilization itself, I would rather view it as part of a great renewal in academic life.[6]

Before I discuss these issues in detail, I want to stress the importance of recognizing that the university is not simply a place to accumulate disciplinary knowledge that can be exchanged for decent employment and upward mobility. Neither is it a place whose purpose is merely to cultivate the life of the mind or reproduce the cultural equivalent of "Masterpiece Theater." I firmly believe that the institutions of higher education, regardless of their academic status, represent places that affirm and legitimate existing views of the world, produce new ones, and authorize and shape particular social relations; put simply, they are places of moral and social regulation "where a sense of identity, place, and worth is informed and contested through practices, which organize knowledge and meaning."[7] The university is a place that produces a particular selection and ordering of narratives and subjectivities. It is, furthermore, a place that is deeply political and unarguably normative.

Unfortunately, questions concerning higher education in general and liberal arts in particular are often discussed as if they have no relation to existing arrangements of social, economic, and political power. Central to this chapter are the arguments that as a social, political, and pedagogical site, the university is a terrain of contestation and that one can neither understand the nature of the struggle itself nor the nature of the liberal arts unless one raises the question of what the purpose of the university actually is or might be. Or, as Jacques Derrida has put it, "To ask whether the university has a reason for being is to wonder why

there is a university, but the question 'why' verges on 'with a view to what?' "[8]
It is this question of purpose and practice that illuminates what the limits and
possibilities are that exist within the university at a given time in history. Putting
aside Derrida's own political agenda, this is essentially a question of politics, power,
and possibility. As we know, the liberal arts and various other programs and schools
within the university presuppose and legitimate particular forms of history, community, and authority. Of course, the question is what and whose history, community, knowledge, and voice prevails? Unless this question is addressed, the issues
of what to teach, how to teach, how to engage our students, and how to function
as intellectuals becomes removed from the wider principles that inform such issues
and practices.

The sphere of higher education represents an important public culture that
cultivates and produces particular stories of how to live ethically and politically;
its institutions reproduce selected values, and they harbor in their social relations
and teaching practices specific notions regarding "what knowledge is of most worth,
what it means to know something, and how one might construct representations
of [themselves], others, and the social environment." In many respects, the normative and political language taught in the university can be compared to what
Ernst Bloch called the utopian impulse of daydreams.

> Dreams come in the day as well as the night. And both kinds of dreaming are
> motivated by the wishes they seek to fulfill. But daydreams differ from night
> dreams; for the day dreaming "I" persist throughout, consciously, privately, en-
> visaging the circumstances and images of a desired, better life. The content of
> the daydream is not, like that of the night dream, a journey back into repressed
> experiences and their association. It is concerned with, as far as possible, an
> unrestricted journey forward, so that instead of reconstituting that which is no
> longer conscious, the images of that which is not yet can be fantasized into life
> and into the world.[9]

Bloch's analysis points to an important relation between daydreaming and the
liberal arts that is often overlooked. As an introduction to, preparation for, and
legitimation of social life, a liberal arts education inscribes students in a present
informed by a past that presupposes a particular citizen, society, and future. In
other words, like the process of daydreaming, the liberal arts is fundamentally
involved in the production of narratives of that which is "not yet." As Roger Simon
points out, "the utopian impulse of such programs is represented in the notion
that without a perspective on the future, conceivable as a desired future, there can
be no human venture."[10] In this respect, the language of education that students
take with them from their university experience should embody a vision capable
of providing them with a sense of history, civic courage, and democratic community. It is important to emphasize that visions are not only defined by the
representations they legitimate and the practices they structure, but also by the
arguments they embody for justifying why meaning, knowledge, and social action
matter as part of the rewriting and remapping of the events that make up daily

life as well as the dynamics of the larger world. The question becomes To what version of the future do the visions of our students speak? To whom do such visions matter and why? As a matter of pedagogical practice, students need to take up these questions through a language of obligation and power, a language that cultivates a capacity for reasoned criticism, for undoing the misuses of power and the relations of domination, and for exploring and extending the utopian dimensions of human potentiality. Needless to say, such a language is at odds with the language of cultural despair, conservative restoration, and aristocratic elitism trumpeted by the educational theorists of the New Right.[11]

It serves us well to remember that the visions presupposed in the structure and discourse of the liberal arts are neither ideologically neutral nor politically innocent. Visions always belong to someone, and to the degree that they translate into curricula and pedagogical practices, they not only denote a struggle over forms of political authority and orders of representation, but also weigh heavily in regulating the moral identities, collective voices, and the futures of others.[12] As institutionalized practices, visions draw upon specific values, uphold particular relations of power, class, gender, ethnicity, and race, and often authorizes official forms of knowledge. For this reason, visions always have a moral and political dimension. Moreover, they become important not as a signal for a single-minded preoccupation with academic achievement or social status but as a context from which to organize the energies of a moral vision, to believe that one can make a difference both in combating domestic tyranny and assaults on human freedom and in creating a society that exhibits in its institutional and everyday relations moral courage, compassion, and cultural justice. This is, after all, what university life should be all about: the politics and ethics of dreaming, dreaming a better future, and dreaming a new world.

The current debate about education represents more than a commentary on the state of public and higher education in this country, it is basically a debate about the meaning of democracy, social criticism, and the status of utopian thought in constituting both our dreams and the stories that we devise in order to give meaning to our lives. This debate has taken a serious turn in the last decade and now as before its terms are being set principally by extremists and antiutopians. Critics such as Allan Bloom, Lynne V. Cheney, Roger Kimball, and John Silber have presented an agenda and purpose for shaping higher education that abstracts equity from excellence and cultural criticism from the discourse of social responsibility. Under the guise of attempting to revitalize the language of morality, these critics and politicians have, in reality, launched a serious attack on some of the most basic aspects of democratic public life and the social, moral, and political obligations of responsible, critical citizens. What is being valorized in this language is, in part, a view of higher education based on a celebration of cultural uniformity and a rigid view of authority; in addition, the neoconservative agenda for higher education includes a call to remake higher education an academic beachhead for defending and limiting the curriculum to a narrowly defined patriarchal, Eurocentric version of the Western tradition and a return to the old transmission model of teaching.

Within this new public philosophy, there is a ruthlessly frank expression of doubt about the viability of democracy.[13] What at first sight appears to be a debate about the meaning and purpose of the canon has become a struggle for "the moral definition of tomorrow's elites."[14] Unfortunately, this is not a debate being conducted within the parameters of critical exchange. It is increasingly taking on the shades of McCarthyism rampant in the 1950s in the United States, with those in power using their influence in the press, in well-funded public symposiums, and through highly financed private think tanks to conjure up charges that academics who are questioning the relationship between the liberal arts and the discourse of power and citizenship are to be judged by their motives rather than their arguments. With great burst of melodramatic rhetoric, we are told, for example, by Roger Kimball, the editor of *The New Criterion*, that politically motivated academic radicals, regardless of their particular theoretical orientation, have as their goal nothing less than the destruction of the values, method, and goals of Western civilization. Equating advocates for a multicultural curriculum with the forces of barbarism, Kimball constructs a reductionistic opposition in which conservatives become the defenders of civilization itself. Kimball spares no words on the importance of *his* messianic struggle:

> The multiculturalists notwithstanding, the choice facing *us* today is not between a "repressive" Western culture and a multicultural paradise, but between culture and barbarism. *Civilization* is not a gift, it is an achievement—a fragile achievement that needs constantly to be shored up and defended from besiegers inside and out.[15]

Critics such as Allan Bloom and John Silber extend the tone and logic of such attacks by arguing that the very nature of Western civilization is under attack by the infusion of critics in the humanities who constitute a monolithic party (surely an embarrassing overstatement given the endless fragmentation and divisions that characterize the American left). There is more at stake here than the rise of a new nativism; there is also the nature of academic freedom as it has developed in the liberal arts in the last few decades. The poison of McCarthyism is once again being used to limit debate and constrain the so-called excesses of democracy. For instance, instead of addressing the complexity of issues being waged over the nature of the liberal arts and the ideological construction of the canon, John Silber, the President of Boston University, has urged fellow conservatives to abandon any civility toward scholars whose work is considered political. Instead of encouraging rigorous debate, Silber has urged his fellow conservatives to name names, to discredit educators who have chosen to engage in forms of social criticism (work the New Right considers political) at odds with the agenda of the New Rights's mythic conception of the university as a warehouse built on the pillars of an unproblematic and revered tradition.[16] In the Bush Era, there are, sadly, few attempts to engage in dialogue about the assumptions that inform the traditional view of the curriculum and canon; on the contrary, the privileged and the powerful in academia and in government positions now openly advocate crude policing functions as a way to regulate university life. So much for the spirit of democracy and academic freedom.

The loss of utopian vision that characterizes this position is no where more evident than in Allan Bloom's *The Closing of the American Mind* and E. D. Hirsch's *Cultural Literacy*.[17] For Bloom, the impulse to egalitarianism and the spirit of social criticism represent the chief culprits in the decay of higher learning. Bloom argues that the university must give up educating intellectuals, whose great crime is that they sometimes become adversaries of the dominant culture or speak to a wider culture about the quality of contemporary politics and public life. He would prefer that the university curriculum be organized around the Great Books and be selectively used to educate students from what he calls the top twenty elite schools to be philosopher-kings. What Bloom appears to suggest by reform is nothing less than an effort to make explicit what women, people of color, and working-class students have always known: The precincts of higher learning are not for them, and the educational system is meant to reproduce a new mandarin class.

Hirsch, like Bloom, presents a frontal attack aimed at providing a programmatic language with which to defend schools as cultural sites; that is, as institutions responsible for reproducing the knowledge and values necessary to advance the historical virtues of Western culture. Hirsch presents his view of cultural restoration through a concept of literacy that focuses on the basic structures of language, and he applies this version of cultural literacy to the broader consideration of the needs of the business community as well as to maintenance of American institutions. For Hirsch, the new service economy requires employees who can write a memo, read within a specific cultural context, and communicate through a national language composed of the key words of Western culture.

Central to Hirsch's concept of literacy is a view of culture removed from the dynamics of struggle and power. Culture is seen as the totality of language practices of a given nation and merely "presents" itself for all to participate in its language and conventions. Not unlike Bloom's position, Hirsch's view of culture expresses a single durable history and vision, one at odds with a critical notion of democracy and difference. Such a position maintains an ideological silence, a political amnesia of sorts, regarding either how domination works in the cultural sphere or how the dialectic of cultural struggle between different groups over competing orders of meaning, experience, and history emerges within unequal relations of power and struggle. By depoliticizing the issue of culture, Hirsch ends up with a view of literacy cleansed of its own complicity in producing social forms that create devalued others. This is more than a matter of cultural forgetting on Hirsch's part; it is also an attack on difference as possibility. Hirsch's discourse also attempts to undermine the development of a curriculum committed to reclaiming higher education as an agency of social justice and critical democracy and to developing forms of pedagogy that affirm and engage the often silenced voices of subordinate groups.

In the most general sense, Bloom, Hirsch, Cheney, Kimball, and Silber represent the latest cultural offensive by the new elitists to rewrite the past and construct the present from the perspective of the privileged and the powerful.[18] They disdain the democratic implications of pluralism and argue for a form of cultural uniformity in which difference is consigned to the margins of history or to the museum of the disadvantaged. From this perspective, culture, along with the authority it sanctions becomes merely an artifact, a warehouse of goods, posited either as a canon of knowledge or a canon of information that simply has to be transmitted as a means for promoting social order and control. In this view, pedagogy becomes an afterthought, a code word for the transmission and imposition of a predefined and unproblematic body of knowledge. For educators like Bloom and Cheney, pedagogy is something one does in order to implement a reconstituted body of knowledge or information. The notion that pedagogy is itself part of the production of knowledge, a deliberate and critical attempt to influence the ways in which knowledge and identities are produced within and among particular sets of social relations, is far removed from the language and ideology of the neoconservatives.

What is at stake here is not simply the issue of bad teaching, but the broader refusal to take seriously the categories of meaning, experience, and voice that students use to make sense of themselves and the world around them. It is this refusal to enable speech for those who have been silenced, to acknowledge the voices of the other, and to legitimate and reclaim student experience as a fundamental category in the production of knowledge that the character of the current dominant discourse on the canon reveals its totalitarian and undemocratic ideology.

Put in Bloch's terms, this new conservative public philosophy represents a form of daydreaming in which tradition is not on the side of democracy and difference, but is a form of the "not yet" expunged of the language of hope and strangled by a discourse in which history and culture are closed. It is a public philosophy in which teaching is reduced to a form of transmission, the canon is posited as a relationship outside of the restless flux of knowledge and power, and intellectuals are cheerfully urged to take up their roles as clerks of the empire.[19]

It is worth noting that Bloom, Cheney, and other neoconservatives have been able to perform a task that humanists and progressives have generally failed to do. They have placed the question of curriculum at the center of the debate about both education and democracy, but they have argued for a view of the liberal arts fashioned as part of an antiutopian discourse that serves to disconnect the purpose of higher education from the task of reconstructing democratic public life. This is not to suggest that they have not invoked the notions of democracy and citizenship in their arguments. But in doing so they have reduced democracy to gaining access to an unproblematic version of Western civilization and defined learning as the training of good citizens, that is, "willing subjects and agents of hegemonic authority."[20] By refusing to link democracy to forms of self and social empowerment, neoconservatives have been able to suppress the relationship between learning, social justice, and critical citizenship. This new cultural offensive presents a formidable challenge to humanists who have attempted to defend liberal arts education from the perspective of a highly specialized, self-referential discipline that holds up either a plurality of canons or a canon that serves as a model of scientific rigor and sophisticated methodological inquiry. In such cases, the purpose of the liberal arts is defined, though from different ideological perspectives, from within the perspective of creating a free, enterprising, educated, well-rounded individual. Though well meaning, this discourse discounts the most important social relations that are constitutive of what it means to be educated. That is, it ignores the social and political function of particular knowledge/power/pedagogy relations and how they serve to construct students individually and collectively within the boundaries of a political order that they often take for granted.

The liberal arts cannot be defended either as a self-contained discourse legitimating the humanistic goal of broadly improving the so-called life of the mind or as a rigorous science that can lead students to indubitable truths. Similarly, it is insufficient to defend the liberal arts by rejecting technocratic education as a model of learning. All of these positions share the failure of abstracting the liberal arts from the intense problems and issues of public life. Moreover, the defense of the liberal arts as a gateway to indubitable truths, whether through the discourse of Western civilization or science, often collapses into a not too subtle defense of higher education as a training ground for a "dictatorship of enlightened social engineers."[21] This issue at stake is not one of merely creating a more enlightened or scientific canon but of raising more fundamental questions about how canons are used, what interests they legitimate, what relations they have to the dominant society, and how students are constituted within their prevailing discourses and social relations. How we read or define a "canonical" work may not be as important as challenging the overall function and social uses the notion of the canon has served. Within this type of discourse, the canon can be analyzed as part of a wider set of relations that connect the academic disciplines, teaching, and power to more political considerations defined through broader, intersecting political and cultural concerns such as race, class, gender, ethnicity, and nationalism. What is in question here is not merely a defense of a particular canon, but the issue of struggle and empowerment.[22]

The debate over the canon must be refigured in order to address issues of struggle in which power and knowledge intersect to produce and legitimate specific orders of representations, values, and identities. As such, the issue of canon formation must be engaged in terms that address the historical formation of the canon and the pedagogies through which it is taught and how these pedagogies have either provided or excluded the conditions and knowledge necessary for marginal people to recover their own histories and to speak and learn in places occupied by those who have the dominant power to shape policy and act. In other words, the liberal arts should be defended in the interest of creating critical rather than "good" citizens. That is, the notion of the liberal arts has to be reconstituted around a knowledge–power relationship in which the question of curriculum is seen as a form of cultural and political production grounded in a radical conception of citizenship and public wisdom.

By linking the liberal arts to the imperatives of a critical democracy, the debate on the meaning and nature of higher education can be situated within a broader context of issues concerned with critical citizenship, politics, and the dignity of human life. In this view, it becomes possible to provide a rationale and purpose for higher education, which aims at developing critical citizens and reconstructing community life by extending the principles of social justice to all spheres of economic, political, and cultural life. This position is not far from the arguments posed by John Dewey, George S. Counts, C. Wright Mills, and more recently Hannah Arendt and Alvin Gouldner. These theorists fashioned the elements of a public philosophy in which the liberal arts was seen as a major social site for revitalizing public life. Dewey, for example, argued that a liberal education afforded people the opportunity to involve themselves in the deepest problems of society, to acquire the knowledge, skills, and ethical responsibility necessary for "reasoned participation in democratically organized publics."[23] Mills urged intellectuals to define the liberal arts and their own roles through a commitment to the formation of a critical and engaged citizenry. He envisioned the liberal arts as social site from which intellectuals could mobilize a moral and political vision committed to the reclamation and recovery of democratic public life.[24] In the most general sense, this means fashioning the purpose of higher education within a public philosophy committed to a radical conception of citizenship, civic courage, and public wisdom. In more specific terms, this means challenging the image of higher education as an adjunct of the corporation and rejecting those ideologies and human capital theories that reduce the role of university intellectuals to the status of industrial technicians and academic clerks whose political project or, lack of one, is often betrayed by claims to objectivity, certainty, and professionalism. It means challenging the sterile instrumentalism, selfishness, and contempt for democratic community that has become the hallmark of the Reagan–Bush Era.[25] It means recognizing and organizing against the structured injustices in society that prevent us from extending our solidarity to those others who strain under the weight of various forms of oppression and exploitation. It also means enhancing and ennobling the meaning and purpose of a liberal arts education by giving it a truly central place in the social life of a nation where it can become a public forum for addressing preferentially the needs of the poor, the dispossessed, and the disenfranchised.

A public philosophy that offers the promise of reforming liberal arts education as part of a wider revitalization of public life raises important questions regarding what the notion of empowerment would mean for developing classroom pedagogical practices. That is, if liberal arts education is to be developed in relation to principles consistent with a democratic public philosophy, it is equally important to develop forms of critical pedagogy that embody these principles and practices, a critical pedagogy in which such practices are understood in relation *to* rather than *in* isolation from those economies of power and privilege at work in wider social and political formations.

Critical Pedagogy as a Form of Cultural Politics

For many educators, pedagogy is often theorized as what is left after curriculum content is determined. In this view, knowledge "speaks" for itself and teaching is often a matter of providing an occasion for the text to reveal itself. Guided by a concern with producing knowledge that is academically correct or ideologically relevant, educational theorists have largely sidestepped the issue of how a teacher can work from sound ethical and theoretical principles and still end up pedagogically silencing students. Put another way, if educators fail to recognize that the legitimating claims they make in defense of the knowledge they teach is not enough to ensure that they *do not* commit forms of symbolic violence in their pedagogical relations with students, they will not adequately understand the ways in which students are both enabled and disabled in their own classrooms.

Central to the development of a critical pedagogy is the need to explore how pedagogy functions as a cultural practice to *produce* rather than merely *transmit* knowledge within the asymmetrical relations of power that structure teacher–student relations. There have been few attempts to analyze how relations of pedagogy and relations of power are inextricably tied not only to what people know but also to how they come to know in a particular way within the constraints of specific cultural and social forms.[26] Rendered insignificant as a form of cultural production, pedagogy is often marginalized and devalued as a means of recognizing that what we teach and how we do it are deeply implicated not only in producing various forms of domination but also in constructing active practices of resistance and struggle. Lost here is an attempt to articulate pedagogy as a form of cultural production that addresses how knowledge is produced, mediated, refused, and re-presented within relations of power both in and outside of the university.

Critical pedagogy as a form of cultural politics rejects the reduction of teaching to a narrowly defined concern with instrumental techniques, skills, and objectives. The instrumentalization of teaching erases questions of power, history, ethics, and self-identity. Absent from this discourse is any attempt to understand how pedagogical and institutional practices produce, codify, and rewrite disciplinary practices, values, and social identities in relation to, rather than outside of, the discourse of history, power, and privilege. Critical pedagogy also rejects the notion of knowledge as accumulated capital. Instead, it focuses on the production of knowledge and identities within the specificity of educational contexts and the broader institutional locations in which they are located. Critical pedagogy refers to a deliberate attempt to construct specific conditions through which educators and students can think critically about how knowledge is produced and transformed in relation to the construction of social experiences informed by a particular relationship between the self, others, and the larger world. Rather than reducing classroom practice to forms of methodological reification governed by a pragmatic concern for generating topologies or a reductionist fetish for empirical verification, critical pedagogy stresses the realities of what happens in classrooms by raising a number of crucial questions. These include how identities and subjectivities are produced differently in relation to particular forms of knowledge and power; how cultural differences are coded within the center and margins of power; how the discourse of rationality secures, ignores, or dismisses the affective investments that organize the daily experiences of students; how education might become the practice of liberation; and what it means to know something as part of the broader discourses of cultural democracy and citizenship.[27]

The notion of pedagogy being argued for here is not organized in relation to a choice between elite or popular culture, but as part of a political project that takes issues of liberation and empowerment as its starting point. It is a pedagogy that rejects the notion of culture as an artifact immobilized in the image of a storehouse. Instead, the pedagogical principles at work here analyze culture as a set of lived experiences and social practices developed within asymmetrical relations of power. Culture in this sense is not an object of unquestioning reverence but a mobile field of ideological and material relations that are unfinished, multilayered, and always open to interrogation. Moreover, this view of culture is defined pedagogically as social practices that allow both teachers and students to construe themselves as agents in the production of subjectivity and meaning. Such a pedagogy transcends the dichotomy of elite and popular culture by defining itself through a project of educating students to feel compassion for the suffering of others, to engage in a continual analysis of their own conditions of existence, to construct loyalties that engage the meaning and importance of public life, and to believe that they can make a difference, that they can act from a position of collective strength to alter existing configurations of power. This notion of pedagogy is predicated on a notion of learned hope, forged amidst the realization of risks, and steeped in a commitment to transforming public culture and life. It is a notion of critical pedagogy that stresses the historical and transformative in its practice.

In the debate about the importance of constructing a particular canon, the notion of naming and transmitting from one generation to the next what can be defined as "cultural treasures" specifies what has become the central argument for reforming the liberal arts.[28] For that reason, perhaps, it appears as though the debate is reducible to the question of the contents of course syllabi. The notion of critical pedagogy for which I am arguing provides a fundamental challenge to this position. For in the great challenges that we confront as university educators, what is called for is a more critical and fundamental argument that transcends the limited focus on the canon. What the issue of critical pedagogy raises in this debate is that the crisis in liberal arts education is one of historical purpose and meaning that challenges us to rethink in a critical fashion the relationship between the role of the university and the imperatives of a democracy in a mass society.

Historically, the liberal arts education was conceived of as the essential prep-aration for governing, for ruling—more specifically, as the preparation and outfitting of the governing *elite*. The liberal arts curricula, composed of the "best" that had been said or written, was intended, as Elizabeth Fox-Genovese has observed, "to provide selected individuals with a collective history, culture, and epistemology so that they could run the world effectively."[29] The canon, considered a possession of the dominant classes or groups, was fashioned as a safeguard to insure that the cultural property of such groups was passed on from generation to generation along with the family estates. Thus, in these very terms it seems most appropriate that the literary canon should be subject to revision—as it has been before in the course of the expansion of democracy—such that it might also incorporate and reflect the experience and aspirations of the women, minorities, and children of the working class who have been entering the academy.

As conceived above, a radical vision of liberal arts education is to be found within its elite social origins and purpose. But this does not suggest that the most important questions confronting liberal arts reform lie in merely establishing the content of the liberal arts canon on the model of the elite universities. Instead, the most important questions become that of reformulating the meaning and purpose of higher education in ways that contribute to the cultivation and regen-eration of an informed critical citizenry capable of actively participating in the shaping and governing of a democratic society. Within this discourse, the peda-gogical becomes political and the notion of a liberal arts canon commands a more historically grounded and critical reading. The pedagogical becomes more political in that it proposes that the ways in which students engage and critically examine knowledge is just as important an issue as the choosing of texts to be used in a class or program. That is, a democratic notion of liberal education rejects those views of the humanities that would treat texts as sacred and instruction as merely transmission. This notion of the canon undermines the possibility for dialogue, argument, and critical thinking. Moreover, it treats knowledge as a form of cultural inheritance that is beyond considerations regarding how it might be implicated, as I previously noted, in social practices that exploit, infantilize, and oppress.

The canons we have inherited, in their varied forms, cannot be dismissed as simply part of the ideology of privilege and domination. Instead, the privileged texts of the dominant or official canons should be explored with respect to the important role they have played in shaping, for better or worse, the major events of our time. Moreover, there are forms of knowledge that have been marginalized by the official canons. There are noble traditions, histories, and narratives that speak to important struggles by women, Afro-Americans, minorities, and other silenced groups that need to be heard so that such groups can lay claim to their own voices as part of a process of both affirmation and critical inquiry. At issue here is a notion of pedagogy as a form of cultural politics that rejects a facile restoration of the past and rejects history as a monolog. A critical pedagogy rec-ognizes that history is constituted in dialogue and that some of the voices that make up that dialogue have been eliminated. Such a pedagogy calls for a public debate regarding the dominant memories and repressed stories that constitute the historical narratives of a social order. In effect, a critical pedagogy recognizes that canon formation is a matter of both rewriting and reinterpreting the past, that canon formation embodies the ongoing "process of reconstructing the 'collective reflexivity' of lived cultural experience . . . which recognizes that the 'notions of the past and future are essentially notions of the present.' "[30] Such notions are central to the politics of identity and power and to the memories that structure how experience is individually and collectively authorized and experienced as form of cultural identity.

As a historical construct, critical pedagogy functions in a dual sense to address the issue of what kinds of knowledge can be put in place that enable rather than subvert the formation of a democratic society. On one level, it authorizes forms of counter-memory. It excavates, affirms, and interrogates the histories, memories, and stories of the devalued others who have been marginalized from the official discourse of the canon. It attempts to recover and mediate those knowledge forms and social practices that have been decentered from the discourses of power. Surely, such knowledge might include the historical and contemporary writings of feminists such as Mary Wollstonecraft, Charlotte Perkins Gilman, and Adrienne Rich; Afro-American writers such as W.E.B. Dubois, Martin Luther King, Jr., and Zora Neale Hurston, as well as documents that helped shape the struggles of labor movements in the United States. The pedagogical practice at work here is not meant to romanticize these subjugated knowledges and "dangerous memories" as much as to critically appropriate and renew them as part of the reconstruction of a public philosophy that legitimates a politics and pedagogy of difference.

On another level, critical pedagogy recognizes that all educational work is at root contextual and conditional. This pedagogy refuses the totalizing unity of discourses that expunge the specific, contingent, and particular from their formulations. In this case, a critical pedagogy can only be discussed from within the historical and cultural specificity of space, time, place, and context. A critical pedagogy does not arise against a background of psychological, sociological, or anthropological universals but from within tasks that are strategic and practical, guided by imperatives that are both historical and ethical.

A critical pedagogy also rejects a discourse of value neutrality. Without subscribing to a language that polices behavior and desire, a critical pedagogy aims at developing pedagogical practices informed by an ethical stance that contests racism, sexism, class exploitation, and other dehumanizing and exploitative social relations as ideologies and social practices that disrupt and devalue public life. This is a pedagogy that rejects detachment, though it does not silence in the name of its own ideological fervor or correctness, acknowledges social injustices, and examines with care and in dialogue with itself and others how injustice works through the discourses, experiences, and desires that constitute daily life and the subjectivities of the students who invest in them. That is, it is a pedagogy guided by ethical principles that correspond to a radical practice rooted in historical experience. It is a pedagogy that comprehends the historical consequences of what it means to take a moral and political position with respect to the horror of, for example, the Gulag, the Nazi holocaust, or the Pol Pot regime, events that not only summon images of terror, domination, and resistance, but also provide *a priori* examples of what principles have to be both defended and fought against in the interest of freedom and life.

Within this perspective, ethics becomes more than the discourse of moral relativism or a static transmission of reified history. Ethics becomes instead a continued engagement in which the social practices of everyday life are interrogated in relation to the principles of individual autonomy and democratic public life—not as a matter of received truth but as a constant engagement. This provides the opportunity for individual capacities to be questioned and examined so that they can serve both to critically analyze and advance the possibilities inherent in all social forms. Community, difference, remembrance, and historical consciousness become central to the language of public life. This particular ethical stance is one that cannot be separated from the issue of how a socialized humanity develops within ideological and material conditions that either enable or disable the enhancement of human possibilities. It moves beyond moral outrage, attempting instead to provide a critical account of how individuals are constituted as human agents within different moral and ethical discourses and experiences. At the heart of such a pedagogy is the recognition that it is important to stare into history in order to remember the suffering of the past and that out of this remembrance a theory of ethics should be developed in which solidarity, compassion, and care become central dimensions of an informed social practice.

Essential to a critical pedagogy is the need to affirm the lived reality of difference as the ground on which to pose questions of theory and practice. Moreover, a critical pedagogy needs to function as a social practice that claims the experience of lived difference as an agenda for discussion and a central resource for a project of possibility. It must be constructed as part of a struggle over assigned meanings, the viability of different voices, and particular forms of authority. It is this struggle that makes possible and hence can redefine the possibilities we see both in the conditions of our daily lives and in those conditions that are "not yet."

A critical pedagogy for the liberal arts is one that affirms for students the importance of leadership as a moral and political enterprise that links the radical responsibility of ethics with the possibility of having those who are not oppressed understand the experience of oppression as an obstacle to democratic public life. Thus, critical pedagogy as a form of cultural politics is a call to celebrate responsible action and strategic risk taking as part of an ongoing struggle to link citizenship with the notion of a democratic public community, civic courage to a shared conception of social justice. Chantal Mouffe argues that a critical conception of citizenship should be "postmodern" in that it recognizes the importance of a politics of difference in which the particular, heterogeneous, and the multiple play a crucial role in the forming of a democratic public sphere:

The struggle for democratic citizenship is one strategy among others. It is an attempt to challenge the undemocratic practices of neoliberalism by constructing different political identities. It is inspired by a view of politics, which assumes a community of equals who share rights, social responsibility, and a solidarity based on a common belonging to a political community whose political ends—freedom and equality for all—are pursued in participating institutions. This is a long way from ... a privatized conception of citizenship that intends to whisk away the notion of political community. Democratic citizenship, on the contrary, aims at restoring the centrality of such a notion.[31]

Mouffe's view of citizenship and my view of a critical pedagogy include the idea that the formation of democratic citizens demands forms of political identity that radically extend the principles of justice, liberty, and dignity to public spheres constituted by difference and multiple forms of community. Of course, this is as much a pedagogical issue as it is a political issue. These political identities have to be constructed as part of a pedagogy in which difference becomes a basis for solidarity and unity rather than for competition and discrimination.

If pedagogy is to be linked with the notion of learning for empowerment, it is important that educators understand theoretically how difference is constructed through various representations and practices that name, legitimate, marginalize, and exclude the cultural capital and voices of subordinated groups in American society. Difference in this case does not become an empty marker for registering such differences within the language of harmony and conflict resolution. On the contrary, difference has to be taken up as a historical and social construction situated within hierarchies of domination and resistance. Hence, differences must be understood historically as part of larger political processes and systems tied to specific forms of exclusion, resistance, and transformation. In this case, difference is about how pedagogical and political practices work within and outside of the university to rewrite, codify, and reshape the practices of some groups within the discourse of privilege, while simultaneously erasing the cultural identities and histories of others.

As part of this theoretical project, a pedagogy of difference must address the question of how representations and practices that name, marginalize, and define difference as the devalued Other are actively learned, internalized, challenged, or transformed. In addition, such a pedagogy needs to address how understanding these differences can be used in order to change the prevailing relations of power that sustain them. It is also imperative to acknowledge and critically interrogate how the colonizing of differences by dominant groups is expressed and sustained through representations: in which the Other is seen as a deficit, in which the humanity of the Other is posited either as cynically problematic or ruthlessly denied. At the same time, it is important for a pedagogy of difference not only to critically unravel the ways in which the voices of the Other are colonized and repressed by the principle of identity that runs through the discourse of dominant groups, but also to understand how the experience of marginality at the level of everyday life lends itself to forms of oppositional and transformative consciousness.[32] This understanding must be based on the Others' reclamation and recreation of their own histories, voices, and visions as part of a wider struggle to change those material and social relations that deny radical pluralism as the basis of democratic political community. For it is only through such an understanding that teachers can develop a pedagogy of difference, one characterized by what Teresa de Lauretis calls "an ongoing effort to create new spaces of discourse, to rewrite cultural narratives, and to define the terms of another perspective—a view from 'elsewhere.' "[33]

What is suggested is a pedagogy in which there is a critical questioning of the omissions and tensions that exist between the master narratives and hegemonic discourses that make up the official curriculum of the university, department, or program and the self-representations of subordinated groups as they might appear in "forgotten" histories, texts, memories, experiences, and community narratives. Not only does a pedagogy of difference seek to understand how difference is constructed in the intersection of the official canon of the school and the various voices of students from subordinate groups, it also draws upon student experience as both a narrative for agency and a referent for critique. This requires forms of pedagogy that both confirm and critically engage the knowledge and experience through which students author their own voices and construct social identities. In effect, we must take seriously, as an aspect of learning, the knowledge and experiences that constitute the individual and collective voices by which students identify and give meaning to themselves and others by first using what they know about their own lives as a basis for criticizing the dominant culture. The student experience has to be first understood and recognized as the accumulation of collective memories and stories that provide students with a sense of familiarity, identity, and practical knowledge. Such experience has to be both affirmed and critically interrogated. In addition, the social and historical construction of such experience has to be affirmed and understood as part of a wider struggle for voice, but it also has to be remade, reterritorialized in the interest of a social imaginary that dignifies the best traditions and possibilities of those groups learning to speak from a position of enablement, that is, from the discourse of dignity and governance. In her analysis of the deterritorialization of women as Other, Caren Kaplan articulates this position well.

> Recognizing the minor cannot erase the aspects of the major, but as a mode of understanding it enables us to see the fissures in our identities, to unravel the seams of our totalities. ... We must leave home, as it were, since our homes are often sites of racism, sexism, and other damaging social practices. Where we come to locate ourselves in terms of our specific histories and differences must be a place with room for what can be salvaged from the past and made anew. What we gain is a reterritorialization; we reinhabit a world of our making (here "our" is expanded to a coalition of identities—neither universal nor particular).[34]

Furthermore, it is important to extend the possibilities of experience by making it both the object of critical inquiry and by appropriating in a similarly critical fashion, when necessary, the codes and knowledges that constitute broader and less familiar historical and cultural traditions. We need not necessarily indiscriminately abandon the traditions of Western civilization; instead, we need to engage the strengths and weaknesses of such a complex and contradictory tradition as part of a wider effort to deepen the discourse of critical democracy and responsible citizenship.

At issue here is the development of a pedagogy that replaces the authoritative language of recitation with an approach that allows students to speak from their own histories, collective memories, and voices while simultaneously challenging the grounds on which knowledge and power are constructed and legitimated. Critical pedagogy contributes to making possible a variety of human capacities that expand the range of social identities that students may become. It points to the importance of understanding in both pedagogical and political terms how subjectivities are produced within those social forms in which people move but of which they are often only partially conscious. Similarly, it raises fundamental questions regarding how students make particular investments of meaning and affect, how students are constituted within a triad of knowledge, power, and pleasure, and what it is we as teachers need to understand regarding why students should be interested in the forms of authority, knowledge, and values that we produce and legitimate within our classrooms and university. It is worth noting that not only does such a pedagogy articulate a respect for a diversity of student voices, it also provides a referent for developing a public language rooted in a commitment to social transformation.

Another serious challenge of reforming the liberal arts necessitates that university teachers rethink the nature of their role with respect to issues of politics, social responsibility, and the construction of a pedagogy of possibility. Instead of weaving dreams fashioned in the cynical interests of industrial psychology and cultural sectarianism, university educators can become part of a collective effort to build and revitalize critical public cultures that provide the basis for transformative democratic communities. This means, among other things, that they can educate students to work collectively to make "despair unconvincing and hope practical" by refusing the role of the disconnected expert, technician, or careerist and adopting the practice of the engaged and transformative intellectual. This is not a call for educators to become wedded to some abstract ideal that turns them into prophets of perfection and certainty; on the contrary, it represents a call for educators to perform a noble public service, that is, to undertake teaching as a form of social criticism, to define themselves as engaged, critical public intellectuals who can play a major role in animating a democratic public culture.[35] It begs intellectuals to construct their relationship to the wider society by making organic connections with the historical traditions that provide themselves and their students with a voice, history, and sense of belonging. This view resonates with Gramsci's call to broaden the notion of education by seeing all of society as a vast school. It also resonates with his call for critical intellectuals to forge alliances around new historical blocks.[36]

Educators need to encourage students by example to find ways to get involved, to make a difference, to think in global terms, and to act from specific contexts. The notion of teachers as transformative intellectuals is marked by a moral courage and criticism that does not require them to step back from society but only to distance themselves from being implicated in those power relations that subjugate, corrupt, exploit, or infantilze. This is what Michael Walzer calls criticism from within, the telling of stories that speak to the historical specificity and voices of those who have been marginalized and silenced.[37] It is a form of criticism wedded to the development of pedagogical practices and experiences in the interest of a utopian vision that in Walter Benjamin's terms rubs history against the grain, one that gives substance to the development of a public culture that is synonymous with the spirit of a critical democracy.

Educators must therefore develop a public language that refuses to reconcile higher education with inequality, that actively abandons those forms of pedagogical practice that prevent our students from becoming aware of and offended by the structures of oppression at work in both institutional and everyday life. We need a language that defends liberal arts education neither as a servant of the state nor as authoritarian cultural ideology but as the site of a counter-public sphere where students can be educated to learn how to question and, in the words of John Dewey, "break existing public forms."[38] This is a language in which knowledge and power are inextricably linked to the presupposition that to choose life, so as to make it possible, is to understand the preconditions necessary to struggle for it. As engaged public intellectuals committed to a project of radical pedagogy and the reconstruction of democratic public life, academics can create forms of collegiality and community forged in social practices that link their work in the university with larger social struggles. This suggests redefining the borders of knowledge–power relationships outside of the limitations of academic specialties so as to broaden the relationship of the university with the culture of public life. Academic interventions can thus provide the basis for new forms of public association, occasions informed by and contributing to moral and political commitments in which the meanings we produce, the ways in which we represent ourselves, and our relation to others contribute to a wider public discussion and dialogue of democratic possibilities not yet realized. This is a call to transform the hegemonic cultural forms of the wider society and the academy into a social movement of intellectuals intent on reclaiming and reconstructing democratic values and public life rather than contributing to their demise. This is a utopian practice that both critiques and transcends the culture of despair and disdain that has characterized education in the Reagan–Bush Era. It also provides a starting point for linking liberal arts education with a public philosophy in which the curriculum is not reduced to a matter of cultural inheritance, but is posed as part of an ongoing struggle informed by a project of possibility that extends the most noble of human capacities while simultaneously developing the potentialities of democratic public life.

REFERENCES

[1] Of course, a caveat has to be noted here. For many liberal and left academics, the university is generally regarded as a site constituted in relations of power and representing various political and ethical interests. On the other hand, some neoconservative educators believe that the true interests of the university transcend political and normative concerns and that the latter represent an agenda being pushed exclusively by left-wing academics who are undermining the most basic principles of university life. For example, former Secretary of Education William J. Bennett has argued that most universities are controlled "by a left-wing political agenda" pushing the concerns of feminists, Marxists, and various ethnic groups. The neoconservative argument is often made in defense of an objective, balanced, and unbiased academic discourse. The claim to objectivity, truth, and principles that transcend history and power may be comforting to neoconservatives, but in reality the discourse of such groups is nothing more than a rhetorical mask that barely conceals their own highly charged, ideological agenda. The neoconservative ongoing attacks against affirmative action, ethnic studies, radical scholarship, modernity, and any thing else that threatens the traditional curriculum and the power relations it supports represent a particularized, not universalized view of the university and its relationship with the wider society. The most recent example of neoconservative "objectivity" and public conscience was displayed in a recent meeting in Washington, D.C., of 300 conservative scholars whose major agenda was to reclaim the universities and to find ways to challenge those left-wing academics, referred to by one of the participants as "the barbarians in our midst" (p. 14), who are challenging the authority of the traditional canon. Underlying this form of criticism is the not so invisible ideological appeal to the "white man's burden" to educate those who exist outside of the parameters of civilized culture; the rhetoric betrays the colonizing logic at the heart of the "reactionary" political agenda that characterizes the new cultural offensive of such groups as the National Association of Scholars. The report on the conference appeared in Joseph Berger, "Conservative Scholars Attack 'Radicalization' of Universities," *New York Times*, November 15, 1988, 14. For a discussion of the conservative offensive in establishing a traditional reading of the liberal arts and the notion of the canon, see William V. Spanos, *Repetitions: The Postmodern Occasion in Literature and Culture* (Baton Rouge, 1987); a special issue on "The Politics of Education," *South Atlantic Quarterly* 89:1, (1990); a special issue on "The Politics of Teaching Literature," *College Literature* 17:2/3 (1990); Henry A. Giroux, *Schooling and the Struggle for Public Life* (Minneapolis, 1988).

[2] A characteristic form of this type of evasion can be found in John Searle, "The Storm Over the University," *The New York Review of Books* 37:1 (December 6, 1990); Allan Bloom, *Giants and Dwarfs: Essays 1960–1990* (New York: Simon and Schuster, 1990); and Roger Kimball, *Tenured Radicals: How Politics has Corrupted Our Higher Education* (New York: Harper and Row, 1990). All of these books share the lament that progressives and radicals have corrupted the university by politicizing the curriculum. Central to this charge is the assumptions that conservatives are politically neutral and that their call for educational reform is objective and value-free. Searle's claim is a bit more sophisticated, though no less confused. He alleges that because social critics link university reform with the broader goal of social transformation that they must by necessity engage in forms of political indoctrination. Searle cannot, unfortunately, distinguish between rooting one's pedagogy in a particular set of expectations that serve as a referent for engaging students and a pedagogical approach designed to beat them into ideological submission. In other words, Searle collapses the particular ideological values that educators individually profess and the pedagogy they exercise. While I believe that students should be educated to not simply adapt to the system but be able to change it when necessary, the nature of my pedagogy does not have to be reduced to the inculcation of a specific ideology in the service of social transformation. My immediate goal is to get students to think critically about their lives; the specific objectives and ideologies they choose to address and take up are not something that can be forced upon them. Any pedagogy that acts in the service of only one outcome generally constitutes a form of terrorism.

³ Henry Louis Gates, Jr., "The Master's Pieces: On Canon Formation and the African-American Tradition," *The South Atlantic Quarterly* 89:1 (1990), 89–111.

⁴ Gayatri C. Spivak, "The Making of Americans, the Teaching of English, and the Future of Cultural Studies," *New Literary History* 21:4 (Autumn 1990), 785.

⁵ Philip Corrigan, "In/Forming Schooling," in David W. Livingstone, *Critical Pedagogy and Cultural Power* (New York, New York: Bergin and Garvey, 1987), 17–40.

⁶ I am borrowing this idea from Peter Brooks, "Western Civ at Bay," *New York Times Literary Supplement*, January 25, 1991, 5.

⁷ Roger I. Simon, "Empowerment as a Pedagogy of Possibility," *Language Arts* 64:3 (April 1987), 372.

⁸ Jacques Derrida, "The Principle of Reason: The University in the Eyes of Its Pupils," *Diacritics* 13:3 (Fall 1983), 3.

⁹ Ernst Bloch, *The Philosophy of the Future* (New York, 1970), 86–87.

¹⁰ The quotes before and after the passage by Bloch are from Roger Simon, "Empowerment, as a Pedagogy of Possibility," 371, 372. I am indebted to Simon for a number of the ideas in this section on Bloch and the relationship between daydreaming and the process of schooling.

¹¹ Leon Botstein illuminates some of the ideological elements at work in the language of cultural despair characteristic of the educational discourse of the New Right:

> In particular, the new conservativism evident in the most influential educational critiques and Jeremiads utilizes the language and images of decline and unwittingly makes comparisons to an idealized American past during which far fewer Americans finished high school. It challenges implicitly (Hirsch) and explicitly (Bloom) the post–World War II democratic goal of American schooling: to render excellence and equity incompatible in reality. In the 1980s, the call for educational reform is not being framed, as it was in the late 1950s (when America was concerned about Sputnik and Harvard's Conant studied the American high school), in terms of what might be achieved. Rather the discussion begins with a sense of what has been lost.

See Leon Botstein, "Education Reform in the Reagan Era: False Paths, Broken Promises," *Social Policy* (Spring 1988), 7. For a critique of the ideology of cultural decline among universities, see Jerry Herron, *Universities and the Myth of Cultural Decline* (Detroit, 1988).

¹² Simon, "Empowerment as a Pedagogy of Possibility."

¹³ This criticism is more fully developed in Stanley Aronowitz and Henry A. Giroux, *Postmodern Education* (Minneapolis: University of Minnesota Press, 1991); Henry A. Giroux, *Schooling and the Struggle for Public Life*; Stanley Aronowitz and Henry A. Giroux, *Education Under Siege* (Granby, Mass., 1985).

¹⁴ Brooks, "Western Civ at Bay," 5.

¹⁵ Roger Kimball, *"Tenured Radicals"*: As Postscript," *The New Criterion* (January 1991), 13.

¹⁶ Silber, cited in Carolyn J. Mooney, "Scholars Decry Campus Hostility to Western Culture at a Time When More Nations Embrace Its Values," *The Chronicle of Higher Education*, January 30, 1991, A16.

¹⁷ Allan Bloom, *The Closing of the American Mind: How Higher Education Has Failed Democracy and Impoverished the Souls of Today's Students* (New York, 1987). E.D. Hirsch, Jr., *Cultural Literacy: What Every American Needs to Know* (Boston, 1987).

¹⁸ Allan Bloom, *The Closing of the American Mind*; E.D. Hirsch, Jr., *Cultural Literacy*; Kimball, *Tenured Radicals*; Lynne V. Cheney, *Humanities in America: A Report to the President, the Congress, and the American People* (Washington, D.C.: National Endowment for the Humanities, 1988).

¹⁹ This position is more fully developed in Jim Merod, *The Political Responsibility of the Critic* (Ithaca, 1987); Aronowitz and Giroux, *Education Under Siege*, 1985; Frank Lentricchia, *Criticism and Social Change* (Chicago, 1983).

²⁰ William V. Spanos, *Repetitions*, 302.

[21] Christopher Lasch, "A Response to Fischer," *Tikkun* 3:6 (1988), 73.

[22] Mas'ud Zavarzadeh and Donald Morton, "War of the Words: The Battle of (and for) English," *In These Times* (October 28–November 3, 1987), 18–19. Hazel Carby, in "The Canon: Civil War and Reconstruction," *Michigan Quarterly Review* (Winter 1989), 36–38, is clear on this point and is worth quoting at length:

> ... I would argue that debates about the canon are misleading debates in many ways. Arguments appear to be about the inclusion or exclusion of particular texts and/or authors or about including or excluding types of books and authors ("women" and "minorities" are usually the operative categories). It also appears as if debates about the canon are disagreements about issues of representation only. ... Contrary to what the debate appears to be about, talking about the canon means that we avoid the deeper problem. Focusing on books and authors means that we are not directly addressing ways in which our society is structured in dominance. We live in a racialized hierarchy which is also organized through class and gender divisions. Reducing these complex modes of inequality to questions of representation on a syllabus is far too simple a method of appearing to resolve those social contradictions and yet this is how the battle has been waged at Columbia and Stanford, to take two examples of campuses engaged in debating the importance of canonical works of western culture. What is absurd about these hotly contested and highly emotive battles is that proponents for radical change in canonical syllabi are forced to act as if inclusion of the texts they favor would somehow make accessible the experience of women or minorities as generic types. The same people who would argue in very sophisticated critical terms that literary texts do not directly reflect or represent reality but reconstruct and represent particular historical realities find themselves demanding that the identity of a social group be represented by a single novel. Acting as if an excluded or marginalized or dominant group is represented in a particular text, in my view, is a mistake. ... Our teaching needs to make connections with, as well as provide a critique of, dominant ideologies and meanings of culture which structure the curricula of departments of English and American studies.

See also Toni Morrison, "Unspeakable Things Unspoken: The Afro-American Presence in. American Literature," *Michigan Quarterly Review* (Winter 1989), 1–34.

[23] This particular quote is cited in Frank Hearn, *Reason and Freedom in Sociological Thought* (Boston, 1985), 175. The classic statements by Dewey on this subject can be found, of course, in John Dewey, *Democracy and Education* (New York, 1916) and John Dewey, *The Public and Its Problems in The Later Works of John Dewey, Volume 2, 1925–1927*, Jo Ann Boydston, ed. (Carbondale, 1984), 253–372.

[24] See, for example, C. Wright Mills, *Power, Politics, and People: The Collected Essays of C. Wright Mills*, Irving Louis Horowitz, ed. (New York, 1963), especially the "Social Role of the Intellectual" and "Mass Society and Liberal Education."

[25] For a critical treatment of this issue, see Robert N. Bellah, Richard Madsen, William M. Sullivan, Ann Swidler, and Steven M. Tipton, *Habits of the Heart: Individualism and Commitment in American Life* (Berkeley, 1985); for an excellent analysis and criticism of American life and the decline of community as portrayed in *Habits of the Heart*, see Fredric R. Jameson, "On Habits of the Heart," in Charles H. Reynolds and Ralph V. Norman, eds., *Community in America* (Berkeley, 1988), 97–112.

[26] A number of representative essays that deal with pedagogy as a form of cultural production can be found in Henry A. Giroux and Peter McLaren, eds., *Critical Pedagogy, The State and Cultural Struggle* (Albany: SUNY Press, 1988); Henry A. Giroux and Roger I. Simon, eds., *Popular Culture and Critical Pedagogy* (New York: Bergin and Garvey, 1989); Patricia Donahue and Ellen Quandahl, eds., *Reclaiming Pedagogy: The Rhetoric of the Classroom* (Carbondale: Southern Illinois University Press, 1989); Aronowitz and Henry A. Giroux, *Postmodern Education*; and Roger I. Simon, *Teaching Against the Grain* (New York: Bergin and Garvey Press, 1991).

[27] Democracy, in this case, is linked to citizenship understood as a form of self-management constituted in all major economic, social, and cultural spheres of society. Democracy as it is being used here takes up the issue of transferring power from elites and executives authorities, who control the economic and cultural apparatuses of society, to those producers who wield power at the local level.

[28] The next two pages draw from Henry A. Giroux and Harvey J. Kaye, "The Liberal Arts Must Be Reformed to Serve Democratic Ends," *The Chronicle of Higher Education*, March 29, 1989, A44.

[29] Elizabeth Fox-Genovese, "The Claims of a Common Culture: Gender, Race, Class and the Canon," *Salmagundi* 72 (Fall 1986), 133.

[30] Gail Valaskakis, "The Chippewa and the Other: Living the Heritage of Lac Du Flambeau," *Cultural Studies* 2:3 (October 1988), 268.

[31] Chantal Mouffe, "The Civics Lesson," *New Statesman and Society* (October 7, 1988), 30.

[32] bell hooks, "Choosing the Margin as a Space of Radical Openness," *Yearning* (Boston: South End Press, 1990), 145–52.

[33] Teresa de Lauretis, *Technologies of Gender* (Bloomington, 1987), p. 25.

[34] Caren Kaplan, "Deterritorialization: The Rewriting of Home and Exile in Western Feminist Discourse," *Cultural Critique* 6 (Spring 1987), 187–98.

[35] On this point, see Russell Jacoby, *The Last Intellectuals* (New York, 1987); Terry Eagleton, *The Function of Criticism* (London, 1984).

[36] Antonio Gramsci, *Selections from the Prison Notebooks* (New York, 1971).

[37] Michael Walzer, *Interpretation and Social Criticism* (Cambridge, 1985).

[38] John Dewey, *The Public and Its Problems in The Later Works of John Dewey, Volume 2, 1925–1927*, Jo Ann Boydston, ed., (Carbondale, 1984), 253–372.

5

Redefining the Boundaries of Race and Ethnicity: Beyond the Politics of Pluralism

Introduction

Within the current historical conjuncture, the political and cultural boundaries that have long constituted the meaning of race and cultural politics are beginning to shift. The question of race figures much differently in the United States at the beginning of the 1990s than it did a decade ago for a number of reasons. First, the legacies of anticolonial and postcolonial struggles have ruptured the ability of Eurocentric discourses to marginalize and erase the many-faceted voices of those Others who have struggled under the yoke of colonial oppression. Second, the population of America's subordinated groups are changing the cultural landscapes of our urban centers. According to recent demographic projections, Blacks and Hispanics will "constitute a decided majority in nearly one-third of the nation's 50 largest cities . . . and Blacks alone will be the major racial group in at least nine major cities, notably Detroit, Baltimore, Memphis, Washington, D.C., New Orleans, and Atlanta."[1] In this case, populations traditionally defined as the Other are moving from the margin to the center and challenging the ethnocentric view that people of color can be relegated to the periphery of everyday life.

Third, while people of color are redrawing the cultural demographic boundaries of the urban centers, the boundaries of power appear to be solidifying in favor of rich, white, middle and upper classes. The consequences of this solidification will have a dramatic effect on race relations in the next decade. For example, escalating unemployment among Afro-American teenage youth poses a serious threat to an entire generation of future adults; in many urban cities the dropout rate for nonwhite children exceeds 60 percent (with New York City at 70%);[2] the civil rights gains of the 1960s are slowly being eroded by the policy-makers and judicial heirs of the Reagan Era, and the tide of racism is aggressively rising in the streets, schools, workplaces, and campuses of the United States.[3] In the Reagan and Bush Eras, equity and social justice are given low priority next to the "virtues" of collective greed, individual success, and expanding the defense budget. As class divisions grow deeper, intraclass and racial tensions mask the need for collective struggles for social and political justice. As the white working class sees its dream of moving up the social and economic ladder imperiled, it is increasingly coming to view affirmative action, social policy programs, and the changing nature of national and cultural identity as a threat to its own sense of security and possibility. Instead of embracing Afro-Americans and other ethnic groups as allies in the struggle to dismantle the master narratives of Eurocentric domination with the discourse of democratic struggle and solidarity, the legacy of institutional and ideological racism appears to have once again reached a dangerous threshold that impedes rather than extends such a goal. As we move into a postmodern world that is progressively redrawing the boundaries established by nationalism, ethnocentrism, and Eurocentric culture, the United States appears to be refiguring its political, social, and cultural geography in a manner that denies rather than maintains a democratic community. Instead of engaging a politics of difference, community, and democracy with respect to the principles of justice, equality, and freedom, the current neoconservative government appears eager to sever "the links between democracy and political equality."[4]

The shadow of totalitarianism is darkening the future of American democracy. Its primary expression is found in the resurgence of racism in this country. Racial slurs are now regularly incorporated into the acts of some rock stars and stand-up comedians;[5] the dominant culture seems indifferent or even hostile to the deepening poverty and despair affecting a growing population of Afro-Americans in the underclass in our nation's cities; the growing dropout rate among Afro-American students is met with insulting diatribes and the refusal to engage the racism prevalent in our nation's schools;[6] the Afro-American family is not highlighted for its resiliency amidst the most degrading economic and social conditions but is condemned as a cause of its own misery.[7] Increasingly, racial hatred is erupting into racist terror. Growing racial tensions have resulted in outbreaks of violence in Chicago's Marquette Park, Baltimore's Hampden section, Philadelphia's Fishtown and Feltonville, and a number of other cities in the last decade. In two highly publicized murders, black youths Michael Griffith and Yusuf Hawkins were killed by racists in Howard Beach and Bensonhurst, New York. Civil rights demonstrations have been met by overt white hostility and racist attacks. What needs to be stressed is not only that minorities are increasingly open to ideological and physical assaults, but that the very fate of our society as a democratic nation is at risk. Central to the effort to reconstruct this nation as a democratic society is the need to rethink the project of race, and cultural and economic justice. Moreover, this is not merely a political issue; it is eminently a pedagogical one as well. Racism is an ideological poison that is learned; it is a historical and social construction that seeps into social practices, needs, the unconscious, and rationality itself. If it is to be challenged at the institutional level, at the very centers of authority, racism must first be addressed as an ideological concern for the ways in which it is produced, sustained, and taken up within a cultural politics secured within wider dominant relations of power.

These are not new insights and generations of Afro-American leaders have raised them in elegant and courageous ways. The fight against racism has always been seen as an important political objective by those committed to democratic struggle. But in most cases, this concern has been framed within a discourse of modernism that has failed to place race and ethnicity at the center of a radical politics of democracy, difference, and cultural struggle. In what follows, I want to argue for a postmodern discourse of resistance as a basis for developing a cultural politics and antiracist pedagogy as part of a larger theory of difference and democratic struggle. In developing this perspective, I will first address in general terms the failings of various versions of modernist discourse; next I will argue that the foundations for an antiracist pedagogy can be taken up by drawing selectively upon the discourses of a critical postmodernism, the discourse of narrative and difference that has largely emerged in the work of Afro-American feminist writers, and a neo-Gramscian discourse that links difference with the notion of a democratic public philosophy. I will conclude by suggesting how these discourses provide some important elements for developing specific pedagogical practices.

Refiguring the Boundaries of Race as Modernism

The dominant discourses of modernity have rarely been able to address race and ethnicity as an ethical, political, and cultural marker in order to understand or self-consciously examine the notions of justice inscribed in the modernist belief in change and the progressive unfolding of history.[8] In fact, race and ethnicity have been generally reduced to a discourse of the Other, a discourse that, regardless of its emancipatory or reactionary intent, often essentialized and reproduced the distance between the centers and margins of power. Within the discourse of modernity, the Other not only sometimes ceases to be a historical agent, but is often defined within totalizing and universalistic theories that create a transcendental rational white, male, Eurocentric subject that occupies the centers of power while simultaneously appearing to exist outside of time and space. Read against this Eurocentric transcendental subject, the Other is shown to lack any redeeming community traditions, collective voice, or historical weight—and is reduced to the imagery of the colonizer. By separating the discourse of the Other from the epistemic and material violence that most postmodernist critics have identified as central to the character and definition of Western notions of progress, modernist discourses were never able to develop an adequate understanding of racism that could serve as a form of cultural criticism capable of redefining the boundaries and articulations between itself and the subordinate groups it continually oppressed.

In this sense, modernism in its various forms served to repress the possibility of linking the construction of its own master narratives and relations of power with the simultaneous creation of alternative narratives woven out of the pain, misery, and struggle of subordinate groups.[9] Modernist discourses, in part, have served to solidify the boundaries of race and ethnicity either by creating biological and scientific theories that "proved" the inferiority of Afro-American and other subordinated groups, or in its more liberal forms created the self-delusion that the boundaries of racial inequality and ethnicity were always exclusively about the language, experiences, and histories of the Other and had little to do with power relations at the core of its own cultural and political identity as the discourse of white authority. In the first instance, the ideology of racism and degraded Otherness can be found, as Cornel West points out, in the logics of three central European traditions: the Judeo-Christian, scientific, and psychosexual. He is worth quoting at length on this issue:

> The Judeo-Christian racist logic emanates from the biblical account of Ham looking upon and failing to cover his father Noah's nakedness and thereby receiving divine punishment in the form of blackening his progeny. Within this logic, black skin is a divine curse owing to disrespect for and rejection of paternal authority. The scientific racist logic rests upon a modern philosophical discourse guided by Greek ocular metaphors, undergirded by Cartesian notations of the primacy of the subject and the preeminence of representation and buttressed by Baconian ideas of observation, evidence, and confirmation that promote and encourage the activities of observing, comparing, measuring, and ordering physical characteristics of human bodies. Given the renewed appreciation and appropriation of classical aesthetic and cultural norms. Within this logic, the notions of black ugliness, cultural deficiency, and intellectual inferiority are legitimated by the value laden, yet prestigious, authority of science. The psychosexual racist logic arises from the phallic obsessions, Oedipal projections, and anal-sadistic orientations in European culture that endow African men and women with sexual prowess; view Africans as either cruel, revengeful fathers; frivolous, carefree children; or passive, long-suffering mothers; and identify Africans with dirt, odious smell, and feces. In short, Africans are associated with acts of bodily defecation, violation, and subordination. Within this logic, Africans are walking abstractions, inanimate things or invisible creatures. For all three white supremacist logics, which operate simultaneously in the modern West, Africans personify degraded Otherness, exemplify radical alterity, and embody alien difference.[10]

It is important to emphasize that the Eurocentric drive to systematize the world by mastering the conditions of nature and human life represents a form of social modernism that must not be confused with the more emancipatory elements of political modernism. On the one hand, the project of social modernity has been carried out under the increasing domination of relations of capitalist production characterized by a growing commodification, bureaucraticization, homogenization, and standardization of everyday life. Such a project has been legitimized, in part, through an appeal to the Enlightenment project of rationality, progress, and humanism. On the other hand, the legacy of political modernism provides a discourse that inaugurates the possibility of developing social relations in which the principles of liberty, justice, and equality provide the basis for democratic struggles. If the ravages of modernism has led to overt forms of racism and colonialization, its victories have provided a discourse of rights, universal education, and social justice.

As I mentioned in Chapter 3, modernity is not a unified discourse, and its networks of meanings and social practices have included a Western-style counterdiscourse that also offered liberals and radicals spaces for challenging racist practices and ideologies.[11] This challenge can be seen, of course, in the traditions of rupture and dissent in this country that extend from the abolitionist movement to the civil rights legislation of the 1960s and to the more recent efforts by contemporary activists and artists to counter the increasing racism of the 1980s and perhaps the 1990s as well. As noble as these responses have been, at least in intent, few of them have adequately theorized racism as part of a wider discourse of ethics, politics, and difference.[12] Unable to step beyond the modernist celebration of the unified self, totalizing notions of history, and universalistic models of reason, liberal and radical discourses have generally failed to explore the limits of the absolutist character of their own narratives regarding race and difference. Within these discourses, ethics and politics have been removed from any serious attempt to engage contingency, particularity, partiality, and community within a notion of difference free from binary oppositions, hierarchical relations, and narratives of mastery and control. But modernity has also failed to challenge with any great force the white supremacist logics embedded in the ideological traditions cited by Cornel West. Similarly, it has failed to account for the power of its own authority as a central component in structuring the very notion of Otherness as site for objectification and marginalization.

The emancipatory promise of plurality and heterogeneity as the basis for new forms of conversation, solidarity, and public culture never fully materialized within the more liberal and radical discourses of Western modernity. Caught within the limiting narratives of European culture as the model of civilization and progress, liberal and radical theorists have never been able to break away from Western models of authority that placed either the individual white male at the center of history and rationality or viewed history as the unproblematic progressive unfolding of science, reason, and technology.

For example, dominant strains of liberal ideology have fashioned their antiracist discourses on a Eurocentric notion of society that subordinates the discourse of ethics and politics to the rule of the market, an unproblematic acceptance of European culture as the basis of civilization, and a notion of the individual subject as a unified, rational self that is the source of all cultural and social meaning. The central modernist political ideology at work here, as Stanley Aronowitz has pointed out, is "that a free market and a democratic state go hand in hand."[13] Unfortunately for liberals, it is precisely this assumption that prevents them from questioning how they, as a dominant group, actually benefit from racist ideologies and social relations, even as they allegedly contest such practices. By assuming that the middle class, which bears the values of individualism and free-market rationality, is the only agent of history, liberals are blind to the corruptions implicated in the exercise of their own authority and historical actions.[14]

Within this multilayered liberal discourse, the attack on racism is often reduced to policy measures aimed at eliminating racist institutional barriers in the marketplace, providing compensatory programs to enhance the cultural capital and skills of Afro-Americans as in various remedial programs in education or the workplace such as Headstart or the now defunct Job Corps project, or is relegated to patronizing calls for Afro-Americans to muster the courage and fortitude to compete in a manner consistent with the drive and struggle of other ethnic groups who have succeeded in American society.

Though the theoretical sweep is broad and oversimplified here, the basic issue is that modernist discourse in its various forms rarely engages how white authority is inscribed and implicated in the creation and reproduction of a society in which the voices of the center appear either invisible or unimplicated in the historical and social construction of racism as an integral part of their own collective identity. Rather than recognizing how differences are historically and socially constructed within ideologies and material practices that connect race, class, and gender within webbed connections of domination, liberals consign the struggle of subordinate groups to master narratives that suggest that the oppressed need to be remade in the image of a dominant white culture in order to be integrated into the heavenly city of Enlightenment rationality.

Eurocentric radical discourses of modernity have also failed to develop a complex and adequate theory of racism as part of a wider theory of difference and democratic struggle. The classic instance in this case in represented by those versions of Marxism that have reduced struggle and difference to a reductionist logocentricism that universalizes the working class as the collective agent of history. Marxism buys the productivist discourse of modernity but rejects the liberal notion of the middle class as the agent of history. Marxist economics rejects the rule of the market as the end of ideology and inserts in its place the rule of the working class as the projected end of history. In this view, racism is historically tied to the rise of capitalism and is afforded no independent status as an irreducible source of either exploitation or struggle. In this instance, the notion of historical agency loses its pluralist character. As a consequence, racism is subsumed within the modernist logic of essentialism in which reason and history seem to move according to some inner logic outside of the play of difference and plurality. In effect, class struggle becomes the all-embracing category that relegates all other struggles, voices, and conflicts to simply a distraction in the march of history.[15]

Radical social theorists have long offered a challenge to the classical Marxist theory of race, but it is only within the last few decades that such work has advanced the category of difference beyond the essentialism of Afro-American nationalism, cultural separatism, staged pluralism, and the discourse of avant-garde exoticism.[16]

The failure of modernism around race can be seen in the ways in which it has structured the discourse of educational reform on this issue.

Educational Theory and the Discourse of Race and Ethnicity

Within the discourse of modernism, dominant educational approaches to race and ethnicity imitate many of the worst dimensions of liberal ideology and radical essentialism.[17] Questions of Otherness are generally fashioned in the discourse of multicultural education, which in its varied forms and approaches generally fails to conceptualize issues of race and ethnicity as part of the wider discourse of power and powerlessness. Questions of representation and inclusion suppress any attempts to call into question the norm of whiteness as an ethnic category that secures its dominance by appearing to be invisible. Modernism's emancipatory potential within multicultural education finds expression in the call to reverse negative images of Afro-American and other ethnic groups as they appear in various forms of texts and images. Missing here is any attempt to either critique forms of European and American culture that situate difference in structures of domination or reconstruct a discourse of race and ethnicity in a theory of difference that highlights questions of equality, justice, and liberty as part of an ongoing democratic struggle. Multiculturalism is generally about Otherness, but is written in ways in which the dominating aspects of white culture are not called into question and the oppositional potential of difference as a site of struggle is muted.[18] Modernism and dominant forms of multicultural education merge in their refusal to locate cultural differences in a broader examination of how the boundaries of ethnicity, race, and power make visible how whiteness functions as a historical and social construction, "an unrecognized and unspoken racial category that secures its power by refusing to identify culture as a problem of politics, power, and pedagogy."[19] As a critical discourse of race and pedagogy, multiculturalism needs to break its silence regarding its role in masking how white domination colonizes definitions of the normal.[20] In effect, critical educators need to move their analyses and pedagogical practices away from an exotic or allegedly objective encounter with marginal groups and raise more questions with respect to how the dominant self is always present in the construction of the margins. As Toni Morrison points out, the very issue of race requires that the bases of Western civilization will require rethinking.[21] It means that the central question may not be why Afro-Americans are absent from dominant narratives, but "What intellectual feats had to be performed by the author or his critic to erase (Afro-Americans) from a society seething with (their) presence, and what effect has that performance had on the work? What are the strategies of escape from knowledge?"[22] This means refiguring the map of ethnicity and difference outside of the binary oppositions of modernism.

What is at stake here is more than the politics of representation. Issac Julien and Kobena Mercer state the issue clearly:

> One issue at stake, we suggest, is the potential break-up or deconstruction of structures that determine what is regarded as culturally central and what is regarded as culturally marginal. . . . Rather than attempt to compensate the "structured absences" of previous paradigms, it would be useful to identify the relations of power/knowledge that determine which cultural issues are intellectually prioritized in the first place. The initial stage in any deconstructive project must be to examine and undermine the force of the binary relation that produces the marginal as a consequence of the authority invested in the centre.[23]

Implicit in this perspective are a number of political and pedagogical challenges that can be taken up by radical educators as part of a broader theoretical attempt to deconstruct and displace some of the more powerful ideological expressions of a hegemonic theory of multicultural education. First, critical educators need to reveal the political interests at work in those forms of multicultural education that translate cultural differences into learning styles; the ideological task here is to challenge those mystifying ideologies that separate culture from power and struggle while simultaneously treating difference as a technical rather than a political category. Second, critical educators need to challenge those educational discourses that view schooling as a decontextualized site free from social, political, and racial tensions. What has to be stressed here is the primacy of the political and the contextual in analyzing issues of culture, language, and voice. Third, critical educators must ideologically engage theories of multicultural education that attempt to smother the relationship between difference and power/empowerment under the call for harmony and joyful learning. At the same time, they must further the development of a theory of difference that takes as its starting point issues of power, domination, and struggle.[24] But an antiracist pedagogy must do more than reconceptualize the political and pedagogical struggle over race, ethnicity, and difference as merely part of the language of critique. It must also retrieve and reconstruct possibilities for establishing the basis for a progressive vision that makes schooling for democracy and critical citizenship an unrealized yet possible reality. In doing so, it is necessary to provide some central theoretical principles for developing the foundation for an antiracist pedagogy. In what follows, I will argue that there are elements of a postmodern discourse that offer valuable insights for engaging in such a task.

Postmodernism and the Shifting Boundaries of Otherness

Postmodernism is a culture and politics of transgression. It is a challenge to the boundaries in which modernism has developed its discourses of mastery, totalization, representation, subjectivity, and history.[25] Whereas modernism builds its dream of social engineering on the foundations of universal reason and the unified subject, postmodernism questions the very notion of meaning and representation. Postmodernism not only opens up a new political front within discourse and representation. It also criticizes the notion of the unified subject as a Eurocentric construct designed to provide white, male, Christian bosses and workers with a legitimating ideology for colonizing and marginalizing those Others who do not measure up to the standards of an "I" or "We" wielding power from the center of the world.[26]

Postmodernism also rejects the modernist distinction between art and life. In doing so, it also rejects the modernist distinctions between elite culture and the culture of everyday life. As a discourse of disruption and subversion, postmodernism does not argue that all referents for meaning and representation have disappeared; rather, it seeks to make them problematic and reinscribes and rewrites the boundaries for establishing the conditions for the production of meaning and subjectivity.[27] For example, in treating cultural forms as texts, postmodernism multiplies both the possibilities of constructing meaning as well as the status of meaning itself. In this sense, postmodernism redraws and retheorizes the objects and experiences of politics by extending the reach of power and meaning to spheres of the everyday that are often excluded from the realm of political analysis and pedagogical legitimation. In this case, the field of political contestation is not restricted to the state or the workplace, but also includes the family, mass and popular culture, the sphere of sexuality, and the terrain of the refused and forgotten. In the discourse of modernism, there is a world held together by the metanarrative of universal reason and social engineering.[28] Therefore, the central question for modernists has been "How can I interpret and master this world? How do I constitute myself within it?" Postmodernism does not begin from such a comfortable sense of place and history. It subordinates reason to uncertainty and pushes its sense of distrust into transgressions that open up entirely different lines of inquiry.

Sygmunt Bauman captures the political and epistemological shifts between modernism and postmodernism in the different questions and lines of inquiry they each pursue. He writes:

> [Postmodernists] have hardly any axioms they may use as a confident start, nor do they have a clear address. Before they turn to exploring the world, they must find out what world(s) there is (are) to be explored. Hence: "Which world is it? What is to be done in it? Which of my selves is to do it?"—in this order . . . the typically modern questions are, among others: "What is there to be known? Who knows it? How do they know it, and with what degree of certainty?" The typically postmodern questions do not reach that far. Instead of locating the task for the knower, they attempt to locate the knower himself [sic]. "What is a world? What kinds of worlds are there? How are they constituted, and how do they differ?" Even when sharing concern about knowledge, the two types of inquiry articulate their problems differently: "How is knowledge transmitted from one knower to another, and with what degree of reliability?" as against "What happens when different worlds are placed in confrontation, or when boundaries between worlds

are violated?" Not that postmodern questions have no use for "certainty"; not even reliability. The one-upmanship of modernist epistemology looks hopelessly out of place in that pluralist reality to which the postmodern ontological inquiry is first reconciled and then addressed. Here that overwhelming desire of power which animated the search for the ultimate (and which alone could animate it) raises little passion. Only eyebrows are raised by the self-confidence, which once made the pursuit of the absolute look as a plausible project.[29]

Bauman articulates an antagonism that has become a central feature of postmodernist discourse. That is, postmodernism rejects those aspects of the Enlightenment and Western philosophical tradition that rely on master narratives "which set out to address a transcendental subject, to define an essential human nature, to prescribe a global human destiny or to proscribe collective human goals."[30] Within this perspective, all claims to universal reason and impartial competence are rejected in favor of the partiality and specificity of discourse. Abstractions that deny the specificity and particularity of everyday life, that generalize out of existence the particular and the local, and that smother difference under the banner of universalizing categories are rejected as totalitarian and terroristic.

But there is more at stake here than simply an argument against master narratives or the claims of universal reason. There is also an attack on those intellectuals who would designate themselves as the emancipatory vanguard, an intellectual elite who have deemed themselves to be above history only to attempt to shape it through their pretensions to what Dick Hebdige calls an "illusory Faustian omnipotence."[31] In some versions of the postmodern, not only do totality and foundationalism not lead to the truth or emancipation; they actually lead to periods of great suffering and violence. The postmodernist attack on master narratives is simultaneously a criticism of an inflated teleological self-confidence, a dangerous transcendentalism, and a rejection of the omniscient narrator.[32] Read in more positive terms, critical postmodernists are arguing for a plurality of voices and narratives, that is, for narratives of difference that recognize their own partiality and present the unrepresentable, those submerged and dangerous memories that provide a challenge to white supremacist logic and recover the legacies of historically specific struggles against racism. Similarly, postmodern discourse is attempting with its emphasis on the specific and the normative to situate reason and knowledge within rather than outside particular configurations of space, place, time, and power. Partiality in this case becomes a political necessity as part of the discourse of locating oneself within rather than outside of history and ideology.

Related to the critique of master narratives and theories of totality is another major concern of critical postmodernism: the development of a politics that addresses popular culture as a serious object of aesthetic and cultural criticism on the one hand and one that signals and affirms the importance of minority cultures as historically specific forms of cultural production on the other.[33] Postmodernism's attack on universalism, in part, has translated into a refusal of modernism's relentless hostility to mass culture and its reproduction of the elitist division between high and low culture.[34] Not only has postmodernism's reaffirmation of popular culture challenged the aesthetic and epistemological divisions supportive of academic disciplines and the contours of what has been considered "serious" taste, it has also resulted in new forms of art, writing, film-making, and types of aesthetic and social criticism.[35] Similarly, postmodernism has provided the conditions necessary for exploring and recuperating traditions of various forms of Otherness as a fundamental dimension of both the cultural and the sociopolitical sphere. In other words, postmodernism's stress on the problematic of Otherness has included a focus on the importance of history as a form of counter-memory;[36] an emphasis on the value of the everyday as a source of agency and empowerment;[37] a renewed understanding of gender as an irreducible historical and social practice constituted in a plurality of self and social representation;[38] and an insertion of the contingent, the discontinuous, and the unrepresentable as coordinates for remapping and rethinking the borders that define one's existence and place in the world.

Another important aspect of postmodernism is that it provides a series of referents for both interrogating the notion of history as tradition and for redrawing and rewriting how individual and collective experience might be struggled over, understood, felt, and shaped. For example, postmodernism points to a world in which the production of meaning has become as important as the production of labor in shaping the boundaries of human existence. Three issues are at stake here. First, the notion that ideological and political structures are determined and governed by a single economic logic is rejected. Cultural and social forms contain a range of discursive and ideological possibilities that can only be grasped within the contextual and contradictory positions in which they are taken up; moreover, while such forms are reproduced under the conditions of capitalist production, they influence and are influenced by such relations. This is not a rejection of materialist analyses of culture as much as a rejection of the vulgar reductionism that often accompanies its classical interpretation. Second, labor does not provide the exclusive basis either for meaning or for understanding the multiple and complex ensemble of social relations that constitute the wider society. In this case, social antagonisms grounded in religious, gender, racial, and ethnic conflicts, among others, possess their own dynamism and cannot be reduced to the logic of capitalist relations. More specifically, the various discourses of historical materialism no longer describe the social order. Third, how subjects are constituted in language is no less important than how they are constructed as subjects within relations of production. The world of the discursive, with its ensemble of signifying terms and practices, is essential to how people relate to themselves, Others, and the world around them. It is a textual world through which people develop a sense of self and collective identity and relate to each other, not a world that can be explained merely in terms of causal events that follow the rule-bound determinations of physical and economic laws.[39] The political economy of the sign does not displace political economy; it simply assumes its rightful place as a primary category for understanding how identities are forged within particular relations of privilege, oppression, and struggle. In pursuing this line of inquiry, postmodernism serves to deterritorialize the map of dominant cultural understanding. That is, it rejects European tradition as the exclusive referent for judging what constitutes historical, cultural, and political truth. There is no tradition or story that can speak with authority and certainty for all of humanity. In effect, critical postmodernism argues that traditions should be valued for their attempts to name the partial, the particular, and the specific; in this view, traditions demonstrate the importance of constituting history as a dialogue among a variety of voices as they struggle within asymmetrical relations of power. Traditions are not valued for their claims to truth or authority, but for the ways in which they serve to liberate and enlarge human possibilities. In other words, tradition does not represent the voice of an all-embracing view of life; instead, it serves to place people self-consciously in their histories by making them aware of the memories constituted in difference, struggle, and hope. Tradition in postmodern terms is a form of counter-memory that recovers those complex yet submerged identities that constitute the social and political construction of public life.[40]

Postmodernism rejects the modernist discourse on history that views it as uniform, chronological, and teleological. In contrast, postmodernism argues for a view of history that is decentered, discontinuous, fragmented, and plural. Jim Collins rightly argues that postmodernism challenges this view of historiography by problematizing "histories that seek to minimize heterogeneity in pursuit of a dominant style, collective spirit, or any other such unitary conception."[41] He elaborates on this by arguing:

> The common denominator of all such histories, from Oswald Spengler's *The Decline of the West* to Will Wright's *Six Guns in Society*, has been the privileging of homogeneous structures that allow historians to draw rather neat generalizations that support far more grandiose claims about culture "as a whole." Emphasis has been placed repeatedly on the diachronic changes between periods, movements, moods, etc. instead of on synchronic tensions within those subdivisions—which would naturally undermine any unitary formulations concerning a particular period's representation of itself in a specific time. . . . The chief way to break this spell is to begin with a different set of priorities—specifically that most periods are a "mixture of inconsistent elements," and that different art forms, discourses, etc., all have their own history as well as a societal history . . . To account for these differences, histories that have been predicated on theories of evolution, mass consciousness, or Zeitgeist, must be replaced by histories that emphasize synchronic tensions, the fragmentation of mass consciousness, and the possibility of more than one Zeitgeist per culture."[42]

It is worth emphasizing that postmodernism not only raises central questions about not simply how to rethink the meaning of history and traditions. It also forces us in the absence of a discourse of essences and foundationalism to raise new and different questions. As Chantal Mouffe has pointed out, postmodernism provides the possibility of understanding the limits of traditions so we can enter into dialogue with them, particularly with respect to how we may think about the construction of political subjects and the possibility of democratic life.[43]

Finally, as I have stated in Chapter 3, and at the risk of great simplification, a postmodernism of resistance challenges the liberal, humanist notion of the unified, rational subject as the bearer of history.[44] In this instance, the subject is neither unified nor can such a subject's action be guaranteed in metaphysical or trans-historical terms. Postmodernism not only views the subject as contradictory and multilayered, it also rejects the notion that individual consciousness and reason are the most important determinants in shaping human history. It posits instead a faith in forms of social transformation that are attentive to the historical, structural, and ideological limits that shape the possibility for self-reflection and action. It points to solidarity, community, and compassion as essential aspects of how we develop and understand the capacities we have for how we experience the world and ourselves in a meaningful way.[45] But it does so by stressing that in the absence of a unified subject, we can rethink the meaning of solidarity through a recognition of the multiple antagonisms and struggles that characterize both the notion of the self and the wider social reality. By recognizing the multiplicity of subject positions that mediate and are produced by and through contradictory meanings and social practices, it becomes possible to create a discourse of democratic values that requires a "multiplication of democratic practices, institutionalizing them into ever more diverse social relations . . . [so that] we be able not only to defend democracy but also to deepen it."[46] In different terms, postmodernism offers a series of referents for rethinking how we are constituted as subjects within a rapidly changing set of political, social, and cultural conditions.

What does this suggest for the way we look at the issue of race and ethnicity? Postmodern discourse provides a theoretical foundation for deconstructing the master narratives of white supremacist logics and for redrawing the boundaries between the construction of experience and power. In the first instance, by challenging the concept of master narratives, critical postmodernism has opened up the possibility for launching a renewed attack on the underlying assumptions that have allowed the dominant culture to enforce its own authority and racist practices through an unproblematic appeal to the virtues of Western civilization. In challenging the notions of universal reason, the construction of a white, humanist subject, and the selective legitimation of high culture as the standard for cultural practice, postmodern criticism has illuminated how Eurocentric-American discourses of identity suppress difference, heterogeneity, and multiplicity in the effort to maintain hegemonic relations of power. Not only does postmodernism provide new ways to understand how power works in constructing racist identities and subjectivities, but it also redefines culture and experience within multiple relations of difference that offer a range of subject positions from which people can struggle against racist ideologies and practices. By calling into question the themes of "degraded Otherness and subaltern marginality" postmodernism offers new theoretical tools for attacking "notions of exclusionary identity, dominating hetero-

geneity, and universality—or in more blunt language, white supremacy."[47] Postmodern engagements with foundationalism, culture, difference, and subjectivity
provide the basis for questioning the modernist ideal of what constitutes a decent,
humane, and good life. Rather than celebrate the narratives of the "masters,"
postmodernism raises important questions about how narratives get constructed,
what they mean, how they regulate particular forms of moral and social experience,
and how they presuppose and embody particular epistemological and political views
of the world. Similarly, postmodernism attempts to delineate how borders are
named; in fact, it attempts to redraw the very maps of meaning, desire, and
difference, inscribing the social and individual body with new intellectual and
emotional investments and calling into question traditional forms of power and
their accompanying modes of legitimation. All of these developments redefine
theory by moving it far beyond—and in opposition to—the concerns embodied in
the ideologies and questions that have defined the underlying racist principles that
have remained unchallenged as a central aspect of modernist discourse.

For educators interested in developing an antiracist pedagogy, postmodernism
offers new epistemologies for rethinking both the broader and specific contexts in
which democratic authority is defined; it offers what Richard Bernstein calls a
healthy "suspiciousness of all boundary-fixing and the hidden ways in which we
subordinate, exclude, and marginalize."[48] Postmodernism also offers educators a
variety of discourses for interrogating modernism's reliance on totalizing theories
based on a desire for certainty and absolutes.

In order for postmodernism to make a valuable contribution to the development of a critical pedagogy of race, educators must combine its most important
theoretical insights with those stories and narratives that illuminate how difference
and resistance are concretely expressed within communities of struggle organized
around specific antiracist practices. In this way, the project of an antiracist pedagogy
can be deepened by expanding its discourse to increasingly wider spheres of social
relations and practices. But postmodern discourse must do more than redefine
difference as an integral aspect of the construction of educational life. It must also
do more than reconstruct the theoretical discourse of resistance by recovering
knowledge, histories, and experiences that have traditionally been left out of dominant accounts of schooling, everyday life, and history. Most important, it is vital
that postmodernism open up and establish public spheres among nonacademic
audiences and work with them as part of the struggle to fight racism and other
forms of domination while simultaneously struggling to revitalize democratic public
life. What is important to recognize is that a critical postmodernism needs to
provide educators with a more complex and insightful view of the relationship
between culture, power, and knowledge. When linked with the language of democratic public life, the notions of difference, power, and specificity can be understood as part of a public discourse that broadens and deepens individual liberties
and rights through rather than against a radical notion of democracy.

In what follows, I want to develop how a postmodern discourse of resistance
might be elaborated and advanced through the discourse of Afro-American fem-

inists and writers whose work serves to rewrite and reinscribe the relations between power and issues of difference, struggle, identity-politics, and narrative. In choosing to focus on the writings of Afro-American feminists, I make no claim to speak as, for, or within a similar politics of location. My own politics of location as a white, academic male positions me to speak to issues of racism and gender by self-consciously recognizing my own interests in taking up these practices as part of a broader political project to expand the scope and meaning of democratic struggle and a politics of solidarity. Border crossing in this instance is part of an attempt to further rupture a politics of historical silence and theoretical erasure that serves to repress and marginalize the voices of the Other. At stake here is the need to understand the specificity of cultural production in its own terms as it is produced through the diverse voices of Afro-American feminists constituted in different relations of power. In addition, border crossings of this sort need to challenge the authority and practices of dominant representation in order to refigure the possibility for building new forms of identification and solidarity across a politics of difference. What is at issue here is not an attempt to merely develop forms of self-criticism and understanding, although these are not to be easily discounted, but to rewrite the conditions for forms of solidarity by making visible the varied contributions that women of color are developing in their attempts both to come to voice and to voice critical and transformative narratives that deeply refigure the meaning of justice, liberty, and freedom as a condition for making difference essential to democratic life. Such a position rewrites the relationship between the margins and the centers by resisting the tendency to construct the world through the conceptual baggage of a Eurocentric colonial discourse while simultaneously creating new critical public spheres as sites of resistance and transformation that challenge existing neocolonial ideological and institutional centers of power.

Afro-American Feminist Writers and the Discourse of Possibility

Afro-American women feminists have been writing against the grain for a long time in this country.[49] Most importantly, they have given the politics of resistance and solidarity a new meaning in the diverse ways in which they have struggled, as Barbara Christian puts it, "to define and express our totality rather than being defined by Others."[50] Within the diverse body of material that makes up their work, there is a language both of critique and possibility. It is woven out of forms of testifying, narrativizing, and theorizing that reconstruct the meaning of difference while simultaneously rewriting the meaning of history as a basis for sustaining community memories and enveloping viable forms of collective struggle. The tensions that permeate this work range from suffering and resistance to a sense of healing and transcendence. For example, in the work of the novelist Paule Marshall we encounter the attempts to reconstruct "the past and the need to reverse the present social order."[51] In the work of political writers such as June Jordan, Audre Lorde, bell hooks, Michele Wallace, and Hazel Carby there is an ongoing attempt to retheorize the notion of voice as part of the shifting construction of identities forged in differences, especially those constituted out of class, race, and gender.[52] There is also an attempt to theorize voice as a historically specific cultural site from which one learns to create an oppositional consciousness and identity, a standpoint that exists not only as one that opposes domination, but one that also enables and extends individual and social capacities and possibilities for making human connections and compassionate communities of resistance and liberation.[53]

Within this work, a discourse of difference and solidarity emerges which is multilayered and dialectical. First, all of these Afro-American women offer, in different ways, a critique of difference as it is constructed through the codes and relations of the dominant culture. Second, Afro-American feminist writers have criticized the emancipatory notion of difference put forward by white feminists in the last decade while simultaneously developing a more radical notion of the politics of difference and identity politics. Third, there is a brilliant reconstruction of difference in these works through the development of narratives as forms of dangerous memory that provide the foundation for communities of resistance and a radical ethics of accountability. In what follows, I will analyze each of these elements of difference before addressing their pedagogical implications for developing what I call a border pedagogy of resistance.

Unlike many radical and postmodern theories, the work of Afro-American feminists is deeply concerned with developing a politics of difference that locates the dynamics of domination in the center of rather than on the margins of power. In effect, Afro-American feminists have attempted to uncover how complex modes of inequality are structured through racial, class, and gender divisions that lie at the heart of the dominant culture and that by definition serve to shape its most basic institutional and ideological forms. A number of issues are at work here. First, there is the need to establish that racial identities are also white and must be seen as specific historical and social constructions. It is imperative to see questions of ethnicity as part of a broader discussion of racism in order to understand how whiteness serves as a norm to privilege its own definitions of power while simultaneously concealing the political and social distinctions embedded in its essentialist constructions of difference through the categories of race, gender, and class.

Within this perspective, difference cannot be understood outside of the dynamics of silencing, subjugation, and infantilzation. By focusing on the ways in which white ethnicity exercises power, designates Otherness in term that degrade and cheapen human life, and hides its own partiality in narratives of universality and common sense, Afro-American feminists have been able to redefine what it means for people of color to come to voice and to speak in their own terms. To struggle within a politics of voice, within these practices, means that Afro-Americans have to reject a politics of the center in which the Other is reduced to an object whose experiences and traditions are either deemed alien by whites or whose identity has to bear exclusively the historical weight of Otherness and racialization. Hazel Carby suggests that:

> one way to rethink the relationship between the social, political, and cultural construction of blackness and marginality, on the one hand, and assumptions of a normative whiteness within the dominant culture, on the other, is to examine the ways in which that dominant culture has been shaped and transformed by the presence of the marginalized. This means a public recognition that the process of marginalization itself is central to the formation of the dominant culture. The first and very important stage is . . . to recognize the cultural and political category of whiteness. It seems obvious to say it but in practice the racialization of our social order is only recognized in relation to racialized "others."[54]

What Carby points to is part of a broader theoretical attempt by Afro-American feminists to reject narrow notions of Afro-American identity while also calling into question the cultured absences that historically and socially locate white ethnicity within subject positions that blind many whites to the mechanisms of cultural apartheid and relations of power that are constitutive of what it means to be part of a dominant Eurocentric culture in America. As Coco Fusco puts it, "Endemic to this history are structured absences that function to maintain relations of power. To put it bluntly, no one has yet spoken of the 'self' implicit in the 'other,' or of the ones who are designating the 'others.' Power, veiled and silent, remains in place."[55] Afro-American feminists have provided an enormous service by shifting the discussion of difference away from an exclusive concern with the margins and in doing so have made it clear that any analysis of racial identity must include an analysis of how the dominant Other functions to actively and systematically conceal its own historical and cultural identity while devaluing the identity of other racial groups. By challenging how boundaries of difference have been constructed through dominant Eurocentric codes and binarisms, it becomes possible to deepen our understanding of not only how white ethnicity is constructed in its attempts to position others. It also becomes possible to rethink the issue of subjectivity and resistance outside of the crippling essentialisms that have characterized dominant humanist theory. Identity is no longer something that is fixed but fluid, shifting, and multiple. At the same time, oppression can now be seen in its multiple antagonisms and social relations. Once dominant culture is racialized within the discourse of ethnicity and existing power relations, it becomes possible to write history from the perspective of those engaged in the struggle against cultural genocide. Voices now begin to emerge from different locations and are no longer authorized to speak only through a Eurocentric perspective that defines them in its own interests. Bell hooks links this emergence of multiple voices as part of a wider struggle for a politics and identity that is crucial to the reconstruction of Afro-American subjectivity. She writes:

> We return to "identity" and "culture" for relocation, linked to political practice— identity that is not informed by a narrow cultural nationalism masking continued fascination with the power of the white Hegemonic other. Instead identity is

evoked as a stage in a process wherein one constructs radical black subjectivity. Recent critical reflections on static notion of black identity urge transformation of our sense of who can we be and still be black. Assimilation, imitation, or assuming the role of rebellious exotic other are not the only available options and never have been. This is why it is crucial to radically revise notions of identity politics, to explore marginal locations as spaces where we can best become whatever we want to be while remaining committed to liberatory black liberation struggle.[56]

Central to the notion of difference put forth by many black theorists is a notion of antiracism that refigures the meaning of ethnicity as a social and historical construct. Such a view signals the end of the essentialist black subject as well as the structured absence of whiteness as a racial category. For example, Stuart Hall suggests that the notion of the black subject as a social and historical construction points to a new conception of identity and a redefinition of a cultural politics of difference. He writes:

> Constituting oneself as "black" is another recognition of self through difference: certain clear polarities and extremities against which one tries to define oneself. . . . It has long been thought that this is really a simple process: a recognition— a resolution of irresolutions, a coming to rest in some place which was always there waiting for one. The "real me". . . . The fact is "black" has never been just there either. It has always been an unstable identity, psychically, culturally, and politically. It, too, is a narrative, a story, a history. Something constructed, told, spoken, not simply found.[57]

The strategic importance of making Afro-American identity both complex and visible has been theoretically developed in the writing of a number of Afro-American feminists. More specifically, these writers have criticized the ways in which the notion of difference and race have been taken up in essentialist terms by many white middle-class feminists in the struggle over sexuality and gender. Audre Lorde is a powerful voice in this struggle.

> Those of us who have been forged in the crucibles of difference—those of us who are poor, who are lesbians, who are Black, who are older—know that survival is not an academic skill. It is learning how to stand alone, unpopular and sometimes reviled, and how to make common cause with those others identified as outside the structures in order to define and seek a world in which we can all flourish. It is learning how to take our differences and make them strengths. For the master's tools will never dismantle the master's house. They may allow us temporarily to beat him at his own game, but they will never enable us to bring about change.[58]

In this quote, she uses the notion of difference as a referent for critique and as a basis for advancing the emancipatory possibilities in a radicalized notion of difference. In the first instance, she argues against various versions of contemporary feminism that limit domination to the sphere of sexual relations and, in doing so, develop a discourse of difference that excludes questions of racism, class domination, and homophobia. Under the banner of feminist struggle and liberation, many contemporary feminists have unconsciously reconstructed the Eurocentric logocentrism they claimed they were attacking. In effect, while the center was being reconstructed as an affirmation of feminism in the service of an attack on patriarchy, it functioned to recreate existing margins of power while denying the voices of working-class women, lesbians, and women of color. As Lorde points out:

> The absence of these considerations weakens any feminist discussion of the personal and the political. It is a particular academic arrogance to assume any discussion of feminist theory without examining our many differences, and without a significant input from poor women, Black and Third World Women, and lesbians.[59]

Lorde is not merely criticizing a feminist perspective that refuses to examine differences as they are constructed outside of the world of white, middle-class women. She is also arguing that in this refusal of difference lie the seeds of racism and homophobia. She recognizes that whites have a heavy cultural, political, and affective investment in ignoring differences. To recognize such differences is to immediately call into play the asymmetrical relations of power that structure the lives of white and Afro-American women differently. For white middle-class women, this often invokes guilt and forces them to "allow women of Color to step out of stereotype . . . [and] it threatens the complacency of these women who view oppression only in terms of sex."[60] Lorde is eloquent on this issue:

> Poor women and women of Color know there is a difference between the daily manifestations of marital slavery and prostitution because it is our daughters who line 42nd Street. If white American feminist theory need not deal with the differences between us, and the resulting difference in our oppressions, then how do you deal with the fact that the women who clean your houses and tend your children while you attend conferences on feminist theory, are for the most part, poor women and women of Color? What is the theory behind racist feminism? In a world of possibility for us all, our personal visions help lay the groundwork for political action. The failure of academic feminists to recognize difference as a crucial strength is a failure to reach beyond the first patriarchal lesson. In our world, divide and conquer must become define and empower.[61]

But Lorde, like a number of Afro-American writers, is not content either to limit her analysis to the racism inherent in narrowly defined feminist theories of difference or to deconstruct forms of cultural separatism that argue that Afro-Americans only need to bear witness to the positive moments in their own stories. These are important political and strategic issues, but Lorde is also concerned about developing a politics of solidarity and identity that views difference as a dynamic human force that is "enriching rather than threatening to the defined self when there are shared goals."[62] In this case, Afro-American women writers have attempted to develop a politics of difference that celebrates its creative function while simultaneously arguing for new forms of community rooted in definitions of power and patterns of relating that allow diverse groups of people to reach out beyond their own interests to forge living connections with a multitude of differences for the purpose of developing a democratic culture and society.

At issue here is a politics of resistance in which difference is explored through the category of voice and solidarity. It is important to stress, even at the expense of overstating the issue, that Afro-American feminists have attempted to develop a notion of Afro-American subjectivity and voice that portrays Afro-American women outside of the narrow confines of an essentialist and stereotypical reading. In this case, there is an attempt to develop a notion of self and identity that links difference to the insistence of speaking in many voices, to fasten a notion of identity that is shifting and multiple rather than static and singular. Central here is the need to engage voice as an act of resistance and self-transformation, to recognize that as one comes to voice one establishes the precondition for becoming a subject in history rather than an object.[63] In analyzing a portion of her own experience in attending all-black segregated schools, hooks comments on how she learned to recognize the value of an education that allowed her to speak in many voices. She writes:

> In part, attending all-black segregated schools with black teachers meant that I had come to understand black poets as being capable of speaking in many voices . . . The black poet, as exemplified by Gwendolyn Brooks and later Amiri Baraka, had many voices—with no single voice being identified as more or less authentic. The insistence on finding one voice, one definitive style of writing and reading one's poetry, fits all too neatly with a static notion of self and identity that was pervasive in university settings. It seemed that many black students found our situations problematic precisely because our sense of self, and by definition our voice, as not unilateral, monologist, or static but rather multidimensional. We were at home in dialect as we were in standard English. Individuals who speak languages other than English, who speak patois as well as standard English, find it a necessary aspect of self-affirmation not to feel compelled to choose one voice over another, not to claim one as more authentic, but rather to construct social realities that celebrate, acknowledge, and affirm differences, variety . . . to claim all the tongues in which we speak, to make speech of the many languages that give expression to the unique cultural reality of a people.[64]

As part of a politics of difference, an antiracist pedagogy would have to investigate the relationship between language and voice as part of a wider concern with democratic struggle and antagonisms. Instead of talking about literacy, radical educational theory would have to educate teachers and administrators to speak and listen to many languages and ways of understanding the world. Not only would this open up the possibility for many people to speak from the decided advantage of their own experiences, it would also multiply and decidedly transform the discursive and nondiscursive sites from which administrators, teachers, students, parents, and neighborhood people could engage in dialogue and communities of solidarity. A radical educational discourse would also educate people to the tyranny that lies beneath logocentric narratives, truths that appear to exist beyond criticism, and language that undermines the force of democratic encounters. In this context,

June Jordan is illuminating in sharply contrasting the implications of a language difference with the reality that most people find themselves in at the current historical juncture in the United States.

> I am talking about majority problems of language in a democratic state, problems of a currency that someone has stolen and hidden away and then homogenized into an official "English" language that can only express non-events involving nobody responsible, or lies. If we lived in a democratic state our language would have to hurtle, fly, curse, and sing, in all the common American names, all the undeniable and representative participating voices of everybody here. We would not tolerate the language of the powerful and, thereby, lose all respect for words, per se. We would make our language conform to the truth of our many selves and we would make our language lead us into the equality of power that a democratic state must represent . . . This is not a democratic state. And we put up with that. We have the language of the powerful that perpetuates that power through the censorship of dissenting views.[65]

Another important element in the theory and politics of difference that has emerged in the writings of Afro-American feminists is the importance of stories, of narrative forms that keep alive communities of resistance while also indicting the collective destruction that mobilizes racism, sexism, and other forms of domination. Barbara Christian argues that Afro-American people have always theorized in narrative forms, "in the stories we create, in riddles and proverbs, in the play with language, since dynamic rather than fixed ideas seem more to our liking."[66] The narratives that are at work here are grounded in the discourse of everyday life—they are polyphonic, partial, and vibrant. And yet they are produced amid relations of struggle. Toni Cade Bambara claims that such stories are grounded in relations of survival, struggle, and wide-awake resistance. She writes:

> Stories are important. They keep us alive. In the ships, in the camps, in the quarters, field, prisons, on the road, on the run, underground, under siege, in the throes, on the verge—the story teller snatches us back from the edge to hear the next chapter. In which we are the subjects. We, the hero of the tales. Our lives preserved. How it was, how it be. Passing it along in the relay. That is what I work to do: to produce stories that save our lives.[67]

The development of narrative forms and stories in the work of writers like Zora Neale Hurston, Paule Marshall, Toni Morrison, Alice Walker, and Toni Cade Bambara challenge the ways in which knowledge is constructed, illuminate the relationship between knowledge and power, and redefine the personal and the political so as to rewrite the dialectical connection between what we learn and how we come to learn given our specific location in history, experience, and language.[68] The literature of Afro-American feminist writers extends and challenges postmodernism's view of narratives. Their writings link the form and substance of narrative storytelling with issues of survival and resistance and add a more progressive political character to narrative structure and substance than is developed in postmodern analyses. The development of these stories becomes a medium for developing forms of historical consciousness that provide the basis for new relations of solidarity, community, and self-love. For example, Michelle Gibbs Russell links the political and the pedagogical in the use of storytelling and, in doing so, demonstrates the radical potential it assumes as a form of self and social empowerment,

> The oldest form of building historical consciousness in community is storytelling. The transfer of knowledge, skill, and value from one collective memory, has particular significance in diaspora culture. . . . Political education for Black women in America begins with the memory of four hundred years of enslavement, diaspora, forced labor, beating, bombings, lynchings, and rape. It takes on inspirational dimension when we begin cataloguing the heroic individuals and organizations in our history who have battled against those atrocities, and triumphed over them. It becomes practical when we are confronted with the problem of how to organize food cooperatives for women on food-stamp budgets or how to prove one's fitness as a mother in court. It becomes radical when, as teachers, we develop a methodology that places daily life at the center of history and enables Black women to struggle for survival with the knowledge that they are making history. One setting where such connections can be made is the classroom. In the absence of any land, or turf, which we actually control, the classroom serves as a temporary space where we can evoke and evaluate our collective memory of what is done to us, and what we do in turn.[69]

As a pedagogical practice, the recovery and affirmation of stories that emanate from the experience of marginal groups can also serve in an emancipatory way to recenter the presence of white authority. Such stories cannot be used exclusively as a basis for whites to examine their own complicity in the construction of racism; they can also help privileged groups listen seriously to the multiple narratives that constitute the complexity of Others historically defined through reifications and stereotypes that smother difference within and between diverse subordinate groups. Of course, such stories also need to provide the opportunity to raise questions about what kinds of common claims regarding a discourse of ethics, accountability, and identity politics can be developed between whites and people of color around such narrative forms. I believe that by making visible and interrogating the variety of textual forms and voices that inform such narratives, students can deconstruct the master narratives of racism, sexism, and class domination while simultaneously questioning how these narratives contribute to forms of self-hatred and contempt that surround the identities of blacks, women, and other subordinated groups.[70] Similarly, the stories of marginal groups provide counter-narratives that call into question the role that whites and other dominant groups have and continue to play in perpetuating oppression and human suffering. Sharon Welch is instructive on this issue. She argues that listening to and engaging the stories of the Other can educate members of white, Eurocentric culture to a redefinition of responsibility through what she calls an ethic of risk and resistance. She writes:

> Particular stories call us to accountability. As dangerous memories of conflict, oppression and exclusion, they call those of us who are, often unknowingly,

complicit in structures of control to join in resistance and transformation. For those of us who are members of the Western elite, by reason of race, gender, education, or economic status, we are challenged by the stories of the marginalized oppressed to grasp the limits of our ethical and political wisdom—the limited appeal of our capitalist economic system, our limited appreciation of the vitality and determination of the other people to shape their own identities. . . . We in the first World are not responsible for others; we are responsible for ourselves— for seeing the limits of our own vision and for rectifying the damages caused by the arrogant violation of those limits.[71]

Welch is arguing for a dialectical notion of narrative. She rightly argues that the narratives of subordinate groups needs to be recovered as "dangerous memories" that rewrite and reinscribe the historical threads of community forged in resistance and struggle. She also argues that such stories are needed to construct an ethical discourse that indicts Eurocentric-American master narratives so they can be critically interrogated and discarded when necessary in the interests of constructing social relations and communities of struggle that provide healing, salvation, and justice. At the same time, Michele Wallace offers a critical qualification on the praise and use of narrative structure in the writings of Afro-American women.[72] She argues that the success of contemporary Afro-American women's novel writing is privileged by dominant groups to the exclusion of other forms of discursive representation. This is not to undermine what I have said about the importance of narrative structure in Afro-American feminist works. I mean only to locate how such work can be appropriated by the dominant culture in ways that reproduce and reinforce forms of inequality and racism. In this case, theoretical cultural criticism becomes the exclusive discourse of mostly white academics, while theoretical cultural criticism by Afro-American feminists is either ignored or marginalized.

Border Pedagogy as the Practice of Struggle and Transformation

If the construction of antiracist pedagogy is to escape from a notion of difference that is silent about other social antagonisms and forms of struggle, it must be developed as part of a wider public discourse that is simultaneously about the discourse of an engaged plurality and the formation of critical citizenship. This must be a discourse that breathes life into the notion of democracy by stressing a notion of lived community that is not at odds with the principles of justice, liberty, and equality.[73] Such a discourse must be informed by a postmodern concern with establishing the material and ideological conditions that allow multiple, specific, and heterogeneous ways of life to come into play as part of a border pedagogy of postmodern resistance. In other words, educators must prepare students for a type of citizenship that does not separate abstract rights from the realm of the everyday and does not define community as the legitimating and unifying practice of a one-dimensional historical and cultural narrative. Postmodernism radicalizes the emancipatory possibilities of teaching and learning as part of a wider struggle for democratic public life and critical citizenship. It does this by refusing forms of knowledge and pedagogy wrapped in the legitimizing discourse of the sacred and the priestly; rejecting universal reason as a foundation for human affairs; claiming that all narratives are partial; and performing a critical reading on all scientific, cultural, and social texts as historical and political constructions.

In this view, the broader parameters of an antiracist pedagogy are informed by a political project that links the creation of critical citizens to the development of radical democracy; that is, a political project that ties education to the broader struggle for a public life in which dialogue, vision, and compassion remain critically attentive to the rights and conditions that organize public space as a democratic social form rather than as a regime of terror and oppression. It is important to emphasize that difference and pluralism in this view do not mean reducing democracy to the equivalency of diverse interests; on the contrary, what is being argued for is a language in which different voices and traditions exist and flourish to the degree that they listen to the voices of Others; a language that engages in an ongoing attempt to eliminate forms of subjective and objective suffering and maintains those conditions in which the act of communicating and living extends rather than restricts the creation of democratic public spheres. This is as much a political project as it is a pedagogical project, one that demands that antiracist pedagogical practices be developed within a discourse that combines a democratic public philosophy with a postmodern theory of resistance. Within this perspective, the issue of border pedagogy is located within those broader cultural and political considerations that are beginning to redefine our traditional view of community, language, space, and possibility. It is a pedagogy that is attentive to developing a democratic public philosophy that respects the notion of difference as part of a common struggle to extend and transform the quality of public life. In short, the notion of border pedagogy presupposes not merely an acknowledgment of the shifting borders that both undermine and reterritorialize dominant configurations of power and knowledge. It also links the notion of pedagogy with the creation of a society in which there is available a multiplicity of democratic practices, values, and social relations for students to take up within different learning situations. At stake here is a view of democracy and learning in which multiplicity, plurality, and struggle become the raison d'etre of democratic public life. Chantal Mouffe has elaborated this position in neo-Gramscian terms:

> If the task of radical democracy is indeed to deepen the democratic revolution and to link together diverse democratic struggles, such a task requires the creation of new subject-positions that would allow the common articulation, for example of antiracism, antisexism, and anticapitalism. These struggles do not spontaneously converge, and in order to establish democratic equivalences, a new "common sense" is necessary, which would transform the identity of different groups so

that the demands of each group could be articulated with those of others according to the principle of democratic equivalence. For it is not a matter of establishing a mere alliance between given interests but of actually modifying the very identity of those forces. In order that the defense of workers' interests is not pursued at the cost of the rights of women, immigrants, or consumers, it is necessary to establish an equivalence between these different struggles. It is only under these circumstances that struggles against power becomes truly democratic.[74]

Mouffe's position should not suggest that this is merely a political task to be established and carried out by an elite, a party, or a specific group of intellectuals. It is more importantly a pedagogical task that has to be taken up and argued for by all cultural workers who take a particular political stand on the meaning and importance of radical democracy as a way of life. Such a position not only rejects the one-sided and undemocratic interests that inform the conservative argument that collapses democracy into the logic of the market or buttresses the ideology of cultural uniformity, but also rejects leftist versions of an identity politics that excludes the Other as part of a reductive discourse of assertion and separatism. Stanley Aronowitz extends Mouffe's emphasis on difference as a central feature of democracy by linking democracy with citizenship understood as a form of self-management constituted in all major economic, social, and cultural spheres.[75] Democracy in this context takes up the issue of transferring power from elites and executive authorities, who control the economic and cultural apparatuses of society, to those producers who wield power at the local levels. Aronowitz's argument is important because he not only critiques the discourse of liberal pluralism and "chic" difference in his analysis of democratic struggle and call for the construction of popular public spheres, but he also places the issue of power, politics, and struggle at the heart of the debate over radical democracy. What is being called for here is a notion of border pedagogy that provides educators with the opportunity to rethink the relations between the centers and the margins of power. That is, such a pedagogy must address the issue of racism as one that calls into question not only forms of subordination that create inequities among different groups as they live out their lives, but as I have mentioned previously, also challenges those institutional and ideological boundaries that have historically masked their own relations of power behind complex forms of distinction and privilege.

What does this suggest for the way we develop the basic elements of an antiracist pedagogy? First, the notion of border pedagogy offers students the opportunity to engage the multiple references that constitute different cultural codes, experiences, and languages. This means providing the learning opportunities for students to become media-literate in a world of changing representations. It means offering students the knowledge and social relations that enable them to critically read not only how cultural texts are regulated by various discursive codes, but also how such texts express and represent different ideological interests. In this case, border pedagogy establishes conditions of learning that define literacy inside of the categories of power and authority. This suggests developing pedagogical practices that address texts as social and historical constructions; it also suggests developing pedagogical practices that allow students to analyze texts in terms of their presences and absences. Most important, such practices should provide students with the opportunity to read texts dialogically through a configuration of many voices, some of which offer resistance, some of which provide support. Border pedagogy also stresses that students must be provided with the opportunity to critically engage the strengths and limitations of the cultural and social codes that define their own histories and narratives. In this case, partiality becomes the basis for recognizing the limits built into all discourses. At issue here is the need for students to not merely develop a healthy skepticism toward all discourses of authority, but also to recognize how authority and power can be transformed in the interest of creating a democratic society.

Within this discourse, students engage knowledge as border-crossers, as people moving in and out of borders constructed around coordinates of difference and power.[76] These are not only physical borders, but cultural borders historically constructed and socially organized within maps of rules and regulations that serve to either limit or enable particular identities, individual capacities, and social forms. Students cross borders of meaning, maps of knowledge, social relations, and values that are increasingly being negotiated and rewritten as the codes and regulations that organize them become destabilized and reshaped. Border pedagogy decenters as it remaps. The terrain of learning becomes inextricably linked to the shifting parameters of place, identity, history, and power. By reconstructing the traditional radical emphasis of the knowledge–power relationship away from the limited emphasis of mapping domination to the politically strategic issue of engaging the ways in which knowledge can be remapped, reterritorialized, and decentered, in the wider interests of rewriting the borders and coordinates of an oppositional cultural politics, educators can redefine the teacher–student relationship in ways that allow students to draw upon their own personal experience as real knowledge.

At one level this means giving students the opportunity to speak, locate themselves in history, and become subjects in the construction of their identities and the wider society. It also means defining voice not merely as an opportunity to speak, but to engage critically with the ideology and substance of speech, writing, and other forms of cultural production. In this case, "coming to voice" for students from both dominant and subordinated cultures means engaging in rigorous discussions of various cultural texts, drawing upon one's personal experience, and confronting the process through which ethnicity and power can be rethought as a political narrative that challenges racism as part of a broader struggle to democratize social, political, and economic life. In part, this means looking at the various ways in which race implicates relations of domination, resistance, suffering, and power within various social practices and how these are taken up in multiple ways by students who occupy different ethnic, social, and gender locations. In this way, race is never discussed outside of broader articulations nor is it merely about people of color.

Second, a border pedagogy of postmodern resistance needs to do more than educate students to perform ideological surgery on master narratives based on white, patriarchal, and class-specific interests. If the master narratives of domination are to be effectively deterritorialized, it is important for educations to understand how such narratives are taken up as part of an investment of feeling, pleasure, and desire. The syntax of learning and behavior must be rethought outside of the geography of rationality and reason. For example, this means that racism cannot be dealt with in a purely limited analytical way. An antiracist pedagogy must engage how and why students both make particular ideological and affective investments and occupy particular subject positions that give them a sense of meaning, purpose, and delight. As Hall argues, this means uncovering both for ourselves as teachers as well as for the students we are teaching "the deep structural factors which have a tendency persistently not only to generate racial practices and structures but to reproduce them through time which therefore account for their extraordinarily immovable character."[77] In addition to engaging racism within a politics of representation, ideology, and pleasure, any serious analysis of racism must also be historical and structural. It has to chart out how racist practices develop, where they come from, how they are sustained, how they affect dominant and subordinate groups, and how they can be challenged. This is not a discourse about personal preferences or dominant tastes but a discourse about economics, culture, politics, and power.

Third, a border pedagogy offers the opportunity for students to air their feelings about race from the perspective of the subject positions they experience as constitutive of their own identities. Ideology in this sense is treated not merely as an abstraction but as part of the student's lived experience. This does not mean that teachers either reduce their role to that of intellectual voyeur or collapse their authority into a shabby form of relativism. Nor does border pedagogy suggest that students merely express or assess their own experiences. Rather, it points to a particular form of teacher authority grounded in a respect for a radically decentered notion of democratic public life, a view of authority that rejects the notion that all forms of authority are expressions of unwarranted power and oppression. Instead, border pedagogy argues for forms of authority that are rooted in democratic interests and emancipatory social relations. Authority that, in this case, rejects politics as aesthetics, that retains instead the significance of the knowledge/power relationship as a discourse of criticism and politics necessary for the achievement of equality, freedom, and struggle. This is not a form of authority based on an appeal to universal truths; rather, it is a form of authority that recognizes its own partiality while simultaneously asserting a standpoint from which to engage the discourses and practices of democracy, freedom, and domination. Put another way, this is a notion of authority rooted in a political project that ties education to the broader struggle for public life in which dialogue, vision, and compassion remain critically attentive to the liberating and dominating relations that organize various aspects of everyday life.[78]

This suggests that teachers use their authority to establish classroom conditions in which different views about race can be aired but not treated as simply an expression of individual views or feelings.[79] Andrew Hannan rightly points out that educators must refuse to treat racism as a matter of individual prejudice and counter such a position by addressing the "structural foundations of [the] culture of racism."[80] An antiracist pedagogy must demonstrate that the views we hold about race have different historical and ideological weight, forged in asymmetrical relations of power, and that they always embody interests that shape social practices in particular ways. In other words, an antiracist pedagogy cannot treat ideologies as simply individual expressions of feeling, but as historical, cultural, and social practices that serve to either undermine or reconstruct democratic public life. These views must be engaged without silencing students, but they must also be interrogated next to a public philosophy that names racism for what it is and calls racist ideologies and practices into account on political and ethical terms.

Fourth, educators need to understand how the everyday experience of marginality lends itself to forms of oppositional and transformative consciousness. For those designated as Others need to both reclaim and remake their histories, voices, and visions as part of a wider struggle to change those material and social relations that deny radical pluralism as the basis of democratic political community. It is only through such an understanding that teachers can develop a border pedagogy that opens up the possibility for students to reclaim their voices as part of a process of empowerment and not merely as what some have called an initiation into the culture of power.[81] It is not enough for students to learn how to resist power that is oppressive, that names them in a way that undermines their ability to govern rather than serve, and that prevents them from struggling against forms of power that subjugate and exploit. For example, Lisa Delpit's call for educators to integrate Afro-American students into what she unproblematically addresses as "the culture of power" appears to be linked to how such power is constructed in opposition to democratic values and used as a force for domination.[82]

I do not mean to suggest the authority of white dominant culture is all of one piece, nor do I mean to imply that it should not be the object of study. What is at stake here is forging a notion of power that does not collapse into a form of domination, but is critical and emancipatory, which allows students to both locate themselves in history and to critically, not slavishly, appropriate the cultural and political codes of their own and other traditions. Moreover, students who have to disavow their racial heritage in order to succeed are not becoming "raceless" as Signithia Fordham has argued; they are being positioned to accept subject positions that are the source of power for a white, dominant culture.[83] The ability of white, male, Eurocentric culture to normalize and universalize its own interests works so well that Fordham underemphasizes how whiteness as a cultural and historical construction, as a site of dominant narratives, exercises the form of authority that prevents black students from speaking through their own memories, histories, and experiences. Delpit and Fordham are right in attempting to focus on issues of powerlessness as they relate to pedagogy and race, but they both obscure this relation by not illuminating more clearly how power works in this society within the schools to secure and conceal various forms of racism and subjugation. Power is multifaceted, and we need a better understanding of how it works not simply as a force for oppression but also as a basis for resistance and self and social empowerment. Educators need to fashion a critical postmodern notion of authority, one that decenters essentialist claims to power while simultaneously fighting for relations of authority and power that allow many voices to speak so as to initiate students into a culture that multiplies rather than restricts democratic practices and social relations as part of a wider struggle for democratic public life.

Fifth, educators need to analyze racism not only as a structural and ideological force, but also in the diverse and historically specific ways in which it emerges. This is particularly true of the most recent and newest expressions of racism developing in the United States and abroad among youth, in popular culture, and in its resurgence in the highest reaches of the American government.[84] Any notion of antiracist pedagogy must arise out of specific settings and contexts and must allow its own character to be defined, in part, by the historically specific and contextual boundaries from which it emerges. At the same time, such a pedagogy must disavow all claims to scientific method or for that matter to any objective or transhistorical claims. As a political practice, an antiracist pedagogy has to be constructed not on the basis of essentialist or universal claims but on the concreteness of its specific encounters, struggles, and engagements. Roger Simon outlines some of the issues involved here in his discussion of critical pedagogy.

> Such a form of educational work is at root contextual and conditional. A critical pedagogy can only be concretely discussed from within a particular "point of practice"; from within a specific time and place and within a particular theme. This means doing critical pedagogy is a strategic, practical task not a scientific one. It arises not against a background of psychological, sociological, or anthropological universals—as does much educational theory related to pedagogy—but from such questions as: "how is human possibility being diminished here?"[85]

Sixth, an antiracist border pedagogy must redefine how the circuits of power move in a dialectical fashion among various sites of cultural production.[86] That is, we need a clearer understanding of how ideologies and other social practices that bear down on classroom relations emerge from and articulate with other spheres of social life. As educators, we need a clearer understanding of how the grounds for the production and organization of knowledge are related to forms of authority situated in political economy, the state, and other material practices. We also need to understand how circuits of power produce forms of textual authority that offer readers particular subject positions, that is, ideological references that provide but do not rigidly determine particular views of the world.[87] In addition, educators need to explore how the reading of texts is linked with the forms of knowledge and social relations that students bring into the classroom. In other words, we need to understand in terms of function and substance those social and cultural forms outside of the classroom that produce the multiple and often contradictory subject positions that students learn and express in their interaction with the dominant cultural capital of American schools.

Finally, central to the notion of border pedagogy is a number of important pedagogical issues regarding the role that teachers might take up in making a commitment to fight racism in their classrooms, schools, communities, and the wider society. The concept of border pedagogy can help to locate teachers within social, political, and cultural boundaries that define and mediate in complex ways how they function as intellectuals who exercise particular forms of moral and social regulation. Border pedagogy calls attention to both the ideological and the partial as central elements in the construction of teacher discourse and practice. To the degree that teachers make the construction of their own voices, histories, and ideologies problematic, they become more attentive to Otherness as a deeply political and pedagogical issue. In other words, by deconstructing the underlying principles that inform their own lives and pedagogy, educators can begin to recognize the limits underlying the partiality of their own views. Such a recognition offers the promise of allowing teachers to restructure their pedagogical relations in order to engage in an open and critical fashion fundamental questions about how knowledge is taught, how knowledge relates to students' lives, how students can engage with knowledge, and how pedagogy actually relates to empowering both teachers and students. Within dominant models of pedagogy, teachers are often silenced through a refusal or inability to make problematic with students the values that inform how they teach and engage the multifaceted relationship between knowledge and power. Without the benefit of dialogue and understanding of the partiality of their own beliefs, teachers are cut off from any understanding of the effects their pedagogies have on students. In effect, their infatuation with certainty and control serves to limit the possibilities inherent in their own voices and visions. In this case, dominant pedagogy serves not only to disable students, but teachers as well. In short, teachers need to take up a pedagogy that provides a more dialectical understanding of their own politics and values; they need to break down pedagogical boundaries that silence them in the name of methodological rigor or pedagogical absolutes; more important, they need to develop a power-sensitive discourse that allows them to open up their interactions with the discourses of various Others so that their classrooms can engage, rather than negate the multiple positions and experiences that allow teachers and students to speak in and with many complex and different voices.[88]

What border pedagogy makes undeniable is the relational nature of one's own politics and personal investments. But at the same time, border pedagogy emphasizes the primacy of a politics in which teachers assert rather than retreat from the pedagogies they use in dealing with the differences represented by the students who come into their classes. For example, it is not enough for teachers to merely affirm uncritically their student's histories, experiences, and stories. To take student voices at face value is to run the risk of idealizing and romanticizing them. It is equally important for teachers to help students find a language for critically examining the historically and socially constructed forms by which they live. Such a process involves more than allowing students to speak from their own histories and social formations. It also raises questions about how teachers use power to cross borders that are culturally strange to them.

At issue here is not a patronizing notion of understanding the Other, but a sense of how the self is implicated in the construction of Otherness, how exercising critical attention to such a relationship might allow educators to move out of the center of the dominant culture toward its margins in order to analyze critically the political, social, and cultural lineaments of their own values and voices as viewed from different ideological and cultural spaces. It is important for teachers to understand both how they wield power and authority and how particular forms of authority are sedimented in the construction of teachers' own needs along with the limited subject positions offered them in schools. Border pedagogy is not about engaging just the positionality of our students but about the nature of our own identities as they have and are emerging within and between various circuits of power. If students are going to learn how to take risks, to develop a healthy skepticism towards all master narratives, to recognize the power relations that offer them the opportunity to speak in particular ways, and be willing to critically confront their role as critical citizens who can animate a democratic culture, they need to see such behavior demonstrated in the social practices and subject positions that teachers live out and not merely propose.

If an antiracist pedagogy is to have any meaning as a force for creating a democratic society, teachers and students must be given the opportunity to put into effect what they learn outside of the school. In other words, they must be given the opportunity to engage in antiracist struggles in their effort to link schooling with real life, ethical discourse to political action, and classroom relations to a broader notion of cultural politics. School curriculum should make antiracist pedagogies central to the task of educating students to enliven a wider and more critically engaged public culture. It should allow students not merely to take risks but also to push against the boundaries of an oppressive social order. Such projects can be used to address the relevance of the school curriculum and its role as a significant public force for linking learning and social justice with the daily institutional and cultural traditions of society and reshaping them in the process. All schools should have teachers and students participate in antiracist curriculum that in some way link with projects in the wider society. This approach redefines not only teacher authority and student responsibility, but places the school as a major force in the struggle for social, economic, and cultural justice. A critical postmodern pedagogy of resistance can challenge not only the oppressive boundaries of racism, but all of those barriers that undermine and subvert the construction of a democratic society.

142 BORDER CROSSINGS

REFERENCES

[1] Editorial, "The Biggest Secret of Race Relations: The New White Minority," *Ebony Magazine* (April 1989), 84; John B. Kellog, "Forces of Change," *Phi Delta Kappan* (November 1988), 199–204.

[2] Michelle Fine, *Framing Dropouts* (Albany: SUNY Press, 1991).

[3] Kirk Johnson, "A New Generation of Racism Is Seen," *The New York Times*, August 27, 1989, 20; Kathy Dobie, "The Boys of Bensonhurst," *The Village Voice*, 54:36 (September 5, 1989), 34–39.

[4] Chantal Mouffe, "Hegemony and New Political Subjects: Toward a New Concept of Democracy," in Cary Nelson and Lawrence Grossberg, ed., *Marxism and the Interpretation of Culture* (Urbana: University of Illinois Press, 1988), 102. For a lengthy discussion of a notion of democracy similar to my own, see Stanley Aronowitz, *The Crisis in Historical Materialism* (Minneapolis: University of Minnesota Press, 1990), especially Chapter 8.

[5] John Pareles, "There's a New Sound in Pop Music: Bigotry," *The New York Times*, Sect. 2, Sunday, September 10, 1989, 10, 32; See also Lawrence Grossberg, *We Gotta Get Out of This Place: Rock, Politics, and Postmodernity* (Routledge, forthcoming).

[6] This theme is take up in Stanley Aronowitz and Henry A. Giroux, *Postmodern Education: Politics, Culture, and Social Criticism* (Minneapolis: University of Minnesota Press, 1991).

[7] This position was first made famous in Daniel Moynihan, *The Negro Family: The Case for National Action* (Washington, D.C.: U.S. Department of Labor, 1985). For two critical responses to this report, see Marian Wright Edelman, *Families in Peril: An Agenda for Social Change* (Cambridge: Harvard University Press, 1987), and Hortense J. Spillers, "Mamma's Baby, Papa's Maybe: An American Grammar Book," *Diacritics* 17:2 (Summer 1987), 65–81; See also a special issue of *The Nation* (July 24/31, 1989), entitled "Scapegoating the Black Family: Black Women Speak."

[8] Ernesto Laclau, "Politics and the Limits of Modernity," in Andrew Ross, ed. *Universal Abandon? The Politics of Postmodernism* (Minneapolis: University of Minnesota Press), 63–82; Nelly Richard, "Postmodernism and Periphery," *Third Text* 2 (1987/1988), 5–12.

[9] Gayatri C. Spivak, *In Other Worlds: Essays in Cultural Politics* (London: Metheun, 1987); See also Abdul R. JanMohamed and David Lloyd, eds., *The Nature and Context of Minority Discourse* (New York: Oxford University Press, 1990).

[10] Cornel West, "Marxist Theory and the Specificity of Afro-American Oppression," In Nelson and Grossberg, eds., *Marxism and the Interpretation of Culture*, 17–26.

[11] David Kolb, *The Critique of Pure Modernity: Hegel, Heidegger, and After* (Chicago: University of Chicago Press, 1986), especially the first and last chapters. See also Anthony Giddens, *The Consequences of Modernity* (Stanford: Stanford University Press, 1990).

[12] Stuart Hall, "Gramsci's Relevance for the Study of Race and Ethnicity," *Journal of Communication Inquiry* 10:2 (Summer 1986), 5–27; Of course, a number of writers, especially those of color, have begun to place the issue of race within a broader context. In addition to the feminist works cited in this chapter, see bell hooks, *Yearning: Race, Gender, and Cultural Politics* (Boston: South End Press, 1990); Michele Wallace, *Invisibility Blues* (London: Verso Press, 1991); Trinh T. Minh-ha, *Women, Native, Other* (Bloomington: Indiana University Press, 1989). See also the various articles in Russell Ferguson, Martha Gever, Trinh T. Minh-ha, Cornel West, eds., *Out There: Marginalization and Contemporary Cultures* (Cambridge: MIT Press, 1990); David Theo Goldberg, ed., *Anatomy of Racism* (Minneapolis: University of Minnesota Press, 1990); Henry Louis Gates, Jr., ed., *Reading Black, Reading Feminist* (New York: Meridian, 1991); Gloria Anzaldua, ed., *Making Face, Making Soul: Creative and Critical Perspectives by Women of Color* (San Francisco: An Aunt Lute Foundation Book, 1990). Chandra Talpade Mohanty, Ann Russo, & Lourpes Torres, eds., *Third World Women and the Politics of Feminism* (Bloomington: Indiana University Press, 1991).

[13] Stanley Aronowitz, "Postmodernism and Politics," *Social Text* 18 (1987/88), 113.

[14] Scott Lash and John Urry, *The End of Organized Capitalism* (Madison: University of Wisconsin Press, 1987); Scott Lash, *Sociology of Postmodernism* (New York: Routledge, 1990).

[15] Of course, this type economistic crudeness is a bit exaggerated but its spirit lives on in more updated orthodoxies; for example, see Jim Sleeper, "The Economics Beyond Race," *Democratic Left* 19:2 (March–April 1991), 9, 19. See also Jim Sleeper, *The Closest of Strangers: Liberalism and the Politics of Race in New York* (New York: W. W. Norton, 1989). For a critique of this position, see Stanley Aronowitz, *The Crisis of Historical Materialism* (Minneapolis: University of Minnesota Press, 1990); Ernesto Laclau and Chantal Mouffe, *Hegemony and Socialist Strategy* (London: Verso Books, 1985).

[16] See sources listed in note #12. In addition, two important references on these issues are Cornel West, *Prophesy Deliverance: An Afro-American Revolutionary Christianity* (New York: Westminister Press, 1982); Cornel West, *The American Evasion of Philosophy* (Madison: University of Wisconsin Press, 1989); Coco Fusco, "Fantasies of Oppositionality: Reflections on Recent Conferences in Boston and New York," *Screen* 29:4 (Autumn 1988), 80–93.

[17] This theme is taken up in Henry A. Giroux, *Schooling and the Struggle for Public Life* (Minneapolis: University of Minnesota Press, 1989). See also, Aronowitz and Giroux, *Postmodern Education*.

[18] Some exceptions include John Young, ed., *Breaking the Mosiac: Ethnic Identities in Canadian Society* (Toronto: Gramond Press, 1987); Lisa Albrecht and Rose Brewer, eds., *Bridges of Power: Women's Multicultural Alliances* (Santa Cruz, CA: New Society Publishers, 1990); Cameron McCarthy, *Race and Curriculum: Social Inequality and the Theories and Politics of Difference in Contemporary Research on Schooling* (New York: Falmer Press, 1990); Christine E. Sleeter, ed., *Empowerment Through Multicultural Education* (Albany: SUNY Press, 1991); Lucy R. Lippard, *Mixed Blessings: New Art in Multicultural America* (New York: Pantheon Books, 1990).

[19] Hazel V. Carby, "The Canon: Civil War and Reconstruction," *Michigan Quarterly Review* 28:1 (Winter 1989), 39.

[20] On the issue of engaging whiteness as a central racial category in the construction of moral power and political/cultural domination, see Richard Dyer, "White," *Screen:* 29:4 (Autumn 1988), 44–64; Cornel West, "The New Cultural Politics of Difference," *October* 53 (Summer 1990), 93–109, especially 105; Russell Ferguson, "Introduction: Invisible Center," in Russell Ferguson, et al., *Out There* (Cambridge: MIT Press, 1991), 9–14; Robert Young, *White Mythologies: Writing History and the West* (New York: Routledge, 1990).

[21] Toni Morrison, "Unspeakable Things Unspoken: The Afro-American Presence in American Literature," *Michigan Quarterly Review* 28:1 (Winter 1989), 34.

[22] Ibid., 11.

[23] Issac Julien and Kobena Mercer, "Introduction: De Margin and de Centre," *Screen* 8:2 (1987), 3.

[24] Hazel V. Carby, "Multi-Culture," *Screen Education* 34 (Spring 1980), 3; hooks, *Yearning*.

[25] For an elaboration of the distinction between critical and conservative forms of postmodernism, see Stanley Aronowitz and Henry A. Giroux, *Postmodern Education*.

[26] Robert Merrill, "Ethics/Aesthetics: A Post-Modern Position," in Robert Merrill. ed., *Ethics/Aesthetic: Postmodern Positions* (Washington, D.C.: Maisonneuve Press, 1988), 7–13.

[27] Hal Foster, ed., *The Anti-Aesthetic: Essays on Postmodern Culture* (Towsend, Washington: Bay Press, 1983); Hal Foster, ed., *Discussions in Contemporary Culture* No. 1 (Seattle: Bay Press, 1987); Linda Hutcheon, *A Poetics of Postmodernism* (New York: Routledge, 1988).

[28] Jean-Francois Lyotard, *The Postmodern Condition: A Report on Knowledge* (Minneapolis: University of Minnesota Press, 1984).

[29] Sygmunt Bauman, "Strangers: The Social Construction of Universality and Particularity," *Telos* 78 (Winter 1988–1989), 12.

[30] Dick Hebdige, "Postmodernism and 'the other side' ", *Journal of Communication Inquiry* 10:2 (1986), 81.

[31] Ibid., 91.

[32] Frenc Feher, "The Status of Postmodernity," *Philosophy and Social Criticism* 13:2 (1988), 195–206.

[33] Jim Collins, *Uncommon Cultures: Popular Culture and Post-Modernism* (New York: Routledge, 1989).

[34] For a variety of essays on this issue, see Brian Wallis ed., *Art After Modernism: Rethinking Representation* (Boston: Godine Publishing, 1989); Foster, *The Anti-Aesthetic*.

[35] For instance, Dennis Farber employs painting and photography in a way that makes the distinction between them seem moot. In photography, this tradition is most manifest in the work of Sherri Levine, Barbara Kruger, and Cindy Sherman. For both examples and analyses of the new forms of representation and social criticism that has emerged out of postmodernism, see Hutcheon, *A Poetics of Postmodernism*; Brian Wallis, (ed.), *Blasted Allegories* (Cambridge: MIT, Press, 1988); Brian Wallis, (ed.), *Art After Modernism*; Hal Foster, *Recordings: Art, Spectacle, Cultural Politics* (Seattle: Bay Press, 1985); Robert Hewison, *Future Tense: A New Art for the Nineties* (London: Metheun, 1990); Abigail Solomon-Godeau, *Photography at the Dock*; Hugh J. Silverman, *Postmodernism-Philosophy and the Arts* (New York: Routledge, 1990).

[36] Caren Kaplan, "Deterritorializations: The Rewriting of Home and Exile in Western Feminist Discourse," *Cultural Critique* 6 (1987), 187–98; Iain Chambers, *Border Dialogues: Journeys in Postmodernity* (New York: Routledge, 1990).

[37] See especially the excellent treatment of this issue in Grossberg, *We Gotta Get Out of This Place*.

[38] Teresa de Lauretis, *Technologies of Gender* (Bloomington: Indiana University Press, 1987); Meaghan Morris, *The Pirate's Fiancee: Feminism, Reading, Postmodernism* (London: Verso Press, 1988).

[39] These themes are taken up in Ernesto Laclau and Chantal Mouffe, *Hegemony and Socialist Strategy* (London: Verso Press, 1985); Ernesto Laclau, *New Reflections on the Revolution of Our Time* (London: Verso Books, 1990); Stanley Aronowitz, *The Crisis in Historical Materialism*. On different interpretations of the changing economic, political, and cultural conditions that characterize the postmodern condition, see Lash Urry, *The End of Organized Capitalism*; David Harvey, *The Condition of Postmodernity* (New York: Basil Blackwell, 1989); Steven Connor, *Postmodernist Culture* (New York: Blackwell, 1989).

[40] Richard Terdiman, *Discourse/Counter Discourse* (New York: Cornell University Press, 1985); George Lipsitz, *Time Passages: Collective Memory and American Popular Culture* (Minneapolis: University of Minnesota Press, 1990); Renato Resaldo, *Culture and Truth* (Boston: Beacon Press, 1989).

[41] Jim Collins, *Uncommon Cultures*, 115.

[42] Ibid.

[43] Chantal Mouffe, "Radical Democracy: Modern or Postmodern," in Ross (ed.), *Universal Abandon?*, 41.

[43] Of course, this theme is taken up in an endless number of discussions of postmodernism. One important analysis can be found in Laclau and Mouffe, *Hegemony and Socialist Strategy*. See also Slavoj Zizek, *The Sublime Object of Ideology* (London: Verso Books, 1989).

[45] Sharon Welch, *A Feminist Ethic of Risk* (Minneapolis: Fortress Press, 1990).

[46] Mouffe, Op. cit., in Ross (ed.), 1988, 41.

[47] Cornel West, "Black Culture and Postmodernism," in Barbara Kruger and Phil Mariani eds., *Remaking History* (Seattle: Bay Press, 1989), 90.

[48] Richard Bernstein, "Metaphysics, Critique, and Utopia," *The Review of Metaphysics* 42 (1988), 267.

[49] The literature on this issue is vast. Three representative works on black women writers include: Paula Giddings, *When and Where I Enter: The Impact of Black Women on Race and Sex in America* (New York: Bantam Books, 1984); Mari Evans ed., *Black Women Writers (1950–1980): A Critical Evaluation* (New York: Anchor Press, 1984); Henry Louis Gates, Jr., *Reading*

Black, Reading Feminist. Important theoretical works discussing the writings of black women include: Barbara Christian, *Black Feminist Criticism* (New York Pergamon, 1985); Susan Willis, *Specifying: Black Women Writing—The American Experience* (Madison: University of Wisconsin, Press, 1987); Hazel V. Carby, *Reconstructing Womanhood: The Emergence of the Afro-American Women Novelist* (New York: Oxford University Press, 1987); Michele Wallace, *Black Macho and the Myth of the Superwoman* (London: Verso Books, 1990); Michele Wallace, *Invisibility Blues*, especially 129–255; Sharon Welch, A *Feminist Ethic of Risk*.

[50] Christian, *Black Feminist Criticism*, 159.

[51] Cited in John McCluskey, Jr., "And Call Every Generation Blessed: Theme, Setting and Ritual in the Works of Paule Marshall," in Evans, ed., *Black Women Writers*, 316.

[52] See, for example, Audre Lorde, *Sister Outsider* (Freedom, CA: The Crossing Press, 1984); hooks, *Talking Back* (Boston: South End Press, 1989), *Yearnings* (Boston: South End Press, 1990); Wallace, *Black Macho* June Jordan, *On Call* (Boston: South End Press, 1989); and Carby, *Reconstructing Womanhood*.

[53] Lorde, *Sister Outsider*.

[54] Carby, "The Canon: Civil Way and Reconstruction," 39.

[55] Fusco, "Fantasies of Oppositionality," 90.

[56] bell hooks, "The Politics of Radical Black Subjectivity," *Talking Back*, (Boston: South End Press, 1989), 54.

[57] Stuart Hall, "Minimal Selves," in *ICA Documents 6, Postmodernism and the Question of Identity* (London: ICA, 1987), 45.

[58] Lorde, *Sister Outsider*, p. 112.

[59] Ibid.

[60] Ibid., p. 118.

[61] Ibid.

[62] Ibid., p. 45.

[63] Christian, *Black Feminist Criticism*.

[64] bell hooks, op. cit., *Talking Back*, 11–12.

[65] June Jordan, *On Call*, 30–31.

[66] Barbara Christian, "The Race for Theory," *Cultural Critique* 6 (Spring 1987), 52.

[67] Toni Cade Bambara, "Evaluation Is the Issue," in Evans, *Black Women Writers*, 46.

[68] See Willis, *Specifying*, 1987.

[69] Michelle Gibbs Russell, "Black Eyed Blues Connections; From the Inside Out," in Charlotte Bunch and Sandra Pollack, eds., *Learning Our Way; Essays in Feminist Education* (Trumansburg, N.Y.: The Crossing Press, 1983), 274, 275.

[70] June Jordan, "Where Is the Love?" in Barbara H. Andolsen, Christine Gurdorf, and Mary Pellauer, eds., *Women's Consciousness Women's Conscience* (New York: Harper and Row, 1985), 203.

[71] Welch, A *Feminist Ethic of Risk*, 139.

[72] Michele Wallace, *Invisibility Blues*, 1–10.

[73] Henry A. Giroux, *Schooling and the Struggle for Public Life*; Mouffe, "Hegemony and New Political Subjects: Toward a New Concept of Democracy," in Nelson and Grossberg, eds., *Marxism and the Interpretation of Culture*, 89–104.

[74] Mouffe, "Radical Democracy," *Marxism and the Interpretation of Culture*, in Ross, ed., *Universal Abandon?*, 42.

[75] Aronowitz, *The Crisis in Historical Materialism*.

[76] D. Emily Hicks, "Deterriorialization and Border Writing," in Robert Merrill, ed., *Ethics/ Aesthetics: Post-Modern Positions* (Washington, D.C.: Maisonneuve Press, 1988), 47–58.

[77] Stuart Hall, "Teaching Race," in Alan Jones and Robert Jeffcoate, eds., *The School in Multicultural Society* (London: Harper and Row, 1981), 61.

[78] I have taken up this issue in Giroux, *Schooling and the Struggle for Public Life*, especially chapters 2 & 3. See also two excellent pieces on authority and pedagogy in Patricia Bizzell,

"Classroom Authority and Critical Pedagogy," *American Literary History* (forthcoming), and Patricia Bizzell, "Power, Authority, and Critical Pedagogy," *Journal of Basic Writing* (forthcoming).

[79] Chandra Mohanty is excellent on this issue. See "On Race and Voice: Challenges for Liberal Education in the 1990s," *Cultural Critique* (Winter 1989–1990), 179–208.

[80] Andrew Hannan, "Racism, Politics, and the Curriculum," *British Journal of Sociology of Education*, 8:2 (1987), 127.

[81] Lisa Delpit, "The Silenced Dialogue: Power and Pedagogy in Educating Other People's Children," *Harvard Educational Review* 58:3 (1988), 280–98.

[82] Ibid.

[83] Signithia Fordham, "Racelessness as a Factor in Black Students' School Success: Pragmatic Strategy or Pyrrhic Victory?" *Harvard Educational Review* 58:3 (1988), 54–82.

[84] Hall, "Teaching Race," in Jones and Jeffcoate, eds., *The School in Multicultural Society*, 58–69.

[85] Roger I. Simon, "For a Pedagogy of Possibility," *Critical Pedagogy Networker* 1:1 (1981), 54–82.

[86] Richard Johnson, "What is Cultural Studies Anyway?" *Social Text* 16 (Winter 1986/87), 38–80.

[87] These issues are taken up in Catherine Belsey, *Critical Practice* (New York: Metheun, 1980); Tony Bennett, "Texts in History: The Determinations of Readings and Their Texts," in Derek Atridge, Geoff Bennington, and Robert Young, eds., *Post-Structuralism and the Question of History* (New York: Cambridge University Press, 1987); Aronowitz and Giroux, *Postmodern Education*.

[88] For specific ways in which voice and difference are treated in critical pedagogical terms, see various chapters in this book. Also see hooks, *Talking Back*; hooks, *Yearning*; Giroux, *Schooling and the Struggle for Public Life*.

II

CULTURAL WORKERS AND CULTURAL PEDAGOGY

6

Critical Pedagogy and Cultural Power:
An Interview with Henry A. Giroux*

For nearly two decades education theorist Henry A. Giroux has worked to broaden our understanding of the relationship between schooling and political life. In challenging traditional roles of students, teachers, and the institutional structures that bring them together, Giroux has formulated a range of radical educational subject positions and new discursive spaces for learning. Giroux's work is of particular interest to artists for the way he draws cultural workers into the circle of pedagogy, whether they practice in the classroom, the gallery, or the street. As discussed in the conversation below, such efforts to form alliances among progressive artists and educators have assumed even greater urgency in recent years, as conservatives have recognized the strategic role of arts and humanities education in producing identities.

At the center of Giroux's writing and teaching lies a moral commitment to a set of democratic practices that engages all citizens in common governance. He argues that these practices can never be inherited but must be learned and relearned by each successive generation. In espousing these views, Giroux has emerged as one of the most outspoken proponents of the "critical pedagogy" movement, an amalgam of educational philosophies that first gained wide public recognition in the 1960s through the writings of Brazilian expatriate Paulo Freire. At the heart of this philosophy lies a belief in the centrality of education in determining political and social relations. As practiced by Freire in countries throughout the third world, the doctrines of critical pedagogy were used by colonized citizens to analyze their roles in relations of oppression and to devise programs for revolutionary change.

---

* David Trend is a San Francisco-based editor and critic.

During the 1970s and 1980s the philosophies of critical pedagogy were adapted throughout the industrialized world as a means of addressing power imbalances there. As a result much of the vocabulary of "empowerment," "dialogue," and "voice" has entered the lexicon of Western social reform movements. At the same time the principles of critical pedagogy have undergone significant modifications that adapt them to the needs of contemporary technocratic societies. In a world that is rapidly redefining relations between its centers and margins and questioning the legitimacy of master narratives, critical pedagogy has borrowed significantly from postmodernism, feminism, literary theory, cultural studies, and psychoanalysis.

Since 1983 Giroux has taught in the School of Education and Allied Professions at Miami University in Oxford, OH, where he is a professor of education and director of the Center for Education and Cultural Studies. A secondary school teacher from 1969 to 1975, he earned his Ph.D. in curriculum theory, sociology of education, and history at Carnegie-Mellon University in 1977. He later taught at Boston and Tufts universities.

Giroux is the author of numerous books, five of which were named by the American Educational Studies Association as among the most significant books in education in the years of their publication: *Ideology, Culture and the Process of Schooling, Education Under Siege: The Conservative, Liberal, and Radical Debate over Schooling* (with Stanley Aronowitz), *Theory and Resistance in Education, Teachers as Intellectuals: Toward a Critical Pedagogy of Learning,* and *Schooling and the Struggle for Public Life: Critical Pedagogy in the Modern Age.* His other works include *Curriculum Discourse as Postmodernist Critical Practice, Postmodern Education: Politics, Culture, and Social Criticism* (with Stanley Aronowitz)[1], and over 150 articles and essays.

Giroux has edited books including *Critical Pedagogy, the State, and the Struggle for Culture* (with Peter McLaren), *Popular Culture, Schooling and Everyday Life* (with Roger Simon), and *Postmodernism, Feminism, and Cultural Politics: Rethinking Educational Boundaries.*[2] He is a member of the consulting editorial board of the Boston University *Journal of Education* and a contributing editor of *Curriculum Inquiry.* He is coeditor with Freire of the series *Critical Studies in Education,* published by Bergin and Garvey Press, and coeditor with Peter McLaren of *Teacher Empowerment and School Reform,* a series published by SUNY Press.

This interview was recorded on August 4, 1990, in San Francisco and subsequently revised for publication in *Afterimage.*

David Trend: By way of introduction, I think we should discuss the language of critical pedagogy and perhaps address the issue of discursive terminology itself.

Henry Giroux: The struggle over language in these fields often stems from arguments about clarity, complexity, and the redfinition of terms. Many people reading pedagogical language mistakenly say that you simply have to explain it or write in a style that is clear and uncomplicated. This position is too reductionist.

Actually, we're talking about how educational paradigms begin to generate a new language and raise new questions. These points shouldn't be confused. We're pointing to a theory that examines how you view the very realities you engage. When people say that we write in a language that isn't as clear as it could be, while that might be true they're also responding to the unfamiliarity of a paradigm that generates questions suppressed in the dominant culture.

When you discuss language, you must consider what public you are addressing. Is there one public? What's the relationship between intellectuals and the public sphere? In there a universalized standard of language that becomes a referent for all others? How do you begin to ask that question in a way that remains aware of the possibility of ghettoization on one hand but that also recognizes different publics in different contexts? You should consider those multiple publics and their multiple political strategies. I think the question is a very important one.

Producing Knowledge and Power

DT: What are the new paradigms that pedagogical language conveys? Isn't the discourse of critical pedagogy based on critiques of conventional models of schooling, the interests they embody, the values they promote, the groups they favor and disfavor?

HG: Critical pedagogy has arisen from a need to name the contradiction between what schools claim they do and what they actually do. This position has both strengths and weaknesses.

DT: You mean that it's a reactive discussion?

HG: Historically schools were rarely self-critical about their purposes and means, and the few movements challenging them were very marginal. But something happened in the 1970s. Samuel Bowles and Herbert Gintis published a book called *Schooling in Capitalist America: Educational Reform and the Contradictions of Economic Life*[3] that launched a form of analysis tied to theories of social reproduction. This wasn't critical pedagogy but an attempt to unravel certain political and economic injustices within education. As important as it was in politicizing the issue of school, it was still built upon an Orwellian notion of domination that was overpowering and without a discourse of resistance.

Also it focused almost exclusively on labor functions. Schools were said to reproduce the social relations necessary for maintaining a market economy. Rather than creating managers they produced passive workers who would adjust to the imperatives of the capitalist order. That language exercised a powerful influence in mobilizing the critical pedagogy movement, but it exhausted itself in its inability to take up power dialectically or to consider what schools could do to apply power productively. So it doesn't have much of an impact except in academic circles. In 1978 I could count 10 people in education who had established public reputations writing about those ideas.

DT: In this country?

HG: Yes. And those whose works were imported from abroad you could count on one hand: people like Paul Willis, Geoff Witty, and Basil Bernstein. The new feminist work wasn't emerging then in education because the emphasis was on materialist theories of class reproduction. Also no one addressed the question of pedagogy outside the realm of schooling.

DT: This is in the late 1970s? Why was educational thinking evolving in such a vacuum?

HG: Marxism seemed to offer the only discourse available to people interested in analyzing the relationship of schools and politics. Even the most radical educational theory was overwhelmed by an economic orthodoxy. The importance of other disclosures wasn't recognized. However, you have to remember that, while orthodox Marxism reigned from around 1977 to 1980, a new version of reproductive theory emerged in the work of Pierre Bourdieu and others. It wasn't simply about laborers being socialized by the hidden curriculum into dead-end futures. It also addressed cultural reproduction. Bourdieu brought forward an old Gramscian line in which schools were said to create cultural capital for those who occupy positions of power as intellectuals within the cultural apparatus of the larger society. Dominant forms of cultural capital had a certain exchange rate on the market but were accessible to very few people—those who are white and upper middle class. Regrettably, Bourdieu's work was similarly overdetermined by theories of domination and had no programmatic notion of power in the Foucauldian sense.

DT: Coincidentally, this was also a period of great government largesse. It's difficult to discuss the era without considering its very generous social programs: educational initiatives, CETA (Comprehensive Employment and Training Act) programs, and the growth of the National Endowment for the Arts, for example. What about the impact of the Reagan revolution in catalyzing some of this thinking, perhaps some of your thinking?

HG: Reagan comes along and introduces the idea of education as a popular struggle. The Reagan administration said that social reproduction is a terrific idea: We absolutely need workers, and that's what schools should do. We'll define education precisely in those terms; we believe that progressives really missed the point of living in a capitalist society. Schools aren't neutral. They're political sites, and we're going to fight for them on those grounds. We're going to engage the notion of power by saying that schools create character and identities, and we're going to show you how to inscribe students in specific roles. And they will take them up very cheerfully. After all, students are not just dupes. What are you people on the Left talking about? It's demeaning to say that people are stupid and that they don't make choices.

Then comes Allan Bloom. This is one of the most important moments in the history of education in the United States, as the Right begins to wage an overactive struggle on the cultural front. It says that schools exist to preserve Western civilization. We need not only a structure to train workers but also a means of taking up the issues of ideology and cultural formations, particularly as they are linked to traditions that we think are vital to American hegemony. But the conservative argument goes even further and says that probably the place in which traditions are most dangerously undermined is within the discourse of democracy.

DT: Turning democracy on its head?

HG: Yes, invoking the infamous Trilateral Commission Study of 1965, the one that said that we should limit the excesses of democracy, control social criticism, and police the universities. Bloom offers no apology at all. He argues that the nation is engaged in a cultural politics in which democracy becomes subversive, criticism becomes dangerous, and intellectuals who do not take up the mantle of tradition should not teach in the university. So it seems to me that what Bloom and E.D. Hirsch Jr. did—along with Dianne Ravitch, John Silber, Chester Finn Jr., and William Bennett—was really to help us rethink schooling as a form of cultural politics—as opposed to simply thinking of it as a form of cultural domination.

They certainly forced me, among others, to rethink how we were going to redefine schools as sites of struggle, where power is productive and where the axis isn't simply between reproduction and resistance. It's more about the complexity with which power works and the multilayered and contradictory identities that are taken up. It's about the production of particular ways of life. Because of the attack from the Right, we began to make this incredible shift. We no longer simply said, in classic Left pedagogical terms, "Okay, here's a school, let's identify the dominant ideological interests at work that serve to oppress teachers and students."

DT: Nevertheless, that is an important point to reach.

HG: Of course; it's an essential moment. But there are at least two other central questions in the configuration of cultural politics. Beyond identifying interests, we need to ask how these interests function. How do they produce particular ways of life? Even more importantly, we need to consider how they're taken up. Without considering the question of how they're taken up, we assume that ideologies are absorbed by virtue of their existence rather than fought over continually.

DT: By "taken up" do you mean how they are integrated into everyday life?

HG: Yes, how people respond to them. Where does a theory of agency come in here? Simply because a curriculum is racist, does this mean everyone in the class will become a racist? Simply because a curriculum is based on an *Afterimage* notion of culture, does this mean that everyone will come out thinking that way? We should be concerned with how students actually construct meaning, what the categories of meaning are, and what ideologies students bring to their encounters with us. In the interaction between text, teacher, and student something is always created around the specificity of the situation in which you find yourself.

DT: Meaning is a negotiated part of the transaction.

HG: Given the different variables in each context, people are writing meaning rather than simply receiving it. That seems dangerous to the Right because it makes knowledge problematic. It means taking the identities of subordinate cultures seriously. It means you can't have standardized curricula. When we enlarge our notion of how ideology works, a circle of power begins to develop that has more to do with what a cultural politics of schooling should be about. For me there are four major points. First, obviously there's a material apparatus at work in the state, in textbook companies, in banks, etc. Second, there is the question of text. Who authorizes them, who produces them, what is the historical weight of the range of meanings they make available or legitimize? And texts include everything from visual images to curricula. Third, there is the question of ideology. What ideologies and lived experiences enter the context of a particular classroom? Finally, there are communities. One should examine communities to understand how ideologies accumulate historical weight for kids, how they provide the conditions for specific intellectual and emotional investments. Beyond addressing the ideologies that kids bring to the classroom, I'm concerned with the historical, social, and political conditions that create lived experiences for those kids in the first place. Although those four issues circle round and round, unfortunately most people on the Left are focused on the first moment.

Struggle and Democracy

DT: What about the ways theories of schooling and cultural politics work in practical application? How do these premises actually function in schools, for instance?

HG: Schools and teachers need to gain a vision of why they're doing what they're doing. For this reason you need to define intellectual work within some notion of authority that you can fight for. That means that it has to have an ethical and political referent. For me this means defining schools as democratic public spheres. We need to make a link between schooling and the reconstruction of public life, because in this country the language of democracy has been removed from the language of schooling except as a pejorative term.

DT: The Right has appropriated the language of democracy. They say its values bind us all together, that its heritage is what makes us whole. Of course, we both know that isn't so, but they've adopted that terminology.

HG: Actually there are two versions of that position. The Blooms say that democracy is dangerous to higher education.

DT: Ultimately anarchistic.

HG: Yes; then there are the Ravitches and the Hirsches who, while they use the language of democracy, always manipulate it in a way that does the same thing. They remove its central and basic tenets and substitute expressions like "tradition" or "common culture." By never discussing democracy as a radical social practice, they recode the term and displace its meaning.

Left cultural workers need to address democracy as a site of struggle and to reclaim it in terms that take seriously issues of quality, justice, freedom, and difference. That's a very practical matter for me. We need to reclaim progressive notions of the *public* in public schooling so that education can become a real public service, just as one might say maybe the arts need to be taken up pedagogically in the same ways.

In this regard the debate over Robert Mapplethorpe's photographs isn't simply a matter of censorship. The real issue concerns a fight for democracy beyond the arts. It's also about difference as it's constituted in public life and in schools. This business that cultural works or intellectual knowledge can only be ordered in very particular ways according to government mandates and surveillances—I see the struggle against this idea as central to the notion of democracy itself.

What I find in my field, and I know this may sound terribly bizarre, is that teachers have no vocabulary to link schools to a critical notion of democracy. The language is absent. Even when democracy is evoked, it is evoked in a way that doesn't expand human capacities to engage issues of justice and struggle.

DT: What do you mean they don't have a language?

HG: The language of teacher education, the language in the places where they're educated or trained.

DT: But it's like that in every field.

HG: Some have more room than others. Where you get a field that defines itself as applied, you often find a confused relationship between principles and applications. Larger questions of vision can be relegated quickly to the dustbin of academic involvement. So teachers come along and demand 25 different ways to teach social studies or deconstruction. They become focused on a fetishized methodology that precludes examination of their roles as a public intellectuals, of the institutions in which they work, and of society at large. The language they learn or take up is depoliticized; it is largely a language or procedure and technique.

DT: What would you say makes that happen? The commodification of knowledge? Is it job standardization and professionalization?

HG: The ideology of positivism is very powerful in American education. It represents strong interests, and it complements capitalist social relations very well. It breaks knowledge down. It makes people into consumers. It exalts the language of commodification. At the same time there's a legacy of McCarthyism in American education that is making a comeback.

DT: Not to mention books like Charles Sykes's *Profscam* (1988) that cast the university as a hideout for lazy, tenured academics.

HG: The attack on tenure is really an attack on the civil rights of educators who dare to raise their voices. It's another form of censorship that is forcing educators and cultural workers to rethink the function of struggle in an ongoing reconstruction of democratic public life. As a pedagogue I am constantly working to remind people both inside and outside my field that just as democracy is given it can also be taken away.

You can define democracy within the narrow limits of electoral politics, or you can define it as an ongoing contest within every aspect of daily life. By understanding that, we can make articulations between the specific cultural work we do and other fields. You and I know that knowledges and identities always concern the relationships among power, language, imagery, social relations, and ethics. Although we may do different things, there's something connecting us when we have the sense of being in the fight for democracy. We operate in different terrains, but that difference doesn't become antagonistic, it becomes a basis for articulation.

DT: You've made the point before that this is always a dynamic process. Conservatives often argue that we're now in a democracy that's perfect and shouldn't be questioned.

HG: The Mapplethorpe case brings the point home so powerfully. In Cincinnati curator Dennis Barrie was actually put on trial. His life is on the line not for a particular photography exhibition but for the kind of social criticism that's endemic to the very nature of democracy. His struggle is much broader than the arts. [Barrie and the Cincinnati Contemporary Arts Center have since been acquitted.] The fight is over our ability to name realities in ways that aren't simply functions of government surveillance. When you say that democracy has reached its ultimate form you're stepping into the world of terrorism. The U.S. is getting closer to describing democracy as a totality of one, a democracy in which social criticism is no longer pragmatic because it's dangerous. Ironically, we've reached a point where democracy actually can be taken up in terms that suggest that any struggle for it is a struggle against it—which immediately proves that it's always a struggle.

But there's also the other side. No tradition should ever be seen as received, because when it is received it becomes sacred, its terms suggest reverence, silence, and passivity. Democratic societies are noisy. They're about traditions that need to be critically reevaluated by each generation. The battle to extend democratic possibilities has to be fought in education at a very primal level. The very notions of knowledge, values, testing, evaluation, ethics all ultimately relate to social criticism and its role in democratic struggle.

Authority and Agency

DT: To play the devil's advocate for a minute, what about the argument that teaching operates within relations of unequal power, despite theories of agency and resistance, and that even the principles of critical pedagogy are transmitted through a dominant teacher to a student? If we're talking about what constructs us all and motivates us in what we do, how does a teacher practicing critical pedagogy not deliver an ideology to someone else in his or her own interests?

HG: Two issues. I would reiterate that knowledge is produced rather than received. That raises a very interesting question about the notion of authority. You can exercise authority in ways that do not establish the conditions for knowledge to be produced and engaged. I would call that authoritarianism. Or you can exercise authority to establish conditions in which a central tension lies at the heart of how we teach. The latter method encourages self-reflection, learning from others, and refiguring forms of cultural practice.

Therefore it's conceivable to be theoretically correct and pedagogically wrong. It's conceivable that I can go into a class and say that this knowledge is absolutely worthwhile because it's an antiracist pedagogy that takes up questions of difference in a profoundly utopian way. We can certainly justify doing that, but what we can't justify is assuming that that's all we should do. We also have to consider how knowledge can be taken up in ways that make it the object of analysis rather than of reverence. We also need to consider how knowledge is understood within the contexts of the experiences students bring to our classes. We are there not merely to produce knowledge so that it can be debated but also to be self-critical ourselves and learn from the forms of knowledge produced as they come from the class, from our students, from the community, and from their texts.

Nevertheless, we should always be mindful of our obligation not to run away from authority but to exercise it in the name of self- and social formation. That means always reminding ourselves that power must be exercised within a framework that allows students to inform us and to be more critical about their own voices, as well as aware of the codes and cultural representations of others outside the immediacy of their experience. As cultural workers we must be aware of the partial nature of our own views.

I don't want to argue simply that as a white, middle-class intellectual I have no right to do anything but listen to the voices of the oppressed. That suggests that social location and identity politics absolutely determine and guarantee the way one takes up political questions. I have no trouble at all in exorcising authority as long as I'm constantly self-critical about the limits of my own knowledge. One needs to recognize what it means to place students in relations of difference and articulation that consistently push them toward forms of struggle with themselves, teachers, and the society at large.

DT: That's a very difficult question. I know teachers who have become frustrated with student-centered techniques because they don't work. Students resist because they don't really believe the teacher is yielding authority to them. They instinctively recognize that the institution is exerting an overdetermining influence over what happens in the classroom.

HG: It's naive to deny the existence of authority. Instead one should investigate how it is exercised.

DT: You can't avoid authority, because it's a psychological condition. It creates a relationship of transference.

HG: The problem of authority raises several other issues. We're not merely free-floating intellectuals. We're inscribed within institutions that have the historical weight of particular kinds of power. Whether we like it or not, particularly as university professors or people involved in other cultural institutions, we don't just represent ourselves. We are representations of authority, and to say to students that institutions and practices of power don't exist is actually to be deceptive about the ways those institutions shape our own roles. This is why we must become self-conscious through the exercise of oppositional forms of authority: not only to question those roles but to undo them where necessary.

I find too many students who come from places where they're afraid to speak. They've been silenced all their lives. It is now becoming very popular to say that intellectuals have no right to speak, that we have no right to appropriate the voice of the other. I certainly have no right to totalize the other and to say that I can speak for the other. I can speak to and about racism, sexism, and other issues as considerations that must be challenged in a democratic society, but what happens when we find ourselves in classes with students who have been mutilated and are afraid to speak? How do we raise issues that encourage them to speak? If I try to so do, does that mean that as a white man I've violated some category that says that only blacks can speak about oppression?

Experience has to be read critically; it never speaks for itself. This points to the need to exercise authority as a politics of engagement rather than as politics of assertion or as a politics of the personal/confessional. Authority must be used to provide the pedagogical conditions that empower students not only to speak but also to develop the critical capacities and courage to transform the conditions that oppress them and others in the first place.

DT: Obviously one has to be very careful about doing this.

HG: Given the power that public intellectuals sometime have, I'm suggesting that we have obligations at least to inaugurate a discourse around the unrepresentable, that which cannot be spoken within social relations, particularly within groups that know that generally to speak is to be punished. I want to help create those oppositional spaces without dominating them. I don't want to say this is the only truth that will prevail. But as a public intellectual I have the obligation to rewrite the narratives of possibility for those who have occupied subject positions where that hasn't been possible before.

Teachers and Communities

DT: At this point we should move our theoretical discussion to other issues of practice.

HG: A specific point that we've just begun to discuss is the notion of teachers as intellectuals. How do teachers assume positions in which they can engage in real struggles over what forms of knowledge count? How do we approach questions of social relations? How do racism, sexism, and classism work? How do we begin to deconstruct textbooks in order to identify the ways of life and the stories that they tell?

DT: This applied perfectly to artists and other cultural workers.

HG: Yes; how can we begin to produce our own materials? How do we begin to take seriously the production of content-specific curricula? We see this happening all over the San Francisco Bay Area, as Mexican, Chicano, and Latino kids are suddenly becoming historians of their own cultures, going out and doing oral histories, taking photographs. They're reappropriating their own identifies within forms of historical memory that represent a complete reconfiguration of how they look at knowledge. Another example is Tim Rollins's KOS (Kids of Survival) project in the Bronx. In their classrooms knowledge is not simply about something that's been produced in New York City or about Dick and Jane and their little dog in Greenwich, CT. It's about reappropriating history as part of the struggle over power, knowledge, culture, and identify.

The fight for curricular democracy and our roles as public intellectuals requires more than rethinking the relationship between knowledge and power. It also means that educators must form alliances with people like you who are doing this work in other ways. We need to enlarge the possibility for other groups to see schools as political sites where they can make a contribution.

There are a number of things we can do in this regard. First, the historical isolation of people who work in schools from other cultural workers needs to be overcome. This means we must make an attempt to develop a shared language around the issue of pedagogy and struggle, develop a set of relevancies that can be recognized in each other's work, and articulate a common political project that addresses the relationship between pedagogical work and the reconstruction of oppositional public spheres. Second, we need to form alliances around the issue of censorship both in and out of the schools. The question of representation is central to the issue of pedagogy as a form of cultural politics and cultural politics as a practice related to the struggles of everyday life. Third, we need to articulate these issues in a public manner, in which *Artforum* and *Afterimage* can say we're really addressing a variety of cultural workers and not simply a narrowly defined audience. This points to the need to broaden the definition of culture and political struggle and in doing so invite others to participate in both the purpose and practice central to such tasks.

DT: How do we do that? It's a question many people have been grappling with.

HG: There are at least three ways in which it has to be done. First we begin to talk about an organization that frames itself around the struggle for democracy and cultural politics.

DT: What kind of organization?

HG: I'm not sure if it is a formal organization or not. As a loose entity the cultural studies movement might yield some answers, but it has no frame or political project. Cultural studies for what? It should involve issues like the reconstruction of public life, questions of pedagogy, politics, identity, and power, breaking down the disciplines and bringing groups together, and ways to explore the perimeters or borderlands where they can meet.

Maybe we should discuss a public sphere created in the form of conferences or in new kinds of journals, or new kinds of relationships in neighborhoods. Maybe we should focus on breaking down the lines between academics and cultural workers around different kinds of local projects.

DT: Unfortunately, it sounds like this revolution is going to take place inside a university. There are many factors preventing it from taking place elsewhere. It's difficult to get people to think otherwise, because there are so few support structures to encourage people to bridge these gaps.

HG: The gaps need to be bridged by people who have the resources and time to do so. They's why people both inside and outside academia should begin to reformulate the ghettoization of academic public life. Politics is not simply about theoretical work that takes place around symposia. The academy is important, but there is also a network of people who work in communities. Since I work primarily in public education, I find myself addressing communities of people, and they don't just talk about school. They talk about drugs and crime, and they want to know where resources can be found in their communities. We need academics to come into our communities with their resources and possibilities so that we can begin to create borderlands for dialogue and struggles.

DT: We try to name these new discursive spaces, but it's difficult because they don't exist.

HG: There are many things that stand in the way. How do the notions of professionalism and expertise get perpetuated even in the most radical of languages? How are we implicated in these forms of exclusions? A battle has to be fought in the academic sector, because it has resources that other communities don't really have.

DT: One of the saddest things is the strength of material pressure. You and I both know people who began their careers as grassroots radicals only to find themselves at a point in their lives with very few choices. Very few support structures, and very few places to go except the university. And that's where they go, because it's the only place where they can practice what they want. But the tacit understanding is that you keep your practice sequestered within the academy.

HG: That's why pedagogy is both exhilarating and dangerous. It's one of the few forms of cultural politics that cannot simply be consigned to academia. Its central questions of ideology and politics ask how people take up what they take up; that is, how they participate in, produce, and challenge particular ways of life. The issue is not simply how people are inserted into particular subject positions but also how they create them. To raise that question is automatically to engage the language of specificity, community, diversity, difference, and the struggle for public life.

REFERENCES

[1] Published by, respectively, Temple University Press (1981). Bergin and Garvey (1983); Bergin and Garvey (1985), Bergin and Garvey (1988); University of Minnesota Press (1988), Deakin University Press (1990); and University of Minnesota (1991).

[2] Published by, respectively, SUNY Press (1989), Bergin and Garvey (1989), and SUNY Press (1991).

[3] Published simultaneously by Basic Books (New York) and Routledge and Kegan Paul (London) in 1976.

7

Cultural Studies, Resisting Difference, and the Return of Critical Pedagogy

All those men and women in South Africa, Namibia, Zaire, Ivory Coast, El Salvador, Chile, Philippines, South Korea, Indonesia, Grenada, Fanon's 'Wretched of the Earth', who have declared loud and clear that they do not sleep to dream, 'but dream to change the world'.[1]

Introduction

American public education is in crisis. It is not an isolated crisis affecting a specific aspect of American society; it is a crisis that is implicated in and produced by a transformation in the very nature of democracy itself. This is not without a certain irony. As a number of countries in Eastern Europe move toward greater forms of democraticization, the United States presents itself as the prototype for such reforms and leads the American people to believe that democracy in the United States has reached its penultimate form. The emptiness of this type of analyses is best revealed by the failure of the American public to actively participate in the election of its own government officials, to address the growing illiteracy rates among the general population, and to challenge the increasing view that social criticism and social change are irrelevant to the meaning of American democracy. In part, this is an illiteracy built on the refusal of a large segment of the American public to "dream to change the world." But the failure of formal democracy is most evident in the refusal of the American government and general population to view public schooling as fundamental to the life of a critical democracy. At stake here is the refusal to grant public schooling a significant role in the ongoing process of educating people to be active and critical citizens capable of fighting for and reconstructing democratic public life.

The struggle over public schools cannot be separated from the social problems currently facing this society. These problems are not only political in nature but are pedagogical as well. That is, whenever power and knowledge come together, politics not only functions to position people differently with respect to the access of wealth and power, but it also provides the conditions for the production and acquisition of learning. Put another way, it offers people opportunities to take up and reflect on the conditions that shape themselves and their relationship with others. The pedagogical in this sense is about the production of meaning and the primacy of the ethical and the political as a fundamental part of this process. This means that any discussion of public schooling has to address the political, economic, and social realities that construct the contexts that shape the institution of schooling and the conditions that produce the diverse populations of students who constitute its constituencies. This perspective suggests making visible the social problems and conditions that affect those students who are at risk in our society while recognizing that such problems need to be addressed in both pedagogical and political terms, inside and outside of the schools.

The problems that are emerging do not augur well for either the fate of public schooling or the credibility of the discourse of democracy itself as it is currently practiced in the United States. For example, it has been estimated that nearly 20% of all children under the age of 18 live below the poverty line. In fact, the United States ranks first among the industrialized nations in child poverty; similarly, besides South Africa, the United States is the only industrialized country that does not provide universal health care for children and pregnant women. Moreover, economic inequality is worsening with the poor getting poorer while the rich are getting richer. In fact, the division of wealth was wider in 1988 than at any other time since 1947. As Sally Reed and Craig Sautter have pointed out, "the poorest 20% of families received less than 5% of the national income, while the wealthiest 20% received 44% . . . 1% of families own 42% of the net wealth of all U.S. families."[2] At the same time, it is important to note that neoconservative attempts to dismantle public schooling in this country during the last decade have manifested themselves not only in the call for vouchers and the development of school policy based on the market logic of choice, but also in the ruthless cutbacks that have affected those most dependent on the public schools, i.e., the poor, people of color, minorities, the working class, and other subordinated groups. The Reagan "commitment" to education and the underprivileged manifested itself shamefully in policies noted for slashing federal funds to important programs such as Aid to Families with Dependent Children, drastically reducing federal funding for low income housing and, in general, cutting over 10 million dollars from programs designed to aid the poor, homeless, and the hungry. At the same time the Reagan government invested $1.9 trillion dollars in military spending.

Within this perspective, the discourse of democracy was reduced to conflating patriotism with the cold war ideology of military preparedness, and the notion of the public good was abstracted from the principles of justice and equality in favor of an infatuation with individual achievement. Greed became respectable in the 1980s while notions of community and democratic struggle were either ignored or seen as subversive. Absent from the neoconservative public philosophy of the 1980s was any notion of democracy that took seriously the importance of developing a citizenry that could think critically, struggle against social injustices, and develop relations of community based on the principles of equality, freedom, and justice. This should not suggest that as educational and cultural workers we have nothing to do but to offer a language of critique. On the contrary, we need a new language of educational and cultural criticism that provides the basis for understanding how different social formations are structured in dominance within specific pedagogical and cultural practices. Cultural workers also need to rupture the relationship between difference and exploitation through a vision and social movement that transforms the material and ideological conditions in which difference, structured in the principles of justice, equality, and freedom, becomes central to a postmodern conception of citizenship and radical democracy.[3]

In what follows, I want to argue that cultural studies needs to be reconstructed as part of a broader discourse of difference and pedagogical transformation, one that is forged in the dialectic of critique and possibility. In effect, I want to argue that cultural studies offers a theoretical discourse for a new cultural politics of difference, pedagogy, and public life. Central to the reconstruction of cultural studies is the need to develop a discourse that accentuates the organic connections between cultural workers and everyday life on the one hand and schooling and the reconstruction of democratic public culture on the other. In effect, I develop the proposition that cultural studies provides the opportunity for educators and other cultural workers to rethink and transform how schools, teachers, and students define themselves as political subjects capable of exhibiting critical sensibilities, civic courage, and forms of solidarity rooted in a strong commitment to freedom and democracy.

Cultural Studies as Pedagogical Practice

> When I moved into internal University Teaching . . . we started teaching in ways that . . . [related] history to art and literature, including contemporary culture, and suddenly so strange was this to the Universities that they said 'My God, here is a new subject called Cultural Studies.' . . . The true position . . . was not only a matter of remedying deficit, making up for inadequate educational resources in the wider society, nor only a case of meeting new needs of the society, though those things contributed. The deepest impulse was the desire to make learning part of the process of social change itself.[4]

Raymond Williams reminds us that the relationship between cultural studies and education has a long history, one that appears to have been forgotten in the United States. More specifically, the theoretical and historical legacy of cultural studies has largely been ignored by progressive American educators. In part, this is because radical educational theory has never adequately escaped from an overly orthodox concern with the relationship between schooling and political economy and has refused to engage the complex and changing traditions that have informed the diverse formations and projects in which cultural studies has developed.[5]

While it is not my intention to reconstruct either the history of cultural studies or to present an analyses of its everchanging theoretical strengths and weaknesses, I do want to focus on some of the implications it has for providing a set of categories that deepens the radical democratic project of schooling while theoretically advancing the discourse and practice of critical pedagogy as a form of cultural politics. In what follows, I want to cast cultural studies as a political and pedagogical project that provides a convergence between a species of modernism that takes up questions of agency, voice, and possibility with those aspects of a postmodern discourse that have critically deconstructed issues of subjectivity, language, and difference. In effect, I will argue that cultural studies offers a theoretical terrain for rethinking schooling as a form of cultural politics and provides a discourse of intervention and possibility.

Cultural studies is important to critical educators because it provides the grounds for making a number of issues central to a radical theory of schooling. First, it offers the basis for creating new forms of knowledge by making language constitutive of the conditions for producing meaning as part of the knowledge/power relationship. Knowledge and power are reconceptualized in this context by reasserting not merely the indeterminacy of language but also the historical and social construction of knowledge itself. In this case, the cultural studies strategy of interrogation points to an evaluation of the disciplines within which intellectual knowledge is configured. Holding these disciplines to be constructed under historically specific circumstances leads to the discovery that as these conditions have been surpassed, the legitimacy of dominant forms of knowledge are in doubt. Therefore, efforts to preserve the distinctions between natural, social, and human sciences and between the arts can be viewed as exemplars of the politics and historicity of the academic disciplines. Rather than holding knowledge in some kind of correspondence with a self-enclosed objective reality, a critical cultural study views the production of knowledge in the context of power. The consequences of these views are: to reshape knowledge according to the strategy of transgression; to define the traditional disciplines as much by their exclusions as by their inclusions; and to reject the distinctions between high and low culture.

Of central concern is not merely how aesthetic standards emerge, but how "our interpretations of society, culture, history and our individual lives, hopes, dreams, passions and sensations, involve attempts to *confer* sense rather than to *discover* it."[6] There is more at stake here than the crisis of representation. What cultural studies makes visible is the need to underscore questions of culture, change, and language with the equally important concerns of agency and ethic. Questions of culture are deeply political and ethical and necessitate theoretical and pedagogical practices in which educators and cultural workers engage in a continual dialogue and struggle that take up the obligations of critical citizenship and the construction of public spheres that provide "the justification for a cultural pluralism, which seeks to address the needs and interests of a range of audiences . . . and be effective on a range of levels."[7] This suggests more than a politics of discourse and difference. It also points to a politics of social and cultural forms in which new possibilities open up for naming in concrete terms what struggles are worth taking up, what alliances are to be formed as a result of these struggles, and how a discourse of difference can deepen the political and pedagogical struggle for justice, equality, and freedom.

Second, by defining culture as a contested terrain, a site of struggle and transformation, cultural studies offers critical educators the opportunity for going beyond cultural analyses that romanticize everyday life or take up culture as merely the reflex of the logic of domination.[8] A more critical version of cultural studies raises questions about the relations between the margins and the center of power, especially as they are configured through and around the categories of race, class, and gender. In doing so, a critically and politically informed version of cultural studies offers educators the opportunity to challenge hegemonic ideologies, to read culture oppositionally, and to deconstruct historical knowledge as a way of re-claiming social identities that give collective voice to the struggles of subordinate groups. In this case, culture is taken up not merely as a marker for the specificity of different cultural identities. Culture also refigures itself as a political and pe-dagogical discourse for calling into question not only forms of subordination that create inequities among different groups as they live out their lives, but also as a basis for challenging those institutional and ideological boundaries that have his-torically masked their own relations of power behind complex forms of distinction and privilege. Hence, cultural studies points to the need to analyze the relationship between culture and power as historical differences that manifest themselves in historical, textual, and public struggles.

Third, cultural studies offers the opportunity to rethink the relationship be-tween the issue of difference as it is constituted within subjectivities and between social groups. This suggests understanding more clearly how questions of subjec-tivity can be taken up so as not to erase the possibility for individual and social agency. As such, subjectivities are seen as contradictory and multiple, produced rather than given, and are both taken up and received within particular social and historical circumstances. What is important to note is developing a pedagogical practice based on what Larry Grossberg calls a theory of articulation. He writes:

> A theory of articulation denies an essential human subject without giving up the active individual who is never entirely and simply 'stitched' into its place in social organizations of power. . . . There are always a multiplicity of positions, not only available but occupied, and a multiplicity of ways in which different meanings, experiences, powers, interests, and identities can be articulated together.[9]

Finally, cultural studies provides the basis for understanding pedagogy as a form of cultural production rather than as the transmission of a particular skill, body of knowledge, or set of values. In this context, critical pedagogy is understood as a cultural practice engaged in the production of knowledge, identities, and desires. As a form of cultural politics, critical pedagogy suggests inventing a new language for resituating teacher/student relations within pedagogical practices that open up rather than close down the borders of knowledge and learning. Disciplines can no longer define the boundaries of knowledge or designate the range of questions that can be asked. Similarly, critical pedagogy within the tradition of an older cultural studies ruptures the dominant notion that culture as pedagogy is about transmission and consumption. As risky as this approach is, it serves to reinvent the project and possibility of teaching and learning within a context that engages its own ideological assumptions rather than suppress them. In doing so, critical pedagogy can assert itself on the terrain of convictions through forms of ethical address and cultural work that freely engages real problems confronting everyday life. In effect, as a form of cultural production, critical pedagogy becomes a critical referent for understanding how various practices in the circuit of power inscribe institutions, texts, and lived cultures in particular forms of social and moral regulation which presuppose particular visions of the past, present and future. In what follows, I want to further develop the relationship between cultural studies and some of the issues mentioned above as part of a broader debate on language, difference, voice, and pedagogy.

Schooling and the Politics of Language

Education may well be, as of right, the instrument whereby every individual, in a society like our own, can gain access to any kind of discourse. But we all know that in its distribution, in what it permits and prevents, it follows the well-trodden battle lines of social conflict. Every educational system is a political means of maintaining or modifying the appropriation of discourse with the knowledge and powers it carries with it.[10]

There is a long tradition in the United States of viewing schools as relatively neutral institutions whose language and social relations mirror the principles of equal opportunity. For example, liberal theories of education are grounded upon the belief that students have open access to the language and knowledge that schools provide as part of their public responsibility to educate. More recently, radical educators have drawn on a number of theoretical traditions that link language and power to disprove this assumption.[11] Not only do they expose the naivete of such views by revealing the social and political constraints that operate upon language, they also provide an intricate reading of how school language functions through a web of hierarchies, prohibitions, and denials to reward some students and deny other students access to what can be both learned and spoken within the confines of dominant schooling.[12] For radical educators, schools are sites where knowledge and power enter into relations that articulate with conflicts being fought out in the wider society. Central to this thesis is the assumption that the language of schooling is implicated in forms of racism that attempt to silence the voices of subordinated groups whose primary language is not English and whose cultural capital is either marginalized or denigrated by the dominant culture of schooling.

There are three important elements in this view of language that need to be reiterated. First, language has a social foundation and must be viewed as a site of struggle implicating the production of knowledge, values, and identities. Second, as a social phenomenon, language cannot be abstracted from the forces and conflicts of social history. In other words, the historicity of the relationship between dominant and subordinate forms of language offer insights into countering the assumption that the dominant language at any given time is simply the result of a naturally given process rather than the result of specific historical struggles and conflicts. In effect, the literature on social linguistics, deconstruction, and post-structuralism provides an important lesson in refusing to analyze the language/power relationship in simply synchronic and structural terms. While radical educators are acutely concerned with taking up the ideologies that structure dominant language paradigms and the ways of life they legitimate, they do not abstract this type of inquiry from particular forms of historical and social analyses. That is, rather than developing an analysis that is simply concerned with the codes, classifications, orderings, and distribution of discourse, they also attend to the historical contexts and conflicts that are central to the purpose and meaning of discourse.[13] In effect, this work builds upon Bakhtin's insight that specific languages cannot be uprooted from the historical struggles and conflicts that make them heteroglossic rather than unitary. Bakhtin is clear on this issue and argues that:

> at any given moment of its historical existence, language is heteroglot from top to bottom: it represents the coexistence of socio-ideological contradictions between the present and the past, between differing epochs of the past, between different socio-ideological groups in the present, between tendencies, schools, circles, and so forth, all given a bodily form. These 'languages' of heteroglossia intersect each other in a variety of ways, forming new socially typifying 'languages.'[14]

More recent analyses have argued that any claim to a totalizing and unitary language is the result of forms of social, moral, and political regulation that attempt to erase their own histories.[15] At stake here is the need to make clear that language is always implicated in power relationships expressed, in part, through particular historical struggles over how established institutions such as education, law, medicine, social welfare, and the mass media produce, support, and legitimate particular ways of life that characterize a society at a given time in history. Language makes possible both the subject positions that people use to negotiate their sense of self and the ideologies and social practices that give meaning and legitimacy to institutions that form the basis of a given society.

Third, radical educators more recently have not been content to simply situate the analysis of language in the discourse of domination and subjugation. They are also concerned with developing a "language of possibility."[16] In this case, the emphasis is on perceiving language as both an oppositional force and an affirmative force. That is, discursive practices are viewed as deconstructing and reclaiming not only new forms of knowledge but also providing new ways of reading history through the reconstruction of suppressed memories that offer identities that challenge and contest the very conditions through which history, desire, voice, and place are experienced and lived. It is within this context that radical education offers educators a critical approach to pedagogy forged in the discourse of difference and voice.

The Politics of Voice and Difference

So, if you want to really hurt me, talk badly about my language. Ethnic identity is twin skin to linguistic identity—I am my language. Until I can accept as legitimate Chicano Texas Spanish, Tex-Mex and all the other languages I speak, I cannot accept the legitimacy of myself . . . and as long as I have to accommodate . . . English speakers rather than having them accommodate me, my tongue will be illegitimate. I will no longer be made to feel ashamed of existing. I will have my voice: Indian, Spanish, White. I will have my serpent's tongue—my women's voice, my sexual voice, my poet's voice. I will overcome the tradition of silence.[17]

Difference must be not merely tolerated, but seen as a fund of necessary polarities between which our creativity can spark like a dialectic. Only then does the necessity for interdependency become unthreatening. . . . Within the interdependence of mutual (nondominant) differences lies that security, which enables us to descend into the chaos of knowledge and return with true visions of our future, along with the concomitant power to effect those changes, which can bring that future into being. . . . As women, we have been taught either to ignore our differences, or to view them as causes for separation and suspicion rather than as forces for change. Without community there is no liberation, only the most vulnerable and temporary armistice between an individual and her oppression. But community must not mean a shedding of our differences, nor the pathetic pretense that these differences do not exist.[18]

The discourse of difference as used by both Gloria Anzaludua and Audre Lorde provides a glimpse of the multiple and shifting ground that the term suggests. Defined in opposition to hegemonic codes of culture, subjectivity, and history, a number of social theorists have begun recently to use a discourse of difference to challenge some of the most fundamental dominant assertions that characterize mainstream social science. As I have pointed out in other chapters, theorists writing in anthropology, feminism, liberation theology, critical education, literary theory, and a host of other areas firmly reject mainstream assumptions regarding culture as a field of shared experiences defined in Western ethnocentric terms; in addition, critical theorists have rejected the mainstream humanist assumption that the individual is both the source of all human action and the most important unit of social analysis; moreover, many critical theorists reject the view that objectivity and consensus are the privileged and innocent concerns of dominant social science research. Reading in opposition to these assumptions, the notion of difference has played an important role in making visible how power is inscribed differently in and between zones of culture, how cultural borderlands raise important questions regarding relations of inequality, struggle, and history, and how differences are expressed in multiple and contradictory ways within individuals and between different groups.

While theories of difference have made important contributions to a discourse of progressive politics and pedagogy, they have also exhibited tendencies that have been theoretically flawed and politically regressive. In the first instance, the most important insights have emerged primarily from feminist women of color. These include: "the recognition of a self that is multiplicitous, not unitary; the recognition that differences are always relational rather than inherent; and the recognition that wholeness and commonality are acts of will and creativity, rather than passive discovery."[19] In the second instance, the discourse of difference has contributed to paralyzing forms of essentialism, ahistoricism, and a politics of separatism. In what follows, I first want to explore the dialectical nature of the relationship between difference and voice that informs a discourse of critical pedagogy. I conclude by pointing to some of the broader implications that a discourse of difference and voice might have for what I call a liberatory border pedagogy.

It is important for critical educators to take up culture as a vital source for developing a politics of identity, community, and pedagogy. In this perspective, culture is not seen as monolithic or unchanging, but as a site of multiple and heterogeneous borders where different histories, languages, experiences, and voices intermingle amidst diverse relations of power and privilege. Within this pedagogical cultural borderland known as school, subordinated cultures push against and permeate the alleged unproblematic and homogeneous borders of dominant cultural forms and practices. It is important to note that critical educators cannot be content to merely map how ideologies are inscribed in the various relations of schooling, whether they be the curriculum, forms of school organization, or in teacher-student relations. While these should be important concerns for critical educators, a more viable critical pedagogy needs to go beyond them by analyzing how ideologies are actually taken up in the voices and lived experiences of students as they give meaning to the dreams, desires, and subject positions that they inhabit. In this sense, radical educators need to provide the conditions for students to speak so that their narratives can be affirmed and engaged along with the consistencies and contradictions that characterize such experiences. More specifically, the issue of student experiences has to be analyzed as part of a broader politics of voice and difference.

As bell hooks points out, coming to voice means "moving from silence into speech as a revolutionary gesture . . . the idea of finding one's voice or having a voice assumes a primacy in talk discourse, writing, and action. . . . Only as subjects can we speak. As objects, we remain voiceless—our beings defined and interpreted by others. . . . Awareness of the need to speak, to give voice to the varied dimensions of our lives, is one way [to begin] the process of education for critical consciousness."[20] This suggests that educators need to approach learning not merely as the acquisition of knowledge but as the production of cultural practices that offer students a sense of identity, place, and hope. To speak of voice is to address the wider issue of how people either become agents in the process of making history or function as subjects under the weight of oppression and exploitation within the various linguistic and institutional boundaries that produce dominant and subordinate cultures in any given society. In this case, voice provides a critical referent for analyzing how students are made voiceless in particular settings by not being allowed to speak, or how students silence themselves out of either fear or ignorance regarding the strength and possibilities that exist in the multiple languages and experience that connect them to a sense of agency and self-formation. At the same time, voices forged in opposition and struggle provide the crucial conditions by which subordinated individuals and groups can reclaim their own memories, stories, and histories as part of an ongoing collective struggle to challenge those power structures that attempt to silence them.

By being able to listen critically to the voices of their students, teachers become border-crossers through their ability to not only make different narratives available to themselves and other students but also by legitimating difference as a basic condition for understanding the limits of one's own voice. By viewing schooling as a form of cultural politics, radical educators can bring the concepts of culture, voice, and difference together to create a borderland where multiple subjectivities and identities exist as part of a pedagogical practice that provides the potential to expand the politics of democratic community and solidarity. Critical pedagogy serves to make visible those marginal cultures that have been traditionally suppressed in American schooling. Moreover, it provides students with a range of identities and human possibilities that emerge among, within, and between different zones of culture. Of course, educators cannot approach this task by merely giving equal weight to all zones of cultural difference; on the contrary, they must link the creation, sustenance, and formation of cultural difference as a fundamental part of the discourse of inequality, power, struggle, and possibility. Difference is not about merely registering or asserting spatial, racial, ethnic, or cultural differences but about historical differences that manifest themselves in public and pedagogical struggles. The possibilities for making difference and voice a central aspect of critical pedagogy can be further elaborated around a number of concerns that are integral to a politics of border pedagogy.

Resisting Difference: Toward a Liberatory Theory of Border Pedagogy

Difference is not difference to some ears, but awkwardness or incompleteness. Aphasia. Unable or unwilling? Many have come to tolerate this dissimilarity and have decided to suspend their judgments (only) whenever the other is concerned.

Such an attitude is a step forward. . . . But it is a very small step indeed, since it serves as an excuse for their complacent ignorance and their reluctance to involve themselves in the issue. You who understand the dehumanization of forced removal, relocation, reeducation, redefinition, and the humiliation of having to falsify your own reality, your voice-you know. And often cannot *say* it. You try and keep on trying to unsay it, for if you don't, they will not fail to fill in the blanks on your behalf, and you will be said.[21]

To take up the issue of difference is to recognize that it cannot be analyzed unproblematically. In effect, the concept has to be used to resist those aspects of its ideological legacy used in the service of exploitation and subordination as well as to develop a critical reference for engaging the limits and strengths of difference as a central aspect of a critical theory of education. In what follows, I want to look briefly at how the concept of difference has been used by conservatives, liberals, and radicals in ways that either produce relations of subordination or undermine its possibility for developing a radical politics of democracy.

Conservatives have often used the term difference in a variety of ways to justify relations of racism, patriarchy, and class exploitation by associating difference with the notion of deviance while simultaneously justifying such assumptions through an appeal to science, biology, nature, or culture. In many instances, difference functions as a marker of power to name, label, and exclude particular groups while simultaneously being legitimated within a reactionary discourse and politics of public life, i.e., nationalism, patriotism, and "democracy."[22] What needs to be noted here is that there is more at stake than the production of particular ideologies based on negative definitions of identity. When defined and used in the interests of inequality and repression, difference is "enacted in violence against its own citizens as much as it is against foreigners."[23]

Liberals generally take up a dual approach to the issue of difference. This can be illuminated around the issue of race. On the one hand, liberals embrace the issue of difference through a notion of cultural diversity in which it is argued that race is simply one more form of cultural difference among many that make up the population of a country like the United States. The problem with this approach is that "by denying both the centrality and uniqueness of race as a principle of socio-economic organization, it redefines difference in a way that denies the history of racism in the United States and, thus, denies white responsibility for the present and past oppression and exploitation of people of color."[24] In this view, the systems of inequalities, subordination, and terror that inform the dominant culture's structuring of difference around issues of race, gender, and class are simply mapped out of existence. On the other hand, liberals often attempt to both appropriate and dissolve cultural differences into the melting pot theory of culture. The history, language, experiences, and narratives of the Other are relegated to invisible zones of culture, borderlands where the dominant culture refuses to hear the voice of the Other while celebrating a "white, male, middle-class, European, heterosexuality [as] the standard of and the criteria for rationality and morality."[25]

Under the rubric of equality and freedom, the liberal version of assimilation wages "war" against particularity, lived differences, and imagined futures that challenge culture as unitary, sacred, and unchanging and the identity, as unified, static, and natural.

On the other hand, radical educational theorists have taken up the issue of difference around two basic considerations. First, difference has been elaborated as part of an attempt to understand subjectivity as fractured and multiple rather than as unified and static.[26] Central to this approach is the notion that subjectivities and identities are constructed in multilayered and contradictory ways. Identity is seen not only as a historical and social construction, but also as part of a continual process of transformation and change. This position is of enormous significance for undermining the humanist notion of the subject as both unified and the determinate source of human will and action. As significant as this position is, it is fraught with some theoretical problems.

By arguing that human subjectivities are constructed in language through the production and availability of diverse subject positions, many radical theorists have developed a theory of subjectivity that erases any viable notion of human agency. In effect, subjectivity becomes an effect of language, and human agency disappears into the discredited terrain of humanist will. Lost here is any understanding of how agency works within the interface of subject positions made available by a society and the weight of choices constructed out of specific desires, forms of self-reflection, and concrete social practices. There is little sense of how people actually take up particular subject positions, what individuals and groups are privileged in having access to particular positions, and what the conditions are that make it impossible for some groups to take up, live, and speak particular discourses.[27]

The second approach to difference that radical educational theorists have taken up centers on the differences between groups. A number of theorists, particularly feminists, have developed what can be called a discourse of identity politics.[28] In the most general sense, identity politics refers to "the tendency to base one's politics on a sense of personal identity—as gay, as Jewish, as Black, as female."[29] This politics of identity celebrates differences as they are constructed around the categories of race, class, gender, and sexual preference. Again, I will first point to the limitations that have emerged around this position and then later highlight the importance of identity politics within a broader notion of difference, politics, and culture.

Initially, identity politics offered a powerful challenge to the hegemonic notion that Eurocentric culture is superior to other cultures and traditions by offering political and cultural vocabularies to subordinated groups by which they could reconstruct their own histories and give voice to their individual and collective identities. This was especially true for the early stages of the feminist movement when the slogan, "the personal is the political," gave rise to the assumption that lived experience offered women the opportunity to insert themselves back into history and everyday life by naming the injustices they had suffered within a society constructed in patriarchal social relations. A number of problems emerged from the conception of difference that informed this view of identity politics. A number of theorists argued that there was a direct correlation between one's social location and one's political position. At stake here was the assumption that one's identity was rooted in a particular set of experiences that led rather unproblematically to a particular form of politics. This position is questionable on a number of grounds. To accept the authority of experience uncritically is to forget that identity itself is complex, contradictory, and shifting and does not unproblematically reveal itself in a specific politics. Second, the emphasis on the personal as a fundamental aspect of the political often results in highlighting the personal through a form of confessional politics that all but forgets how the political is constituted in social and cultural forms outside of one's own experiences. Bell hooks puts the issue well.

> While stating "the personal is the political" did highlight feminist concern with the self, it did not insist on a connection between politicization and the transformation of consciousness. It spoke most immediately to the concerns women had about self and identity. . . . Feminist focus on self was then easily linked not to a process of radical politicization, but to a process of depoliticization. Popularly, the important quest was not to radically change our relationship to self and identity, to educate for critical consciousness, to become politically engaged and committed, but to explore one's identity, to affirm and assert the primacy of the self as it already existed."[30]

Another problem with the radical notion of difference is that it sometimes produces a politics of assertion that is both essentialist and separatist. By ignoring the notion that "the politics of any social position is not guaranteed in advance,"[31] identity politics often reproduced the very problems it thought it was attacking. As I have pointed out in another chapter, the essentialism at work in particular constructions of feminism has been made clear by Audre Lorde, Angela Harris, bell hooks, and others who have criticized white women not only for privileging patriarchy over issues of race, class, sexual preference, and other forms of oppression, but also for defining patriarchy and the construction of women's experiences in terms that excluded the particular narratives and stories of women of color.[32] In this case, racial and class differences among women are ignored in favor of an essentializing notion of voice that romanticizes and valorizes the unitary experience of white, middle-class women who assumed the position of being able to speak for all women. Moreover, forms of identity politics that forgo the potential for creating alliances among different subordinated groups run the risk of reproducing a series of hierarchies of identities and experiences, which serves to privilege their own form of oppression and struggle. All to often this position results in totalizing narratives that fail to recognize the limits of their own discourse in explaining the complexity of social life and the power such a discourse wields in silencing those who are not considered part of the insider group. June Jordan captures this sentiment well in her comment that "Traditional calls to 'unity' on the base of only one of these factors—race or class or gender—will fail, finally, and again and again,

I believe, because no simple one of these components provides for a valid fathoming of the complete individual."[33]

Far from suggesting that critical educators should dispense with either the notion of difference or an identity politics, I believe that we need to learn from the theoretical shortcomings analyzed above and begin to rethink the relationship among difference, voice, and politics. What does this suggest for a liberatory theory of border pedagogy? I want to end by pointing briefly to a number of suggestions.

First, the notion of difference must be seen in relational terms that link it to a broader politics that deepens the possibility for reconstructing democracy and schools as democratic public spheres. This means organizing schools and pedagogy around a sense of purpose and meaning that makes difference central to a critical notion of citizenship and democratic public life. Rather than merely celebrating specific forms of difference, a politics of difference must provide the basis for extending the struggle for equality and justice to broader spheres of everyday life. This suggests that the discourse of difference and voice be elaborated within, rather than against, a politics of solidarity. By refusing to create a hierarchy of struggles, it becomes possible for critical educators to take up notions of political community in which particularity, voice, and difference provide the foundation for democracy. Chantal Mouffe persuasively argues that this view of difference is central to developing a postmodern notion of citizenship.

> An adequate conception of citizenship today should be "postmodern" if we understand by that the need to acknowledge the particular, the heterogeneous, and the multiple. . . . Only a pluralistic conception of citizenship can accommodate the specificity and multiplicity of democratic demands and provide a pole of identification for a wide range of democratic forces. The political community has to be viewed, then, as a diverse collection of communities, as a forum for creating unity without denying specificity."[34]

Second, critical educators must provide the conditions for students to engage in cultural remapping as a form of resistance. That is, students should be given the opportunity to engage in systematic analyses of the ways in which the dominant culture creates borders saturated in terror, inequality, and forced exclusions. Similarly, students should be allowed to rewrite difference through the process of crossing over into cultural borders that offer narratives, languages, and experiences that provide a resource for rethinking the relationship between the center and margins of power as well as between themselves and others. In part, this means giving voice to those who have been normally excluded and silenced. It means creating a politics of remembrance in which different stories and narratives are heard and taken up as lived experiences. Most importantly, it means constructing new pedagogical borders where difference becomes the intersection of new forms of culture and identity.

Third, the concept of border pedagogy suggests not simply opening diverse cultural histories and spaces to students, but also understanding how fragile identity is as it moves into borderlands crisscrossed with a variety of languages, experiences, and voices. There are no unified subjects here, only students whose voices and experiences intermingle with the weight of particular histories that will not fit into the master narrative of a monolithic culture. Such borderlands should be seen as sites for both critical analysis and as a potential source of experimentation, creativity, and possibility. This is not a call to romanticize such voices. It is instead a suggestion that educators construct pedagogical practices in which the ideologies that inform student experiences be both heard and interrogated.[35] There is more at risk here than giving dominant and subordinated subjects the right to speak or allowing the narratives of excluded differences to be heard. There is also the issue of making visible those historical, ideological, and institutional mechanisms that have both forced and benefited from such exclusions. It is here that the borderland between school and the larger society meet, where the relevancies between teachers and cultural workers come into play, and where schooling is understood within the larger domain of cultural politics. More specifically, the pedagogical borderlands where blacks, whites, latinos, and others meet demonstrate the importance of a multicentric perspective that allows teachers, cultural workers, and students to not only recognize the multilayered and contradictory ideologies that construct their own identities but to also analyze how the differences within and between various groups can expand the potential of human life and democratic possibilities.

Fourth, the notion of border pedagogy needs to highlight the issue of power in a dual sense. First power has to be made central to understanding the effects of difference from the perspective of historically and socially constructed forms of domination. Second, teachers need to understand more clearly how to link power and authority in order to develop a pedagogical basis for reading differences critically. Difference cannot be merely experienced or asserted by students. It must also be read critically by teachers who, while not being able to speak as or for those not who occupy a different set of lived experiences, can make progressive use of their authority by addressing difference as a historical and social construction in which all knowledges are not equally implicated in relations of power. Teacher authority can be used to provide the conditions for students to engage difference not as the proliferation of equal discourses grounded in distinct experiences, but as contingent and relational constructions that produce social forms and identities that must be made problematic and subject to historical and textual analyses. Teachers and cultural workers must take responsibility, as Stuart Hall points out, for the knowledge they organize, produce, mediate, and translate into the practice of culture.[36]

At the same time, it is important for teachers and cultural workers to construct pedagogical practices that neither position students defensively nor allow students to speak simply by asserting their voices and experiences. A pedagogy of affirmation is no excuse for refusing students the obligation to interrogate the claims or consequences their assertions have for the social relationships they legitimate. Larry Grossberg is correct in arguing that teachers who refuse to assert their authority or take up the issue of political responsibility as social critics and committed intellectuals often end up "erasing themselves in favor of the uncritical reproduction of the audience [students]."[37]

Fifth, border pedagogy also points to the importance of offering students the opportunity to engage the multiple references and codes that position them within various structures of meaning and practice. In part, this means educating students to become media literate in a world of changing representations. It also means teaching students to critically read not only how cultural texts and images are regulated by various discursive codes but also how such texts express and represent different ideological interests and how they might be taken up differently by students. More generally, border pedagogy points to the need to establish conditions of learning that define literacy inside rather than outside of the categories of power and authority. This suggests providing students with the opportunities to read texts as social and historical constructions, to engage texts in terms of their presences and absences, and to read texts oppositionally. This means teaching students to resist particular readings while simultaneously learning how to write their own narratives. At issue here is not merely the need for students to develop a healthy skepticism towards all discourses of authority, but also to recognize how authority and power can be transformed in the interest of creating a democratic society.

Finally, border pedagogy points to the need for educators to rethink the syntax of learning and behavior outside of the geography of rationality and reason. For example, racist, sexist, and class discriminatory narratives cannot be dealt with in a purely limited, analytical way. As a form of cultural politics, border pedagogy must engage how and why students make particular ideological and affective investments in these narratives. But this should not suggest that educators merely expand their theoretical and pedagogical understanding of how meaning and pleasure interact to produce particular forms of investment and student experience; rather, it points to a pedagogical practice that takes seriously how ideologies are lived, experienced, and felt at the level of everyday life as a basis for student experience and knowledge.[38] It means restructuring the curriculum so as to redefine the everyday as an important resource for linking schools to the traditions, communities, and histories that provide students with a sense of voice and relationship to others.

All of these concerns are relevant to the discourses of cultural studies. While it is true that cultural studies cannot be characterized by a particular ideology or position, it does offer a terrain through which cultural borders can be refigured, new social relations constructed, and the role of teachers and cultural workers as engaged critics rethought within the parameters of a politics of resistance and possibility. It is within this shifting and radical terrain that schooling as a form of cultural politics can be reconstructed as part of discourse of opposition and hope.

REFERENCES

[1] Ngugi Wa Thiong'o, *Decolonizing the Mind: The Politics of Language in African Literature* (Portsmouth, NH: Heinemann, 1986), 3.

[2] Sally Reed and R. Craig Sautter, "Children of Poverty: The Status of 12 Million Young Americans," *Phi Delta Kappan* (June 1990), K5.

[3] The issue here is to develop a politics of difference that would allow various cultural workers to rethink and deepen the purpose and meaning of a radical democracy. Chantal Mouffe is useful on this issue.

> If the task of radical democracy is indeed to deepen the democratic revolution and to link together diverse democratic struggles, such a task requires the creation of new subject-positions that would allow the common articulation, for example, of antiracism, antisexism, and anticapitalism. These struggles do not spontaneously converge, and in order to establish democratic equivalences, a new "common sense" is necessary, which would transform the identity of different groups so that the demands of each group could be articulated with those of others according to the principle of democratic equivalence. For it is not a matter of establishing a mere alliance between given interests but of actually modifying the very identity of these forces. In order that the defense of workers' interests is not pursued at the cost of the rights of women, immigrants, or consumers, it is necessary to establish an equivalence between these different struggles. It is only under these circumstances that struggles against power becomes truly democratic.

In Chantal Mouffe, "Radical Democracy: Modern or Postmodern," in Andrew Ross, ed., *Universal Abandon: The Politics of Postmodern* (Minneapolis: University of Minnesota Press, 1988), 42.

[4] Raymond Williams, "Adult Education and Social Change," *What I Came to Say* (London: Hutchinson-Radus, 1989), 162, 158.

[5] Some of the better commentaries on both the history and central assumptions that informed cultural studies, at least in its British versions, since the 'fifties can be found in Lawrence Grossberg, "The Formations of Cultural Studies: An American in Birmingham," *Strategies* 2 (1989), 114–49; Lawrence Grossberg, *It's a Sin* (Sydney, Australia: Power Publications, 1988); Richard Johnson, "The Story So Far: and Further Transformations?" in David Punter, ed., *Introduction to Cultural Studies*, (New York: Longman, 1986), 277–313, Stuart Hall, "Cultural Studies: Two Paradigms," *Media, Culture and Society* 2 (1980), 57–82; Meachan Morris, "Banality in Cultural Studies," *Discourse* 10:2 (1988), 3–29.

[6] Iain Chambers, *Border Dialogues: Journeys in Postmodernity* (New York: Routledge, 1990), 11.

[7] Rita Felski, "Feminism, Realism, and the Avant-Garde," in Andrew Milner, Philip Thomson, and Chris Worth, eds., *Postmodern Conditions* (New York: Berg Publishers, 1990), 76, 75.

[8] For an excellent analyses of some of the theoretical pitfalls various forms of cultural studies have fallen into, see Meaghan Morris, "Banality in Cultural Studies," *Discourse*, 10:2 (1988), 3–29; Cary Nelson, "Always Already Cultural Studies: Two Conferences and a Manifesto," *The Journal of the Midwest Modern Language Association* 24:1 (1991), 24–38.

[9] Lawrence Grossberg, "The Formations of Cultural Studies," 137.

[10] Michel Foucault, "The Discourse on Language," *The Archaeology of Knowledge* (London: Tavistock, 1972), 227.

[11] For a summary of the various discourses now being taken up by radical educators, see Diane Macdonell, *Theories of Discourse*, (London: Blackwell, 1986).

[12] I take this issue up in Henry A. Giroux, *Schooling and the Struggle for Public Life*, (Minneapolis: University of Minnesota Press, 1988).

[13] See, for example, Noelle Bisseret, *Education, Class Language, and Ideology*, (London: Routledge & Kegan Paul, 1979); Cleo Cherryholmes, *Power and Criticism: Poststructural Investigations in Education*, (New York: Teachers College Press, 1988); Tony Crowley, *Standard English and the Politics of Language*, (Urbana: University of Illinois Press, 1989).

[14] M.M. Bakhtin, *The Dialogic Imagination* (Austin: University of Texas Press, 1981), 291.

[15] Stanley Aronowitz and Henry A. Giroux, *Postmodern Education: Politics, Culture and Social Criticism*, (Minneapolis: University of Minnesota Press, 1991).

[16] Henry A. Giroux, *Teachers as Intellectuals* (New York: Bergin and Garvey Press, 1988).

[17] Gloria Anzaldua, *Borderlands/La Frontera: The New Mestiza* (San Francisco: Spinsters/ Auntlute Press, 1987), 59.

[18] Audre Lorde, *Sister Outsider* (Freedom, CA.: The Crossing Press, 1984), 111–12.

[19] Angela P. Harris, "Race and Essentialism in Feminist Legal Theory," *Stanford Law Review* 42 (February 1990), 581. For an analysis of women of color who have contributed significantly to a theory of difference, see Kimberle Crenshaw, "Demarginalizing the Intersection of Race and Sex: A Black Feminist Critique of Antidiscrimination Doctrine, Feminist Theory and Antiracist Politics," *The University of Chicago Legal Forum* (1989), 139–67; Regina Austin, "Sapphire Bound!" *Wisconsin Law Review* (Fall 1989), 539–78. I am deeply indebted to Linda Brodkey for bringing this literature to my attention. Also see Linda Brodkey's excellent piece, "Toward a Feminist Rhetoric of Difference," (University of Texas at Austin, 1990).

[20] bell hooks, *Talking Back* (Boston: South End Press, 1989), 12.

[21] Trinh T. Minh-ha, *Women, native, Other* (Bloomington: Indiana University Press, 1989), 80.

[22] Of course, we have a vast literature of anticolonialism that points this out very clearly. For example, see Chapter 2 in this book and Frantz Fanon, *Black Skin, White Masks* (New York: Grove Weidenfeld, 1967); Albert Memmi, *The Colonizer and the Colonized* (Boston: Beacon Press, 1965). For a particularly powerful example of the use of language in the production of difference as a marker of colonialism, see Wa Thiong'o, *Decolonizing the Mind*. See also Edward W. Said, *Orientalism* (New York: Vantage Books, 1979). Of course, most of the anti-colonial literature constructs difference through the modernist dichotomies of colonized versus colonizer, enemy versus foe. More recently, especially in the racist discourse being developed by the French Right, the concept of difference is being affirmed through themes that appear to eschew racism (the right to be different), while in actuality are used to reproduce its effects. On this issue, see Alain Policar, "Racism and Its Mirror Images," *Telos*, No. 83 (Spring 1990), 99–108; Pierre-Andre Taguieff, "The New Cultural Racism in France," *Telos*, No. 83 (Spring 1990), 109–22.

[23] Sean Cubitt, "Introduction: Over the Borderlines," *Screen* 30:4 (Autumn 1989), 5.

[24] Paula Rothenberg, "The Construction, Deconstruction, and Reconstruction of Difference," *Hypatia* 5:1 (Spring 1990), 47.

[25] Ibid., 43.

[26] Julian Henriques, Wendy Hollway, Cathy Urwin, Couze Venn, and Valerie Walkerdine, *Changing the Subject: Psychology, Social Regulation, and Subjectivity* (New York: Methuen, 1984).

[27] Lawrence Grossberg, "The Context of Audiences and the Politics of Difference," *Australian Journal of Communication*, No. 16 (December 1989), 29.

[28] For some insightful comments on this issue, see hooks, *Talking Back*; Brodkey, "Toward a Feminist Rhetoric of Difference"; Regina Austin, "Sapphire Bound!," *Wisconsin Law Review* (Fall 1989), 539–78; Henry A. Giroux, "Rethinking the Boundaries of Educational Discourse: Modernism, Postmodernism, and Feminism," *College Literature* (in press).

[29] Diana Fuss, "Lesbian and Gay Theory: The Question of Identity Politics," in D. Fuss, *Essentially Speaking: Feminism, Nature, and Difference* (New York: Routledge, 1989), 97.

[30] hooks, *Talking Back*, 106.

[31] Lawrence Grossberg, "The Context of Audience and the Politics of Difference," 28.

[32] In this book, see Chapter 5, "Redefining the Boundaries of Race and Ethnicity."

[33] June Jordan, "Waiting for a Taxi," *The Progressive* (June 1989), 16. Of course, the call to move beyond a politics of difference and identity that reproduces totalizing narratives should not be mistaken as a criticism of all theorists and social movements that take up particular issues in order to promote specific struggles against racism, sexism, or class exploitation. Such a criticism is warranted only when these issues are developed as part of a politics of assertion and separatism that functions to silence other progressive voices and oppressed groups. In this case, identity politics and the discourse of difference collapse into a hegemonic narrative. The complexity of

the issues surrounding the relationship between a politics of location, difference, and essentialism are taken up in Teresa de Lauretis, "The Essence of the Triangle or, Taking the Risk of Essentialism Seriously: Feminist Theory in Italy, the U.S., and Britain." *Difference* 1:1 (Summer 1989), 3–37; Cornel West, "The New Cultural Politics of Difference," *October*, No. 53 (Summer 1990), 93–109; Rita Felski, "Feminism, Postmodernism, and the Critique of Modernity," *Cultural Critique* No. 13 (Fall 1989), 33–56.

[34] Chantal Mouffe, "The Civics Lesson," *The New Statesman and Society* (October 7, 1988), 30.

[35] Renato Rosaldo, *Culture and Truth* (Boston: Beacon Press, 1989).

[36] Stuart Hall, "The Emergence of Cultural Studies and the Crisis of the Humanities," *October* 53 (Summer 1990), 11–23.

[37] Lawrence Grossberg, "The Context of Audiences and the Politics of Difference," 30.

[38] Lawrence Grossberg, "Teaching the Popular," Cary Nelson, ed., *Theory in the Classroom* (Urbana: University of Illinois Press, 1986), 177–200; Henry A. Giroux and Roger Simon, eds., *Popular Culture, Schooling and Everyday Life* (New York: Bergin and Garvey Press, 1989).

8

Popular Culture as a Pedagogy of Pleasure and Meaning: Decolonizing the Body*

In the past decade, radical educators have begun to take seriously the issue of student experience as a central component in developing a theory of schooling and cultural politics.[1] The ways in which student experience is produced, organized, and legitimated in schools has become an increasingly important theoretical consideration for understanding how schools function to produce and authorize particular forms of meaning and to implement teaching practices consistent with the ideological principles of the dominant society. Rather than focusing exclusively on how schools reproduce the dominant social order through forms of social and cultural reproduction or how students contest the dominant logic through various forms of resistance, radical educators have attempted more recently to analyze the terrain of schooling as a struggle over particular ways of life. In this view the process of being schooled cannot be fully conceptualized within the limiting parameters of the reproduction/resistance model. Instead, being schooled is analyzed as part of a complex and often contradictory set of ideological and material processes through which the transformation of experience takes place. In short, schooling is understood as part of the production and legitimation of social forms and subjectivities as they are organized within relations of power and meaning that either enable or limit human capacities for self and social empowerment.[2]

While the theoretical service that this position has provided cannot be overstated, radical educational theorists have nonetheless almost ignored the importance of popular culture both for developing a more critical understanding of student

---

* Roger I. Simon co-author.

experience and for posing the problem of pedagogy in a critical and theoretically expanded fashion. The irony of this position is that while radical educators have argued for the importance of student experience as a central component for developing a critical pedagogy, they have generally failed to consider how such experience is shaped by the terrain of popular culture. Similarly, they have been reluctant to raise the question of why popular culture has not been a serious object of study either in the school curriculum or in the curriculum reforms put forth by critically minded liberal educators. This lacunae can be partly explained by the fact that radical educators often legitimate in their work a theory of pedagogy in which the ideological correctness of one's political position appears to be the primary determining factor in assessing the production of knowledge and exchange that occurs between teachers and students. Guided by a concern with producing knowledge that is ideologically correct, radical theorists have revealed little or no understanding of how a teacher can be both politically correct and pedagogically wrong. Nor can there be found any concerted attempts by radical theorists to analyze how relations of pedagogy and relations of power are inextricably tied not only to what people know but also to how they come to know in a particular way within the constraints of specific social forms.[3]

We want to argue in this chapter that the lack of an adequate conception of critical pedagogical practice is in part responsible for the absence of an adequate politics of popular culture. Within critical educational theories, the issue of pedagogy is often treated in one of two ways: (1) as a method whose status is defined by its functional relation to particular forms of knowledge or (2) as a process of ideological deconstruction of a text. In the first approach, close attention is given to the knowledge chosen for use in a particular class. Often the ways in which students actually engage such knowledge is taken for granted. It is assumed that if one has access to an ideologically correct comprehension of that which is to be understood, the only serious question that needs to be raised about pedagogy is one of procedural technique; that is, should one use a seminar, lecture, or some other teaching style?[4] In the second approach, pedagogy is reduced to a concern with and analysis of the political interests that structure particular forms of knowledge, ways of knowing, and methods of teaching. For example, specific styles of teaching might be analyzed according to whether or not they embody sexist, racist, and class-specific interests, serve to silence students, or promote practices that deskill and disempower teachers.[5] In both approaches, what is often ignored is the notion of pedagogy as a form of cultural production and exchange that addresses how knowledge is produced, mediated, refused, and represented within relations of power both in and outside of schooling.

In our view, the issue of critical pedagogy demands an attentiveness to how students actively construct the categories of meaning that prefigure how they produce and respond to classroom knowledge. By ignoring the cultural and social forms that are both authorized by youth and simultaneously serve to empower or disempower them, educators run the risk of complicity in silencing and negating their students. This is unwittingly accomplished by educators' refusing to recognize the importance of those sites and social practices outside of schools that actively shape student experiences and through which students often define and construct their sense of identity, politics, and culture. The issue at stake is not one of relevance but of empowerment. We are not concerned with simply motivating students to learn, but rather with establishing the conditions of learning that enable students to locate themselves in history and to interrogate the adequacy of that location as both a pedagogical and political question.[6]

Educators who refuse to acknowledge popular culture as a significant basis of knowledge often devalue students by refusing to work with the knowledge that students actually have. In doing so, these educators eliminate the possibility of developing a pedagogy that links school knowledge with the differing subject relations that help to constitute students' everyday lives. A more critical pedagogy demands that pedagogical relations be seen as relations of power structured primarily through dominant but always negotiated and contested forms of consent.

We wish to stress that the basis for a critical pedagogy cannot be developed merely around the inclusion of particular forms of knowledge that have been suppressed or ignored by the dominant culture, nor can it only center on providing students with more empowering interpretations of the social and material world. Such a pedagogy must be attentive to ways in which students make both affective and semantic investments as part of their attempts to regulate and give meaning to their lives.[7] This is an important insight that both problematizes and provides a corrective to the traditional ways in which radical educators have explained how dominant meanings and values work as part of a wider ideology to position, address, and limit the ways in which students view both themselves and their relationships to the larger society. The value of including popular culture in the development of a critical pedagogy is that it provides the opportunity to further our understanding of how students make investments in particular social forms and practices. In other words, the study of popular culture offers the possibility of understanding how a politics of pleasure serves to address students in a way that shapes and sometimes secures the often contradictory relations students have to both schooling and the politics of everyday life. If one of the central concerns of a critical pedagogy is understanding how student identities, cultures, and experiences provide the basis for learning, we need to grasp the totality of elements that organize such subjectivities.

In this chapter we shall particularly emphasize that while the production of meaning provides one important element in the production of subjectivity, it is not enough. The production of meaning is also tied to emotional investments and the production of pleasure. In our view, the production of meaning and the production of pleasure are mutually constitutive of who students are, the view they have of themselves, and how they construct a particular version of their future. In what follows, we first want to argue that critical educators need to retheorize the importance of popular culture as a central category for both understanding and developing a theory and practice of critical pedagogy. In developing this position, we first want to examine some conservative and radical views of popular culture and then analyze the pedagogical practices implicit in these positions. Second, we will attempt to develop the basic elements that constitute a theory of popular culture, one that would support a critical pedagogical practice. Third, we will analyze a particular Hollywood film as a popular form, treating the film as an exemplary text in order to demonstrate how the formation of identities takes place through attachments and investments that are as much a question of affect and pleasure as they are of ideology and rationality. Finally, we will discuss the implications of this analysis for the practice of a critical pedagogy.

Radical and Conservative Approaches to Popular Culture

Historically, the concept of popular culture has not fared well either as part of the discourse of the Left or of the Right.[8] For the Left, two positions have held center stage in different terrains of Marxist theory. In the first, popular culture lacks the possibility for creative, productive, or authentic forms of expression. In this view, popular culture is simply that terrain of ideology and cultural forms imposed by the culture industry on the masses in order to integrate them into the existing social order. Within this discourse, popular culture becomes commodified and produces people in the image of its own logic, a logic characterized by standardization, uniformity, and passivity. The structuring principle at work in this view of popular culture is one of total dominance and utter resignation. People become synonymous with cultural dupes incapable of either mediating, resisting, or rejecting the imperatives of the dominant culture.

The paradigmatic example of this position comes from Theodor Adorno and Max Horkheimer.[9] Within their discourse, popular culture was equated with mass culture. This was seen as a form of psychoanalysis in reverse; that is, instead of curing socially induced neuroses, mass culture produced them. Similarly, popular forms such as television, radio, jazz, or syndicated astrology columns were seen as nothing more than a form of ideological shorthand for those social relations that reproduced the social system as a whole. For Adorno, in particular, popular culture was simply a form of mass culture whose effects had no redeeming political possibilities. The people or "masses" in this view lacked any culture through which they could offer either resistance or an alternative vision of the world. Adorno is clear on this issue:

> The total effect of the culture industry is one of antienlightenment, in which, as Horkheimer and I have noted, enlightenment, that is the progressive technical domination of nature, becomes mass deception and is turned into a means for fettering consciousness. It impedes the development of autonomous, independent individuals who judge and decide consciously for themselves. . . . If the masses have been unjustly reviled from above as masses, the culture industry is not among

the least responsible for making them into masses and then despising them, while obstructing the emancipation for which human beings [might be] ripe.[10]

Adorno's views represent one of the central paradoxical theses of the Frankfurt School theorists. According to them, reason is not only in eclipse in the modern age, it is also the source of crisis and decline. Progress has come to mean the reification, rationalization, and standardization of thought itself, and the culture industry plays a key role in transforming culture and reason into their opposite, culture as ignorance and commodification. Within this perspective, the distinction between high culture and mass/popular culture is preserved. In this case, high culture becomes a transcendent sphere, one of the few terrains left in which autonomy, creativity, and opposition can be thought and practiced. While arguing that mass culture is an expression of the slide into ignorance, Frankfurt theorists such as Adorno and Horkheimer fall back upon a unfortunate legitimation of high culture in which particular versions of art, music, literature, and the philosophic tradition become a utopian refuge for resisting the new barbarism.[11]

The second view of popular culture that is predominant in Marxist theory is developed mostly in the work of historians and sociologists who focus on various aspects of "peoples' history" or the practices of subcultural groups. In this view, popular culture becomes a version of folk culture and its contemporary variant. That is, as an object of historical analysis, working-class culture is excavated as an unsullied expression of popular resistance. Within this form of analysis the political and the pedagogical emerge as an attempt to reconstruct a "radical and . . . popular tradition in order that 'the people' might learn from and take heart from the struggles of their forebears," or it appears as an attempt to construct " 'the people' as the supporters of [a] 'great culture' so that they might eventually be led to appropriate that culture as their own."[12]

A similar and more contemporary version of this discourse opposes the high or dominant culture to the alternative culture of the working class or various subcultural groups. This is the culture of authenticity, one which is allegedly uninfluenced by the logic and practices of the culture industry or the impositions of a dominant way of life. At work here is a romanticized view of popular experience that somehow manages to escape from the relations and contradictions at work in the larger society. This view falls prey to an essentialist reading of popular culture. It deeply underestimates the most central feature of cultural power in the twentieth century. In failing to acknowledge popular culture as one sphere in a complex field of domination and subordination, this view ignores the necessity of providing an understanding of how power produces different levels of cultural relations, experience, and values that articulate the multilayered ideologies and social prac-tices of any society.[13]

Both of these leftist traditions have played a powerful role in defining popular culture within a theoretical framework that helps to explain why the people have not risen up against the inequities and injustices of capitalism. Ironically, the Right has not ignored the underlying logic of this position, and, in fact, has appropriated it for its own ideological interests. For example, as Patrick Brantlinger points out, the category of popular culture has been "just as useful for helping to explain and condemn the failures of egalitarian schools and mass cultural institutions such as television and the press to educate 'the masses' to political responsibility."[14] Conservative critics such as Arnold Toynbee, José Ortega Y Gasset, Ezra Pound, and T. S. Eliot have viewed popular culture as a threat to the very existence of civilization as well as an expression of the vulgarization and decadence of the masses.

In the conservative attack on mass culture, the category of true culture is treated as a warehouse filled with the goods of antiquity, waiting patiently to be distributed anew to each generation. Knowledge in this perspective becomes sacred, revered, and removed from the demands of social critique and ideological interests.[15] The pedagogical principles at work here are similar to those at work in the Left's celebration of high culture. In both cases, the rhetoric of cultural restoration and crisis legitimates a transmission pedagogy consistent with a view of culture as an artifact and students as merely bearers of received knowledge. Though starting from different political positions, advocates of high culture on the Left and Right often argue that the culture of the people has to be replaced with forms of knowledge and values that are at the heart of ruling culture. In these perspectives, the modalities of revolutionary struggle and conservative preservation seem to converge around a view of popular culture as a form of barbarism, a notion of "the people" as passive dupes, and an appeal to a view of enlightenment that reduces cultural production and meaning to the confines of high culture. Questions regarding the multidimensional nature of the struggles, contradictions, and reformations that inscribe in different ways the historically specific surface of popular cultural forms are completely overlooked in both the dominant radical and conservative positions developed above.

Dominant Left views of popular culture have not provided an adequate discourse for developing a theory of cultural analysis that begins with the issue of how power enters into the struggles over the domains of common sense and everyday life.[16] Nor do such accounts provide sufficient theoretical insight into how the issues of consent, resistance, and the production of subjectivity are formed by pedagogical processes whose structuring principles are deeply political. Of course, in the exaggerations that characterize popular culture as one that is either imposed from above or generated spontaneously from below there are hints of the political reality of cultural power both as a force for domination and as a condition for collective affirmation and struggle. The point is not to separate these different elements of cultural power from each other as binary oppositions but to capture the complexity of cultural relations as they are manifested in practices that both enable and disable people within sites and social forms that give meaning to the relations of popular culture.[17]

Hegemony as a Pedagogical Process

The work of Antonio Gramsci represents an important starting point for both redefining the meaning of popular culture and for advancing its pedagogical and political importance as a site of both struggle and domination.[18] Gramsci did not directly address himself to modern manifestations of popular culture such as cinema and radio, nor did he write anything noteworthy on the symbolic forms of popular culture that existed in the urban centers of Europe in the early part of the twentieth century; but he did formulate an original and profound theory of culture, power, and hegemony that provides a theoretical basis for moving beyond the impasse of viewing popular culture within the bipolar alternatives of a celebratory populism or a debilitating cultural stupor.[19] Gramsci's theory of hegemony redefines the structuring principles that maintain relations between dominant and subordinate classes in the advanced capitalist societies. For Gramsci, the exercise of control by the ruling classes is characterized less by the excessive use of officially sanctioned force than it is through what he calls the struggle for hegemonic leadership. Hegemonic leadership refers to the struggle to win the consent of subordinated groups to the existing social order. In substituting hegemonic struggle for the concept of domination, Gramsci points to the complex ways in which consent is organized as part of an active pedagogical process on the terrain of everyday life. In Gramsci's view such a process must work and rework the cultural and ideological terrain of subordinate groups in order to legitimate the interests and authority of the ruling bloc.

Gramsci's concept of hegemony broadens the question of which social groups will hold and exert power. More importantly, it raises a number of theoretical considerations regarding how power as a cultural, economic, and political set of practices works to define, organize, and legitimate particular conceptions of common sense.[20] Gramsci's hegemony needs to be articulated as both a political and pedagogical process. Moral leadership and state power are tied to a process of consent, as a form of learning, which is secured through the elaboration of particular discourses, needs, appeals, values, and interests that must address and transform the concerns of subordinated groups. In this perspective hegemony is a continuing, shifting, and problematic historical process. Consent is structured through a series of relations marked by an ongoing political struggle over competing conceptions and views of the world between dominant and subordinated groups. What is worth noting here is that this is not a political struggle framed within the polarities of an imposing dominant culture and a weak or "authentic" subordinate cultures. On the contrary, by claiming that every relation of hegemony is necessarily an educational relationship, Gramsci makes clear that a ruling bloc can only engage in a political and pedagogical struggle for the consent of subordinate groups if it is willing to take seriously and articulate some of the values and interests of these groups.[21]

Inherent in the attempt by dominant groups to transform rather than displace the ideological and cultural terrain of subordinated groups, dominant ideology itself is compromised and exists in a far from pure, uncontaminated state. Needless to say, the culture of subordinated groups never confronts the dominant culture in either a completely supine or totally resistant fashion. In the struggle to open up its own spaces for resistance and affirmation, subordinated cultures have to negotiate and compromise around *both* those elements they give over to the dominant culture and those they maintain as representative of their own interests and desires.[22]

From this view of struggle within the hegemonic process, it is clear that the relationship between popular culture and the processes of consent require rejecting any concept of popular culture articulated in essentialist terms. That is, the concept of popular culture cannot be defined around a set of ideological meanings permanently inscribed in particular cultural forms. On the contrary, because of the location of cultural forms within and as part of the dynamics of consent, their meaning can only be ascertained through their articulation into a practice and set of historically specific contextual relations that determine their political meaning and ideological interests. Break dancing, punk dress codes, or heavy metal music may be sufficiently oppositional and congruent within one social and historical context to be considered a legitimate radical expression of popular culture and yet in another social field may be mediated through the consumer ideology and investments of mass culture. What is important to recognize here is that *the key structuring principle of popular culture does not consist in the contents of particular cultural forms*. Stuart Hall illuminates this issue well:

> The meaning of a cultural form and its place or position in the cultural field is not inscribed inside its form. Nor is its position fixed once and forever. This year's radical symbol or slogan will be neutralized into next year's fashion; the year after, it will be the object of a profound cultural nostalgia. Today's rebel folksinger ends up, tomorrow, on the cover of *The Observer* color magazine. The meaning of the cultural symbol is given in part by the social field into which it is incorporated, the practices with which it articulates and is made to resonate. What matters is not the intrinsic or historically fixed objects of culture, but the state of play in cultural relations.[23]

We want to extend further this insight and argue that not only are popular cultural forms read in complex ways, but they also mobilize multiple forms of investment. In other words, the popular has a dual form of address: it serves as a semantic and ideological referent for marking one's place in history and also brings about an experience of pleasure, affect, and corporeality. This is not to suggest that these forms of address posit a distinction in which pleasure takes place outside of history or forms of representation. What is being posited is that the popular as both a set of practices and a discursive field has a variety of effects that may be mediated through a combination of corporeal and ideological meanings or through the primacy of one of these determinants. For instance, while popular cultural forms are productive around historically constructed sets of meanings and practices, their effects may be primarily affective. That is, how these forms are mediated and taken up, how they work to construct a particular form of investment, may depend less on the production of meanings than on the affective relations that they construct with their audiences. For example, pleasure as a terrain of commodification and struggle never exists completely free from the technology of gendered representations, but its power as a form of investment cannot be reduced to its signifying effects. This means that the practices associated with a particular cultural form such as punk can never be dismissed as being merely ideologically incorrect or as simply a reflex of commodity logic. The importance of both the semantic and the affective in the structuring the investments in popular cultural forms provides new theoretical categories for linking the terrain of the everyday with the pedagogical processes at work in the notion of consent.

In summary, we are arguing that there is no popular culture outside of the interlocking processes of meaning, power, and desire that characterize the force of cultural relations at work at a given time and place in history. What this suggests more specifically is that the content of popular culture cannot be understood as prespecified content; instead, its content is produced as the ideological and institutional structuring relations of a given society's function to sustain the differences between what constitutes the dominant culture and what does not. Underlying this struggle in North America today to maintain both a difference and an accommodation of dominant and subordinate cultures is a configuration of institutions, ideologies, and social practices that constitute those features that mark a generic distinction between the realms of popular and dominant culture.

In the context of this distinction, popular culture is, in a sense, an empty cultural form. That is, its form or representation does not guarantee an unproblematic, transcendent meaning. At the same time, popular culture can be understood as a social practice constituted by a particular site and features that point to a distinctive field of political action. The general distinctiveness of popular culture as a sphere of social relations can be made more clear by further elaborating its basic theoretical features.

To begin with the concept of hegemony clarifies how cultural power is able to penetrate into the terrain of daily life, transforming it into both a struggle over and accommodation to the culture of subordinate groups. Second, it is important to acknowledge that the cultural terrain of everyday life is not only a site of struggle and accommodation, but one in which the production of subjectivity can be viewed as a pedagogical process whose structuring principles are deeply political. Third, the notion of consent that lies at the heart of the process of hegemony underscores the importance of specifying the limits and possibilities of the pedagogical principles at work within cultural forms that serve in contradictory ways to empower and disempower various groups. In what follows, we want to extend these insights by pointing to those specific features and activities that illuminate more specifically what constitutes popular culture as both a site and field of pedagogical work.

Culture as a Site of Struggle and Power Relations

We enter the process of theorizing the relation between popular culture and critical pedagogy by arguing for educational practice as both a site and form of cultural politics. In this regard, our project is the construction of an educational practice that expands human capacities in order to enable people to intervene in the formation of their own subjectivities and to be able to exercise power in the interest of transforming the ideological and material conditions of domination into social practices that promote social empowerment and demonstrate possibilities. Within this position we are emphasizing popular culture as a site of differentiated politics; a site with multiple ideological and affective weightings. It represents a particular historical place where different groups collide in transactions of dominance, complicity, and resistance over the power to name, legitimate, and experience different versions of history, community, desire, and pleasure through the availability of social forms structured by the politics of difference. Some of the theoretical and political implications at work in this view of popular culture are captured in Larry Grossberg's discussion of a theory of articulation:

> . . . people are never merely passively subordinated, never entirely incorporated. People are engaged in struggles with, within, and sometimes against, real tendential forces and determinations, in their efforts to appropriate what they are given. Consequently, their relations to particular practices and texts are complex and contradictory: they may win something in the struggle against sexism and lose something in the struggle against economic exploitation; they may both gain and lose something economically; and while they lose ideological ground, they may win some emotional strength. If peoples' lives are never merely determined by the dominant position, and their subordination is always complex and active, then understanding [popular] culture requires us to look at how they are actively inserted at particular sites of everyday life and at how particular articulations empower and disempower its audience.[24]

The key theoretical concepts for further specifying popular culture as a particular site of struggle and accommodation can be initially organized around the category of what we label "the productive." In the more general sense, we use the term "productive" to refer to the construction and organization of practices engaged in by dominant *and* subordinated groups to secure a space for producing and legitimating experiences and social forms constitutive of different ways of life forged in asymmetrical relations of power. The term "productive" points to two distinctly different sets of relations within the sphere of the popular.

The first set of relations refers to the ways in which the dominant culture functions as a structuring force within and through popular forms. In this case, the dominant culture attempts to secure both semantically and affectively, through the production of meaning and the regulation of pleasure, the complicity of subordinated groups. Rather than merely dismiss and ignore the traditions, ideologies, and needs that emerge from the cultures of subordinated groups, the dominant culture attempts to appropriate and transform the ideological and cultural processes that characterize the terrain of the popular. At issue here are processes of selective production, controlled distribution, and regulated notions of narrative and consumer address.

In the second set of relations, the notion of productive refers to the ways in which subordinated groups articulate a distinct set of contents and/or a level of involvement in popular forms that is less distancing and more social in nature than that found in the cultural forms of dominant bourgeois groups. This articulation and set of relations are characterized by a refusal to engage in social practices defined by an abstract rationality, a theoretical mapping, so to speak, that structures cultural forms through a denial of the familiar affective investments and pleasures. For the dominant class, such refusal is often understood as a surrender to the moment, the fun of the event, or the "horror of the vulgar." A more critical reading might suggest that the affective investment and level of active involvement in popular forms such as neighborhood sports, punk dancing, or at working-class weddings represent an important theoretical signpost. In this case, it is a particular form of sociality that signals something more than vulgarity, cooption, or what Bloch calls the swindle of fulfillment. Instead, the sociality that structures popular forms may contain the unrealized potentialities and possibilities necessary for more democratic and humane forms of community and collective formation.[25] This can be made clearer by analyzing the structuring principles that often characterize dominant cultural forms.

Pierre Bourdieu argues that the cultural forms of dominant bourgeois groups can be characterized by the celebration of a formalism, an elective distance from the real world, with all of its passions, emotions, and feelings. The social relations and attendant sensibility at work in bourgeois cultural forms are those that often maintain an investment of form—a celebration of stylized detachment. On the other hand, there is often a space in cultural forms embraced by subordinated groups that is organized around a sensibility in which the needs, emotions, and passions of the participants largely resonate with the material and ideological struc-tures of everyday life. Underlying these social relations one often finds a richly textured collective investment of play and affective engagement in which there is no great disjunction/interruption between the act and its meaning. In other words, there is an active, communal set of experiences and social practices at work in subordinated cultural forms, including a form of public participation in which the dominant practice of distancing the body from reflection is refused. This is the productive moment of corporeality. Mercer illuminates this point in his discussion of Bourdieu's concept of "popular forms."

> 'Nothing' argues Pierre Bourdieu, 'more radically distinguishes popular specta-cles—the football match, Punch and Judy, the circus, wrestling, or even in some cases the cinema—from bourgeois spectacles, than the form of participation of the public.' For the former, whistles, shouts, pitch invasions are characteristic, for

the latter the gestures are distant, heavily ritualized—applause, obligatory but discontinuous and punctual cries of enthusiasm—'author, author' or 'encore'.' Even the clicking of fingers and tapping of feet in a jazz audience are only a 'bourgeois spectacle, which mimes a popular one' since the participation is reduced to 'the silent allure of the gesture.' A certain distance, Bourdieu argues, has been central in the bourgeois economy of the body: a distance between 'reflexion' and corporeal participation.[26]

Since corporeality may be inscribed in either repressive or emancipatory actions, any uncritical celebration of the body is theoretically and politically misplaced. At the same time, it is important to recognize that a discourse of the body is needed that recognizes a sensibility and set of social practices that both define and exhibit a possibility for extending unrealized and progressive moments in the production of corporeality. For example, punk culture's lived appropriation of the everyday as a refusal to let the dominant culture encode and restrict the meaning of daily life suggests the first instance of a form of resistance that links play with the reconstruction of meaning. This particular popular form, filled as it is with abortive hopes, signifies within bourgeois a "tradition of the scorned." That is, punk culture (or for that matter any lived relation of difference that doesn't result in dominance or infantilization) ruptures the dominant order symbolically and refuses to narrate *with* permission. It is scorned by the bourgeoisie because it not only challenges the dominant order's attempt to suppress all differences through a discourse that asserts the homogeneity of the social domain but presents the possibility of a social imaginary in which a politics of democratic difference offers up forms of resistance in which it becomes possible to rewrite, rework, recreate, and reestablish new discourses and cultural spaces that revitalize rather than degrade public life. Whether conscious or not, punk culture partly expresses social practices that contain the basis for interrogating and struggling to overthrow all those forms of human behavior in which difference becomes the basis for subjecting human beings to forms of degradation, enslavement, and exploitation. Of course, there is more at work in punk culture than the affirmation of difference; there is also the difference of affirmation, that is, affirmation becomes the precondition for claiming one's experience as a legitimate basis for developing one's own voice, place, and sense of history. It is this dialectic of affirmation, pleasure, and difference that constitutes some of the basic elements of the notion of the productive. Bourdieu is helpful here, for he defines the productive as that dialectical mixture of pleasure, consent, and unselfconscious involvement that maps out a significant aspect of the popular within everyday life. As Bourdieu points out,

> The desire to enter into the game, identifying with the characters' joys and sufferings, worrying about their fate, espousing their hopes and ideals, living their life, is based on a form of investment, a sort of deliberate "naivety", ingenuousness, good-natured credulity ("we're here to enjoy ourselves"), which tends to accept formal experiments and specifically artistic effects only to the extent that they can be forgotten and do not get in the way of [the affirmation and dignity of everyday life].[27]

As we have stressed, it would be a political mistake to place too much faith in the level of participation and nature of spontaneity that characterizes many cultural forms of subordinated groups. Many of these forms are not innocent. As an area and site of exchange between the dominant and subordinated classes, popular culture embodies a violence inherent in both sides of the processes of hegemony as well as the unrealized potentiality of those needs and desires that reflect a respect for human dignity and a commitment to extend their most ethical and empowering capabilities. We stress here that innocence is not an intrinsic feature of the popular. There is a violence inextricably inscribed in popular forms that must also be addressed as part of the multilayered and contradictory invest-ments and meanings that constitute its changing character.

Popular Culture and Consent: The Dialectic of Ideology and Pleasure

If the popular is to be understood in terms of the unrealized potentialities that inform it, critical educators need to analyze how the production of subjectivity and cultural alliances can emerge within the grammar and codes that make the terrain of the popular significant in peoples' everyday lives. As a site of struggle and possibility, popular culture needs to be understood not only in terms of its productive elements, but also in terms of how its cultural forms articulate processes through which the production, organization, and regulation of consent takes place around various social practices and struggles at the level of everyday life. These processes can be elaborated through the category we call "the persuasive." In the most general sense, the term refers to the ways in which hegemony functions on the terrain of popular culture through a variety of pedagogical processes that work not only to secure dominant interests but to offer as well the possibility of a politics of resistance and social transformation.

The notion of the persuasive illuminates the insight that political power never works without an ideological mediation. For example, instances of domination and hegemony raise questions as to how domination is produced and organized within processes of motivation and legitimation. By introducing the element of persua-sion—that is, how ideological mediation actually functions as a pedagogical process—domination along with resistance can be connected to a broader notion of cultural politics in which the very act of learning can be analyzed as a fundamental aspect of hegemony. More specifically, the category of the persuasive in popular culture is important because it provides a starting point for understanding how the complex relations of dominance and resistance are organized and structured through par-ticular pedagogical forms and practices. Theorizing about popular culture in this way helps to lay bare the practical grounds on which transformations are worked and represented through the important and related categories of consent, invest-ment, ideology, and pleasure.

Consent is an important feature of the practice of persuasion. As the term is generally defined in radical theories of hegemony, consent refers to two somewhat different perspectives on how people come to be engaged within the ideologies and social relations of the dominant culture. In the more orthodox version, consent often refers to the ways in which the dominant logic is imposed on subordinated groups through the mechanizations of the culture industry. In the revisionist radical version, consent is defined through more active forms of complicity in that subordinated groups are now viewed as partly negotiating their adaptation and place within the dominant culture. As either imposition or negotiated complicity, consent defines the relationship between power and culture as nothing more than the equivalence of domination. We want to modify these notions of consent so as to illuminate its dialectical importance as a political and pedagogical process.

In our view, the notion of consent rightly points to the ways in which people are located within and negotiate elements of place and agency as a result of their investments in particular relations of meaning constructed through popular forms. At work in this notion of consent is the central question of what it is that people know, how they come to know, and how they come to feel in a particular way that secures for the hegemonic or counter-hegemonic order their loyalties and desires. This perspective is important as a political and social practice and as a framework of inquiry because it raises important questions about how the modern apparatuses of moral and social regulation, as well as resistance and counter-discourse, define what kind of knowledge counts, how it is to be taught, how subjectivities are defined, and how the very dynamic of moral and political regulation is constantly worked and reworked. The political implications of these insights for a politics of popular culture are significant and need further theoretical elaboration.

That consent is learned begs the question of what kinds of pedagogical processes are at work through which people actively rather than passively identify their own needs and desires with particular forms and relations of meaning. Unfortunately, the pedagogical issue of how people come to learn such identities and pleasures through particular forms of identification and cathexis has not been the central focus of study in most radical analysis of culture. Instead, radical analyses have often focused either on deconstructing the ideologies at work in particular cultural forms or on how readers organize texts according to their own meanings and experiences. In both cases, the issue of pedagogy has been subordinated to and subsumed within a rather limited notion of ideology production. The concern over ideology is limited to a particular view of consent in which the study of popular culture is reduced to analyses of texts or to popular culture as merely forms of consumption.[28] Ideology as a pedagogical process in this case is restricted to how meanings are produced by texts and mediated by audiences or to analyses that attempt to uncover how the market organizes needs in order to commodify popular culture.

What is particularly missing from these perspectives are questions regarding how cultural forms can be understood as mobilizing desire in a way that elaborates how such forms are engaged. For example, through what processes do cultural forms induce an anger or pleasure that has its own center of gravity as a form of meaning? How can we come to understand learning outside of the limits of rationality, as a form of engagement that mobilizes and sometimes reconstructs desire? These questions suggest that pedagogy is not so neatly ensconced in the production of discourse. Rather, pedagogy also constitutes a moment in which the body learns, moves, desires, and longs for affirmation. These questions also suggest a rejection of the pedagogy of modernism, one that serves up "ideal" forms of communication theory in which the tyranny of discourse becomes the ultimate pedagogical medium,[29] that is, talk embodied as a logic abstracted from the body itself. We need to reemphasize that the issue of consent opens up pedagogy to the uncertain, that space that refuses the measurable, that legitimates the concrete in a way that is felt and experienced rather than merely spoken. In this argument, we are not trying to privilege the body or a politics of affective investments over discourse as much as we are trying to emphasize their absence in previous theorizing as well as their importance for a critical pedagogy.

It is worth stressing that the relationship we are posing between affective and discursive investment is neither ahistorical nor ideologically innocent. Nor are we suggesting that ideology and affect as particular forms of investment can best be understood by positing a rigid conceptual opposition between meaning and desire. The cultural forms that mobilize desire and affect along with the struggles that take place over re-producing and investing desire, pleasure, and corporeality are constructed within power relations, which are always ideological *in nature* but which produce an experience or form of investment that cannot be understood merely as an ideological construction—an experience re-presented and enjoyed through the lens of meaning rather than through the primacy of pleasure and affect. Put another way, interpellations in the Althusserian sense are not merely ideological, they are also a summons to particular forms of pleasure, which are always historically situated but not discursively privileged. In what follows, we will argue that by retheorizing the notion of ideology through a reconstructed theory of pleasure, educators can begin to develop a pedagogy that offers a more critical possibility for addressing the purpose and meaning of popular culture as a terrain of struggle and hope.

We are arguing that the relationship between power and complicity is not framed simply around the organization of knowledge and meaning. The power of complicity and the complicity of power are not exhausted simply by registering how people are positioned and located through the production of particular ideologies structured through particular discourses. The relationships that subordinated groups enter into with respect to cultural forms cannot be understood and exhausted simply through what often amounts to a search and destroy mission based on uncovering the particular meanings and messages that mediate between a particular film, popular song, or text and its audience. The limits of ideology and rationality as the interests that structure behavior and move us within particular social forms is neither understood nor made problematic in this position. This position represents a basic misrecognition of the central and important role that pleasure (or its absence) plays in structuring the relationships and investments that one has to a particular cultural form. Colin Mercer emphasizes the point we are trying to make here:

> Barthes has it that 'ideology passes over the text and its reading like the blush over a face (in love, some take erotic pleasure in this colouring)' and this signals something of the contemporary concern for the contradictory play of ideology. There is a general unease that, within the plethora of ideology analysis, which has emerged in recent years, something has quite crucially been missed out: that it may now be important to look over our shoulders and try to explain a certain 'guilt' of enjoyment of such and such in spite of its known ideological and political provenance. . . . Any analysis of the pleasure, the modes of persuasion, the consent operative with a given cultural form would have to displace the search for an ideological, political, economic or, indeed subjective, meaning and establish the coordinates of that 'formidable underside' (i.e., pleasure, joy) . . . because what we are really concerned with here is a restructuring of the theoretical horizon within which a cultural form is perceived.[30]

Drawing upon the work of Walter Benjamin, Roland Barthes, and others, Mercer has called attention to an issue that is central to a politics of popular culture. That is, he has focused on the ways in which consent is articulated not only through the structuring of semantically organized meanings and messages, but also through the pleasures invoked in the mechanisms and structuring principles of popular forms. The theoretical insight at work in this position is in part revealed through the question of why "we not only consent to forms of domination which we know, rationally and politically, are 'wrong', but even enjoy them."[31] The importance of this issue is made somewhat clear in the limits of an ideological analysis that might reveal the sexist nature of the lyrics in a popular song or video. Such a critique is important but it does not tell us or even seem capable of raising the question as to why people enjoy the song or video even though they might recognize the sexist ideologies that such texts embody. It is important to stress that an overreliance on ideology critique has limited our ability to understand how people actively participate in the dominant culture through processes of accommodation, negotiation, and even resistance.

In short, the investments that tie students to popular cultural forms cannot be ascertained simply through an analysis of the meanings and representations that we decode in them. On the contrary, affective investments have a real cultural hold and such investments may be indifferent to the very notion of meaning itself as constructed through the lens of the ideological. This suggests a number of important political and pedagogical principles. First, in hegemonic and counter-hegemonic struggles, the production and regulation of desire is as important as the construction of meaning. This means that the constitution and the expression of such desire is an important starting point for understanding the relations that students construct to popular and dominant forms. Second, the idea and experience of pleasure must be constituted politically so that we can analyze how the body becomes not only the object of [his-patriarchal] pleasure,[32] but also the subject of pleasure. In this case "pleasure becomes the consent of life in the body," and provides an important corporeal condition of life affirming possibility.[33] This argues for a discriminatory notion of pleasure that is not only desirable in and of itself, but that also suggests "at one and the same time . . . a figure for utopia in general, and for the systemic revolutionary transformation of society as a whole."[34] Third, we must recognize how popular culture can constitute a field of possibilities within which students can be empowered so as to appropriate cultural forms on terms that dignify and extend their human possibilities.

We realize that this raises enormously difficult questions about how, as teachers, we come to analyze a politics of feeling within sites that are at odds with the very notion of the popular. To make the popular the object of study within schools is to run the risk of not only reconstituting the meaning and pleasures of cultural forms but also of forcing students into a discourse and form of analysis that is at odds with their notion of what is considered pedagogically acceptable and properly distant from their everyday lives outside of school. At the same time, the popular cannot be ignored because it points to a category of meanings and affective investments that shape the very identities, politics, and cultures of the students we deal with. Subjectivity and identity are in part constituted on the ground of the popular and their force and effects do not disappear once students enter school. The political issue at stake here and its pedagogical relevance are suggested by Larry Grossberg.

> . . . It is only if we begin to recognize the complex relations between affect and ideology that we can make sense of people's emotional life, their desiring life, their struggles to find the energy to survive, let alone struggle. It is only in the terms of these relations that we can understand people's need and ability to maintain a "faith" in something beyond their immediate existence.[35]

In the section that follows, we will consider a particular Hollywood film as a demonstrative text in order to illuminate how the formation of multiple identities takes place through attachments and investments that are structured as much by affect and pleasure as they are by ideology and rationality. The importance of this cultural text is in part due to the opportunity it offers for further elaborating the elements of a critical pedagogical practice and our affirmation of the centrality of the body in the processes of knowing and learning.

Investment and Pleasure in *Dirty Dancing*

We have argued throughout this chapter that popular forms both shape and are mediated through the investments of rationality and affect. In attempting to make this observation more concrete as both a way of analyzing popular forms as well as using them as part of a critical pedagogical process, we want to take up a specific consideration of the film, *Dirty Dancing*, written by Eleanor Bergstein and released into the North American market during the summer of 1987.

As we have stressed earlier in this chapter, the concept of popular culture cannot be defined around a set of ideological meanings permanently inscribed in particular cultural forms. Rather, the meaning of cultural forms can only be ascertained through their articulation into a practice and set of historically specific contextual relations that determine their pleasures, politics, and meanings. This position straightforwardly implies Roland Barthes' encouragement that "whenever it's the body which writes, and not ideology, there's a chance the text will join us in our modernity."[36] Thus our comments on the text of *Dirty Dancing* are not offered as abstract observations without an observer, but rather as a fully embodied account. The pedagogical significance of this statement should not be minimized. It means that when we engage students through a critical consideration of particular cultural forms (whether they be commodity texts such as films or lived social relations such as local peace or environmental movements), we must begin with an acknowledgement and exploration of how we—our contradictory and multiple selves[fully historical and social]—are implicated in the meanings and pleasures we ascribe to those forms. The interest here is not so much self-knowledge as it is the understanding and consideration of the possibilities and limitations inherent in lived social differences.

The following interpretation of *Dirty Dancing* has been produced through a recognition of our own investments in this film. This combination of reason and pleasure is organized not only by our shared work as educators interested in elaborating the complexities of a critical pedagogical practice but as well by biographies within which our earliest sense of social contradiction was formed within the juxtaposition of body movements, textures, timbre, and clothing. We have lived our lives within and against the grain of very different conjunctions of class, gender, and ethnic relations. But what we have shared is the shock, awe, and production of desire in confronting bodies that knew something we did not. For Simon, this experience of difference and desire was organized, in part, through being born to a marriage constituted across class divisions. Thus, the infrequent visits and family celebrations with working-class relatives and the more frequent moments when adult bodies—father and friends—[in the syntax, semantics, and very volume of speech; in the expansive gestures and use of space]—articulated forms of passion and pleasure suppressed by the detachment offered with middle-class rituals of politeness and formalism. For Giroux, the experience of having a different culture inscribe the body in terms that were at odds with one's own social positioning occurred when affiliations organized through high school sport led to hanging out with working-class blacks. Attending weekend parties, dancing to the music of black blues singers such as Etta James, and learning how to dance without moving one's feet made manifest the fact that the body could speak with a rhythm vastly different from that which structured the Catholic Youth Organization dances organized for white working-class youth. In both of our situations, our bodies were positioned within different sets of experiences and practices that embodied contradictions that we neither understood nor were able to articulate.

Unlike many of the teenage films that have swept the North American and European markets, *Dirty Dancing* locates the formation of youth within a material and social set of contradictory and conflicting practices. That is, this film does not treat youth as an isolated social stratum lacking any wider referent than itself. Questions of class and sexism, culture and privilege come together in a tapestry of social relations that emerge within the unlikely location of an affluent summer resort for the families of the rising class of Jewish businessmen and professionals.[37]

The year is 1963 and Frances "Baby" Houseman; her sister, mother, and father arrive at Kellerman's Resort for their summer vacation. We sense after a few moments into the film that Baby [who is soon to start a university program in the economics of international development and later plans to join the U.S. Peace Corps] is bored and alienated from the pleasures and pastimes of the nouveau Jewish-bourgeoisie who make up the majority of the patrons at Kellerman's. But we also quickly learn that Baby's idealistic political commitments to equality and fairness are just as surely rooted in the rhetorical discourse of liberal democracy historically embraced by her class (embodied particularly by her physician father). Baby is proudly introduced as someone who "is going to change the world" and do it with reason and intelligence.

Except for the college students hired by Kellerman to work the dining room, the hotel staff consists of young people whose experience and corporeality define a location across a solid class and ethnicity barrier that marks the landscape of the resort. Such barriers are familiar to us; we have been on both sides.

One evening after escaping the inanities of "entertainment night" at Kellerman's, Baby wanders the grounds and inadvertently discovers what to her is an unknown, astonishing, and mesmerizing corner of the site of the popular. What she discovers is the terrain of "dirty dancing," a form of music and movement whose coded desires and productive pleasures crumble what to her seem like an empty bourgeois body, only to reconstitute it with new meanings and pleasures. What Baby discovers at this working-class party is the overt sensuality of rock and soul. She learns what we have learned in that shock of displacement when one's ignorant body is called to new forms of participation that promise unfamiliar pleasures. She discovers in Barthes' words that "the human body is not an eternal object, written forever in nature . . . for it is really a body that was constructed by history, by societies, by regimes, by ideologies."[38]

The articulations between Baby's class position and the class location of the working class help are first felt as differences of affective investment in the body. By placing her body with the terrain of working-class pleasures, Baby begins to feel and identify her body as a terrain of struggle, one that suggests a need to reject her family's view of bodily pleasure and desire for the more pronounced terrain of sexuality and bodily abandonment offered by the culture of the working-class help. It is through the sociality of "dirty dancing" that Baby first engages her own class-specific cultural capital and attempts to reclaim her body as a terrain of struggle through a redefined sense of pleasure and identity. For Baby, the body becomes the referent not only for redefining and remaking a sense of her own class and gender identity, but also for investing in a notion of desire and pleasure that reconstitutes her sense of self and social empowerment.

It is from this position of being amazed and attracted to a particular body of knowledge that the film's narrative begins to unfold. Baby is attracted to both the male and female personifications of the new cultural terrain: the dance instructor Johnny Castle and his partner Penny. As the story proceeds, Baby is transformed both by a new body knowledge and a new knowledge of her body and its pleasures. Baby seems to embrace the "abandon" of working-class cultural terrain, finding in it perhaps an arena of feeling and emotion that cannot be totally colonized by the expectations of rationality within which her identity has been formed.[39]

Baby learns that Penny is pregnant and that money is needed to illegally terminate the pregnancy. A "doctor" is only available on the night Penny and Johnny are to perform at a nearby hotel. If they miss the performance, Penny would most likely be fired. Deceiving her family (who place perfect faith in her reason and honesty), Baby obtains the abortion money from her father and agrees to take Penny's place as Johnny's partner. As Johnny begins to teach her the dance routine, their relationship develops.

Baby's substitution for Penny as Johnny's partner is a form of lived fantasy that works a reconstitution of explicitly who and what she is. As McRobbie has written:

> Dance evokes fantasy because it sets in motion a dual relationship projecting both internally towards the self and externally towards the 'other'; which is to say that dance as a leisure activity connects desires for the self with those for somebody else. It articulates adolescence and girlhood with femininity and female sexuality and it does this by and through the body. This is especially important because it is the one pleasurable arena where women have some control and know what is going on in relation to physical sensuality and to their own bodies. Continually bombarded with images and with information about how they should be and how they should feel, dance offers an escape, a positive and vibrant sexual expressiveness.[40]

That Baby's investment in the dance of the Other is being anchored through affect seems clear enough from the often cliched dialogue. As Johnny emphasizes "it is not enough to know the steps; you have to feel the music." And as Baby acknowledges as their relationship deepens: "I'm afraid of never feeling the rest of my whole life as I do when I'm with you."

Even in a setting so well defined to privilege the wealthy, the constraints of class and power move across the terrains of pleasure and work so as to lay bare the relationship between wider social constraints and the formation of differentiated class-specific dreams. In *Dirty Dancing* the desire mobilized by relations of domination runs both ways. Johnny confides to Baby, "I dreamed you and I were walking along and we met your father and he put his arm around me just like Robby [one of the Kellerman dinning room staff who attends medical school]."

Baby's new investments, however, are not independent from the identity position regulated and organized by liberal discourse. Within the complications of the plot [when Johnny is falsely accused of theft], she acts on the belief that she can and should help those in trouble and less fortunate than herself, fully expecting Johnny and his friends to be treated with the same credibility and fairness as anyone else. When they are not, her naivete is shattered and the film seems about to conclude with an honest appraisal of the relations of class power. Even though he is cleared of the theft charge, Johnny is fired when Baby admits to their relationship. They say good-bye to each other and he drives off.

But screenwriter Bergstein was evidently unsatisfied by such a limited sense of possibility. Consequently, she closes the film with what can be either dismissed as Hollywood schmaltz or celebrated as a glimpse of utopian hope keyed by the recognition of the importance of investments in the pleasures of sensuality. Johnny returns to find the closing talent night in progress. Confronting Baby's parents, he leads her on to the stage for a final dance performance that evolves into total audience participation. The film thus ends, magically erasing all social divisions [including the patriarchal one between Mr. and Mrs. Houseman] as all the assembled staff and guests rock and roll to the final dissolve into the film's credits.

This concluding scene constitutes dance as a collectivizing process within which individual differences disappear. Rock and roll, like religious singing, seems to deftly bind people together, uniting young and old, performers and audiences, white and black, the rulers and the ruled in a expression of celebration of the American dream in which the relationship between social power and inequality simply fades away.

What then does our understanding of *Dirty Dancing* display regarding the processes of persuasion? Our argument is that Baby's lived relation to the working-class people she engages is mediated by a dual investment mobilized by both the subject position she takes up within the discourse of liberalism *and* the popular cultural forms of working-class life within which she experiences the pleasures of the body. The emphasis here is how popular cultural forms are important in constituting the identities that influence how we engage new challenges and construct new experiences. In this context we are referring to popular culture as a field within which is mobilized a form of investment that is an elaboration of how any given cultural form (text, song, film, and event) is engaged. It is worth noting how important it is to be able to hold analytically separate both semantic and affective aspects of investment, since they can be mutually contradictory. Thus it is not uncommon to experience contrary investments in relation to a specific cultural text: for example, rock music can provide pleasure while being comprehended as very sexist and racist. Such internal contradictions are integral to experiences of guilt.[41]

Implications for Critical Pedagogical Practice

> Everyday moments of teaching ... incorporate the minds and bodies of subjects, as knowers and as learners. When we are at our best as teachers we are capable of speaking to each of these ways of knowing in ourselves and our students. We may override precedents in the educational project that value the knowing of the mind and deny the knowing of the heart and of the body. Students, the partners in these enterprise of knowing, are whole people with ideas, with emotions and with sensations ... the project must not be confined to a knowing only of the mind; it must address and interrogate what we think we know from the heart and the body.[42]

While we are in agreement with McDade, it is important to clarify that when we consider the relationship between popular cultures and pedagogy, we have a particular form of teaching and learning in mind. This is a critical pedagogical form that affirms the lived reality of difference as the ground on which to pose questions of theory and practice. It is a form that claims the experience of lived difference as an agenda for discussion and a central resource for a pedagogy of possibility.[43] The discussion of lived difference, if pedagogical, will take on a particular tension. It implies a struggle over assigned meaning, a struggle over in what direction to desire, a struggle over particular modes of expression, and ultimately a struggle over multiple and even contradictory versions of "self." It is this struggle that makes possible and hence can redefine the possibilities we see both in the conditions of our daily lives and those conditions that are "not yet." This is a struggle that can never be won, or pedagogy stops.[44]

What we are stressing is the absolutely crucial dimension of a critical pedagogy in which knowledge is conceived as an integral aspect of teaching-learning. As David Lusted writes:

> Knowledge is not produced in the intentions of those who believe they hold it, whether in the pen or in the voice. It is produced in the process of interaction, between writer and reader at the moment of reading, and between teacher and learner at the moment of classroom engagement. Knowledge is not the matter that is offered so much as the matter that is understood. To think of fields or bodies of knowledge as if they are the property of academics and teachers is wrong. It denies an equality in the relations at moments of interaction and falsely privileged one side of the exchange, and what that side 'knows' over the other.[45]

This position *does not require teachers to suppress or abandon what and how they know.* Indeed, the pedagogical struggle is lessened without such resources. However, within this position teachers and students are challenged to find forms within which a single discourse does not become the locus of certainty and certification. Rather, teachers need to find ways of creating a space for mutual engagement of lived difference that does not require the silencing of a multiplicity of voices by a single dominant discourse. Indeed, this is precisely the pedagogical motive in stressing that our account of *Dirty Dancing* must be seen as an embodied interpretation that provides an invaluable resource from which to engage lived difference as a possibility for critical dialogue and self and social formation.

What might a teacher need to understand in order to engage in such a struggle? What might she or he wish to find out? If we take popular culture as that terrain of images, knowledge forms, and affective investments within which meaning and subjectivity function, there are several questions a teacher might pursue. What are the historical conditions and material circumstances within which the practices of popular culture are pursued, organized, asserted, and regulated? Do such practices open up new notions of identities and possibilities? What identities and possibilities are disorganized and excluded? How are such practices articulated with forms of knowledge and pleasure legitimated by dominant groups? What interests and investments are served by a particular set of popular cultural practices and critiqued and challenged by the existence of such? What are the moral and political commitments of such practices, and how are these related to one's own commitments as a teacher [and if there is a divergence, what does this imply]?

What all this means is that we think the analysis of popular culture is not simply a question of "reading" off ideology from either commodity forms or forms of lived everyday relations. Rather, we are moving toward a position within which one would inquire into the popular as a field of practices that constitute Foucault's indissoluble triad of knowledge, power, and pleasure.[46] At the same time we want to raise a note of caution. The teacher engaged in a pedagogy that requires some articulation of knowledge and pleasures integral to student everyday life is walking a dangerous road. Too easily perhaps, encouraging student voice can either become a form of voyeurism or satisfy a form of ego-expansionism constituted on the pleasures of understanding those who appear as "Other" to us. This is why we must be clear on the nature of the pedagogy we pursue. Popular culture and social difference can be taken up by educators either as a pleasurable form of knowledge/ power, which allows for more effective individualizing and administration of forms of physical and moral regulation, or as the terrain on which we must meet our students in a critical and empowering pedagogical encounter.

As teachers committed to the project of a critical pedagogy, we have to read the ground of the popular for investments that both distort and constrict human potentialities and those that give "voice" to unrealized possibilities. This is what the pedagogical struggle is all about—opening up the material and discursive basis of particular ways of producing meaning and representing ourselves, our relations to others, and our relation to our environment so as to consider possibilities not yet realized. This is a utopian practice both to be embraced for its urgent necessity and scrutinized for its inherent limitations, a sentiment captured by John Berger in his short story, "The Accordion Player." He writes:

> Music demands obedience. It even demands obedience of the imagination when a melody comes to mind. You can think of nothing else. It's a kind of tyrant. In exchange it offers its own freedom. All bodies can boast about themselves with

music. The old can dance as well as the young. Time is forgotten. And that night, from behind the silence of the last stars, we thought we heard the affirmation of a Yes.

"la Belle jacqueline" once more! the dressmaker shouted at Felix. I love music! With music you can say everything!

You can't talk to a lawyer with music, Felix replied.[47]

REFERENCES

[1] For example, see Ira Shor, *Critical Teaching and Everyday Life* (Boston: South End Press, 1980); Paul Willis, *Learning to Labor: How Working Class Kids Get Working Class Jobs* (New York: Columbia University Press, 1981); R.W. Connell, D.J. Ashenden, S. Kessler, and G.W. Dowsett, *Making the Difference: Schools, Families, and Social Division* (Sydney, Australia: George Allen & Unwin, 1982); Michael Apple, *Education and Power* (New York: Routledge and Kegan Paul, 1982); Henry A. Giroux, *Theory and Resistance in Education* (South Hadley, Mass.: Bergin and Garvey Publishers, 1983); Peter McLaren, *Schooling as a Ritual Performance* (New York: Routledge and Kegan Paul, 1986).

[2] Examples of this work include: Michael W. Apple and Lois Weis eds., *Ideology and Practice in Schooling* (Philadelphia: Temple University Press, 1983); Margo Culley and Catherine Portuges eds., *Gendered Subjects: The Dynamics of Feminist Teaching* (New York: Routledge and Kegan Paul, 1985); David Livingstone et als., *Critical Pedagogy and Cultural Power* (South Hadley, Mass.: Bergin and Garvey Publishers, 1988); Kathleen Weiler, *Women Teaching for Change* (South Hadley, Mass.: Bergin and Garvey Publishers, 1988); Jay MacLeod, *Ain't No Makin It* (Boulder: Westview Press, 1988).

[3] Exceptions include the work done in *Screen Education* in England during the late 1970s and early 1980s, and the U203 Popular Culture course and writings first offered by the Open University in the 1982 (and only recently terminated). For example, see the entire issue of *Screen Education* No. 34 (Spring 1980), especially Tony Bennett, "Popular Culture: A Teaching Object," *Screen Education* No. 34 (Spring 1980), 17–29; Iain Chambers, "Rethinking 'Popular Culture' " *Screen Education*, No. 36 (Autumn 1980), 113–17; Iain Chambers, "Pop Music: A Teaching Perspective," *Screen Education* No. 39 (Summer 1981), 35–44; Len Masterman, *Teaching About Television* (London: Macmillan, 1980); Len Masterman, "TV Pedagogy," *Screen Education* No. 40 (Autumn/Winter 1981/2), 88–92; David Davies, *Popular Culture, Class, and Schooling* (London; Open University Press, 1981).

[4] Both of these positions can be found in Theodore Mills Norton and Bertell Ollman eds., *Studies in Socialist Pedagogy* (New York: Monthly Review Press, 1987). A classic example of the privileging of knowledge in the educational encounter can be found in Pierre Bourdieu and Jean-Claude Passeron, *Reproduction in Education, Society, and Culture* (London: Sage Publishers, 1977); Rachel Sharp, *Knowledge, Ideology, and the Politics of Schooling* (New York: Routledge and Kegan Paul, 1980).

[5] Much of the radical work dealing with the hidden curriculum fell into the theoretical trap of privileging social relations and pedagogical processes over the relations between knowledge and power; the most well-known example is Samuel Bowles and Herbert Gintis, *Schooling in Capitalist America* (New York: Basic Books, 1976); another example can be found in Robert V. Bullough, Jr., Stanley L. Goldstein, and Ladd Holt, *Human Interests in the Curriculum* (New York: Teachers College Press, 1984).

[6] This issue is taken up in detail in Henry A. Giroux, *Schooling and the Struggle for Public Life* (Minneapolis: University of Minnesota Press, 1988); Valerie Walkerdine, "On the Regulation

of Speaking and Silence: Subjectivity, Class, and Gender in Contemporary Schooling," in *Language, Gender and Childhood* eds., Carolyn Steedman, Cathy Urwin, and Valerie Walkerdine (London: Routledge and Kegan Paul, 1985), 203–41; Roger I. Simon, "Empowerment as a Pedagogy of Possibility," *Language Arts*, 64:4 (April 1987), 370–82; Michelle Fine, *Framing Dropouts* (Albany: SUNY Press, 1991).

[7] The issue of the politics and pedagogy of emotional investment is developed in Larry Grossberg, "Teaching the Popular," in *Theory in the Classroom*, Cary Nelson, ed. (Urbana: University of Illinois Press, 1986), 177–200. For an exceptional analysis of the relationship between pleasure and the popular, see Colin Mercer "Complicit Pleasure," in *Popular Culture and Social Relations*, Tony Bennett, Colin Mercer, and Janet Woollacoot, eds. (London: Open University Press, 1986), 50–68; See also various articles in Fredric Jameson, et al., *Formations of Pleasure* (London: Routledge and Kegan Paul, 1983); Roger I. Simon, *Teaching Against the Grain* (New York: Bergin and Garvey Press, 1992).

[8] For a historical treatment of this theme, see Patrick Brantlinger, *Bread and Circuses: Theories of Mass Culture as Social Decay* (Ithaca: Cornell University Press, 1983). This subject has been treated extensively and we cannot repeat all of the sources here, but excellent analyses of the theoretical and political shortcomings of left and right positions on popular culture can be found in Stuart Hall, "Deconstructing 'the Popular' " in *People's History and Socialist Theory*, Raphael Samuel, ed. (London: Routledge and Kegan Paul, 1981), 227–40; Tony Bennett and Graham Martin eds., *Popular Culture: Past Present* (London: Croom Helm/Open University, 1982); Bennett, Mercer, and Woollacoot eds., *Popular Culture and Social Relations*. It is worth noting that a more recent version of left cultural elitism that disdains the masses can be found in Jean Baudrillard, *In the Shadow of the Silent Majorities*, Paul Foss, trans. (New York: Semiotext(e), Inc., 1983); Jean Baudrillard, *Simulations*, Paul Foss, et al., trans. (New York: Semiotext(e), Inc., 1983). The epitome of cultural conservatism and hatred for popular culture, along with the class content it signifies, can be found in Allan Bloom, *The Closing of the American Mind* (New York: Simon and Schuster, 1987) and in various issues of the American journal, *The New Criterion*.

[9] Max Horkheimer and Theodor W. Adorno, *Dialectic of Enlightenment* (New York: Herder and Herder, [1944], 1972) (see especially "The Culture Industry: Enlightenment as Mass Deception," 120–67); Theodor W. Adorno, "Television and the Patterns of Mass Culture," in *Mass Culture: The Popular Arts in America*, Bernard Rosenberg and David Manning White, eds. (Glencoe, New York: The Free Press, 1957), especially 483–84; Theodor W. Adorno, *Minima Moralia* (London: New Left Books, [1951], 1974).

[10] Theodor W. Adorno, "Culture Industry Reconsidered," *New German Critique* No. 6 (Fall 1975), 18–19.

[11] Horkhiemer and Adorno, *Dialectic of the Enlightenment*.

[12] Tony Bennett, "The Politics of the 'Popular' and Popular Culture," in *Popular Culture and Social Relations*, Bennett, Mercer, and Woollacott, eds., 15.

[13] Examples of this tradition in the United States can be found in the *Journal of Popular Culture*. See also John G. Cawelti, *The Six-Gun Mystique* (Bowling Green: Bowling Green State University Press, 1984). For a discussion of this issue, see Stuart Hall, "Deconstructing 'the Popular'." Examples of work that integrates history and theoretical analyses include John F. Kasson, *Amusing the Million: Coney Island at the Turn of the Century* (New York: Hill and Wang, 1978); Duncan Webster, *Looka*Yonder:The Imaginary America of Populist Culture* (New York: Routledge, 1988).

[14] Brantlinger, *Bread and Circuses*, 23.

[15] For an excellent commentary on this issue, see Robert Scholes, "Aiming a Canon at the Curriculum," *Salmagundi* No. 72 (Fall, 1986), 101–17.

[16] Lawrence Grossberg, *We Gotta Get Out of This Place: Rock, Politics, and Postmodernity* (New York: Routledge, forthcoming).

[17] This issue is taken up in a variety of essays in Henry A. Giroux and Roger I. Simon eds., *Popular Culture, Schooling, and Everydaylife* (New York: Bergin and Garvey Press, 1989).

[18] See Antonio Gramsci, *Selections from Prison Notebooks*, Quintin Hoare and Geoffrey Nowell-Smith, eds. and trans. (New York: International Publishers, 1971); Antonio Gramsci, *Selections From Cultural Writings*, David Forgacs and Geoffrey Nowell-Smith, eds., William Boelhower, trans. (Cambridge: Harvard University Press, 1985).

[19] Larry Grossberg provides a useful theoretical elaboration of hegemony as a struggle for the popular:

> Hegemony is not a universally present struggle; it is a conjunctural politics opened up by the conditions of advanced capitalism, mass communication and culture. . . . Hegemony defines the limits within, which we can struggle, the field of "common sense" or "popular consciousness." It is the struggle to articulate the position of "leadership" within the social formation, the attempt by the ruling bloc to win for itself the position of leadership across the entire terrain of cultural and political life. Hegemony involves the mobilization of popular support, by a particular social bloc, for the broad range of its social projects. In this way, the people assent to a particular social order, to a particular system of power, to a particular articulation of chains of equivalence by which the interest of the ruling bloc come to define the leading positions of the people. It is a struggle over "the popular."

Larry Grossberg, "History, Politics, and Postmodernism: Stuart Hall and Cultural Studies," *Journal of Communication Inquiry* 10:2 (Summer 1986), 69.

[20] By focusing on the relationship between power and domination on the one hand and consent and struggle on the other, Gramsci highlights not only the contradiction between the interests of the ruling bloc and the powerlessness of subordinated groups, but also the contradictions between the choices that subordinated groups make and the reality of the conduct they live out at the level of everyday life. Thought and action, common sense and lived experience, become for Gramsci elements of a contradictory consciousness that should be at the heart of political and pedagogical struggle. Gramsci clarifies what he means by contradictory consciousness in the following passage:

> The active man-in-the-mass has a practical activity, but has no clear theoretical consciousness of his practical activity, which nonetheless involves understanding the world insofar as it transforms it. His theoretical consciousness can indeed be historically in opposition to his activity. One might almost say that he has two theoretical consciousness (or one contradictory consciousness); one which is implicit in his activity and which in reality unites him with all his fellow workers in the practical transformation of the real world; and one, superficially explicit or verbal, which he has inherited from the past and uncritically absorbed. But this verbal conception is not without consequences. It holds together a specific social group, it influences moral conduct and the direction of will, with varying efficacity but often powerfully enough to produce a situation in which the contradictory state of consciousness does not permit of any action, any decision or any choice, and produces a condition of moral and political passivity.

Antonio Gramsci, *Selections from Prison Notebooks*, Hoare and Smith, eds., 333.

[21] Ibid., 350.

[22] Bennett, "Introduction: Popular Culture and 'the Turn to Gramsci'," 15.

[23] Hall, "Notes on Deconstructing 'the Popular'," 235.

[24] Lawrence Grossberg, "Putting the Pop Back into Postmodernism," in Andrew Ross ed., *Universal Abandon? The Politics of Postmodernism* (Minneapolis: University of Minnesota Press, 1988), 169–70.

[25] Ernst Bloch, *The Principle of Hope*, (Cambridge, Mass.: MIT Press [1959] 1986).

[26] Mercer, "Complicit Pleasure," 59.

[27] Pierre Bourdieu, "The Aristocracy of Culture," in *Media, Culture, and Society* 2:2 (1980), 237–38.

[28] The emphasis on the study of texts can be seen most clearly in Roland Barthes, *S/Z* (New York: Hill and Wang, 1974); the emphasis on the relationship between popular culture and consumption is exemplified in Judith Williamson, *Decoding Advertisements: Ideology and Meaning in Advertising* (New York: Marion Boyars, 1978); Judith Williamson, *Consuming Passions: The Dynamics of Popular Culture* (New York: Marion Boyars, 1986).

[29] Jurgen Habermas, *The Theory of Communicative Action*, Vol. 1., Thomas McCarthy, trans. (Boston: Beacon Press, 1973).

[30] Colin Mercer, "Complicit Pleasure," 54–55.

[31] Colin Mercer, "A Poverty of Desire: Pleasure and Popular Politics," in *Formations of Pleasure*, 84.

[32] Laura Mulvey, "Visual Pleasure and Narrative Cinema," *Screen* 16:3 (Autumn 1986), 6–18.

[33] Jameson, "Pleasure: A Political Issue," in *Formations of Pleasure*, 10.

[34] Ibid., 13.

[35] Grossberg, "Putting the Pop Back into Postmodernim," 179.

[36] Roland Barthes, *The Grain of the Voice: Interviews 1962–80*, Linda Coverdale, trans. (New York: Hill & Wang, 1985), 191.

[37] Two qualifications must be made here. First, we reject the notion of class portrayed in *Dirty Dancing* embodies a class nostalgia. That is, class formations in this case are not developed along representative ethnic and racial lines and as such portray class conflict in relatively white, waspy terms. Second, there is a complex articulation of gender differences in this film that we have not addressed. These represent an important subtext regarding the articulation of class and gender relations, particularly in Baby's relationship with Penny.

[38] Roland Barthes, "Encore le Corps," *Critique* 35:425 (August–September 1982), 10.

[39] The worst aspect of *Dirty Dancing* is its construction of the polarities of reason and passion as congruent with the class dichotomy portrayed in the film.

[40] Angela McRobbie, "Dance and Social Fantasy," in Angela McRobbie and Mica Nava, eds., *Gender and Generation* (London: MacMillan, 1984), 144–45.

[41] Larry Grossberg, "Teaching the Popular," in Cary Nelson, ed., *Theory in the Classroom* (Urbana: University of Illinois Press, 1986).

[42] Laurie McDade, "Sex, Pregnancy and Schooling: Obstacles to a Critical Teaching of the Body," *Journal of Education*, in press.

[43] Simon, "Empowerment as a Pedagogy of Possibility."

[44] Magda Lewis and Roger Simon, "A Discourse Not Intended for Her: Learning and Teaching With Patriarchy," *Harvard Educational Review*, 56:4 (1986), 457–72.

[45] David Lusted, "Why Pedagogy," *Screen* 27 (September–October 1986), 4–5.

[46] Michel Foucault, *Power/Knowledge: Selected Interviews and Other Writings, 1972–1980*, Colin Gordon, ed. (New York: Pantheon Books, 1980).

[47] John Berger, *Once in Europa* (New York: Pantheon Books, 1987), 35.

9

Leon Golub's Radical Pessimism: Towards a Critical Pedagogy of Representation*

I think that a powerful society, generally speaking, has a powerful art. It reflects not necessarily the goals of the society but, rather, the society viewing its strengths, how successful it is and what it can get away with. What it reflects is confidence. These kinds of figures in a strange way reflect American power and confidence.

—*Leon Golub*[1]

. . . torture today has acquired new ends and a radical technologization of its means. The attack on the personal identity and the body of the victim is calculated now to undermine the social body as well.

—*Barbara Harlow*[2]

Representation and the Public Face of Power

The art of Leon Golub occupies a noble and precarious position within the contemporary art world precisely because of its refusal to disguise its logic of political opposition. For Golub, art is not the basis for simply establishing a new aesthetic, but it is an attempt to make the issues of ethics, power, and politics primary in the production of aesthetic standards for a democratic life. Golub's art resists subsumption under a crude political didacticism; it invokes images that not only assault the margins of social complacency, but also step outside the conventionalized avant-garde marketplace.

Because Golub's work controversially links questions of representation to issues of power, subjectivity, and meaning, and situates painting in relation to photography

---

* Peter McLaren co-author.

as a form of social criticism, it is particularly appropriate to the development of what we are calling a critical pedagogy of representation.[3]

Historically, Golub's paintings reflect a movement away from the social realism of the 1930s. The project of social realist artists assumed a more blatantly political and polemical stance than that of their contemporary populist regionalists. Artists such as Reginald Marsh, Moses, Isaac, and Raphael Soyer, Ben Shahn, George Grosz, William Gropper, and Philip Evergood sympathetically depicted the isolation, loneliness, and despair of those who were forced to rub up against the hard indifference to poverty, racial prejudice and human suffering churned out by the machineries of privilege and power operating within the discursive economics and material practices of the industrial capitalist state. While Golub remains decidedly dissatisfied with many aspects of social realism, his work shares an undeniable affinity to the works of this transgressive movement in numerous ways. These include its unambiguous condemnation of social injustice; its historical situatedness; its rejection of formalism, abstract expressionism, and naturalism; its search for truth in the zone of politics; its advocacy of art as a weapon of social reform and as a site of resistance to the violence of structural domination; and its frequent use of photographic imagery. However, his work escapes the somewhat sentimental, propagandistic, conventionalized, and naive realism often associated with this tradition.

Golub's work also marks a shift from the Lukácsian socialist educative perspective that suggested that "the right epistemology could secure aesthetic and cognitive value."[4] His paintings have undoubtedly been influenced by a certain dissatisfaction with social realism, which resulted in charges that conventional descriptive and narrative painting had begun to "conventionalize its own critique of ideology." In part, Golub's political and aesthetic direction was influenced by a new type of critical modernism that was beginning to assert itself, a modernist politics of representation that mobilized an oppositional aesthetic around questions of race, class, and gender. In this approach, informed to a large extent by Brecht's criticism of Lukács and by the writings of Althusser, considerable emphasis was placed on "difference" and the production of meaning through the process of signification and the discursive "positioning" of the historical subject. The "aesthetic of absence, discontinuity and montage" that this perspective underscored helped to further expand dimensions of the social realist tradition. According to this critique, postwar representional painting "may have offered us recognition of our unfreedom but not knowledge of its laws." There was also a growing awareness within this perspective that visual information was not able to perceive social reality or social action at the level of structure or absent cause, especially, as it pertained to "the demands of the representation and production of knowledge across questions of gender, class, and race." According to John Roberts, one of the major accomplishments of Golub's work has been its prodigious ability to "replace [the] 'photographic-modernist-structuralist' critique of the unities of conventional descriptive painting, back into the narrative spaces of the social realist tradition."

Golub's work has therefore managed to both rework and reinvigorate social realism and modernism by reconstituting narrative to encourage the viewer to observe the current historical juncture in order to analyze the power-sensitive effects of its social, cultural, technological, and bureaucratic practices. In his treatment of narrative, Golub seeks to recapture the relationships among power, ethics, domination, and human agency. By refiguring the critical relationship between the viewer and the image in terms of historical and political agency, Golub insists, against more academically domesticated strands of poststructuralism, that interrogation and torture are not merely matters of textuality, aesthetics, the discursive machinery of interpellation and inscription, or the fetishistic othering of the historical subject. His work points to the concrete materiality that inhere in forms of social meaning and the way in which discourses both map out regions of the flesh for the production and policing of desire and for the shaping or breaking of human will. Golub further recognizes the fragmented, decentered, and self-referential character of knowledge production within the current historical juncture, yet this recognition does not lure Golub into the sometimes slavish valorization of particularism that has so often rendered strands of postmodern critique politically immobile when addressing issues of cultural, political, and social justice. Golub is able to situate the discontinous and heterogeneous character of knowledge into a larger, but nontotalizing narrative structure that reveals the horror out of which the logic of totalitarianism and colonialism offers up its leering and menacing grin. As Roberts notes:

> Golub's interest is in the discontinuous, fractured, and violent nature of the historical process, and not in imbuing the historical image with any futurist resonance. What emerges from this is a 'doubling' of narrative interest; on the one hand a narrativisation of the injuries of class, gender, and race as moments within a larger oppressive totality (capital) and on the other a narrativisation of power-relations between individuals, groups, and classes as ideologically motivated and intelligible acts.[5]

Golub's paintings very much speak to what Anthony Giddens describes as the "totalitarian possibilities . . . contained within the institutional parameters of modernity."[6] With its military and paramilitary images, Golub's work evokes what Giddens calls the dark side of modernity. Not even thinkers such as Marx, Durkheim, or Weber were able to predict just how dark this side would become, especially when industrial innovation and organization are linked to military power. As Giddens points out:

> The twentieth century is the century of war, with the number of serious military engagements involving substantial loss of life being considerably higher than in either of the two preceding centuries. In the present century thus far, over 100 million people have been killed in wars, a higher proportion of the world's population than in the nineteenth century, even allowing for overall population increase.[7]

Reflecting the diabolical effects of the modern military/industrial complex, Golub's paintings may be seen as rupturing the complacency of bourgeois hegemony and revealing in the most human terms the unstated or silenced social conditions necessary to maintain what we are taught to regard as "freedom." Jon Bird refers to this quality of Golub's art as "an example of the way in which the public face of power conceals the nature of its real operations and relations."[8]

What are effectively produced in Golub's canvases are the representations of hidden, repressed, yet normalized political and social practices as they become intextuated or enfleshed. Enfleshment refers to the mutually constitutive enfolding of social structure and desire; that is, the dialectial relationship between the material organization of interiority and cultural forms and modes of materiality we inhabit subjectively. These representations constitute a series of enthrallingly grotesque and morally repulsive images depicting mercenaries, torturers and their victims, and death squad thugs.

Golub's leering and demonic figures do, in some way, serve the same counter-hegemonic and utopian purposes as the grotesque figures found in Bakhtin's writings on the carnival; yet Bakhtin's characters predominately represent the massified consciousness of humanity or "ancestral body of all the people" and the figures in Golub's work do not.[9] While on the surface resembling the lumpenproletariat of Golub's canvases, Bakhtin's carnival figures attempt to invert, decenter, and parody those "classical bodies" that signify the serious and authoritarian languages of the official or sovereign culture. Such figures often reflect the physical pleasure experienced at the moment the body escapes social and cultural control—what de Certeau calls escaping the "law of the named"[10]—and what Barthes calls *jouissance*.

The grotesque realism of Golub's figures portrays *not an ancestral body but a bureaucratically produced body* in the service of a state-sponsored economy of terror, a generalized network of counterinsurgency in which the ideology of fascism and the materiality of the flesh conjoin in the figures of the torturer and executioner. Unlike Bakhtin's carnivalesque parody of state power, Golub's images represent the *real face of state power* devoid of pretence, unmasked and relentlessly present, a presence that cannot be threatened, let alone seriously challenged, by carnivalesque inversion or the playful or parodic negation of authority. As Terry Eagleton points out, "Carnival releases us from the terrorism of excessive significance, multiplying and so levelling meanings; as such it is never far from ... empty futility."[11] Golub's grotesque figures are not meant to, in a Bakhtinian sense, parody the state; nor are they meant to erase the possibilities of resistance and social struggle. Rather, they *capture the naked edge of power*, circumscribing the legitimating and reifying functions of the state. Golub's brutal portrayal of such power serves as a "dangerous" memory that provides testimony to the false claims of a modernist science, progress, and objectivity that disguise the new technologies of power at work in the construction of contemporary society. This power can only be challenged by direct political intervention and ongoing forms of social and cultural resistance.

In his depictions of blatantly horrific and virulent measures of torture and oppression, Golub reveals the fragility of those bodies that the official culture considers illegitimate, expendible, and polluting and how such bodies always live precariously on the edge of annihilation. (Metaphorically, of course, the victims represent all those whom the state considers to be outcasts: artists, intellectuals, political dissidents, nonconformists, gays and lesbians, the poor, and criminals.) The terrible power of the social body made flesh through licensed acts of physical terror that result in the torture and execution of humans is part of the invisible power behind the laws and protocols of democracy. As Foucault has noted, power is productive but its effects can be either emancipatory or oppressive, or both.

The State as a Colonizing Agent

The images Golub produces variously jar, disrupt, and assail our everyday complacency. But this is more than defamiliarizing the everyday on the model of surrealism's subconscious rearrangement in dreams or deconstruction's fanciful "double readings." Rather, Golub's images puncture our reality by *laying bare the consequences of the lifestyles of the bourgeoisie in the sense that they are made possible and maintained at the expense of the colonized Other*. The stark and unsettling honesty of these paintings implicates and indicts bourgeois complicity with the conditions that make it necessary. The swindle of high culture and its cleansing category of what constitutes art is forcefully challenged in Golub's politics of trangression. This is reflected in Roberts's invitation to view Golub's imagery "as products of, and responses to, a highly spectacularized political culture and its attendant imperialist reflexes—America's saturation by confidence-speak and the rhetoric of 'pacifying' aliens."[12]

Golub's paintings serve as a form of social revenge on our complicity as North Americans in unnamed acts of colonial barbarism in an era unprecedented for its creation of supranational political institutions and global industries of terror. This aspect of Golub's work is captured by a phrase used by Fredric Jameson to describe the work of Cuban writer Roberto Fernandez Ratamar; of Ratamar's work, Jameson writes that it possesses "a constant awareness of all those cultural Others with whom we coexist and from whose existence in some peculiar way our own 'identity' is derived, when it is not more literally based on those other cultures by way of either derivation or of exploitation."[13] This sentiment is particularly evident in images constructed by Golub depicting political barbarism in Latin America in which the complicity of the United States in creating Third World sites of oppression through enforced economic dependency is not lost.

Given space limitations, this chapter will restrict itself to those paintings that appear in the "Interrogators," "Mercenaries," and "White Squad" series. The "Interrogation" series from 1981 and 1986 depicts a politics of political detention, incarceration, and torture. This series illustrates military authorities inflicting torture on victims who are gagged, blindfolded, bound, or suspended by their heels. The "Mercenararies" series from 1979 and 1984 deals with hired military figures engaged in joking, leering (sometimes directly at the viewer), making insults and taunts, and ominously brandishing automatic weapons. The "White Squad" representations from 1982, 1983, and 1987 depict acts of violence committed by police rather than military personel, with specific reference to the infamous right wing death squad that is the clandestine political arm of El Salvador's ruling military regime.

Technologies of Power/Bodies

Evident in the three series is the dialectical quality of Golub's canvases—his art attempts to engage rather than command the viewer. It provides images that in their raw immediacy attempt to both open up and peel away those layers of ideological repression and crusted over experiences and habits that contain the contradictions that tie all of us to prevailing systems of control and oppression. Golub's images of focussed horror and canalized brutality directly confront the viewer with his or her own mortality. They operate by positioning the viewer between the semiotically constituted categories of authority and state control and the fear and the total vulnerability of the body to such control. But such a positioning of the viewer involves another simultaneous splitting, which consists of an identification with both the torturers and their victims. This, in turn, evokes the fear of internalizing the self as Other (and making a moral alliance with the oppressor) and naturalizing the difference between acts of atrocity and the preservation of existing machineries of privilege from which the viewer derives some benefits as a "non-Other."

A singular strength of Golub's art is its attempt to break the monopoly of established reality by engaging the social dynamic of repressed needs at the level of the prelogical and unconscious. In fact, a large majority of images in these three series represent precisely what the dominant structures of oppression and social control attempt to conceal: the raw workings of power behind systoms of cultural maintenance and forms of symbolic production and social practice. Golub, like Foucault and Althusser, has taken as his primary project a revelation of the way in which power works on and through the body in various social and discursive practices.

Golub's figures depict a moral and political economy nurtured by the state and literally stamped into the flesh by instruments of torture as a means of exercising ideological and social mangement. They represent for the viewer a direct challenge to the teaching apparatus of the state, as bodies are depicted as serving as tablets upon which the state displays its 'civilizing' codes objects of a disciplinary rehabilitation. The modernist notion of the self as a disciplined will, as an undecaying center of self-identity and autonomous and self-directed social agency, collapses under the realization that mechanisms of identity-formation never operate in a terrain devoid of both the material and ideological effects of power. In the manner described by Foucault, the body becomes a transcendental signified, in that every form of political rehabilitation or normalization is directed at the body.[14] We see this power in the brutality displayed against the victims in Golub's paintings. *But we also see in it the tensions and contradictions exhibited in the faces and body postures of the aggressors.* It is, in its most gruesome manifestation, a power that works through sets of socially and culturally produced needs and desires that point to the material basis of fascist modes of subjectivity and the barbarism of the will.

De Certeau describes the process by which the law is written on the body as "intextuation."[15] This process refers to how the sovereign discourses of a society is made flesh. John Fiske expresses the process as the following:

> juridical law can be effective only if people have bodies upon which it can be imposed. Thus the history of the law is the history of the tools devised to transform an abstract system of justice into social behavior—the scarifying instruments of torture, the prison cell, handcuffs and riot sticks, the prisoner's box in court, and ultimately, of course, the gallows, the electric chair, and the cross . . . Tools are the means by which the law is written on the body; the body itself is meaningless, until the law, as the agent of social discipline, writes it into a text, and thus inserts itself into the social order.[16]

Viewed from this perspective, Golub's paintings function to disturb and menace the tacit conventions and ontological security that are central to cultural hegemony. Primary to the ideological construction of bourgeois life is the assumption that social dominance is "earned" through superior effort and ability. But what happens in Golub's canvases is that the images effectively redraw the boundaries between the process of self-constitution and identity formation and the power of the state to make invisible a reality of exclusion in which certain groups are accorded the status and material means for oppressing other groups. Golub's paintings have no specific "then" and "now"; rather there exists in the perspective of the viewer room to consider—and perhaps even challenge—his or her complicity with the torturers, and by implication, the contradictions of state power. The masculine images of the torturer invite a narcissistic identification on the part of male viewers, yet the moral consequences of such an identification are not easy to displace. The viewer (primarily the male viewer in this case) osscilates between enthrallment (since the torturers face the viewer, inviting him to join the event) and revulsion. In this way, the imagery of Golub's paintings implicates the viewer directly in the challenge of demarcating the boundaries between real life and art, between meaning and knowledge. Thus, Golub's paintings invite us to comprehend our real and imaginary political position in history, which in this instance is not a linear succession of events but a lived discourse in the contradictory and fractured constructions of time and space. This history provides a vantage point both ethically and politically, not for recovering or discovering the past but for entering into a dialogue with it in order to engage both its strengths and limitations.[17]

Golub's images thus raise for the viewer the following questions: What histories and social constructions provide the conditions for torture and terror? How can we grasp torture as a historical practice that implicates relations between the self and others that must be understood in institutional as well as ideological terms? In what way is the torture of bodies an ethical transgression of human rights while at the same time the necessary effect of the established political machinery of power under both so—called democracies and totalitarian regimes? In what way is the struggle by the U.S. to secure democracy *for* the Other a necessary means for securing control *over* the Other? How is torture as a practice taken up, learned, and inscribed as an affective and rational investment? What are the limits of ideology critique in the analysis of Golub's depictions of human suffering? How does one explain the pleasure felt by some in witnessing Golub's depiction of the infliction of pain on Others? In the sense that Golub's work raises such questions, it constitutes power, ethics, and politics not as marginal but as central to the very notion of aesthetics itself.

We are told that some of the figures in the "Mercenaries" series were "derived from a photo from Pakistan of two soldiers carrying a victim on a crude wooden shoulder hoist."[18] Referring to the early works of "Mercenaries," Golub claims that the figures are positioned to convey "the idea . . . that we're looking at them while they're looking at us, as if they're having their photograph taken." Elaborating on Golub's use of photographs during this time, Rifkin and Gumpert remark:

> With the "Mercenaries," Golub began to use multiple photographic sources for each individual figure. This method of selecting bits of various disjunctive moments and overlapping them to form one figure—all the while scraping off the paint to leave behind a skeletal residue of animated imagery within a flat outline of a figure—allows Golub to depict what he calls "the face of the modern world," a composite portrait constructed from bits of photographic data.[19]

Rifkin and Gumpert also comment on the coincidence between the violent subjects depicted in Golub's paintings and his fascination with the photographic image, noting that "both the gun and the camera are aimed at a target and in both cases they are 'shot'." The authors trace the use of the "shot" in photography to Etienne-Jules Marey's rifle-shaped camera, which yielded his "chrono-photographs."

The relationship to photography in Golub's work is further revealed in may of Golub's figures that appear cut off at the shin. Rifkin and Gumpert suggest this has to do with "Golub's infatuation with photography (a medium whose essence involves the fixing of light and darkness) and his use of the opaque projector to throw enlarged images onto the unstretched 'skins' of his canvases; the large figures act as shadows—flat projections of three-dimensional figures—which are fixed on the surface of the paintings."

Terrorism and the State

In his book, *Shamanism, Colonialism, and the Wild Man: A Study in Terror and Healing*[20] Mick Taussig discusses the role of terror in producing the hegemony of colonial state power. He describes terror as something "which as well as being a physiological state is also a social one whose special features allow it to serve as the mediator par excellence of colonial hegemony: the space of death where the Indian, African, and White gave birth to a New World." He describes this "space of death" as a site "where the social imagination has populated its metamorphosizing images of evil and the underworld ... a common pool of key signifiers binding the transforming culture of the conquereor with that of the conquered."

Following Taussig's depiction of terror, Golub's scenes of torture constitute "spaces of death" not simply by conjuring feelings of abject terror in the viewer, *but by both affectively depicting and discursively naming the structures of terror embodied in state and colonial subjecthood.* It is a structure of terror which is simultaneously being *exercised* in the relations of power depicted by the artist and resisted in the pedagogical practice of the artist as social critic. It is a terror heightened by the matter-of-fact or commonplace quality of the evil at work that gives it an almost mystical inevitability. Golub depicts this common sense quality of evil as politically charged, deconstucting the notion of common sense as a self-sufficient truth and reconstructing it as an historical and social practice. In this case, Golub makes the notion of commonsense complicitous with evil and terror by suggesting its structural dependency upon institutions and ideologies that produce subject positions hospitable to established social conventions and social hierarchies. These institutional and ideological sites constitutive of structurally embedded social evil can only be understood as forms of ideological management and cultural maintenance constructed within particular social formations and unconscious modes of subjectivity that are at root political and pedagogical.

Healing, Death, and Utopia

Rifkin and Gumpert describe Golub as someone who, early in his career, "believed that, through the act of painting, the artist could exorcize evil spirits from the social structure."[21] Golub's paintings can also be taken up in pedagogical terms that bear metaphorical affinities to shamanic practice.[22] As articulated by Taussig,[23] shamanic practice may serve as "a strategic zone of vacuity, a palette of imageric possibility." Taussig points out that the "power of shamanism lies not with the shaman but with the differences created by the coming together of shaman and patient ... the joint construction of the healer and the sick in the semantically generative space of annulment that is the colonial death space." What is taking place in shamanic healing, he argues, is a joint interrogation of the ideological environment. This is similar to what Jon Bird emphasizes with respect to the politics of representation in Golub's work. Golub's work must be seen not only as a form of ideology critique expressed in images of terror and torture, but also as a social text jointly created by artist and viewer—one that offers up the pedagogical issue of what conditions exist for these images to be addressed as more than merely objects of aesthetic consumption.

Both shamanism and Golub's imagery thrive on the theoretical and pedagogical potential that death offers, and death is the primary motif of Golub's work in the three series under consideration. This engagement with death is what promotes the utopian possibilities in his work. A glimpse of this possibility can be seen in comments by Ernst Bloch and T.W. Adorno.[24] According to Bloch, "death most certainly provides a continual motivation [in the struggle against reification]" and the struggle to go beyond death is at the basis of the concept of utopia. In fact, he argues that "death depicts the hardest counter-utopia." Sharing a similar sentiment, Adorno writes that "where the threshold of death is not at the same time considered, there can actually be no utopia" and goes on to suggest that "one can talk about utopia only in a negative way."

By focusing on the images of death or near-death in Golub's images, the viewer is provoked to consider *what is missing*—the promise of utopia. Commenting on the function of utopia, Bloch writes that "each and every criticism of imperfection, incompleteness, intolerance, and impatience already without a doubt presupposes the conception of, and longing for, a possible perfection." Thinking about Golub's images in relation to Bloch's and Adorno's understanding of the relationship between death and utopia enables us to understand Golub's work as both a politics of critique and a politics of hope. That is, while Golub's work confronts the viewer with the possibility of a complete dissolution of even the faintest glimmer of utopian possibility, a threatened negation of all hope; it also provides the conditions for the viewer to reflect on the basis of both his or her despair and longing, and the contradictions at work in at once being absorbed in the facticity of the mutilated and mutilators and simultaneously being horrified by the poetics of terror that Golub has produced.

Golub's work contains a form of radical pessimism that not only serves to deter the "happy consciousness" of political struggle, but it also implicitly points to the necessarily affirmative notion that things must change. While Golub's work initiates important debates over the politics of cultural power and the production of art, it also poses some difficulties. His portrayal of political repression through what he has referred to as "bare-ass reality" may appear to operate from a notion of immediacy of representation that functions to recontain the very social power of terror that his art is aimed at challenging. That is, Golub's images at times seem to lack the mediating element of an historical context and thus border on occupying that place of representation that Adorno argued exists between magic and positivism, i.e., that place where knowledge is recorded and immediately given and as such contains the possibility of being mythologized in a universal imagery. This raises the important question of how the logic of opposition becomes visible within these paintings, especially when the artist uses a representational form that clings to a notion of immediacy that appears to dissolve both history and those discursive practices that reveal the relationship among barbarism, ourselves, and the larger society.

The absence in Golub's work of images which are clearly demarcated as politically oppositional raises the issue of whether it is too closely linked to the logic of domination; his work has a structured silence that says little directly about resistance and struggle. Golub may conceivably be operating almost exclusively within a form of cultural production resting on a notion of power that is defined solely through the logic of domination. The notion of power as a positive instance, of counter-hegemonic struggle as the ever-present underside of domination, runs the risk of being undermined in this work. Thus, the question is raised as to whether Golub in his attempt to empower human agency has in fact created a discourse that works to eliminate it.

A defense that can be raised in response to these questions is one that points to the political nature of Golub's art in which his imagery does not compromise the demands of his own politics. This, of course, does not deny the possibility that different people may read his work in contrasting ways. Within a liberal democracy, the horrors portrayed by Golub stand in stark opposition to the valedictory images of harmony and consensus that characterize the dominant culture. It is in this sense that Golub's images contain a discourse of opposition that is sufficiently engaging to make the negation it attempts to perform politically viable. Of course, this is not to suggest that some viewers will not enjoy or delight in such images of horror, but those who might celebrate such images may simply be confirming the political nature of Golub's message, i.e., that political authoritarianism in its most brute form constructs particular needs and desires which resonate with the cultural logic of fascism. Thus, what becomes problematic in Golub's work is the nature of the relationship between the barbarism expressed by servants of the state and the ideological production within the viewer. It is important to stress that Golub takes a stand on the political nature of his relationship to barbarism and the apparatuses of political terror, but he neither predicts nor presupposes that his art will guarantee the viewer's response.

In another sense Golub's work implies a concept of resistance. Golub's "Interrogation" series from 1981 and 1986 suggests that even in the darkest carceral spaces of his canvases, where in the dialectical figuration of torturer and victim, life becomes reduced to a clusters of anguish and a prurient delight in smashing through flesh and bone, there exists a dim surplus of meaning. Here hope may be held in flickering abeyance but never disappear. Each image in Golub's "Interrogation" paintings formulates what is lacking, what Bloch refers to as "anticipatory illumination." For instance, in the bound and brusied torso of the torture victim in *Interrogation (II)* (1981) there exists a space of flesh that refuses total reduction. Though it bears the ritualized inscription of sovereign power terrorized into the flesh, domination does not signal the end of meaning.

An often hard acknowledgment to make with respect to Golub's images in these series is that while resistance appears hopeless and at best less than complete, *domination is always partial*. In that partiality of domination there is always a space of struggle and hope. Even when domination leads to the death of the body the body still signifies. While physical death surrenders the body to total reification, it also transfigures the body into a symbol that can be brought back to life. In this sense, the viewer is invited to reclaim Golub's corpses and reanimate them with a sense of radical hope by engaging what Bloch calls the "world-in-possibility." Death does not offer an escape from meaning. It demands that we transform meaning into power. A corpse does not signify the victory of the state but rather symbolizes the basis of its moral economy and the transactions of terror necessary to maintain it. Torture and the prospect of death through deliberately inflicted pain push us to the margins of reality and the struggle for a utopian form of hope and an interrogation of what Bloch refers to as modes of objective-real possibilities (objective-real Mögliche). Consequently, viewers of Golub's imagery are not necessarily positioned as either voiceless victims or the generic butcher who commands the gulag and its Third World variants. They are provoked instead to anticipate that which has not yet been (noch nie so gewesen) and to assume a prospective understanding of events in terms of historical praxis and possibility.

The political issue that needs to be underscored is that the circuit of production that results in forms of power exercised by the state involves not only the workings of the economy but the means of symbolic production and the political linkages between the two. The powerful aesthetic and experiential images that confront the viewer in Golub's work helps clarify such linkages. Golub provides us with an aspect of reality that is subversive to the dominant society's "clean" aesthetic and ideology of harmony, elements of a hegemony that attempt to smother the agonies, screams, and horror of domination. Leon Golub's work reveals aspects of domination while simultaneously offering a site of intervention, a site that gratingly posits as its starting point our own repressed needs and silences. His paintings offer us a means of confronting the politics of domination and subverting the poetics of terror in a way that does not draw inspiration from the underlying mythology of colonization. It is in this context that the radical pessimism of Golub's art reveals itself.

Taussig writes that "Today, faced with the ubiquity of torture, terror, and the growth of armies, we in the New World are assailed with a new urgency. There is the effort to understand terror, in order to make others understand."[25] In taking up this challenge, Golub's work has brought us closer to recognizing the urgency of the political and pedagogical task at hand: to transform the world into a public space where individuals as active, social agents for change can engage in the project of creating history for the purpose of greater social transformation and justice.

A Critical Pedagogy of Representation

Pedagogy occurs wherever knowledge is produced, wherever culture is given the possibility of translating experience and constructing truths, even if such truths appear unrelentingly reduntant, superficial, and commonsensical. On the one hand, there are standardized pedagogies that codify experience and shape meaning production in predictable and in conventional ways, and in doing so naturalize meaning an the social structures and cultural forms, which help to reproduce such meaning. (In effect, then, all pedagogies produced certain meaning-effects.) On the other hand, oppositional pedagogies resist such formalized production of meaning by offering new channels of communication, new codifications of experience, and new perspectives of reception which unmask the political linkage between images, their means of production and reception, and the social practices they legitimate. A critical pedagogy of representation recognizes that we inhabit a photocentric culture in which the proliferation of hegemonically scripted photographic and electronically produced images and sounds serves as a form of multi-media catechism through which individuals ritually encode and evaluate the engagements they make in the various discursive contexts of everyday life. It is an approach that understands media representations—whether photographs, television, print, film, or another form—as not merely productive of knowledge but also of subjectivity. In this case, critical pedagogy must be understood as a deliberate attempt to recognize connections among the ideologies and practices that structure pedagogical authority, modes of signification, and those that structure the production and consumption of various kinds of representations. Students can then move from an examination of pedagogical relations in the classroom to those pedagogical relations in everyday life that influence the way in which media representations are both produced and taken up by individuals. In addition, students are encouraged to examine how the way in which they are ensconced within webs of significance and assumptions created by the world of media representations helps to constitute the meanings by which they not only come to understand and negotiate reality but are constituted as political subjects.

Representations are always produced within cultural limits and theoretical borders, and as such are necessarily implicated in particular economies of truth, value, and power. In relation to these larger axes of power in which all representations are embedded, it is necessary to remind the student: Whose interests are being served by the representations in question? Within a given set of representations, who speaks, for whom, and under what conditions? Where can we situate such representations ethically and politically with respect to questions of social justice and human freedom? What moral, ethical, and ideological principles structure our reactions to such representations?

While it is commonplace for some radical educators to emphasize the importance of understanding culture as the struggle over assigned meanings, identities, histories, educators and other cultural workers need to find ways of reading texts of popular and mass culture from a perspective that is not limited to ideology critique. It is not enough to limit a critical pedagogy of representation to simply a question of reading ideology from either the perspective of locating commodity forms or discovering contradictory expressions of everyday social relations, but to situate representations in a complex field of rational and affective economies that explore how individuals both construct meanings and make emotional investments in those constructions.[26]

Two important pedagogical issues are at stake here. First, a critical pedagogy of representation needs to highlight and problematize the notion of textual authority at work in any classroom practice. Textual authority, in this case, refers to the power educators used to legitimate both the value of a particular image or text and the range of interpretations that can be brought to bear in understanding it. Second, it is crucial to repeat that radical educators need to develop pedagogical practices that legitimatize the conditions that allow students to speak from their own experiences without simply being invited to romanticize their own voices. For instance, Golub's work should be partly approached from the experiences that students use to produce meaning out of his work. But such meanings should then be made problematic and theoretically extended for the interests they suggest, the social relations they evoke, the histories they might recover, and the possibilities they might contain for reclaiming art as a domain from which to reconstruct notions of emancipatory struggle and critical citizenship.[27] In this instance, the struggle over art becomes central to forms of self and social formation that are constitutive of the conditions for democracy itself. At work here is a pedagogy in which difference, knowledge, power, and politics are integral to what it means to think critically and act with ethical and civic courage.

A critical pedagogy of representation acknowledges that images are neither objective nor transparent but are produced within discursive and material sites of disjuncture, rupture, and contradiction. The world of images is better understood from a pedagogical perspective as a terrain of contestation that serves as the loci of multivalent practical–discursive structures and powers. This suggests not only examining such images in terms of what they include but also examining them in terms of their exclusions. Such a strategy invites students to understand the way background institutions and the routines of everyday life make possible particular discursive formations and social practices, available to some groups and not to others. Similarly, this approach also encourages students not to sanctify knowledge or to view it as something to be simply revered and received, but rather validates the knowledge that students have acquired from their own personal experiences and struggles for meaning and identity. Consequently, students are more likely to read texts and images productively and critically rather than passively. Images such as Golub's can be questioned and challenged through the experiences that students use to give meaning to the world, the language they use to understand such experiences, and in this way an understanding of the production of knowledge itself can thus become part of the process of a critical pedagogy of representation.

We are emphasizing the idea that the interpretations arising from any given representation are always mutable, contingent, and partial; furthermore, their authority is always provisional and not transcendental. Representations have no meaning other than those rhetorically or discursively assigned to them. Such a pedagogy acknowledges that concept formation is shaped and determined by the forms that are inseparable from it and cannot be characterized by a metaempirical universality that exists independently of the contingencies of differential relations of power and the sensual particularities of material life.

This perspective involves more than a language which simply mimics or parodies the dehumanizing tendencies of the age of mechanical reproduction but rather means exposing and reconstituting the political linkages between signs and structures of representation and the technologies of power which underwrite them. In this sense, a critical pedagogy of representation is necessary in order to be able to uncover how the materiality and discursivity of everyday knowledge shapes social existence in certain ways to reproduce hidden economies of power and privilege that legitimize unequal social arrangements.

Central to a critical pedagogy of representation is an interrogation of the multiple ways in which culture is inscribed through the representations that both produce and legitimate it within particular power/knowledge relations. We are using the term "representation" in a manner similar to that of Stuart Hall, who defines it as the way in which meaning is constructed through the placement, positioning, and situatedness of discourse. Hall writes that "how things are represented and the 'machineries' and regimes of representation in a culture . . . play a constitutive, and not merely a reflexive, after-the-event, role.[28] Hall notes that representation is "possible only because enunciation is always produced within codes which have a history, a position within the discursive formations of a particular time and place." By granting the concept of representation a formative and not merely an expressive place in the constitution of social and political life, questions of culture and ideology and what Hall describes as "the scenarios of representation"—subjectivity, identity, and politics—take on an increasing significance.

Hall's notion of representation presents us with a multilayered, complex, and contradictory subjectivity, and he recognizes the need to develop rather than erase a notion of human agency, identity, and difference. Rejecting the master narratives of bourgeois liberal humanism, Hall articulates a view of identity which does not "universalize" the subject and refuses to treat "otherness" or "difference" as excess, exotic, or unrepresentable—something outside the placement of history, politics, and power. Following Hall's analysis, a critical pedagogy of representation can, for example, begin to contest the practice of essantalizing the historical subject is African-American, Puerto Rican, female, or White, etc.— and to underscore the immense diversity and differentiation of the historical and cultural experiences of such subjects. At issue here is a view of subjectivity constituted within rather than outside of cultural, social, and linguistic determinants. For example, when applied to the politics of racism, a critical pedagogy of representation is able to help educators to retheorize the concept of agency and difference such that, in Hall's terminology, it is able to "decouple" ethnicity from its equivalence with nationalism, imperialism, racism, and the violence of the state. In doing so, it helps educators to recognize, according to Hall, that we are *all* ethnically located and our ethnic identities are important but must be constructed so as not to marginalize, dispossess, or displace the "Other." As Kobena Mercer notes, "What is at issue is to acknowledge differences without necessarily ending up in a divisive situation, how to enact an 'ethics of disagreement,' as Hall says, without recourse to rhetorics that cut off the possibility of critical dialogue."[29]

A critical pedagogy of representation not only denaturalizes the conventions that encode the ideological and make those ideological contents open to interrogation and contestation but also explores the preconditions of its own categorizations and categorically provisional assumptions.[30] That is, to a certain extent, our very acts of naming reality always occur from positions of intelligibility which are complicitous with the moral imperatives of the dominant social order and must be interrogated for the limits of their conditions for enabling transformation. In this sense, a pedagogy of representation provides the basis for educators to be attentive to a politics of location, one which recognizes and interrogates the strengths and limitations of those places one inherits, engages, and occupies and which frame the discourses through which we speak and act.

A critical pedagogy of representation must also take up a discourse of possibility. In this context, resistance to domination and oppression must consist of more than a critique of dominant forms of knowledge and social practices—more than moral injunctions against dominant evaluative judgments and cultural forms. As long as resistance is "reactive," it positions itself as "other-centered" discourse.[31] Within a larger project of possibility, resistance must be an active, and not a reactive transvaluation of dominant perspectives. It must be active if it is to generate new "action-guiding" perspectives that can allow cultural workers to escape the larger logic of domination, which continues to underwrite many anti-colonialist struggles and resistances—the very logic that such local struggles set out to overturn.

In short, we are arguing that a critical pedagogy of representation must establish the relativity of all forms of representations by situating them in historical and social constructions that both inform their content and structure their ideological parameters. Second, a pedagogy of representation must bring to light the strategies that are used to structure how texts are read, used, and received within particular contexts and practices. At stake here is understanding not only how power is inscribed in a pedagogy of representation, but also how such a pedagogy can be used to disrupt the ideological, cultural, and political systems that both inscribe and contain them. This suggests that the practice of reading ideologies be connected to the production of political strategies informed by transformative ideologies. Third, a critical pedagogy of representation must be grounded in projects that provide a connection between representations that operate in particular educational sites and representations that operate in other cultural sites around similar forms of address and relevancies. Fourth, a critical pedagogy of representation must be taken up as a form of ethical address which grounds the relationship between the self and others in practices that promote care and solidarity rather than oppression and human suffering. In this case, a pedagogy of representation cannot be disarticulated from the radical responsibility of both politics and ethics.

The preceding discussion enables us to appreciate that the meanings of Golub's paintings are always bounded by the historical, cultural, and political conditions of their production, the epistemological and interpretive resources available to articulate their meaning as they are received by the viewer, and the reading formations that the viewers bring to the act of reception (which very much depend on the personal histories, experiences and the politics of location of the viewers). Golub's paintings are the product of such constraints just as they point to the way such constraints work in the broader arena of the state; they teach us that people do not possess power as much as they produce it and are produced by it.

Within a transformative pedagogy, Golub's work not only points to the way power works corporeally to inscribe its hegemonic certainties into living tissue, but also how it serves as a dominating cultural force to create, in Lukács's terms, "a charnel house of dead interiorities."[32] Just as the photographs of artists such as Cindy Sherman confront essentialist notions of the self yet retain a point of view, a motivating politics,[33] so, too, do Golub's paintings serve as disturbing provocations against hegemonically articulated understandings of subjectivity and power and dominant understandings of representation yet assume an unambiguous condemnation of structures of brutality and the social logic of fascism. Golub's images present us with an opportunity for locating power not just in the daily disciplinary and incorporative practices of state life, but in the barbaric conjuncture of colonial power and the growth of the capitalist world state.

Golub's paintings can help reveal to students the manner in which they, as individual and collective social actors, are located in history so that to be a servant of state power is often to be its unwitting victim. Furthermore, students can be offered the opportunity to recognize their own socially determined positions within the reality they are attempting to describe and understand. A critical pedagogy of representation must provide students with the opportunity of recognizing the limitations of the languages that are made available in helping them to understand their everyday experiences, the categories they use to represent these experiences, and the relationship between such categories and the cultural forms, modes of subjectivity, and social practices in which they become articulated. A transformative politics of representation makes thematic its own rhetorical artifice, alerts us to its constitutional character, its own ontological foundations, and liberate's us from those sovereign discourses that invite us to relive the existing social arrangements within the dominant culture. Students are then encouraged to envision new cultural forms, modes of subjectivity, and social practices that will enable them to better speak their own truth and transform those conditions that constrain their capacities for critical reflection and their ability to engage in the work of social transformation.

If critical pedagogy is to be taken seriously as a form of cultural struggle, it must seek to create new forms of knowledge not only by breaking down disciplinary boundaries but also by creating new spaces where knowledge can be produced. This means that pedagogy as a form of cultural production must not be limited to canonical texts and social relations that mediate and produce forms of dominant culture. Knowledge must be reinvented and reconstructed by inviting students to be border-crossers, by encouraging them to collapse disciplines that separate high from popular culture, theory from practice, art from life, politics from the everyday, and pedagogy from education.[34] Central to the goal of critical pedagogy is the need to create a public sphere of citizens who are able to exercise power over their lives and especially over the conditions of knowledge production and acquisition. Taking up such a goal means critical educators must demonstrate "that a concern for education is inseparable from issues of geography, race, gender, family, income, law—a myriad of social and political concerns that are often considered irrelevant to the classroom."[35]

Creating new forms of knowledge also suggests creating classroom practices that provide students with the opportunity to work collectively and to develop needs and habits in which the social is felt and experienced as an emancipatory rather than alienating. Put in different terms, a critical pedagogy must reclaim the social as a precondition for collective engagement and struggle. David Trend has described many examples in the arts of pedagogical practices where students are provided with the opportunity to learn how to work collectively in and out of schools, in opposition to the traditional competitive and individualist approaches to pedagogy.[36] This approach suggests that when presenting students with the opportunity of challenging the borders of established disciplines, they should learn to connect the specific and the particular to wider social and historical contexts. At the same time, the reconstruction of knowledge/power relations and classroom social practices must extend the promise and possibility of a critical pedagogy by affirming the importance of not simply over struggling forms of knowledge and classroom relations but by creating new public spheres outside the schools where learning is as important as it is inside the classroom. Of course, this is not meant to suggest an opposition between schools and other public spheres as much as it is to suggest their common project in political and pedagogical struggles within broader social and political contexts.

Finally, it is crucial that the very category of educator as transformative cultural worker not be limited to people who work in schools. Critical pedagogy is a form of cultural politics, discourse, and power-sensitive social practices, which always presuppose particular forms of citizenship, community, and visions of the future. The implication is that all cultural workers should be actively involved in critical pedagogy, regardless of the sites in which they work. Neither can those of us who work in the schools, in the arts, in the social services, or in other institutions retreat into our sites of work and act as if we have no connection with other public spheres or other cultural workers. If critical pedagogy is to contribute to the multiplication of sites of democratic struggles, sites that affirm specific struggles while recognizing the necessity to embrace broader issues that enhance the life of the planet, then all forms of cultural struggle must assert the primacy of cultural workers as active participants in pedagogical practices that deepen a democratic and transformative politics. Specifically, we need a pedagogy that allows us to see how educational work can be connected to a broader struggle to reclaim democratic public life. This is the challenge all educators have to face regardless of the cultural work in which they engage. This represents more than a call for a new dialogue; it points to new forms of struggle over power, human dignity, and social justice.

At issue here is the construction of a project of radical democracy in which power works not just *on* individuals but *through* individuals in the interest of a transformative politics. As Golub himself notes:

> I think that if people really learn that they *have* power then they are going to be a real threat, because there are more people out of power than in power. There are people dissatisfied at one level or another about all kind of issues. They have to be, in one sense, manipulated by the government, the information they receive has to be distorted to keep this a repulbic rather than a democracy. The notion of a republic is more bureaucratic than the notion of a democracy. Democracy means that the majority might actually change something.[37]

Those involved in developing a critical pedagogy for radical democracy do not presume to speak for others or on behalf of others, but *in solidarity with* others whose concerns they happen to share, concerns for a society unburdened by suffering and social injustice. In forging relations with dispossessed groups, it is important that critical educators be able to distinguish claims of moral, ethnic, gender, or political superiority that they exercise as outsiders. A consideration concerning how "cultural others" name experience, place labels on their sense of reality, and use their own history and culture to define their struggle for freedom, should be a primary concern within all forms of critical pedagogy. Critical educators must remember, however, that the experiences of those with whom they engage in a critical pedagogy of representation are never self-evident (since experiences are always the seat of ideology and not a state of unmediated innocence). Consequently, critical cultural workers need to provide conditions for themselves and for other to examine the literalness of their reality, the context in which such a reality is aritculated, and how their experiences are imbricated in contradictory, complex, and changing vectors of power. Critical educators need to explore the pervasiveness and complexity of social evil in this current historical juncture and offer a project of possibility for cultural workers—and themselves—so that they have the opportunity to confront such evil. In pedagogical terms, such a project must constitute more than a reversal of power relations—more than the production of social logics and practices prohibited by the master—but rather the creation of new spaces for the reconstitution of the social imagination, for building new modes of sociality, and for reconsitituting new articulations of the meaning of human emancipation and freedom. Much of this work necessarily involves not only understanding the disabling and emancipatory potential of the media knowledges that are available to us, but also the importance of struggling to overturn current arrangements of extra-communicational forms of power and social realtions that undergird—and in some instances help to overdetermine—the production of such knowledges. In this regard, a critical pedagogy of representation seeks to produce partial, contingent, but necessary historical practices that will provide some of the conditions needed for the emancipation of the many public spheres that make up our social and institutional life, practices that recognize their social constructedness and historicity and the institutional and social arrangements which they legitimate.

As cultural workers whose pedagogical sites are primarily the universities and public schools, we want to issue a caveat regarding the issue of who speaks for whom, and under what conditions. We make no claim to speak *for* others, but rather *with* others. But we want to emphasize that we choose to speak to issues that concern us from a specific political and ideological location that is always under analysis. There is, we feel, a certain irony in claims made by some educators who profess a certain political correctness in their so-called direct involvment with those whom they label as the "working-class." One such claim is that if one is an intellectual or cultural worker within academic settings then this precludes one from speaking at all if the form of oppression addressed is not directly experienced. This position often represents a species of "White" bourgeoise guilt that erases the possibility for political action across and between differences. Given the marginality of most social criticism, we believe that the most urgent issue is not whether you can claim to be spending your time advocating for 'others' by adopting a language of "plainspeak" or the now fashionable discourse of partiality but is rather to explore the following questions: What are the issues that need to be addressed in order to create a more just society? Who is listening? With whom do we form alliances, and for what purposes?

For educators, answering these questions means constructing a hybrid pedagogical space where students do not need the colonizer's permission to narrate their own identities, a space where individual identities find meaning in collective expression and solidarity with other culutral workers, where Eurocentric time and Cartesian anxiety recede into the lived, historical moment of contemporary struggles for identity.

A critical pedagogy of representation seeks what Trinh T. Minh-ha calls "the interval."[38] The interval is a space which simultaneously invites and derides closure—a "space in which meaning remains fascinated by what escapes and exceeds it"; and it is simultaneously a closure of meaning that "can defy its own closure" thereby "displacing and emptying out the establishment of totality."

Golub's images help us to understand the pervasiveness and complexity of social evil in this current historical juncture and offers a project of possibility for cultural workers in the arts and education to confront such evil. In pedagogical terms, such a project must constitute more than a reversal of power relations—more than the production of social logics and practices prohibited by the master—but rather the creation of new spaces for the reconstitution of the social imagination, for building new modes of sociality, and for reconstituting new articulations of the meaning of human emancipation and freedom.

REFERENCES

[1] Leon Golub, quoted in Jon Bird, "Leon Golub: 'Fragments of Public Vision,'" *Leon Golub—Mercenaries and Interrogations: Essays by Jon Bird, Interview with Michael Newman.* (London Institute of Contemporary Art, 1982), 15.

[2] Barbara Harlow, "Political Detention: Countering the University." *October* 53 (Summer 1990), 54.

[3] As commentators on Golub's work have consistently pointed out, many of his "monumentalized figures" are derived from "photographic mass cultural fragments." John Roberts, "Zones of Exclusion: Leon Golub's 'Other America,'" *Leon Golub: Selected Paintings, 1967-1986* (Darry, N. Ireland and the Douglas Hyde Gallery, Dublin, 1988), 8. For instance, in making references to Golub's procedural methods, Jon Bird stresses "the constant reworking of surface and image imprinting a history of activity, the complex montage of photographic references culled from the repertoire of cultural knowledge, and the specific interest in media representations" (Bird, 15).

After spending a year in Italy (1956–1957), Golub increasingly "turned to photographs as source materials, further objectifying his feelings and ideas." The quotes in this and the following paragraphs are from Ned Rifkin and Lynn Gumpert, "On Power and Vulnerability: The Art of Leon Golub," Golub (New York: The New Museum of Contemporary Art, 1984). During this time, Golub worked frequently from photographs of three-dimensional classical sculptures, which are easily recognizable in his early works. Golub later turned to photographic sources taken from news photos such as those depicting the conflict in Vietnam, sports events, public officials, and other media events, while always "enhancing the data available in the news photographs, investing it with pathos via his painting technique." As Rifkin and Gumpert point out, "photographs became increasingly important [to Golub], owing to the manner in which they capture man in the fractured moments of continuity." Golub himself refers to the importance of the documentary photograph in its "splintering experience" and "iconic capacity." What Golub refers to as the photograph's "splintering experience," Rifkin and Gumbert elaborate in relation to Golub's work as "the awkward, fragmentary moment, so that the paintings will resonate with that instantaneous seam between now and then, that time/space continuum from which we normally seek refuge, the 'it-will-pass' feeling of fear and/or complacency . . . [which Golub] . . . has called . . . a 'no-space.'"

Golub has noted that, "Photography has changed our ways of seeing, changed our ways of separation, disjunction and conjunction, changed the way we recognize experience, and ultimately the way we see ourselves." And, as Rifkin and Gumbert explain, "In this sense, the mirror used to reflect the outer world upon the inner has been superseded by the photograph, that two-dimensional record of frozen time that sensitizes us to the disjunction of contemporary life." For instance, in describing Golub's representation of Nelson Rockefeller, Rifkin and Gumpert are quick to mention "his brow furrowed, his teeth clenched, while his lips are pursed, frozen by the unyielding distortion of the fraction-of-a-second shutter speed of a camera."

[4] The quotes in this paragraph are from Roberts, "Zones of Exclusion," 6 and 7. For a further discussion of social realism, see David Shapiro, ed., *Social Realism: Art as Weapon* (New York: Frederick Ungar Publishing Co., 1973) and Patricia Hills, *Social Concern and Urban Realism: American Painting of the 1930s* (Boston: Boston University Art Gallery, 1983).

[5] Roberts, "Zones of Exclusion," 9.

[6] Anthony Giddens, *The Consequences of Modernity* (Stanford: Standford University Press, 1990), p. 8.

[7] Ibid., 9–10.

[8] Bird, 13.

[9] M. Bakhtin, *Rabelais and His World* (Cambridge: Massachusetts Institute of Technology Press, 1968), 19.

[10] M. de Certeau, *The Practice of Everyday Life* (Berkeley: University of California Press, 1984), 149.

[11] Terry Eagleton, "Bakhtin, Schopenhauer, Kundera," *Bakhtin and Cultural Theory*, Ken Hirschkop and David Shepherd, eds. (Manchester and New York: Manchester University Press, 1989), 185.

[12] Roberts, 10.

[13] Fredric Jameson, Forward to Roberto Fernandez Retamar, *Caliban and Other Essays*, Edward Baker, trans. (Minneapolis: University of Minnesota Press, 1989), 13.

[14] N. Fraser, *Unruly Practices: Power, Discourse, and Gender in Contemporary Social Theory*, (Minneapolis: University of Minnesota Press, 1989), 60.

[15] De Certeau, *The Practice of Everyday Life*. See also the discussion of enfleshment in Peter McLaren, "Schooling the Postmodern Body: Cultural Pedagogy and the Politics of Enfleshment," *Journal of Education*, 170:3 (1988), 53–83.

[16] John Fiske, *Understanding Popular Culture* (Winchester, Mass: Unwin Hyman, 1989), 91.

[17] Compare with W. Adamson, *Marx and the Disillusionment of Marxism* (Berkeley: University of California Press, 1985).

[18] Leon Golub, quoted in Bird, 5.

[19] He quotes in this and the next two paragraphs are from Rifkin and Gumpert, "On Power and Vulnerability," 63 and 64.

[20] The quotes in this paragraph are from Mick Taussig, *Shamanism, Colonialism, and the Wild Man: A Study in Terror and Healing* (Chicago: The University of Chicago Press, 1987), 5 and 8.

[21] Rifkin and Gumpert, "On Power and Vulnerability," 13.

[22] For a discussion of ritual, pedagogy and shamanism, see P. McLaren, *Schooling as a Ritual Performance* (London: Routledge, 1986).

[23] This quote and the next are from Taussig, *Shamanism, Colonialism, and the Wild Man*, 444 and 460.

[24] The quotes in this paragraph and the next are from Theodor W. Adorno and Ernst Bloch, "Something's Missing: A Discussion Between Ernst Bloch and Theodor W. Adorno on the Contradictions of Utopian Longing, *The Utopian Function of Art and Literature: Selected Essays*, Jack Zipes and Frank Mecklenburg, eds. (Cambridge: The MIT Press, 1988), 1–17. First published in "Etwas fehlt . . . uber die Widerspuche der utopischen Sehnsucht," *Gesprache mit Ernst Bloch*, Rainer Traub and Harald Wieser (eds.) (Frankfurt am Main, West Germany: Suhrkamp Verlag, 1975).

[25] Taussig, *Shamanism, Colonialism, and the Wild Man*, 9.

[26] See Chapter 8 in this book.

[27] Henry A. Giroux, *Schooling and the Struggle for Public Life* (Minneapolis: University of Minnesota Press, 1988); *Teachers as Intellectuals* (Westport, CT: Bergin and Garvey Press, 1988).

[28] The quotes in this paragraph are from Stuart Hall, "New Ethnicities," *ICA Documents 7: Black Film and British Cinema* (London, 1988), 27, 29.

[29] Lorraine Kenny, "Traveling Theory: The Cultural Politics of Race and Representation: An Interview with Kobena Mercer," *Afterimage* (September, 1990), 9.

[30] Abigail Solomon-Godeau, "Living with Contradictions: Critical Practices in the Age of Supply-Side Aesthetics, *Screen*, (Summer 1987), 2–21.

[31] Paul Redding, "Nietzchean Perspectivism and the Logic of Practical Reason," *The Philosophical Forum*, 22:1 (Fall, 1990), 72–88.

[32] Georg Lukacs, *The Theory of the Novel*, Trans. Anna Bostock (Cambridge: MIT Press, 1971), 64.

[33] Cathy N. Davidson, "Photographs of the Dead: Sherman, Daguerre, Hawthorne," *The South Atlantic Quarterly* 89:4 (Fall 1990), 667–701.

[34] S. Aronowitz and Henry A. Giroux, *Postmodern Education: Politics, Culture, and Social Criticism* (Minneapolis: University of Minnesota Press, 1991); Henry A. Giroux, ed., *Postmodernism, Feminism, and Cultural Politics: Rethinking Educational Boundaries* (Albany: State University of New York Press, 1991).

[35] David Trend, "Cultural Struggle and Educational Activism," *Afterimage* 17:4 (November 1989), 5.

[36] David Trend, "Changing the Subject: From Reproduction to Resistance in Media Education," *Afterimage* 16:4 (November, 1988), 10–13.

[37] Leon Golub "Politics and Election," In Bruce Wallis, ed., *Democracy: A Project by Group Material* (Settle: Bay Press, 1990), 115–16.

[38] Trinh T. Minh-ha. "Documentary is/Not a Name." *October* 52 (Spring, 1990), 96. See also bell hooks, *Yearning*. (Toronto: Between the Lines, 1990).

10

Cultural Workers and the Pedagogy of Cultural Politics: Writing Against the Empire*

Implicit in the politicizing mandate of multiculturalism is an attack on the idea of common culture, the idea that despite our many differences, we hold in comomon an intellectual, artistic, and moral legacy, descending largely from the Greeks and the Bible, supplemented and modified over centuries by innumerable contributions from diverse hands and peoples. It is this legacy that has given us our science, our poltical institutions, and the monuments of artistic and cultural achievement that define us as a civilization. Indeed, it is this legacy, insofar as we live up to it, that preserves us from chaos and barbarism. And it is precisely this legacy that the multiculturalist wishes to dispense with.[1]

Within the last decade, conservatives such as Allan Bloom, E.D. Hirsch, Diane Ravitch, Pat Buchanan, and Senator Jesse Helms have been able to beat progressives at their own game. They have placed the issue of culture and difference at the center of the debate about education and democracy. They have asserted the primacy of the political in invoking the language of culture and in doing so have let it be known that culture is a terrain of political and ideological struggle. The general ideological parameters of this struggle are partly revealed in the words of syndicated columnist Pat Buchanan, who has urged his fellow conservatives "to wage a cultural revolution in the 1990s as sweeping as the political revolution in the 1980s."[2] Its more specific expressions have been made manifest on a number of cultural fronts including the schools and the art world, and the more blatant attacks aimed at rolling back the benefits of civil rights and social welfare reforms constructed over the last three decades. More specifically, the right-wing educa-

* David Trend co-author.

tional and cultural agenda, with its emphasis on heritage rather than liberating memory, literacy rather than literacies, censorship rather than artistic expression, moral regulation rather than self and social empowerment, and testing rather than learning, is mobilized by a vision of the arts, culture, and schooling that presupposes and legitimates particular forms of history, community, and authority. Within such a plethora of exhortations that are allegedly self-evident and self-justifying, there is a structured silence around the issue of how power, history, and culture are organized to secure the authority and interests of specific groups. It is plain that it is not the voice of culturally diverse groups that the center of power defines as marginal because of race, class, ethnic, or gender considerations. Nor is it the voice of those groups struggling to reclaim galleries, schools, and other cultural spaces as agencies of social justice, critical expression, and radical democracy. What is being valorized in the dominant language of the culture industry is an elitist view of self and social development based on a celebration of cultural homogeneity, an undemocratic approach to social authority, and a politically regressive move to reconstruct American life within the script of Eurocentrism, racism, and patriarchy. Similarly, within these discourses, the call to define civilization as synonymous with selected aspects of Western tradition is being matched by a fervent attempt to reduce pedagogy to the old transmission model of teaching and learning.[3]

In what follows, we want to analyze the implications that this struggle over culture has for redefining a language of critique and possibility that is capable of challenging the authoritarianism and cultural amnesia that is the hallmark of a new cultural conservatism. Initially we will focus on the past decade's political battles over education and the arts, then we will describe the common challenges facing all cultural workers involved in these debates. Our argument will stress the importance of broadening such concepts as education and artistic practice into a more integrated category of cultural "writing" that requires a new paradigm of emancipatory practice.

In sketching these interwoven political and pedagogical agendas, we will organize our proposals within the framework of a radical democratic imaginary that speaks in the tradition of history's great emancipatory struggles. As described by Chantal Mouffe, such a practice rejects the conservative deployment of "liberty" as an excuse for exploitation and self-interest, and restores its meaning as a value, which "while belonging to the individual, can only be exercised collectively and presuppose the existence of equal rights for others."[4] Such a political philosophy requires a pedagogy that supports the production of diverse knowledge as a prerequisite for an egalitarian civic order. While honoring difference, a radical democracy resists the temptation to romanticize difference into equivalence. It recognizes that identities are often shaped in asymmetrical power relationships and that the resultant conflicts give democracy its dynamic character. In the context of cultural struggle, this involves a critical reexamination of the way textual signification is constructed, as well as an acknowledgement of the frequent indeterminacy of narrative representations. Yet while rejecting modernism's claim of rationality, we would salvage its most idealistic impulses. If we have learned anything from recent debates over identity and difference, it is that human agency does not vanish in the presumed absence of the humanist subject or the presence of decentered identities. In broadening the notion of education, we seek to develop mutually supportive practices for "contesting dominant forms of cultural production across a spectrum of sites where people shape their identity and their relations with the world."[5] More specifically, we will attempt to draw out the implications that a pedagogical literacy might have across and within various sites of cultural production and what this might mean for future alliances and forms of solidarity among artists, educators, and other cultural workers.

Before we take up these issues in more detail, we want to stress at the outset the fundamental importance of recognizing that the public schools, along with other cultural sites, do not simply provide students with the knowledge and skills they will need to secure employment and positions of privilege or enhance their character through an exposure to "the best that has been thought and known in the world."[6] Beyond the ideological distortions, Western chauvinism, and false sense of equality and opportunity that the schooling often legitimates, it is important to emphasize that public schools and other educational sites are never ideologically and politically innocent. In fact, they are contradictory sites of struggle through which different subject positions, knowledges, forms of address, and values are produced. These institutions harbor in their histories, modes of scholarship, and disciplinary and pedagogical practices specific representations and practices regarding what it means to be a knowledgeable and informed citizen, how one might view the relationship between social identity and political agency, and how one responds to prevailing forms of cultural authority. Put another way, educating students and audiences in and out of schools is really an introduction to how culture is organized, a demonstration of who is authorized to speak about particular forms of culture, what culture is considered acceptable and worthy of valorization, and what forms of culture are considered invalid and unworthy of public esteem.

It is important to remember that as cultural workers, regardless of whether we work in the arts, education, or in other cultural spheres, educators are always deeply implicated in the production of narratives and identities. In part, this is because such cultural spheres produce knowledge and engage in identity formation. Needless to say, such narratives are never neutral; they always framed within articulations and experiences occupied by someone and to the degree that they are implicated in organizing the future for others they are always located in moral and political interests. It is worth noting that the stories produced in these diverse contexts not only create structures of domination, they also serve as a context from which to organize sites of resistance; that is, they offer opportunities for creating critical public cultures where the necessary conditions can develop for people to believe that they can make a difference in constructing a society that exhibits in its institutional and everyday relations civic courage, compassion, and cultural justice.

With this in mind we want to reiterate that the current debate about educational reform and the arts in this country represents more than a commentary and conflict over language, representation, and culture. This debate serves, in part, as an ideological marker for the kind of attacks that will increasingly be waged on workers in other spheres of cultural production. For example, within this new public philosophy forged by the cultural guardians on the right there exists a ruthlessly frank distrust of the perils and promises of democracy. This new public philosophy is nowhere more evident than in the views of critics such as Bloom, Hirsch, and Ravitch. For example, Bloom, who has written the cultural manifesto for the New Right in his book *The Closing of the American Mind*,[7] argues that the impulse to egalitarianism and the spirit of social criticism represent the chief culprits in the decay of higher learning in the United States. Bloom claims that the universities must give up educating intellectuals, whose great crime is that they sometimes become adversaries of the dominant culture or speak to a wider culture about the quality of contemporary politics and public life. For Bloom, the university is a central force and space for maintaining practices that secure and privilege particular forms of culture, language, and identity. Within this perspective, any attempt to tamper with the established canon becomes tantamount to threatening the very nature of Western civilization. The fear, terror, self-righteous anger that characterizes Bloom's position rest on a defensiveness in "which all 'others' are seen as enemies bent on destroying 'our' civilization and way of life."[8] In this sense, Bloom's discourse echoes and gives impetus to the ideological colonialism that has become a rallying point for neoconservatives. It should also be stressed that for Bloom and his cohorts, literacy has become an ideological rallying point to reduce culture to a warehouse of selected works of Western civilization and to deride those expressions of popular culture and cultural differences that question the economies of privilege that separate the center and the margins of power and culture in this society.

Hirsch also calls on schools to reproduce the knowledge and values necessary to advance the historical virtues of Western civilization.[9] He defines literacy as part of an attempt to master a common national culture that represents an assemblage of names, dates, and events that allegedly reveal the master code of cultural literacy. Culture in Hirsch's view is seen as a time capsule of past events, prevalent social idioms, and sanctioned codes of behavior of a given nation and merely presents itself for all to participate in its language and conventions. Culture is thereby reduced to a type of monumentalism, and the pedagogy through which it is expressed is organized around the process of transmission and the practice of moral and political regulation. Hirsch's view of culture ignores how schools and other institutions function as complex sites of cultural production, how such institutions function to freeze certain versions of history, and how schools, in particular, ruthlessly deny their own complicity in reproducing forms of inequality, domination, and oppression. Culture is not simply depoliticized in this discourse, it is recoded around "consecrated relics, tradition and shrines . . . the public school system, the syllabus of 'English'—it is as though, through an undisturbed continuity, the very spirit of 'History' had laid its blessing on the nation."[10] By depoliticizing the issue of culture and difference, Hirsch ends up with a view of literacy that cleanses culture of its dynamic and contradictory character. Supporting this view of literacy is a claim to neutral representation, a legacy of colonial and patrician culture, and a designation of the Other that is fixed, subordinate, and inferior. There is more at stake here than a resurgent nativism. It is an attempt to remove the culture of Otherness and the politics of difference from the language of democracy and social justice.

This attack on difference and cultural diversity has been taken very seriously by cultural conservatives and the New Right and can be seen more recently in attempts by Ravitch and others to rewrite the public school curricula of New York and California in such a way that would cleanse them of the rich legacies, conflicts, and diverse struggles that characterize this nation as one that has been constructed in varied cultural traditions and voices.[11] Ravitch's attempt to silence or marginalize the voices of those who have traditionally been excluded from the school curricula is indicative of how the language of liberalism and pluralism are increasingly being used to give credence to the new nativism and racism that has been resurgent in the last decade in the media, mass culture, and American schools.

Acknowledging the importance of the changing demographic and cultural character of the United States, Ravitch constructs a view of pluralism based on a notion of a common culture that serves as a referent to denounce any attempt by subordinated groups to challenge the narrow ideological and political parameters by which such a culture both defines and expresses itself.[12] Though Ravitch emphasizes that the common culture of the United States is multicultural, she glosses over any attempt to designate how dominant configurations of power privilege some cultures over others, how power works to secure forms of domination that marginalize and silence subordinated groups.

In the name of a common culture, Ravitch performs two hegemonic functions. First, she dehistoricizes and depoliticizes the idea of culture. Absent is any account of how various social movements have struggled historically to transform a Eurocentric curriculum that, in part, has functioned to exclude or marginalize the voices of women, blacks, and other subordinated groups. For example, Ravitch does not mention how various social movements struggled successfully in the late 1960s and early 1970s to add black, ethnic, and women's studies programs and curricula in both public schools and various institutions of higher learning.[13] Nor does she examine how the relationship between culture and social identity is constituted "through hierarchical knowledges and power relations" within the curriculum.[14] Through her insistence on a common culture, Ravitch erases the institutional, economic, and social parameters that actively construct deep structural inequalities and forms of domination that characterize relations between privileged and subordinated groups, as well as the challenges that have been waged against such practices.

Ravitch's common culture denies the necessity for either contesting existing configurations of power or transforming the deep-seated inequalities that characterize institutional and everyday life in the United States. Of course, this is precisely her point. Ravitch invokes pluralism, democracy, and consensus in order to defend a dominant order in which the issues of power, politics, and struggle are coded as forms of disruption and extremism. More important, by discrediting social criticism and struggle waged by subordinate groups against the dominant culture, Ravitch locates the source of oppression and change in individual will and achievement. In this account, the social, economic, cultural, and political centers of power simply disappear. At the same time, broad-based struggle and political action over the curriculum and related issues of social justice are rather pointedly discredited as a threat to a "sense of common nationhood."[15]

Also missing from Ravitch's discourse is a notion of difference and citizenship tied to a project of substantive critical democracy that extends the principles of justice, liberty, and equality to the widest possible set of economic and social relations. Employing a comfortable set of oppositions in which those who struggle over extending the meaning of cultural democracy are dismissed as particularists, Ravitch utilizes the language of desperation and extremism to wipe out any attempt on the part of subordinated groups to learn about how their identities have been forged in ongoing historical struggles for social justice. Ravitch apparently believes that the history of the culture of Otherness should be forged exclusively in positive images organized around events like Black History Month, multicultural dinners, or events celebrating the achievements of women. While such images certainly are pedagogically crucial to any form of critical pedagogy, they cannot be expunged from an ongoing criticism of how the dominant culture has created and sustains the very problems that provided the conditions for such heroic struggles in the first place. Ravitch recognizes that the curriculum should become more inclusive in acknowledging the histories, cultures, and experiences of other groups, but she doesn't want students to engage in forms of social criticism aimed at calling into question the Eurocentric nature of the dominant curriculum.

What emerges here is not simply censorship, but a benevolent form of colonialism that refuses to hold up to critical scrutiny its own complicity in producing and maintaining specific injustices, practices, and forms of oppression that deeply inscribe its legacy and heritage. Ravitch's dismissal of the pedagogical importance of self-esteem as a basis for social identity and critical citizenship is a testimonial to a notion of common culture that self-righteously defines itself outside of a discourse of politics and ethics while simultaneously dismissing those who struggle for a place in history as extremist and particularist. For example, Ravitch claims that the call to give subordinate students a voice in the curriculum, to locate themselves in a sense of history, as part of a broader pedagogical effort to raise their self-esteem is really nothing more than a ploy to inscribe them in just another form of ethnocentricism. She writes:

> Advocates of particularism propose an ethnocentric curriculum to raise the self-esteem and academic achievement of children from racial and ethnic minority

backgrounds. Without any evidence, they claim that children from minority back-grounds will do well in school *only* if they are immersed in a positive, prideful version of their ancestral culture.[16]

Scholars writing in feminist, black, and ethnic studies have continuously called for curriculum relevant to the needs of specific groups of students as part of an effort to broaden and democratize a dominant school curriculum largely shaped by Western traditions.[17] Moreover, the crucial pedagogical issue around the value of student self-esteem is about more than teaching a particular version of knowl-edge, whether cloaked in the mantle of Western civilization or some other cultural tradition. It is also about how teachers can relate the knowledge they teach and legitimate to the histories, traditions, stories, and experiences that students actually bring with them to the schools. Difference is important both as a marker for including specific forms of knowledge into the curriculum and as a basis for developing a pedagogy that takes seriously the notion that students read the world differently, that they produce knowledge and categories of meaning that must be understood if they are to be inserted into, rather than outside of, the process of teaching and learning. At issue here is the fundamental pedagogical principle of acknowledging how different students produce meaning through the diverse social and cultural formations that give them a sense of voice and identity. Teachers and schools have an obligation to make knowledge meaningful for students in order that they can then engage what they learn in critical terms. Again, this does not suggest a pedagogical practice that romanticizes the culture of subordinated groups, nor does it suggest that critical educators ought to simply dismiss a curriculum steeped in Western tradition outright. It does suggest examining critically how the school curriculum constructs relationships between dominant and subordinate cul-tures. It means studying the history of the West dialectically for its strengths and for the role it has played in colonizing cultural differences.

It is the refusal of the dominant culture to acknowledge its complicity in waging of real and symbolic violence on minority children all across this country that isolates the notion of a common culture from considerations of ethics, politics, and history. This is manifest in the common culture's shameless refusal to provide support services for those parents, children, and adults who are homeless, poor, without food, and barely able to survive the struggle of daily living that the character of the current dominant discourse reveals what it actually means by a discourse of pluralism, harmony, and civility.[18]

None of this directly affected the arts community until recently, when con-servative members of Congress recognized the political mileage that "sex panics" and radical cultural criticism could yield them. As Richard Bolton recently noted in the *New Art Examiner*, the "outrage over art was not fueled by popular rebellion, but by extremists with narrow and self-serving agendas, by politicians who like to be in the news, and by a news media driven by sensationalism."[19] Until the past year, even the most politically ambitious artists had achieved only slight public visibility, and the erosion of their expressive rights had advanced at a snail's pace.

In part this is because radical art practices have been marginalized within the discursive precincts of high theory and the institutional ghetto of the "alternative space." It took the catalyzing influence of forces outside the art world to capitalize on the avant-garde's civic alienation and to cast artists as the terror of the heartland.

But these assaults were not without precedent. As explained by Carole S. Vance in her essay "Reagan's Revenge," the overt challenges in early 1990 to agencies like the National Endowment for the Arts and the National Endowment for the Humanities were enabled, at least in part, by the covert erosions of autonomy and political support initiated a decade earlier.[20] Like the educational reformism championed by Bloom, Hirsch, and Ravitch, the cultural reform movement sought to suppress democratic expression with a systematic elimination of opposition or difference. Analyzing the endowments in the 1981 *Mandate for Leadership* transition document, prepared by the Heritage Foundation, Michael S. Joyce wrote that "as a true friend of democracy the NEH can teach the nation the limits of egalitarian impulse," explaining that the agency should "support humanities, rather than social crusades, political action, or political education as demanded by narrowly partisan interests."[21] Based on such recommendations, William Bennett and Frank Hodsoll, the Reagan-appointed stewards of the NEH and NEA, began to impose their own agendas by systematically undermining the processes of peer review. This moved decision making from the arts community into the hands of government bureaucrats. (These unsanctioned actions by Bennett and Hodsoll were ratified as policy in the endowments' 1990 reauthorization bill).

Such institutional erosions were symptoms of a broader cultural backlash against liberal advances of the 1960s and 1970s, when the alternative arts movement grew from a handful of grassroots groups into a network of hundreds of artists spaces, media centers, performance collectives, and avant-garde musical ensembles that, despite their marginality, symbolically challenged the primacy of the museum and the symphony. This development supported the resurgent interest among artists in producing noncommodity works that implicitly criticized the values of the cultural establishment. In the years that followed, perhaps the most telling marker of conservative ire was the 1982 inauguration by publisher Samuel Lipman and *New York Times* critic Hilton Kramer of a periodical funded by the Scaife, Olin, and Heritage Foundations. At the time, Kramer wrote that:

> it is time to apply a new criterion to the discussion of our cultural life—a criterion of truth. This is by no means an easy task. The defense of high culture in a democracy has never been an easy task. It is in the very nature of democracy, with its multiplicity of interests and tastes, for the task to be difficult.[22]

The philosophical roots of this will to cultural homogeneity date to the early days of the republic in the yearning for a distinctly American identity. From Ralph Waldo Emerson through William Carlos Williams, writers sought to create "pure products" from an array of inherited traditions. As U.S. influence grew following the First World War, the production and distribution of American cultural products at home and abroad came to symbolize U.S. dominance. During the Cold War,

Washington bureaucrats touted modern art forms of minimalism and abstract expressionism as proof of the benefits of a free society. Thus in the 1960s atmosphere of competition with the Soviet Union (the nuclear arms build-up, space race, etc.) and domestic government largess (CETA, HUD, Medicare) the national endowments were a natural development.

Since then, politicians have searched for pragmatic rationales for cultural spending that could be equated (at least theoretically) with economic gain: a more intelligent citizen, a more perceptive worker, a more discriminating consumer of goods. This logic has been academically reinforced by views of socialization in which individuals purportedly adapt to the mandates of an unchanging society. Along the way, personal agency inevitably succumbs to the will of existing institutions and behavioral norms. To conservatives, this "functionalist" adaptation is enforced by obliterating any distractions. By placing itself at the center of all value, this attitude toward culture not only excludes other perspectives, but ultimately ignores its own self-justifying tendencies. Gayatri Spivak argues that this blindness is endemic to all dominant social speech, because "when a narrative is constructed, something is left out. When an end is defined, other ends are rejected, and one might not know what those ends are."[23] Although this phenomenon restricts those on both the inside and outside of the dominant regime, it is structured to delegitimize any attempt to reveal these tendencies.

The result is a regressive system of texts and discursive positions. By staging the argument with this functionalist framework, subject/object relations are reinforced in which professionals always speak for nonprofessionals and the value of everyday experience is inherently devalued. This establishes a hierarchy that identifies writers, teachers, artists, and scientists as "experts" to whom "ordinary" people must always look for knowledge, insight, or inspiration. Intellectual products pass from institutionally certified senders to commonplace receivers in a manner that translates very well into the economic metaphors of modern capitalism. Culture is viewed as the reified product of "genius" production. Rather than a dialogic process that develops among people, knowledge becomes a static currency that can be accumulated and exchanged.

This conception of knowledge fails to acknowledge that stories and images change when viewed by different people, at different places, and at different historical moments. It can't recognize that reception is an inherent part of the process and that signification is therefore always local and contextual. Nor does it acknowledge the reciprocal character of speech acts, the realization that knowledge is produced at the moment of reception and that this production needs to be encouraged and expanded.

Of course, the cultural conservatism of the last decade has not gone unchallenged. Increasingly, a number of theorists and groups are arguing that culture does not consists of a single narrative, that the division between high and low culture is itself a historical and political construction, and that the production and reception of culture is constituted within a variety of forms and audiences. These new forms of cultural opposition are rewriting culture as a historical and social construct that can be made and remade within not outside of a myriad of traditions, artistic forms, and experiences. The battle in the universities over the canon, in the public schools over a curriculum of diversity, and in Congress over the arts are not merely a tribute to the resurgent power of the New Right. Such struggles are also indicative of various opposition groups to refuse to allow dominant groups to undermine the basis of democracy in the name of an authoritarian discourse that legitimates culture as the reserve of the privileged and mostly as something that is done to others. A growing number of cultural workers are uniting to challenge the exclusionary and often colonizing discourses of the museum, the training of artists to serve the culture industries, and the distribution of capital and cultural funds in ways that divide artistic production from forms of community participation constituted in subordinated and marginalized traditions. This perspective, as it is being developed in various postcolonial, feminist, and other critical discourses, embraces the diverse borders of culture as potentially vibrant centers of resistance and creativity—places where new identities and alliances can and are being forged in the rewriting of history and the reclamation of pluralistic identities.

Redefining Pedagogy as a Form of Cultural Politics and Production

One major challenge that these concerns pose for educational reformers in the next few years is to construct a new language for engaging the debate over culture and literacy; linked with this is the demand for reclaiming schools and other public spaces in the interest of combating domestic tyranny, preventing assaults on human freedom, and extending democratic possibilities. It is especially important at this time in our history that artists, educators, and other cultural workers develop a broader definition of education and pedagogical practice as a form of cultural politics. Within this context, critical pedagogy is not reduced to the skills and techniques that educators use to meet the predefined instrumental objectives of the marketplace or the ideological demands of canonical culture. The teaching and learning of skills and techniques is insufficient for referencing what educators and other cultural workers actually do in terms of the underlying principles and values that structure their beliefs and work, or for providing the language necessary to critically analyze how school, studio, and other cultural practices relate to future vision of community life. What critical pedagogy as a form of cultural politics refers to in this case is a deliberate attempt on the part of cultural workers to influence how and what knowledge and subjectivities are produced within particular sets of social relations. Critical pedagogy draws attention to the ways in which knowledge, power, desire, and experience are produced under the basic conditions of learning. For example, Abigail Solomon-Godeau in analyzing the work of photographer Connie Hatch makes clear that radical cultural practice needs to do more than expose what is left out of dominant representations:

> Hatch's work in its entirety makes clear that the Benjaminian formula for radical cultural practice—making the invisible visible—can no longer be understood as a matter of supplementing, reconstructing, or repositioning the normative givens of representation in such a way that the real relations of power and domination are functionally exposed. And to the extent that much of her work focuses on issues of gender, the lacunae in the radical cultural theory of the 1930s are made particularly clear. Moreover, Hatch's preoccupation with the dynamics of photographic representation—with what it puts in place—is a cogent reminder that attempts to use photography to effect demystifications or deconstructions must additionally combat the ideological effects of the apparatus itself. . . . The importance of Hatch's work lies not so much in some art-critical conception of "success," be that understood as a formal criterion or as a polemical one. Rather , the significance of her practice lies in the attention given equally to the institutional conditions of cultural production (a radical practice must be integrally constituted to resist commodification), the emphasis placed on the spectator's active engagement in the process of signification (politicizing the spectator requires that the work encourage the production of meaning rather than the consumption of meaning), and an internal critique of those modes of representation that have historically functioned to naturalize, authorize, and validate the status quo.[24]

Both in and out of the academy, critical pedagogy as a form of cultural politics has meant a concern with analyses of the production and representation of meaning and how the practices they provoke are implicated in the dynamics of social power. This approach to critical pedagogy does not reduce educational practice to the issue of what works; instead, it stresses the importance of understanding what actually happens in classrooms and other educational settings by raising questions regarding "what knowledge is of most worth, in what direction should one desire, and what it means to know something."[25] Of course, the language of critical pedagogy does something more. Pedagogy is simultaneously about the knowledge and practices that teachers, cultural workers, and students might engage in together and the cultural politics such practices support. It is in this sense that to propose a pedagogy is at the same time to construct a political vision.

Within the last few years, we have seen artists joining with school people to assert a more activist stance on issues of pedagogy. From last year's "Democracy: Education" program organized in New York City by Group Material to the more recent "Magnetic Youth" video compilation at LACE in Los Angeles, to the practices of groups like Artists/Teachers Concerned, Rise and Shine Productions, and Tim Rollins + Kids of Survival, cultural workers in the studio and the classroom are recognizing the imperative of cooperative practice. For artists this reflects a further dissatisfaction with Kantian models of aesthetic transcendence that separate art from life. Cultural workers are increasingly recognizing the limits of apolitical postmodern appropriation, pastiche, and bricolage in a world of lived homophobia, racial oppression, and escalating economic inequity.

Necessary as it is to struggle on the political terrain of representation, it is becoming equally important to bring those struggles into the world of material relations. Otherwise both art and education run the risk of slipping into abstract solipsism and sustaining a form of textual criticism that ignores its own political constraints and the material dimensions of human suffering and power. As stated by Douglas Crimp in his introduction to *AIDS: Cultural Analysis/Cultural Activism*, this becomes particularly evident at points of crisis:

> art does have the power to save lives, and it is this very power that must be recognized, fostered, and supported in every way possible. But if we are to do this, we will have to abandon the idealist conception of art. We don't need a cultural renaissance; we need cultural practices actively participating in the struggle against AIDS. We don't need to transcend the epidemic; we need to end it.[26]

More than any other issue, the AIDS crisis has demonstrated the need and potential of positive alliances, as it has mobilized cultural workers who never considered themselves to be political activists. The crisis has fostered forms of cultural practice of a directly pedagogical character, works that both disseminate public information and challenge the epidemic's discursive construction. The AIDS activism of such groups and individuals as Gran Fury, Jan Zita Grover, Sunil Gupta, Paula Treichler, the Testing the Limits Collective, and Simon Watney has foregrounded ways that public knowledge of AIDS is produced through language and media. As Crimp suggests, in addition to deploying alternative texts, this writing and picture making entails a critique of the way the cultural world participates in or resists representational conventions. Not so coincidentally, it is exactly such work that so troubles those on the Right. This is because the topic in question is not merely a particular book or film but a challenge to an entire system of thought.

Reclaiming the Discourse of Democracy

Turning more specifically to the schools, we want to argue that the problem within our educational system lies ultimately in the realm of values and politics, not in the realm of management and economics. Consequently, educational reformers and other cultural workers need to address the most basic questions of purpose and meaning. What kind of society do we want? How do we educate students for a truly democratic society? What conditions do we need to provide teachers, artists, and students for such an education to be meaningful and workable? Underlying these questions is the need to reclaim the legacy of defending public schools as democratic spheres responsible for providing an indispensable public service to the nation: that of awakening the moral, political, and civic responsibilities of its youth. At stake here is the need for educators and other cultural workers to fashion a critical politics of representation, difference, and literacy not outside but within a tradition of radical democracy. If the notion of radical democracy is to function as a pedagogical practice that provides a point of articulation between and among various cultural workers, it must be comprehended as a way of life that consistently has to be fought for, struggled over, and rewritten as part of an oppositional politics.

Cultural Workers as Public Intellectuals

Related to the issue of defining public schools and other cultural spheres as democratic spheres is the issue of illuminating the role that educators and cultural workers might play as engaged and transformative critics. This suggests a notion of leadership and pedagogical practice that combines a discourse of hope with forms of self and social criticism that do not require cultural workers to step back from society as a whole or to lay claim to a specious notion of objectivity or authenticity but to unlearn and transform those practices of privilege that reproduce conditions of oppression and human suffering. We believe that cultural workers need to reclaim and reassert the importance of a discourse and politics of location that recognizes how power, history, and ethics are inextricably intertwined so as to position, enable, and limit their work within shifting relations of power. The radical nature of such a discourse points to the roles of cultural workers as public intellectuals who combine a sense of their own partiality with a commitment for justice and an attempt to "keep alive potent traditions of critique and resistance."[27]

Cultural workers dedicated to reforming all spheres of education as part of a wider revitalization of public life also need to raise important questions regarding the relationship among knowledge and power, learning and possibility, social criticism and human dignity, and how these might be understood in relation to rather than in isolation from those practices of domination, privilege, and resistance at work in wider social and political formations. This is essentially a question of not only what people know but also how they come to know in a particular way within the contexts and constraints of specific social and cultural practices. This dimension of cultural politics suggests a critical deconstruction of tradition not as a rejection of history but as an attempt to reclaim tradition as a historical and social construct that always needs to be subjected to critical dialogue rather than unquestioning reverence. Of primary importance for cultural workers is the need to resurrect traditions and social memories that provide a new way of reading history and reclaiming power and identity. Within this view of memory, history, and identity, the concept of academic disciplinary borders breaks down and enables cultural workers to grasp the ultimate arbitrariness of disciplinary divisions, of the forced separations and hierarchies that prevent cultural production from taking place in the interfacing of multiple cultural codes, knowledge forms, and modes of inquiry. Outside of the ghettoization of the disciplines lies the possibility of creating new languages and social practices that connect rather than separate education and cultural work from every day life. It is in the reconstruction of social memory, the role of cultural workers as transformative critics, and the discourse of radical democracy as a basis for social struggle and cultural work that the pedagogical basis exists for a theory of literacy that engages cultural difference as part of a broader discourse of justice, equality, and community.

Most importantly, this is a popular literacy that lives beyond the walls of the university. Often in recent years the forays into popular culture by well-meaning artists and academics have devolved into exercises of intellectual and colonial tourism. The promise of fields like cultural studies and media studies has been undercut by their lack of specificity and contact with the constituencies under analysis. Attention has focussed on the movies, music, or fashion accoutrements of young people as objects for scholarly discourse—but little on young people themselves. This is particularly true when white intellectuals distance themselves from the dominant culture and whiteness by focusing on the popular culture of the "Other" only, after spinning webs of "clever" criticism, to return to it more intensely. Rather than providing a space for young people to speak, the study of popular culture becomes a form of border crossing in which the Other becomes a resource for academic appropriation and valorization. What begins as a critical project is often reduced to an intellectual practice that merely privileges the authoritative persona of the "seer." This peculiarly Western tradition, so valorized in cultural professions, has contributed to the regressively monolithic views of literacy we seek to dismantle.

At the same time the academic objectification of the popular has ironically romanticized the ability of "the people" to escape the economic realities they inhabit. As Meaghan Morris has suggested, the theoretical concept of popular knowledge has been used to subvert an awareness of "real" racism, sexism, homophobia, or economic injustice.[28] For this reason cultural workers must be constantly attentive of their own affective investments in groups they address. Writers, teachers, and artists are never disinterested observers and can easily project their own agendas upon those they study or depict. Yet, cultural workers are rarely so self-conscious of their own politics.

Critical Literacy as the Discourse of Possibility

In taking up the issue of literacy, we want to argue that literacy is fundamentally crucial to how we think about the construction of the political subject in a critical democracy. In this sense, literacy is incompatible with current definitions that reduce it either to learning functional reading and writing skills or to learning the rules and codes of a narrowly defined cultural context. If we view the world as a text, then literacy means engaging the full range of what is in the library (conventional notions of reading), the art gallery (the making and interpretation of art), and the street (popular culture and student experience). It is also hardly equitable with the false definitions of emancipation through which it is typically promoted. A recent example is Barbara Bush's motto "Give them books, give them wings."[29] In this discourse, literacy becomes both an introduction into the "best" of American thinking and a ideological prop that reduces the practice of liberation to the mechanistic learning of reading and writing skills. Bush's literacy campaign succinctly conveys the double articulation of conventional literacy as both social empowerment and ideological oppression. Although conservatives readily draw comparisons between illiteracy, unemployment, poor health, welfare dependency, and mental illness, the notion that illiteracy might result from economic inequities (rather than cause them) is rarely considered.

Literacy in its varied versions is about the practice of representation as a means of organizing, inscribing, and containing meaning. It is also about practices of representation that disrupt or rupture existing textual, epistemological, and ideological systems. Literacy is critical to the degree that it makes problematic the very structure and practice of representation; that is, it focuses attention on the importance of acknowledging that meaning is not fixed and that to be literate is to undertake a dialogue with others who speak from different histories, locations, and experiences. Literacy is a discursive practice in which difference becomes crucial for understanding not simply how to read, write, or develop aural skills, but to also recognize that the identities of Others matter as part of a broader set of politics and practices aimed at the reconstruction of democratic public life.

Literacy as part of a broader politics of difference and democracy points, at the very least, to two important considerations. First, it makes visible the historically and socially constructed strengths and limitations of those places and borders we inherit and which frame our discourses and social relations. Second, literacy is a form of ethical address that structures how we construct relationships between ourselves and others. It marks out the boundaries of difference and inscribes them in borders that "define the places that are safe and unsafe, [that] distinguish *us* from *them*."[30] Borders signal in the metaphorical and literal sense how power is inscribed differently on the body, culture, history, space, land, and psyche. When literacy is defined in monolithic terms, from the center, within a linear logic that erases uncertainty, it only recognizes the borders of privilege and domination.

What is crucial here is that the discourse of literacy cannot be abstracted from the language of difference and power. As such, literacy cannot be viewed as merely an epistemological or procedural issue but must be defined primarily in political and ethical terms. It is political in that how we "read" the world is always implicated in relations of power. Literacy is ethical in that people "read" the world differently depending, for instance, on circumstances of class, gender, race, and politics. They also read the world in spaces and social relationships constructed between themselves and others and in turn demand actions based on judgments and choices about how one is to act in the face of ideologies, values, and experiences that are the mark of "otherness." It is these shifting relations of knowing and identity, which frame our "different modes of response to the Other (e.g., between those that transfigure and those that disfigure, those that care for the other in his/her otherness and those that do not)."[31]

If a politics of difference is to be fashioned in emancipatory rather than oppressive practices, literacy must be rewritten in terms that articulate difference with the principles of equality, justice, and freedom rather than with those interests supportive of hierarchies, oppression, and exploitation. In this case, literacy as an emancipatory practice requires cultural workers to write, speak, and listen in the language of difference, a language in which meaning becomes multiaccentual and dispersed and resists permanent closure. This is a language in which one speaks *with* rather than *for* Others. Put differently, the discourse of critical literacy is one that signals the need to challenge and redefine the substance and effects of cultural borders, the need to create opportunities for students to be border-crossers in order to understand Otherness on its own terms, and the need to create borderlands in which diverse cultural resources allow for the fashioning of new identities within existing configurations of power.[32]

Central here is a notion of literacy that is inseparable from the practice of forms of civic courage and critical citizenship that extends the democratic principles of liberty and equality to the widest possible set of relations. At its best, critical literacy provides students and audiences with the competencies needed to develop and experience a pluralistic conception of citizenship and community that dignifies democracy as a forum for creating unity without denying specificity. Literacy can offer new ways of reading the past and present as a way of reclaiming power, voice, and sense of worth.

As a pedagogical practice, literacy means making one's self present as part of a moral and political project that links the production of meaning to the possibility for human agency, democratic community, and transformative social action. Literacy means more than breaking with the predefined. It also means understanding the details of everyday life through the larger categories of history, culture, and power. As part of the language of possibility, a critical theory of literacy provides a crucial pedagogical insight into the dynamics of the learning process by linking the nature of learning itself with the dreams, experiences, histories, and languages that people bring to the cultural sphere. What is being advocated here is that teachers and other cultural workers learn to confirm student experiences and voices so that students are legitimated and supported as people who matter, as people who can participate in the production and acquisition of their own learning, and as people who in doing so can speak with a voice that is rooted in their sense of history and place.

But if we are to view this insight in a meaningful way, we must understand that it not enough to affirm and give voice to the often multilayered experiences that different constituencies bring to the classroom or the gallery. It is also imperative to examine students' cultural backgrounds and social experiences so that they can understand both the strengths and weaknesses that constitute their often multiple and contradictory voices.

As part of a pedagogy of difference, students must engage the richness of their own communities and histories while struggling against structures of domination. They must be able to move in and out of different cultures so as to appreciate and appropriate the codes and vocabularies of diverse cultural traditions in order to further expand the knowledge, skills, and insights they will need to define and shape, rather than simply serve, in the modern world.

Towards a Discourse of Postmodern Citizenship

We want to end by arguing that cultural workers need a language of critique and possibility that allows for multiple solidarities and political vocabularies, one that also articulates a common concern for extending the democratic principles of liberty, equality, and justice to the widest possible relations. Writers, teachers, and artists need both a shared language that in part provides the foundation for a democratic politics as well as a postmodern view of citizenship that acknowledges the multiple, particular, and heterogeneous as constitutive of the public life. This suggests several considerations for developing a discourse of difference and literacy as part of a broader struggle for cultural democracy. On one level, cultural workers must explore the complexity of culture within power relations that both enable and silence students from diverse traditions. They must also address issues of inequality as they are structured within racial, gender, and class relations and recognize the limitations of the politics of separatism in waging collective struggles against various relations of oppression in their complexity and interrelatedness. At the same time, it is imperative for cultural workers to provide in their work and actions the basis for a language of solidarity and a project of possibility as part of a new vision and attempt to rethink the meaning of democratic citizenship in the postmodern age.

At the very least, this means that cultural workers need to develop a shared network of public spheres from which they can develop a set of relevancies that can be recognized in each others' work.[33] Similarly, cultural workers need to make the issue of representation not only central to the production and deconstruction of ideologies but also primary to the construction of pedagogical practices that address how knowledge and power come together to produce particular ways of being in the world, particular ways of dreaming and desiring, and how these are taken up by dominant and subordinated groups within specific historical and cultural contexts. We should be attentive to the ways that peoples' lived relations can be fictionalized in depictions of race, age, class, and sexual orientation. We need to remember that representation and reality are concepts that determine and are determined by each other. In this context, our task becomes far more subtle than the mere correction of negative stereotypes through the deployment of positive images. As Stuart Hall and others have pointed out, even positive images of "genuine ethnicity" at times bear the imprint of colonial overdetermination or function simply as reversals of a reductionist anticolonial logic.[34] The contradictory and complicitous nature of experience gets lost in this type of analysis and bears all of the problems of exoticizing and romanticizing the Other.

Beyond this level of textual critique, we also need to scrutinize the structures through which such questions are formulated, if for no other reason than to examine the way they divert attention from such dominant categories as "maleness" and "whiteness." In this regard, even the progressive deconstructionist position that interrogates the relationship of the margin to the center must be questioned for the authoritative privilege it affords its European practitioners—even as it critiques them. In effect this means developing a notion of culture and political struggle informed by a language that is simultaneously historical, political, critical, pedagogical, and hopeful. We want to conclude by pointing more specifically to some of the elements that might inform such a language in an attempt to open up and deepen the possibility for cultural democracy.

First, cultural workers should demonstrate the importance of historical memory. By historical memory, we mean the recognition that there is no language, knowledge, or social practice that is beyond the past. In addition, historical memory rejects the notion of the past as a linear progression, history as an unproblematic train of events moving forward toward greater heights of achievement and progress. In this case, historical memory rejects the monologue of totalizing narratives and theories. Instead, it represents:

> a putative shift or movement that is not beyond and away from the past but rather involves a circulating back on it, a return, a stepping back down into its details, earlier silences and margins, into its previously 'blank' spaces and hidden networks, in order to extract from it a more extensive sense of the possible . . . the struggle is not over an absolute truth, the horrifying void of the ultimate referent . . . but over what is 'good' and beneficial for us. Instead of stable foundations and a rational directive accompanying us on our journey down the single road of truth towards the 'real', we seek our liberation in the multiple voices, languages, her- and his-stories, of a world that is altogether less guaranteed, but for that lighter, more open, accessible and, in a profoundly secular sense, more possible.[35]

Historical memory suggests, as Chambers points out, that cultural workers are compelled to confer a sense of the past rather than discover it. Such a task links the notion of historical inquiry to the imperatives of moral and political agency. It is to locate ourselves and our visions inside of rather than outside of the language of history and possibility.

Second, cultural workers need to not only think about representational practices in terms of historical memory, they also need to rewrite the political and pedagogical practice of cultural work. In this case, the pedagogical dimension of cultural work refers to the process of creating symbolic representations and the practices within which they are engaged. This includes a particular concern with the analysis of textual, aural, and visual representations and how such representations are organized and regulated within particular institutional arrangements. Such a practice entails a wariness of the forces that would aestheticize difference and commodify dissent. It also addresses how various people engage such representations in the practice of comprehension and significance. As a cultural practice,

pedagogy both contests and refigures the construction, presentation, and engagement of various forms of images, text, talk, and action that result in the production
of meaning, which informs students and others with regard to their individual and
collective futures. Pedagogy in this sense represents both a discourse of critique
and a project of possibility. The political dimension of cultural work suggests that
cultural workers be attentive to the obvious and covert ideological and institutional
forces that inform, mediate, and constrain their work. It also suggests a critical
recognition of the "rhetorical and formal strategies that determin[es] the work's
meaning, reception, and use."[36]

The political dimension of cultural work recognizes that the symbolic presentations that take place in various spheres of cultural production in society manifest contested and unequal power relations. In this sense, cultural work informs
a project whose intent is to mobilize knowledge and desires that may lead to
significant changes in minimizing the degree of oppression in people's lives. What
is at stake is a political imaginary that extends the possibilities for creating new
public spheres in which the principles of equality, liberty, and justice become the
primary organizing principles for structuring relationships between the self and
others.[37]

Third, cultural workers need to develop what Cornel West has termed "prophetic Criticism." Such criticism is rendered here as the deliberate notion of unveiling,
negating, and problematizing. In part, this suggests keeping "track of the complex
dynamics of institutional and other related power structures in order to disclose
options and alternatives for transformative praxis; it also attempts to grasp the way
in which representational strategies are creative responses to novel circumstances
and conditions."[38] Prophetic criticism engages a politics of difference by linking
structural analyses with cultural analyses as part of a moral and political project
that engages its own assumptions with the same rigor as it does the objects of its
political and social analysis. In short, it means that cultural workers exhibit in their
own work and teaching a language that is self-critical and can question public
forms, address social injustices, and break the tyranny of the present.

Finally, cultural workers need a language of imagination, one that both insists
and enables them to consider the structure, movement, and possibilities in the
contemporary order of things as well as how they might act to prevent the barbaric
and develop those aspects of public life that point to its best and as yet unrealized
possibilities. This is a language of democratic possibilities that rejects the enactment
of cultural difference structured in hierarchy and dominance; it is a language that
rejects cultural, social, and spatial borders as shorelines of violence and terrorism.
In opposition to this view, the concepts of democracy, border, borderlands, and
difference must be rewritten so that diverse identities and cultures can intersect
as sites of creative cultural production, multiple resources, and experimentation
for expanding those human capacities and social forms necessary for a radical
democracy to emerge in this country.

REFERENCES

[1] Roger Kimball, *"Tenured Radicals:* A Postscript," *The New Criterion* (January 1991), 6.

[2] Patrick Buchanan, "In the War for America's Culture, the 'Right' Side is Losing," *Richmond News Leader,* June 24, 1989.

[3] Stanley Aronowitz and Henry A. Giroux, *Postmodern Education: Politics, Culture, and Social Criticism* (Minneapolis: University of Minnesota Press, 1991).

[4] Chantal T. Mouffe, "Radical Democracy: Modern or Postmodern?" in Andrew Ross ed., *Universal Abandon: The Politics of Postmodernism* (Minneapolis: University of Minnesota Press, 1988), 42.

[5] Roger I. Simon, *Teaching Against the Grain* (New York: Bergin and Garvey Press, 1992), 8.

[6] Matthew Arnold, cited in Cornel West, "The New Cultural Politics of Difference," *October* 53 (Summer 1990), 95.

[7] Allan Bloom, *The Closing of the American Mind* (New York: Simon & Schuster, 1987).

[8] Edward W. Said, "Figures, Configurations, Transfigurations," *Polygraph*, No. 4 (1990), 22.

[9] E.D. Hirsch, Jr., *Cultural Literacy* (Boston: Houghton Mifflin, 1987).

[10] Iain Chambers, *Border Dialogues: Journeys in Postmodernity* (New York: Routledge, 1990), 16.

[11] Diane Ravitch, "Multiculturalism: E Pluribus Plures," *The American Scholar* (Summer 1990), 337–54; Diane Ravitch, "What's at Stake with Multicultural Education?" *Clipboard* No. 5 (February 1990), 1–2; Diane Ravitch, "Diversity and Democracy: Multicultural Education in America," *American Educator* (Spring 1990), 16–20, 46–48.

[12] In it important to note that it is precisely neoconservatives like Roger Kimball who use Ravitch's notion of common culture as a basis for dismissing any criticism of Western culture. See Kimball, "Tenured Radicals."

[13] On this issue, see Chandra T. Mohanty, "On Race and Voice: Challenges for Liberal Education in the 1990s," *Cultural Critique*, No. 14 (Winter 1989–1990), 179–208.

[14] Ibid., 196.

[15] Ravitch, "Multiculturalism," 340.

[16] Ibid.

[17] Examples of this work include: Stanley Aronowitz and Henry A. Giroux, *Education Under Siege* (South Hadley, Mass.: Bergin and Garvey Publishers, 1985); David Livingstone, ed., *Critical Pedagogy and Cultural Power* (South Hadley, Mass.: Bergin and Garvey Publishers, 1987); Paulo Freire and Donaldo Macedo, *Reading the Word and the World* (South Hadley, Mass.: Bergin and Garvey Publishers, 1987); Henry A. Giroux and Peter McLaren, eds., *Critical Pedagogy, the State, and Cultural Struggle* (Albany, New York: SUNY Press, 1989); Henry A. Giroux and Roger I. Simon, eds., *Popular Culture, Schooling and Everyday Life* (New York: Bergin and Garvey, 1989); Henry A. Giroux, *Schooling and the Struggle for Public Life* (Minneapolis: University of Minnesota Press, 1988); Deborah P. Britzman, *Practice Makes Practice* (Albany, New York: SUNY Press, 1991); Ivor Goodson and Rob Walker, *Biography, Identity, and Schooling: Episodes in Educational Research* (New York: The Falmer Press, 1991); Aronowitz and Giroux, *Postmodern Education: Politics, Culture, and Social Criticism.*

[18] Mohanty, "On Race and Voice: Challenges for Liberal Education in the 1990s," 207.

[19] Richard Bolton, as quoted in Paul Mattick, Jr., "Arts and the State," *The Nation* 251:10 (October 1, 1990), 354.

[20] Carole S. Vance, "Reagan's Revenge: Restructuring the NEA," *Art in America* (November 1990), 49–59.

[21] Michael S. Joyce, "The National Endowments for the Humanities and the Arts," *Mandate for Leadership* (Washington, DC: The Heritage Foundation, 1981), 1040–1041.

[22] Hilton Kramer, "A Note on the New Criterion," *New Criterion* 1:1 (September 1982), 7.

[23] Gayatri C. Spivak, *The Post-Colonial Critic* (New York: Routledge, Chapman, and Hall, 1990), 19.

[24] Abigail Solomon-Godeau, *Photography At The Dock: Essays on Photographic History, Institutions, and Practices* (Minneapolis: University of Minnesota Press, 1991), 215–16.

[25] Roger I. Simon, "For a Pedagogy of Possibility," *Critical Pedagogy Networker* I:*1* (February 1988), 2.

[26] Douglas Crimp, "AIDS: Cultural Activism/Cultural Analysis," *October* 43 (Winter 1987), 6–7.

[27] West, "The New Cultural Politics of Difference," 108.

[28] Meaghan Morris, "Banality in Cultural Studies," *Block* 14 (1988), 15–26.

[29] Barbara Bush, as quoted in Eden Ross Lipson, "Reading Along with Barbara Bush: The Endings are Mostly Happy," *New York Times Book Review*, May 21, 1989, 36.

[30] Gloria Anzaldua, *Borderlands/La Frontera: The New Mestiza* (San Francisco: Spinsters/ Aunt Lute, 1987), 3.

[31] Richard Kearney, *The Wake of Imagination* (Minneapolis: University of Minnesota Press, 1988), 369.

[32] These themes are developed extensively in Stanley Aronowitz and Henry A. Giroux, *Postmodern Education: Politics, Culture, and Social Criticism* (Minneapolis: University of Minnesota Press, 1991).

[33] On the need for progressives to develop public spheres that allow them to both engage specific issues as well as develop alliances aimed at exercising power and influencing policy, see the various articles on the public sphere in *Social Text*, Nos. 25 & 26. See especially, Nancy Fraser, "Rethinking the Public Sphere, *Social Text*, Nos. 25 & 26 (1990), 56–80, and Patricia Mann, "City College as a Postmodern Public Sphere," *Social Text*, Nos. 25 & 26 (1990), 81–102.

[34] Stuart Hall, "New Ethnicities," in Kobena Mercer, ed. *Black Film/British Cinema*, ICA Document 7 (London: Institute for Contemporary Arts, 1988).

[35] Iain Chambers, *Border Dialogues: Journeys in Postmodernity* (New York: Routledge, 1990), 9–10.

[36] Abigail Solomon-Godeau, "Who is Speaking Thus? Some Questions About Documentary Photography," in Lorne Falk and Barbara Fischer, eds., *The Event Horizon: Essays on Hope, Sexuality, Social Space and Media(tion) in Art* (Toronto: The Coach House Press, 1987), 211.

[37] The ideas in this section draw from an unpublished article by Henry A. Giroux and Roger I. Simon titled "Pedagogy and Cultural Politics," Toronto, Ontario, Canada (1990).

[38] Cornel West, "The New Cultural Politics of Difference," *October*, 53 (Summer 1990), 105.

Index